iption
nty of
lands of
twright
596.

WENS

Mr Cartwrights
Demeans being
12 lands

The Hadland

Wards Ash

Wards Ath peece

Hemp Butts

Butts Peece

Schoole

London Great Road

Croaton Way

Mrs Dropes Close

Mrs Dropes

The Parsonage

Over Church pasture

The Garden

Court

Coach Yard

Husbandmens Yard

The Churchyard

Spitter

Sibwells

Neather Church pasture

The Great Parkway

Copied from the original survey
of James Fish, of Warwick,
by Clement Millard. 1895.

E

S

AYNHO

A Northamptonshire Village

AYNHO

A Northamptonshire Village

by
Nicholas Cooper

Leopard's Head Press
In conjunction with
Banbury Historical Society
Volume 20

Published by the
LEOPARD'S HEAD PRESS
in conjunction with the
Banbury Historical Society
1984

Distributed by
Gulliver Publishing,
White Lion Walk, Banbury, Oxon. OX16 8UD

ISBN 0 904920 09 7 (Leopard's Head Press)
0 900129 21 (Banbury Historical Society)

Printed in Great Britain by
Billing & Sons Limited, Worcester.

To the memory of
Robert Weston,
agent to the Cartwright estate
1777–1814,
and to all who preserve the
records of the past.

Preface

Though my name appears on the title page of this book, I have not done all the work. Years ago Elizabeth Watt commissioned a history of Aynho from Marjorie Kennedy. The vicissitudes of that work included her first draft's being kept for three years by someone who was going to read it (and did not), and its being stolen from my car (and not recovered). As it stands, the book has been entirely written by me, and I have seen most of the sources that Miss Kennedy consulted and others that she did not, and their interpretation is mine. But her researches and her text formed the foundation of it, and the content of some parts of this book is still largely hers. It is by her request that my name alone appears on the title page, but I am glad to be able to acknowledge the enormous generosity with which she allowed me to use her work.

The second acknowledgement must be to Miss Watt, whose interest in the history has been maintained through long periods when its completion must have seemed very doubtful. Also to Jeremy Gibson, who has similarly given encouragement and active help throughout the book's long gestation and latterly has compiled the Index of names and undertaken the tedious but essential work of seeing the book through the press.

The Chief Archivist, Mr. P.I. King, and his staff at the Northamptonshire Record Office have supplied the wants first of Miss Kennedy and then of myself with a willingness that has never faltered, and I include them in my dedication. That this book could be undertaken at all is due to the deposit there of her family's papers by Mrs. Cartwright-Hignett, and in the concluding stages of the work she found for me, and most generously allowed me to reproduce here, pictures of great interest. These were photographed with great skill by Colin Wilson of Bath, while the maps on the end papers, from Delapré, were photographed equally skillfully by Christopher Dalton. The Record Office's own photographer also copied pictures for me. Others are from the Banbury Museum, to whose staff I offer grateful thanks. The plans of houses 42 and 87–92 are founded in part on drawings by Peter Lucas Associates and by James Bailey.

Publication of local history is not normally a paying proposition. That it is possible to publish this work at a price that is not beyond many people's means is due to generous financial help from

Miss Watt and from the Marc Fitch Fund, under whose Leopard's Head Press imprint the book appears. The Fund's Director, Mr. Roy Stephens, has given much help with the book's production, and its continuing sale is assured by the agreement of Mrs. Dianne Coles and the Banbury Bookshop to act as post-publication distributor. Mr. Nick Allen, at one time administrator of Aynho Park under its present ownership, has provided much help with publicity, proof reading and with the book's jacket design. The Northamptonshire Record Society and in particular its present Secretary, Mrs. Margaret Clarke, maintained an interest in the book's progress and helped with advance publicity. The staff at the Banbury Museum have provided an essential focal point for advance sales.

Dr. Sally Howell has given me valuable help over the problem of the Cotman Fields, discussed in Appendix 8. Lawrence Cole told me much of interest about the village under his stewardship, and numerous people in Aynho allowed me into their homes in order that I might see how their predecessors lived. That I cannot thank them all does not indicate any lack of appreciation for their patience. My wife's cheerfulness at the prospect of yet another 'final' visit to Delapré Abbey passed, if possible, that with which she abstracted parish registers for me.

I have tried to write a book that will interest the general reader as well as the historian, and the outsider as well as the inhabitant of Aynho. Local histories are used by other people besides locals, and their contents must therefore be placed in a broader context; on the other hand the local reader may not want to be bothered with too much information about the world beyond the village and which he can better get from other sources. Readers must judge whether I have been able to reconcile these centrifugal demands.

There are no footnotes. The sources are almost all at the Northamptonshire Record Office, among the Cartwright papers, the parish collection and probate records there, and they are admirably calendared and indexed. The exceptions are Quaker records at Friends' House, tax rolls and censuses at the Public Record Office, and some documents relating to Edward Wing and to Joseph Wasse at the Bodleian. If anyone needs a reference in order to follow up in greater detail anything I have touched on, I hope I shall be able to supply it.

Contents

Page

1. The Distant Past 1
2. The Medieval Manor and its Lords 13
3. Villagers and Squires 33
4. The New Broom 56
5. War 73
6. Three Parsons 90
7. The Eighteenth Century: Rich and Poor 99
8. Buildings 132
9. Some Village Institutions 149
10. Enclosure 177
11. Good Living and Hard Times 193
12. High Finance and High Farming 216
13. A Close Village 255
    Epilogue 283

Appendices
1. Poll Tax, tenures and rents, 1544/5 293
2. Households, tenures and rents, 1618 296
3. Farmers: households and tenures, 1740–45 299
4. Farmers: post-enclosure holdings and rents, 1794 300
5. Occupiers of houses, 1790 (rear end-paper) 301
6. Field and furlong names in the early eighteenth
   century 303
7. Field names, c.1960 308
8. The Cotman Fields 312

Pedigree: The Cartwright family tree 314–5

Indexes
Subjects (including places within Aynho) 316
Places outside Aynho 323
Personal Names 326

List of Illustrations

Endpapers

Front — Aynho in 1696. 'The Topographical Description of Aynho in the County of Northampton, being the Lands of the worshipful Thomas Cartwright Esqr., Taken Anno 1696'

Back — Aynho about 1790, just before the Enclosure. Probably drawn by Robert Weston, the Cartwright agent

Plates

Between pages 100 and 101
1. The Aynho landscape in the eighteenth century, with the Fermor brothers hunting
2. Aynho from the air, c.1950
3. The Great House in 1683
4. The old church in 1721
5. The Grammar School in 1823
6. Edward Jarvis's house in 1949
7. Richard Cartwright in 1606
8. John Cartwright

Between pages 164 and 165
9. Thomas Cartwright in 1720–25
10. The Park in 1721
11. William Ralph Cartwright as a boy, c.1785

Between pages 196 and 197
12. The Square in 1815
13. Looking up the Hollow Way in 1815
14. Cottages on Blacksmith's Hill in 1815
15. Cottages on the Lower Green, 1815
16. The same cottages on Blacksmith's Hill in 1949
17. The same cottages on Lower Green, c.1910
18. Looking down Blacksmith's Hill, 1815
19. Lace-making in Watson's Yard, 1815

Between pages 228 and 229
20. General William Cartwright, c.1860
21. The Great House, 1949, from the North East
22. The drawing room at the Rectory, 1846
23. Cottages on the Charlton Road, 1949
24. The almshouses, 1949
25. The Square, c.1910
26. The church, 1949

Between pages 260 and 261
27. The canal, c.1910
28. The railway station, c.1920
29. The Cartwright Arms, c.1900
30. The Post Office, c.1895
31. Prospect Terrace, c.1905
32. The stocks, the hill trees and a waggon, c.1910
33. Coronation Sports, 1910. Ladies' race
34. Flower Show, 1908. Pillow Fight

Maps

		page
1.	Aynho and the Cherwell valley	5
2.	Aynho: topography	10–11
3.	Land and roads after the 1620 Enclosure	100
4.	North, Middle and South Fields in 1680 and 1696	105
5.	The area north of Blacksmith's Hill in c.1690 and c.1790	135
6.	The village centre, c.1950	138–9
7.	Land and roads after the 1792 Enclosure	186
8.	Land use, c.1860	252
9.	Field and furlong names in the early eighteenth century	306–7
10.	Field names, c.1960	310–1

Figures

1.	Births and deaths, 1580–1830	127
2.	Provenance of men marrying in Aynho church 1650–1800	131
3.	Representative house plans	141
4.	Representative house plans	143

Permission to reproduce copyright illustrations is gratefully acknowledged to the following individuals and organisations:

Banbury Museum: Plates 16, 27, 29, 31, 32

British Museum (Crown Copyright): Plates 4, 10

Cambridge University Air Photograph Unit: Plate 2

Mrs. E. Cartwright-Hignett: Plates 7, 12, 13, 14, 15, 18, 19, 22

Courtauld Institute: Plates 1, 8, 9, 11

National Monuments Record (Crown Copyright): Plates 6, 17, 21, 23, 24, 26, 28

Northamptonshire Record Office: Plates 3, 20, 25, 33, 34, endpapers

The late Mrs A. Taylor: Plate 30

Chapter 1

The Distant Past

For most of its existence, Aynho has been quite an ordinary village. It is prettier than many, though it is only in the last fifty years that anyone has told the villagers so, and more recently still that anyone has come to live in Aynho because of that. For centuries life in Aynho proceeded much as in any other village in the southern Midlands. It happens to be in Northamptonshire, though the map shows that that is almost an accident: it is half surrounded by Oxfordshire; Buckinghamshire and Warwickshire are not far off, and what happened in Aynho might have taken place in almost any other village within forty miles or more. But there are more documents surviving from Aynho's history than from a good many villages that might otherwise have provided equally interesting stories, and the papers that make it possible to write about Aynho show, too, that the village is worth writing about.

It stands on the eastern slope of the Cherwell valley, on the edge of the hill. There is light, corn-growing land on the uplands east of the village, and pasture and meadow on the hill slope and in the valley. The parish is roughly rectangular, with its boundaries for the most part following natural features: the river Cherwell on the west, the valley of a tributary stream, the Cuttle Brook, on the south, and a ridge overlooking a broader valley on the north. These boundaries gave the place from the first a good mixture of soils, of upland and lowland, and of woods and fields. They were probably chosen, before records began, for that very purpose — to provide a balance of resources. A spring rising almost from the centre of the village provided water for everyone until the present century, and falls into the river by a stream anciently known as the Ho brook — the brook of the hill. In the past there must have been very few of the necessities of life that the village could not provide for itself.

The houses are built of a greyish-yellow, oolitic limestone that weathers to a slightly brownish grey: geologically a Cotswold stone, though the village is hardly in the Cotswolds, and in contrast to the warm, orange ironstone of most of the villages to the north, east and west. It is a village familiar to many, because it has always lain on one or more main roads, though these have changed

1

their relative importance over the centuries. The ancient ridge way from Buckingham, through Aynho and Deddington to Chipping Norton and the west, still runs through the village, crossing the Cherwell valley between two spurs of the hills. Another road, perhaps equally old, that formerly skirted the village is now almost lost: the Port Way running up the east side of the Cherwell valley and passing on to the Midlands and the North. The most important road now is the A41 from Bicester to Banbury, running close to the village centre and past the Park House that is always noticed with surprise by everyone driving through and which distracts one's attention just before one reaches a particularly dangerous bend in the road. The great house is surprising because it stands so close to the houses of the village, in something of a continental manner rather than being secluded in its park like English country houses so often are. But the house occupies a fine site, looking south over its parkland and with distant views into the river valley, and by standing virtually within the village it expresses forcefully the close relationship that existed between the Lord of the Manor or the Squire and the villagers themselves.

It is thousands of years since men first penetrated into the Aynho region, hunting with rough weapons of stone and bone wild creatures in the dense woods of the hills and in the marshes of the river valleys. Man was then a rarer species than the beasts he was hunting. It was still many generations before men first settled, first making clearings in the edges of the forest for some kind of simple agriculture and probably moving on after a few years to clear new land and letting the first clearance go back to the wild. In the course of ages their settlements became more permanent and their way of life more complex, their society sufficiently organised to heap up barrows where they buried the great among their dead and to build stone circles like that at Rollright, near Chipping Norton, with the aid of which they seem to have undertaken elaborate astronomical observations for purposes we no longer know. But these people left scarcely any trace at Aynho, and a few tools and weapons of stone or bronze, probably lost or thrown away, are all that have ever been found in the village.

It is only from the fifth century before Christ that archaeology has revealed anything about the real lives of the people who lived near. Rainsborough Camp is a fortified enclosure near the edge of the plateau, a little north of the boundaries of the present parish. The first inhabitants lived in wooden huts; they had coarse pottery, grew crops, kept sheep and goats, oxen and pigs, and the richer among them probably had tools and weapons of iron. The place was undefended at first, but it was not many years before they felt the need to fortify it. There are many such Iron Age camps in the southern England; two are at Tadmarton, seven miles away, and at Idbury beyond Deddington, and the British tribes seem constantly to have been at war. Rainsborough stands a little behind the rim of the valley, as though the inhabitants were trying not to attract notice. But they made a thorough job of the defences, with a double line of banks and ditches, a twenty foot drop from top to bottom, the inner banks strengthened with stone and timber and a parapet walk with a stockade on top. The entrance led over the ditches and then between high walls and beneath a wooden bridge from which defenders could hurl missiles onto the heads of attackers crammed into the narrow passage below. Beyond was a pair of stone guardhouses. The place must have seemed very secure to those who built it, and extremely formidable to any possible enemy who passed by.

It is not likely that many people lived there continuously. It is inconvenient to live in a fort and to have to go in and out to drive one's animals in and out by a single gate. In any case, large though the camp was, it was certainly too small for all those who must have built it to live in with their families, and they must have regarded it as a place of refuge in time of danger rather than as a permanent home. They were farmers, probably living on farmsteads among their fields rather than together in villages, and it would have been extremely inconvenient to have lived far from their land. But the fact that the camp could be built at all points to a sizeable population in the Aynho area, and to an effective ruler too, who could organise the men of his tribe to undertake the work.

We do not know what was the danger they feared, or whether it was the same danger, growing again a century later, that led them hurriedly to renew the defences, clean out the ditches, and prepare to fight. But it was too little, and perhaps too late. When the attack did come the fort was taken, pillaged and burnt. The old, dry wood of the palisades on the inner bank burned fiercely and their stone footings crashed into the ditch in a ruin of rubble and blazing timber. The roofs of the guardhouses flamed and fell, burying one of the combatants, dead already from a blow that had smashed his skull. The entrance passage was choked with debris, and the huts inside the camp burnt to the ground. And the victors tossed the severed head of one of the defenders onto the ashes.

A little later a few people returned and left a scatter of their rubbish on the grass that was beginning to cover the ruins. Many years afterwards Rainsborough was again occupied and the defences again patched up: perhaps the Romans had been heard of, first as a distant rumour, now as a real threat — the best trained and most formidable army that the tribes of Britain had ever encountered. The British put up a good resistance: that is clear from the accounts that the Romans wrote, from the Roman army camps that have been found, and from the continuing presence of Roman legions stationed in Britain for three hundred and fifty years in case the natives should rebel. But we know of no fighting around Aynho, and though there must have been many fierce, local fights these have left no record. In the end the Britons acquiesced, and adopted such aspects of the Roman way of life as they cared to or were made to.

The country around Aynho was quite thickly populated under Roman rule, though the Romans themselves must have made up only a tiny fraction of the population — rather like the British in India centuries later. This was a country of small towns — the nearest was Alauna, the modern Alchester near Bicester; Towcester was another. There were villas — country houses with their own farms, where rich landowners lived on their estates often in considerable style. Their owners were probably British, but they were doing their best to live up to the life-style of the country gentlemen of Italy itself with their bath-houses, their underfloor central heating (hypocausts) and their fashionable mosaic pavements (even if these were sometimes rather crude by the standards of the smarter parts of the Empire). There was probably a villa of some kind at Souldern, where in the last century some farm workers dug up some pieces of mosaic, a coin and a bronze statuette. And there were the farms of those who were not in the country landowner class, but who were still well enough off to import luxuries from abroad — and to leave the remains for later generations to find. There was probably such a farm in the valley between Deddington and North Aston; there was a settlement of some kind just north of King's Sutton; and there was probably another farm within the boundaries of Aynho itself in the direction of Croughton, where in the nineteenth century a good deal of pottery was found which included wares from abroad — wine jars, oil jars or just best china. And there must have been many other farms and settlements whose existence will never be known, their barns and houses made of mud and timber and now vanished without a trace.

Generally these more-or-less Romanised Britons seem to have

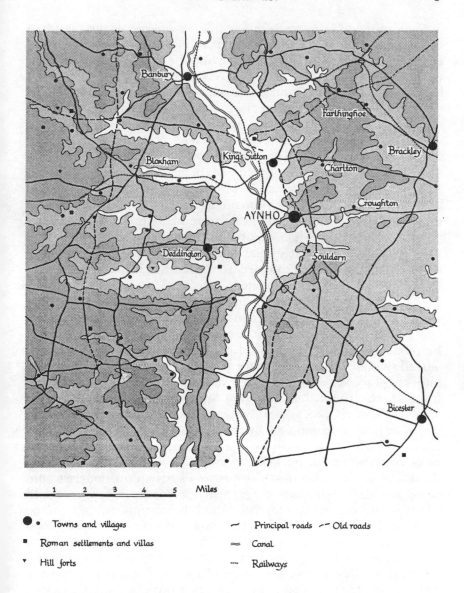

Map 1. Aynho and the Cherwell Valley. Contours at 350 feet and 450 feet.

lived in separate farmsteads rather than in villages, as their modern descendants, the Welsh and Irish, still do. Separate but in no way isolated: there were plenty of them, and the Port Way and the east-west ridgeway probably existed even then. But there must, too, have been villages of some kind where tradesmen and craftsmen lived, who spent their time in making, buying and selling their goods rather than in tilling the fields, and for whom living close together was an economic convenience. For a few modern villages it has been found that they have been continuously occupied since Roman times, though Aynho is not one of them. The fields of Roman farms, too, have been traced elsewhere, though not here. Nevertheless it is conceivable that Aynho might have existed then. Later, the open fields of the medieval village were made up of many smaller divisions in each of which the strips of land that composed them were arranged differently, and it is possible that these divisions may in part have corresponded to fields that had existed before the open-field system was created.

Under Roman rule the county was heavily populated, intensively cultivated, and to Britons whose great-great-grandfathers had known no other rulers it must have seemed that the Roman Empire was eternal. Changes, of course, there were. In the towns, not all the fine buildings that the Romans built in the first flush of Imperial glory lasted into the next century. There were disturbances from time to time: there was even one governor of Roman Britain who had himself proclaimed Emperor and marched on Rome, and when he was defeated and Britain reconquered by the legitimate Emperor there must have been a good many Britons who were made to regret having backed the wrong horse. Perhaps, too, in the third and fourth centuries there were Christian missionaries who came to tell of the new religion that even the Emperor would adopt — the Emperor, who had himself been supposed to be some kind of God! And perhaps, too, some people may have been curious when they first saw among the Roman soldiers men with ruddy faces, with long, fair hair and who talked a strange, gutteral language. If they asked, they would have been told that they were mercenaries from beyond the Empire's frontiers, from Germany, recruited to reinforce legions that had fallen below strength because of fighting in other distant provinces. Perhaps some people considered what this might portend, and felt that all was not well.

We shall never know how people reacted to the final disaster, the withdrawal of the legions themselves soon after 400 AD. No records tell us, and archaeologists, however skilled at finding physical remains, can only infer attitudes from their finds — the buried hoard that tells of the need to hide one's treasures and of the fact that the chance to retrieve them never came, and the earth banks thrown up as defences against a new enemy. When the Romans left, they left a system of government, a network of roads, a settled countryside, a prosperous and civilised country — but they left it without protection from the land-hungry barbarians from the north and beyond the sea. A few were here already, mercenaries retired from the Roman army and pensioned off with a farm in Britain rather than returning to their own less prosperous lands. But Saxon pirates had been raiding the east and south coasts of Britain for a century before the Romans left, and now they were joined by others, seeking new lands to settle as much as the spoils of towns and of defenceless British farms.

From the Dark Ages between the passing of the Romans and the first record of the village we have only a few archaeological finds — a spearhead from somewhere in the Park, and graves from Souldern which were discovered long ago, when their identification was less sure than it would be now. All we can say for certain is that some time a generation or two after the Romans left, Saxons were coming into the Aynho district in search of lands to settle, and that there were already Saxons living in the area a hundred years and more before they were converted to Christianity in the seventh century. These Saxons need not have come straight from Germany: they are just as likely to have been the children of men who were in England already, now pushing on from the Thames up the edge of the Cherwell valley, and coming from the north and east along the ancient roads that had already long served travellers.

It was probably seldom that the Britons were exterminated, though there must often have been fighting: the Anglo-Saxon Chronicle mentions a battle that may have taken place at Stoke Lyne, four miles away, and there are other traditions, too, of fighting among the British warlords who tried to fill the vacuum left by the departure of the legions and whose leader (if he ever existed) was King Arthur. The Saxons cannot have wiped out the natives, but they imposed their way of life very effectively on the places they occupied. There is scarcely a trace in the country round of any pre-Saxon place name, though Walton, a former hamlet and now a farm a mile north of Aynho into King's Sutton, may mean Town of the British: 'Welsh' is the same word. Aynho itself probably means 'Aegon's Hill', whoever Aegon may have been. He may have been the leader of a pioneering band of warriors, farmers

and their dependents; he may have been no more than the head of
a single family, but to him and to his companions it must have
seemed that Aynho was a good place to stop and settle down. The
Saxons buried at Souldern may have known who he was; we never
shall.

Nor shall we know what accommodation, if any, they reached
with the British who were here already. In any case the country
must have been in a state of turmoil, and ancient properties dis-
possessed. In this chaos, land may have gone out of cultivation,
and the newcomers may have had to clear more ground for farming. In some places, scrub may have encroached from neglect onto
previously cultivated land. There were probably swampy areas by
the Cherwell, broad swaithes of damp, tangled undergrowth in the
valley of the Cuttle Brook, and everywhere substantial stretches of
thick woodland. The land was attractive, and had been farmed for
centuries before, but for many generations still there was clearance
to be done. The boundaries of the parish were settled before records
were made, but probably even before that the watermeadows by
the Cherwell were being used for grazing since centuries later the
men of Croughton had the right to pasture their beasts and to cut
hay in one of Aynho's fields by the river.

The most distinctive of all the settlers' introductions were the
open arable fields, farmed co-operatively by the villagers. We shall
return again and again to these open fields: the whole history of
the village revolves around them, and they endured unchanged save
in details for a thousand years. They dominated the life of everyone, for most people had holdings in them, and even those who
did not depended for their livelihood on those who did. Almost
everyone still knows the basic principle: the great open fields where
each man had a scatter of long, narrow strips of land. The strips
were scattered so that each had a share of the good land and the
bad; they were long because the heavy, wooden plough hauled by
six or eight oxen was unwieldy and one wished to turn it as seldom
as possible. The strips were owned and cultivated by individuals,
but managed communally in that each year all the strips in one field
would grow one crop, and all those in the next would grow another
or lie fallow for the soil to recover its fertility, and would be available, meanwhile for grazing. And the crops would rotate annually,
so that each field would grow a different crop or lie fallow, once
every two or three years.

There is still no agreement among historians about how the
open fields began: they existed long before there were records. The

Saxons may have brought the system with them from Germany; they may have evolved it here. In any case the number of strips probably multiplied enormously over the centuries, as holdings were split up among children, were bought and sold, and as new land taken into cultivation by communal effort was divided among those who had worked to reclaim it. The 2,600 or so strips recorded in Aynho in 1618 when they were first (so far as we know) counted were the end result of an immensely long process in which the detailed map of the village must constantly have changed as strips were exchanged, inherited, consolidated, sold and split up again. But for all its complexity, the system worked.

As the country slowly became more settled, so gradually men found themselves to be part of a larger unit, first a part of the Kingdom of Mercia, and later a part of England. And so, from a mixture of choice and compulsion, they came to submit to the King's authority and to the King's justice, administered at the Hundred Court at Sutton. Gradually, too, the power of local leaders was transformed through the greater authority of the King. Sometimes, as small local rulers submitted to a more powerful, they will have found their own powers confirmed and strengthened. Sometimes the King granted a village to one of his own retainers. However it may have happened, by the time that records first exist, Aynho like most other villages in the south Midlands had a Lord of the Manor with an extensive estate — his demesne; with the power to do justice and to administer local customs at the Manor Court — the court of the Lord's house or *mansio*; and with the right to exact tribute of money and services from the villagers in his manor.

These peasants, whether or not they had ever owned freely the land that they and their ancestors had settled, were now willing or even compelled to accept sometimes onerous obligations to their lord. Someone less remote than the King could give them greater security in times of trouble. After a bad harvest, or when crops had been devastated by marauding Danes or fellow Saxons, and all an individual had left was his land and his labour, then if some great man could provide seed corn or new stock, all that could be offered in return was that land and labour. With seed and stock the Lord might return the peasant his land, but henceforth the peasant held it from the Lord by performing whatever services and paying whatever rent his Lord might demand. A similar situation might arise if the King demanded taxes that the poor man could not pay: the only way of raising the money might be by selling his land and his labour to a rich man.

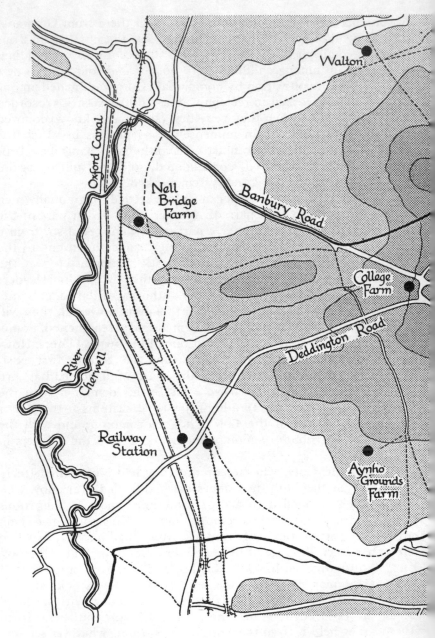

Map 2. Aynho: topography. Contours at 50 foot intervals.

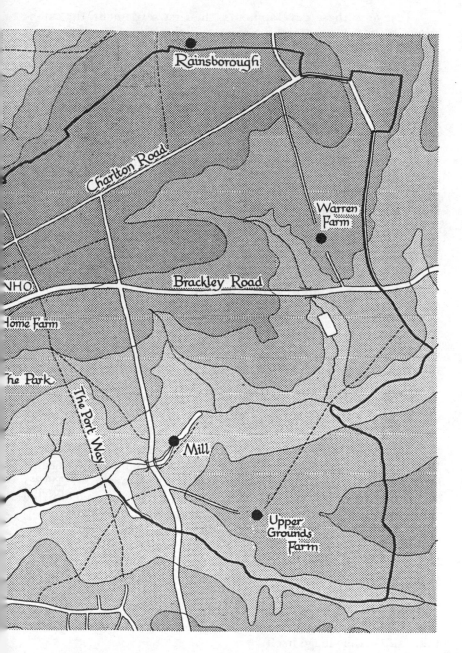

The boundary of the Parish and Manor is shown as a thick line.

Just how these developments, the first settlement, the establishment of the open field system and the manor, took place in
Aynho (or anywhere else in England, for that matter) we do not
know. All we know for certain is that between the arrival of the
Saxons in the fifth and sixth centuries and the Norman conquest
six hundred years later all this had happened. It is a long time, and
it was not an undisturbed process. However well established the
Saxons may have been, almost the whole country was more or less
troubled by the Danish raids of the ninth and tenth centuries, and
by the time that anything like peace returned the Danes were settled
in much of eastern England. There were a good many of them living
permanently by then at the other end of Northamptonshire, and
their raids extended very much further.

In fact it is a Dane, not a Saxon, who is the first recorded Lord
of Aynho, just before the Norman Conquest: Asgar the Staller,
a great landowner who held estates in seven counties. Asgar was
one of the great men of the kingdom. What he did as Staller is not
clear, but he was almost certainly some kind of royal official. His
grandparents were called Tofig the Proud and Gytha, and King
Hartha-Canute is supposed to have been at their wedding when he
dropped to the ground with apoplexy and died soon afterwards,
which is why the wedding was remembered. Asgar himself was
sheriff of London and Middlesex, and commanded the defences of
London against the Normans after Harold's defeat at Hastings.
Aynho may have suffered during the fighting that followed the invasion, but it is unlikely that Asgar gave it much thought; besides
being fully occupied himself against the invaders, Aynho was only
one among his many manors and he may never even have been
there. Aynho was probably (if he could read) no more than a name
on a rent roll. What happened to Asgar is unknown, but Aynho
was granted by the Conqueror to one of the newcomers, Geoffrey
de Mandeville, as great and distant a man as Asgar had been.

But if all has been generalisation and speculation up till now,
with the Norman Conquest we come to firmer ground. What has
been said about Aynho could just as well be said about any of five
hundred other villages where the same institutions had all come to
exist by 1066. The processes that formed them had to be described
in order to understand and to set the scene for what came later.
But now one can begin to abandon generalisation and to say something about the village itself.

Chapter 2

The Medieval Manor and its Lords

It is under Geoffrey de Mandeville that we have the first account of what Aynho was like, through the entry in Domesday Book, written for King William in 1086. The trouble with Domesday is that though its entries are clear and precise, what they actually mean is neither clear nor precise at all. For Aynho the entry reads —

> GEOFFREY DE MANNEVILE holds of the King AIENHO [Aynho] . There are 3 hides and the fifth part of a hide. There is land for 8 ploughs. Of this land 1 hide and the fifth part of 1 hide is in demesne, and there (are) 3 ploughs, and 8 serfs; and (there are) 23 villeins and 9 bordars, with 5 ploughs. There (is) a mill rendering 10 shillings, and 20 acres of meadow. It was worth 6 pounds; now (it is worth) 8 pounds. Asgar held (it) in King Edward's time.

What Domesday says about the people is relatively easy as far as it goes. The serfs were slaves, probably unmarried, working directly for the Lord himself and as much his property as his cattle and ploughs. The bordars were slightly better off; they had cottages and a few acres, and they probably had to do a good deal of work on the Lord's demesne in return for these small holdings. The villeins were simply the mass of the villagers, holding larger amounts of land from the lord in return for services and rent. Richer or poorer, the villagers were indebted to Geoffrey de Mandeville for almost all that they had. And as to how many people there were in the village: if one allows four and a half to five people to a household, this gives a population of around 150. Small by the standard of today's village, but larger than Croughton or Charlton at the time, while Souldern is not recorded at all.

The amount of land that they were farming is a much more difficult matter. The amount sounds exact and circumstantial enough, but Domesday was not intended as an accurate description of the country. For south-western Northamptonshire almost all the places mentioned have two hides of land for every five ploughs, and this too-exact correspondence puts one on one's guard against accepting these figures literally. Aynho has three-and-one-fifth hides and eight ploughs, a proportion of precisely two to five. A slightly earlier document gives a much higher hideage for the district than Domesday does, and it is clear that by Domesday a hide was a unit of taxation rather than a real measurement of land, and that the royal officials had felt that the district was in danger of being over-taxed and had reduced the assessment. We do not know why, but the last Danish army to have devastated this part of England had been active as recently as 1060, and the whole Hundred of King's Sutton had its assessments reduced in the way described.

But though we cannot calculate the amount of land on the Manor from the number of hides, we can do better with the ploughs. On a very rough estimate, one plough could handle a hundred acres or so a year, so that eight ploughs could cultivate around 800 acres. If one allows for half the land's lying fallow at any one time, this represents 1,600 acres under cultivation, compared with 2,300 acres of farmland in the present parish. Of this acreage, about a third was the Lord's demesne, the rest farmed by the 23 villein families mentioned in Domesday Book. Then there were twenty acres of meadow — of permanent pasture, that is, rather than of fallow onto which animals could only be turned at certain times of year. (The acres of 1086, though, may not have been the same as modern ones.) Pasture was on the lower slopes of the valley, and in the valley bottom by the river. There was certainly waste land as well at Domesday, probably on the edges of the Manor furthest from the village and by the streams where, again, the Commons lay centuries later.

A full plough team was eight oxen, and probably each villager except the bordars and slaves would have had two or three beasts and the Lord a few as well. At ploughing time, the villagers would have been expected to work on the Lord's demesne, and to arrange between themselves how their resources were to be pooled in order that each should get his own acres ploughed. Of course, they owned other livestock besides oxen. They would have had a few cows, though as much for breeding draught animals from as for milk. For milk they had sheep which provided them with clothing as well. They had pigs, which were probably left for much of the year to root in the woods and the undergrowth of the wilder places, and even the poorest villagers may have owned a few chickens.

But though much of the land was already being farmed, and over the next 150 years probably all of it, the produce was extremely poor. A fleece probably weighed 1lb - 2lbs, against 4½lbs today. The milk yields from cows were probably no more than a sixth of the modern figures. Manuring was understood, but few peasants owned enough animals to produce manure in worthwhile amounts. The return on seed was very low: around 4 to 1 for wheat, 5 to 1 for barley, and as low as 2½ to 1 for oats. In a bad year the proportions were even worse, so that it might be necessary to keep as much as half the corn for seed.

In a bad year, of course, hunger might mean eating the seed corn just to stave off starvation — but that would probably mean starving for certain the following year. Villagers had reasonable amounts of land; at Domesday, the average villein may have had a virgate, around 30 acres, but he would have needed it in view of these poor yields. He had to do labour services for his Lord in return; perhaps two or three days work a week on the demesne land, and more at harvest; he had to pay 'fines' to the Lord on innumerable occasions such as when his children married, if his son wanted to go to a school, into the church or a monastery, if he wanted to leave the Manor and live elsewhere, or if he wanted to take some waste land into cultivation to ease the ever increasing economic pressures upon him. A peasant was usually permitted to inherit his father's holding, but only on payment of what was called a 'heriot', a price that normally comprised his father's best beast, and a fine of an extra year's rent. And the peasants'|situation was steadily worsening: in 1086 England was on the eve of a population explosion.

Of the villagers' houses we know nothing, except that they were small dark and squalid, and were built of mud and sticks. The average man had a cottage of one or two rooms, with a fire burning in one of them whose smoke went out through the roof. There was no window glass in any except the very grandest houses, and if light was needed it could only be achieved by opening shutters. If, conversely, one wanted warmth it could only be by sitting in the dark and getting kippered. But probably the fug and the smell were a comfort after spending all the daylight hours in the fields, and the absence of light only mattered to craftsmen working at home. The poorer peasants probably shared their houses with such animals as they might possess, or else slept in one of the Lord's barns. It was the villager's responsibility to keep his house in repair and the Lord could fine him if he did not, but wood for repairs (and even for fuel) could only be cut with the Lord's permission: trees and bushes were his property.

There is not much doubt that the life of the peasants in the middle ages was grim, living in conditions of great discomfort and often scarcely at subsistence level. But there were some compensations: holidays for church festivals and after harvest, fairs and markets to visit if one had produce to sell, travellers through the

village to bring news of the outside world and perhaps to provide
entertainment with songs, juggling or a dancing bear, and the
occasional visit of the Lord of the Manor himself with his train of
knights and his retinue for a brief sojourn at the Manor house.

And despite the Lord's overwhelming authority, the villagers
were not entirely without resource if his demands became too
overbearing. The fines due on the occasions described could not be
arbitrarily increased if the villagers declared them to be 'ancient
customs' — that is to say, as established for time out of mind.
(Octogenarians were always in demand as witnesses at the Manor
Court.) A son would normally be allowed to inherit provided he
paid the heriot, even though in principle the Lord could refuse
him and give the holding to someone else. The way in which the
crops were to be sown in the open fields — what crops, when and
where — and the times at which livestock could be turned out to
graze on the stubble after harvest were the sort of decisions that
the Lord left to the villagers. And the village officials, up to the
Reeve whose responsibility it was to see that the Lord received his
due, were chosen from the villagers themselves whose intimate
knowledge of Aynho and its customs was essential if the Lord
was to receive what was owing to him without argument. Of course
a strong and ruthless Lord of a Manor had many ways of exercising
and extending his authority, but he could be sued in the King's
courts, and enterprising villagers in the middle ages did sometimes,
take their Lords to court and — more surprisingly still — even occasionally won.

Geoffrey de Mandeville, who had been given the Manor of
Aynho by William the Conqueror, died about the turn of the century, and the manor passed to his son William and then to another
Geoffrey, one of the more unruly of the barons whose fighting so
disturbed the reign of King Stephen.

> They cruelly oppressed the wretched men of the land with castle-
> works. When the castles were made, they filled them with devils
> and evil men. Then they took those men whom they thought had
> any property, both by day and night, peasant men and women,
> put them in prison for their gold and silver and tortured them
> with unutterable tortures . . . Many thousands they killed with
> hunger . . . The mightest well go on a day's journey, and thou
> shouldst never find a man sitting in a town, or the land tilled.

wrote a contemporary chronicler. The only advantage for the
people of Aynho was that as one of the most powerful, if one of
the worst, of the great landowners of the period, Geoffrey de
Mandeville may have been able to do something to protect them

(in his own interest, of course) from some of the depredations of his rivals and their private armies. Geoffrey disinherited his eldest son, and Aynho passed at his death to his two younger sons in turn, of whom William de Mandeville II gave the manor to the husband of his aunt Alicia, Roger FitzRichard.

(Roger actually exchanged it for his own Manor of Long Compton, but in the complexities of the feudal system, when all land had to be held from an overlord, Roger FitzRichard continued to 'hold' the Manor from the Mandevilles and agreed to provide the services of one-and-a-half knights for it. It was the great man's equivalent of the ploughing and reaping that the villagers had to do. Some money must have been paid for the value of half a knight, and perhaps for the whole knight as well: these feudal services were increasingly commuted into cash rents as the middle ages went on. The de Mandevilles drop out of the story, but four hundred years later, under Queen Elizabeth, the Lords of Aynho still in theory held the Manor from their successors, the Earls of Derby, and rendered him 6s 8d a year.)

The change of landlord probably meant little to the people of Aynho, because Roger FitzRichard was an important man in his own right. He held land in Essex and in the north as well, and he had the exchange of manors witnessed at the royal court at Winchester before the son of the King himself. Probably none of the great men and courtiers who witnessed the charter knew of Aynho, but in those difficult times it was always as well to get good and powerful witnesses to transactions in property. Roger died in 1185 and the Manor passed first to his widow, Alicia, and afterwards to his son Robert, who had close ties with King John. He travelled round the country in the royal retinue, had custody of several royal castles, received various other lucrative appointments from the King and was Sheriff of Northamptonshire. It would be nice to think (though impossible to prove) that this last office had come to him because he spent some time here, or that his father had acquired Aynho because he knew and liked it. Certainly, one of the two founded a hospital at Aynho towards the end of the century, where travellers and poor pilgrims could put up for the night and where one or two priests and brothers could look after them and pray for the souls of the Lord's family. We shall return to the hospital later. But whether or not Robert or Roger ever came to Aynho, it was at best the background to a busy life elsewhere. And their founding the hospital may well have been more because they feared for their souls than because they cared for the village.

Robert's son John was a king's man like his father had been, though he ultimately went over to the barons a few weeks before the famous meeting at Runnymede where he was chosen to be one of the 25 barons who were to enforce the terms of Magna Carta. For this and for his part in the civil war that followed, King John seized his Aynho manor and gave it to a certain Thomas de St. Valery, who held it until John FitzRobert made his peace with the king and had it restored to him. We do not know whether Aynho people were any the worse off for this change of masters; Thomas may have contented himself with the 'reasonable' profits, but it is just as likely that he took the chance to squeeze the villagers for all he could get before the Manor was taken away from him again. If kings could behave high-handedly to their lords, so could lords to their peasants. In any case the king probably made John Fitz-Robert pay heavily for having the Manor restored to him again, and John must have passed the payment on, in one way and another, to the poor villagers. They must often have felt they were mere pawns, exploited by whoever was supposed to be their Lord and protector.

The last 25 years of John FitzRobert's life were uneventful, though he probably came seldom if ever to Aynho. In 1241 he died, leaving a widow and two sons under age. Leaving minors as heirs was a mistake in the middle ages: their wardships belonged to the king who had the right to marry them off to whoever he liked — and their widowed mother too. All too often this meant virtually selling them to the highest bidder. John's widow, Ada de Balliol, offered the king the enormous sum of 2,000 marks (one mark = 13s 4d) if he would grant the wardship over her sons to her. Her request was granted, but her son Roger died when still in his 20's, trampled underfoot in a tournament in France, leaving a child as heir and £100 in debts. Roger's widow, Isabella, was granted the Manor by the king, but the king's brother, William de Valence, was granted the right of finding a suitable husband for her. She too seems to have bought herself off (at least there is no record that she re-married) but if so, it will have made a further hole in the family's fortunes.

There is plenty of evidence from other sources that in the thirteenth century many of the aristocracy were finding it difficult to make both ends meet — or at least finding it increasingly hard to keep up appearances. Going on tournaments in France must have been an expensive pastime. The consequences of this for Aynho will be hinted at in due course: the Lords of Aynho were no exception to the tendencies of the age. Roger's and Isabella's son, another Robert, may have — in a sense — sold his own son, another John. In 1277 he arranged for John, who was probably only about 13, to be married to Hawisia, daughter of a certain Robert de Tybetot, and Robert agreed to give the couple land worth £100 a year when they came of age in return for £400 from Hawisia's father. Hawisia's father, no doubt, was equally cynical: Hawisia was probably less than 13 herself, and he may have been trying to buy his family's way into the aristocracy. It was probably not intended that the children should actually marry until they grew up: many of the stories about child marriages in the middle ages derive from arrangements like this, where although people's futures were decided for them before they had views of their own, the actual marriage took place at a normal time of life. The bargain was made in the King's own presence, with elaborate provisions as to what should happen if either child should die before they were married, or if either parent renegued on the agreement.

John and Hawisia came into the Manor in due course. John took the surname of Clavering, after the family's Essex estates and apparently at the behest of the King himself. (One wishes the family had adopted a surname earlier rather than merely being Fitz-this or Fitz-that; it would have made it easier to keep track of them.) John was a king's man too, and like the rest of his family he got into financial difficulties. He borrowed from Italian merchants (though everyone did that from the King downwards: Edward III's need for money brought about the bankruptcy of two of the leading Florentine banking families). John borrowed from a fellow official of the royal household, Matthew de Columbariis (or Doves), and from two bishops, Walter Langton and Robert Burnell, and to make matters worse, when his father had died royal officials began to press for payment of his father's debts to the King himself.

So in 1311, pressed by creditors and approaching the age of fifty without an heir to leave his property to, John made an arrangement with his creditors whereby the King was to have most of his lands; other land he had already disposed of to other people to whom he was in debt. But Aynho he kept for his lifetime and for Hawisia's, and after his death it was to go to his sister. There were further financial set-backs soon, when John was captured by the Scots at Bannockburn and had to find money to pay the ransom. But one would like to think that he and Hawisia had decided to

hang on to Aynho because they liked the place and actually spent
time here. Certainly, years later, when his financial position had
somewhat improved, he was at Aynho when he paid off a debt
that his father had long owed to Balliol College in Oxford, and it
was at Aynho that he died in 1331. Perhaps he had settled down
in his old age, though 'settled down' was probably a relative term
at best: he was carrying on a violent feud with the men of Dunwich
in Suffolk only a few months before his death. His body was taken
to Langley Abbey in Norfolk, a family foundation (that was another
expensive medieval occupation, founding religious houses) and his
widow Hawisia lived on for another twelve or thirteen years, into
the 1340's.

When she died, the manor passed as had been agreed to her
late husband's nephew, his sister's son Ralph de Neville, who in turn
parted with it to a member of another noble family, Sir John de
Arundel. Once again the village was in the hands of a remote and
aristocratic lord, and the villagers probably saw even less of the
Arundels than they had of previous Lords or the Manor. Certainly
less than of John and Hawisia Clavering, who are the only medieval
lords we know who actually lived in the place. But the 1340's were
a watershed in more ways than one. Of far more immediate concern
to the villagers was the Black Death.

The Black Death was perhaps the greatest single calamity in
English history, though it is possible that if the Black Death had
never struck, the years from 1315 to 1320 might have been remembered as those of the worst harvests, the worst outbreaks of cattle
plague and the worst famine in the middle ages. There are no parish
registers as early as this, but throughout England the famine of
1315 to 1320 put an abrupt stop to the growth of population that
had been continuing since Domesday. And the plague of 1348
killed perhaps one person in every three.

However slow the pace of life in the middle ages, much had
changed since Domesday Book was made. It was a long period —
ten generations — and both prices and population had been increasing all the time. This must have affected everyone, and many people
very severely. The value of the Manor of Aynho — that is to say,
of the Lord's demesne land, of the services that the villagers were
bound to perform and the rents they had to pay — had been £8 at
Domesday. In 1185 its worth was £30. In 1249, on the death of
Roger FitzJohn, its value had gone up to £49. There were several
reasons why the value might increase, and probably all of them
contributed: there were more people to perform services and to

pay rents and dues, and the area under cultivation had probably increased. In 1185 there were four ploughs on the Lord's demesne as against three in 1086, so perhaps a third more land was in hand, reclaimed from the waste. It is known that everywhere the amount of land being farmed had been increasing to feed the ever growing population, and it is unlikely that much of the Manor was uncultivated by then. There were still only four ploughs on the demesne on 1249, though there were by then two mills, one of them the endowment of the Hospital. But it is likely that most of the increase in value over the previous two centuries had been due simply to inflation, and though prices were going up, a villager still had to perform the same services for his lord, had still the same family to feed (or a larger one), and once the limits of cultivation had been reached within the Manor, his over-cropped land would gradually produce less and less return. And the growth of population meant less land per head to feed the village. If the Black Death of 1349 was due to a (now) identifiable virus, the crisis of 1315-20 was the effect of natural disasters striking a population already severely weakened by malnutrition.

Many of the villagers were probably living at subsistence level. Once there was no new land to enclose and to farm, yields would tend to decline, and both a cause and a result of the decline was that villagers did not own enough beasts for the efficient manuring of their lands. Pressure of population meant that ever more land had to be put to arable, ever less to grazing. The value of manure was well understood, but the contraction of grazing meant less manure and so less fertile arable — which meant converting into arable still more of the pasture to remedy the deficiency. In the late thirteenth century Aynho was probably more intensely cultivated than at any time in its history, and the yields per acre and per head were probably lower.

The plight of the villagers could be made worse by the policies of the Lord of the Manor. In 1249 the 'customs' due to the Lord were said to be worth £15. This implies that the services due to him from the villagers had not yet been 'commuted' — that is to say, waived in return for a money rent, and though commutation was to become increasingly common, the situation at Aynho was typical of the times. The Lord of the Manor, at a time of inflation and rising prices, wanted money. All landowners did, though we know at Aynho how pressed the Lord of the Manor was. The best way of raising money was to get as much work out of one's villagers as one could, and to sell the produce of their labour for cash. These

services might not be fully exacted in years of easy farming conditions, but in difficult years or in years of glut harvests when the
villager would need to spend as much time as possible on his own
holdings, in these the Lord would demand his full quota of work.

There were other ways of raising money, too. In 1320 John
Clavering was found by the King's officials to have been fining
butchers and bakers who had been convicted of such offences as
giving short weight, when the proper way of dealing with them
was by pillory and ducking stool — both of which the village was
said to have. And the Lords of the Manor had by then obtained
the right to hold a Market on Tuesdays and a Fair over four days
at Michaelmas, and the reason for getting the grant of such a right
from the King, Edward II, was that the Lord hoped to recoup more
from dues at the Fair and the Market than he had had to pay the
King for the privilege.

The harsh conditions of the time did not affect everyone
equally. Even before the Black Death there was a wide range of
rich and poor. Though most of the villagers were the Lord's men,
holding their land from him, this did not prevent some from pros-
pering. Some worked harder and could afford to take on more
land; others inherited land from parents-in-law (with the Lord's
permission). A tax list for Aynho, early in the fourteenth century,
put John Clavering's contribution at 22s, but next to him was a
William Reeve assessed at 20s. There were two men assessed for 6s,
one of whom, Geoffrey de Camera, is recorded elsewhere as holding
2½ virgates of land, about 70 acres. Then there were three worth
3s, including Richard Berdnell, who was probably an ancestor of
the Brudenells of Deene Park. Thirteen others were assessed at
between two shillings and three, including the two millers. A number of villagers, who may or may not be among those rich enough
to be taxed, probably held small holdings or just a few acres on
what were recorded later as Cotman Fields (see Appendix| 8) —
probably fields given to his serfs and bordars in the twelfth century
by the Lord of the Manor for their maintenance. Others again were
probably already landless labourers, unrecorded because they had
no possessions to tax.

The next survey of Aynho was taken in 1369, a generation
after the Black Death, and though it is a bare, factual document its
implications are fearful enough. Ralph Neville then received rents
from 25 houses and 18 cottages, but nine more were in ruins. For
lack of demand, the value of the land in the demesne had fallen to
2d an acre; three miles away at Newbottle in the 1330's demesne

land had been worth three times that. There were another 200 acres uncultivated, worth only a shilling in all, and which could neither be grazed by the Lord's beasts nor sold because they were too far from the village. That would have been no disincentive during the land hunger of the previous century. Meadow land was worth 1s 5d an acre against 2s for meadow at King's Sutton forty years before, and pasture 3½d against 6d. At the north east corner of the manor, towards Charlton, the boundaries look as though they were drawn round fields, yet three hundred years later there was waste land in that corner of the parish. Was this land that had gone out of cultivation at the Black Death? And in the seventeenth century, too, there were furlongs closer to the village called Deadlands and Nomans Hill: were these too lands left empty then?

The land in hand was worth only £9 in 1369, not much more than half what it had been in the thirteenth century. But there was still income from dues and rents, from the mill and from the Lord's bake house where the villagers had to do their baking, from dovecots, the rabbit warren and from the fishing in the Cherwell. It is clear that some, if not all, of the labour services required from the villagers had by this time been commuted for money payments, and the total cash income from the manor had increased to £25. There was a growing independence among the peasantry as time went on, despite the best attempts of the authorities to keep them in their place. The Statute of Labourers was a piece of legislation designed to maintain wages at pre-Black Death levels, and in the following century there is some indication that the Arundel lords of the Manor of Aynho tried to preserve their bondsmen's services against the trends of the times. We do not know if any Aynho men were involved in the Peasants' Revolt of 1381, when the authorities' repression and the burgeoning ambitions of the peasantry came into head-on collision. But in any case violence was nothing strange to the men of Aynho.

A close connection has recently been established for fourteenth century Northamptonshire between crime and the price of corn. This is as clear proof as could be that people were driven directly to violence by the fear of starvation, and it is a demonstration of the terrible conditions of the time. It is obvious that there was a level of violence in the medieval village that would not have occured later. The survival of records from the middle ages is haphazard at best (though sufficient to provide useful statistics) but we have information on three murders in Aynho in the late thirteenth century that are probably representative of what might happen.

There was a fight between Osmund, one of the brothers at the Hospital, and Geoffrey, brother of a Croughton man, in which Geoffrey grabbed an axe from Osmund's hand and injured him so severely that a week later he was dead. On another occasion a stranger passing through the village was stopped by Alexander, the Lord of the Manor's warrener. On their way to the Manor Court for the stranger to take his pledge — a stranger's good behaviour had to be vouched for — he was set upon and killed. Alexander and an accomplice buried the body in a field that is now a part of the Park, and fled, and since Alexander was the Lord's servant, it was he (Robert FitzRoger) who was fined by the King's justices when Alexander could not be brought to book. Again, a few years later, a stranger was robbed and killed in the house of one William Huwes, though the Aynho jury maintained that William himself was innocent.

Sometimes disturbances were of a different kind, as when in the middle of the fifteenth century rioters attacked the house of William Lambton. It was led by John Newers, Lord of the Manor of Tackley, and among the other attackers were a clerk from Eynsham, men from Begbroke, Bladon and Studley, and a tailor from Bicester. William Lambton was the rector of Aynho and the Master of the Hospital; in the thirteenth century, the Hospital had been given the right to hold an annual fair, and this may have been why so many men from far afield were all at Aynho together.

For villagers were not totally isolated, nor wholly self sufficient. To leave the village for any length of time required permission from the Lord of the Manor, and he liked to keep tabs on where his villagers were in case he should lose sight of them and of their obligations to him. As late as 1544 it was reported at the Manor Court that

> Ther is one William Colyns dwellinge in Crowton bondman to my Lorde
> Also ther is one Thomas Davy of Souldern weddid A bond woman to my Lorde without lycens or agrement with my Lorde or his officers

and most people lived and died in the village. But some travelled far; in the mid thirteenth century there was a certain Jordan of Eynho, for instance, living at Sawbridgeworth and employed to buy cloth for the royal household at fairs all over southern England. Some of the witnesses to charters issued at Aynho have names of nearby villages, as John Adderbury, Thomas Summerton and R. Lukenore.

Men might serve in the retinue of the Lord of the Manor, or in the King's army. In the Hundred Years' War, for instance, a force of Northamptonshire men was picked to guard the French King from Stamford to Woburn. Another Northamptonshire troop were orderd to Sandwich and there to take ship against French raiders, and would probably be unrecorded and forgotten were it not that when they reached Sandwich they made off home with their weapons and their advance of pay, perhaps preferring the risk of imprisonment or outlawry to what they saw of the sea. On another occasion Northamptonshire archers were sent to Wales to fight against Owen Glendour, and the Butts in Aynho, where the local men practiced their archery, is recorded in the sixteenth century when there were still men who kept up their bowmanship.

Even those who stayed at home had opportunities for seeing something of a wider world. Henry III and his son Prince Edward sometimes stayed at Brackley, and tournaments were held there; Woodstock was another royal house frequently visited by the Court. Piers Gaveston, the favourite companion of Edward II and for a time the greatest man in the kingdom, was captured by his enemies at his Castle at Deddington and from there dragged off to execution at Warwick. During the Wars of the Roses, there was a battle at Edgecote, a few miles off, when a rebel army trounced the troops of Edward IV under the Earl of Pembroke. But such events as these, at least, were certainly not regarded by the villagers as either exciting or entertaining. One of the brothers at the Hospital, for instance, had been arrested and accused of giving help to the rebels led by Simon de Montfort, and was only released after he had proved that Earl Hamo Lestrange had come to the Hospital, and seized three horses, and that though the brothers had pursued him they only got two back. Even at the best of times the countryside was never free of robbers and outlaws; armies, even troops of soldiers passing through, meant thieving and hunger and not improbably rape and death.

And within the village itself there were always fears. Of wild men and of wild beasts, seldom seen but often imagined, and always thought to be lurking in the wastes even when it had been generations since anyone had actually seen a boar or a wolf. And of the unseen world of witchcraft, of spells and enchantments, of phantoms and evil spirits. People readily believed that a mumbling old women was a witch, or that men weak in their wits were muttering curses against their neighbours or were themselves accursed. The supernatural was as real to most villagers as was their daily

lives — it was, in fact, a part of it — and they believed in it as strongly
as they believed in what we have, for too long, neglected: the church.

When the first church was built in Aynho is unknown. It
would be surprising if there had been none at Domesday, even
though none is mentioned: scarcely any churches are recorded by
Domesday Book in the whole of Northamptonshire, but this is obviously because the king's officials were not concerned with them.
The fact that the boundaries of the Manor and those of the Parish
are the same is almost certainly because some early Lord, before
the Norman Conquest, had built a church and endowed a priest to
serve his Manor. There was a church by the middle of the twelfth
century anyway, when Geoffrey de Mandeville granted it (that is
to say, its income and the right to appoint a priest) to a new Priory
he had founded at Walden in Essex. The medieval church, much
altered and added to, was pulled down except for the tower in
1723, but we know of its appearance from drawings — a couple of
plans and a sketch (Plate 4) — that were made at the time.

It had a short nave and a long chancel, a clerestory, and the
present tower which stood at its west end. There was a tradition
that it had been built in the reign of Edward III, but it must in
fact have been of many different periods. The piers of the south
arcade were not aligned with those of the north, so the aisles must
have been of different dates, and the clerestory must also have been
an addition: there would have been no need for one before the
aisles were built. The tower is fourteenth century, with niches for
statues of saints in the buttresses and over the west door. The
latter contained a figure of St. Michael killing the dragon, and there
is still a fragment of the winged dragon on the sloping cill beneath
the empty pedestal. And in the sixteenth century the tower housed
four bells, though none now is as old as that.

The arrangements of the east end must have been much the
same as in other medieval churches — a stone altar, with altar cloth
and candles, a piscina in the south wall and possibly an Easter
Sepulchre in the north. A rood screen stood between nave and
chancel, probably a substantial affair with room for singers as well
as for the usual figures of the Crucifixion, and there were besides,
altars to Our Lady and to St. Edmund, probably in the south and
north aisles. And somewhere, too, there was another figure of St.
Michael with candles burning in front of it.

The church must have been the most colourful and gorgeous
place that most villagers would ever see. Authority in the middle
ages, whether ecclesiastical or secular, well knew the power of

ceremonial, of colour and display to impress simple minds. The church walls were probably painted, the windows filled with stained glass, and in the sixteenth century there were at Aynho priests' vestments of red velvet, of white damask and of satin, and a cope of white satin and another of red velvet with the figure of St. Michael embroidered on it. The chancel would have been more difficult for the congregation to see into than in medieval churches today, half hidden by the rood screen, darker with coloured glass and dimly lit by candles, and there the priest would say the Mass in language whose sounds were familiar but of whose words the villagers scarcely understood the meaning. But so much the greater would have been the sense of mystery and awe.

The nave was the villagers' part of the church. There they met to discuss parish business, and there if anywhere would have been a school, always surrounded by reminders (if they needed them) of the supernatural. The pictures painted on the church walls may have been scenes in the Nativity or the Passion, with perhaps a St. Christopher near the door to comfort travellers, and almost certainly with a Last Judgement over the chancel arch, in whose literal representation of the rewards of good and evil most villagers would surely have believed. And there, too, occasional fugitives sought sanctuary, such as Simon atte Walle of Middleton, who stole a coat of russet, and who was pursued to Aynho church.

The parsons of the middle ages are seldom more than names, and when something more is known of them, it is usually something quite unconnected with Aynho. The first recorded, Ralph de Diceto in the twelfth century, was a learned man, but he spent years studying in Paris, he was archdeacon of Middlesex and later Dean of St. Paul's and he cannot often have come to Aynho. In fact he obtained leave from the Prior of Walden to present a vicar to do his duties for him. Turbert was his name, and he — or more likely his son, for simple parish priests did sometimes marry — was still at Aynho fifty years later. But that is almost all that is known about him, and even that little is more than we know of most of his successors. From time to time there were disputes between the Abbots of Walden and the Lords of the Manor about the right of presentation, and occasionally priests exchanged the living with others. There seems in particular to have been a good deal of chopping and changing in the late fourteenth century, a time anyway of rural unrest. The clergy had suffered with everyone else in the plague, and probably parsons could pick and choose their livings then in a way that they never could have done before.

But at the end of the middle ages personalities everywhere begin to become clearer. Two parsons of Aynho in the early sixteenth century — Richard Pearson and Robert Bright — were pluralists and provided priests-in-charge for Aynho. Their stipend was £6 a year, but Christopher Hill, who was a guild priest of Croughton, was able to leave bequests in money at a time when most people still left legacies in kind, and his successor, Edward Wolse (or Wolfe) was even better off. He left £11 in money, legacies to three manservants and three maidservants, and other things that showed a taste for finery that some might have thought improper in a parish priest. He had three coverlets, red, white and green (the liturgical colours!), several doublets of fustian, doeskin or canvas, a jacket, a best and a second-best gown (the best he left to Thomas Hanslope, of whom we shall hear more), and several pair of hose, one of them striped. In contrast, he only left a few books: a Missal, a Breviary or Porteous in two parts, which could be carried about, and a book called *Breviaticus*, all of which were left to various neighbouring parsons. Edward Wolse died in about 1535, and perhaps it would not have been too difficult for worldly parsons like him to adapt to the changes that were in the air.

That the church featured largely in people's lives is obvious. What is surprising is that there was so little opposition to the changes that took place at the Reformation; none at all, so far as one can discover, in Aynho. Whether it was because people accepted what they were told by those put in authority over them, or whether because to many the mysteries of the old religion were beginning to seem empty formulas, one cannot know. Probably there were different considerations for different individuals. But in any case, the changes began gradually. Henry VIII broke with the Pope, placed English bibles in the churches, and told the clergy to exhort their congregations 'not to repose their trust or affiance in any other works devised by men's phantasies beside Scripture', such as going on pilgrimages, repetitious and mechanical telling of beads, and similar superstitions. But it is likely that most people were growing cynical about many of these practices anyway, and though Henry both executed Catholics and burned Lutherans, by retaining such institutions as confession, private Masses and the doctrine of transubstantiation, he saved most people from having to question their most fundamental beliefs. The old-fashioned formulas continued in their wills: leaving their souls to God and Our Lady and to all the Company of Heaven, leaving a strike of barley or a sheep for the upkeep of the Rood light or for candles on the altar or to St. Michael, and money for a priest to say a Mass and for poor men's prayers.

Under Edward VI the pace of change quickened. In 1549 came the first English Prayer Book, and in 1552 a second — the basis of the Church of England's present one. That same year, Commissioners had come to Aynho and made an inventory of the church's furnishings and vestments, and placed them in the hands of Edward Love and of the new Lord of the Manor, Rowland Shakerley (whose arrival is described shortly). He had taken advantage of the dissolution of the monasteries to buy an acre of meadow that had long ago been left to the Priory of Walden for the upkeep of a lamp in Aynho church. And Thomas Bele, who died in 1554, bequeathed his soul to Almighty God, his only Refuge and Comfort, and 12d to the church for its maintenance. Stone altar, candles, Rood and wall paintings had probably all been swept away by then, only to be replaced when Queen Mary restored the old religion and returned England to Rome.

Dutifully, Margaret Cowley at the end of Mary's reign left her soul to God and All the Company of Heaven, two strikes of barley for the Rood, and ten shillings to the parson to pray for her. Yet when Elizabeth succeeded, returned to King Edward's prayer book, adopted Protestant dogma and made the hearing of the Mass tantamount to High Treason, once again the villagers (to judge by their wills) followed without demur. Wills, of course, were public documents, made before witnesses and proved in the church courts, and to adopt the 'wrong' phraseology would be to risk a charge of heresy, if not of treason. Yet whatever private soul-searchings these villagers may have had, they kept them to themselves. When Rowland Shakerley died in 1565, he directed that a chapel should be built onto the church for himself, his son and his family, but there was nothing said about Masses for his soul.

The first whiff of a changed religious climate could have come to the villagers of Aynho fifty years before the Reformation, if they had but sensed it. Not that there was any real reason for them to — but in 1485 the old Hospital in Aynho was dissolved. Aynho Hospital was a tiny religious house, and its dissolution was a foretaste of the Monastic suppression that Henry VIII was to undertake. It had been founded towards the end of the twelfth century by the first of the Claverings, Roger FitzRichard, as a hostel and an infirmary for poor travellers. It stood roughly where College Farm is now, with a courtyard to the west, a hall for the wayfarers to sleep and refresh themselves, and a chapel. There were two or three brothers to look after the inmates and to farm the Hospital's acres, and a Master in charge. Generally the master was a priest, sometimes the rector of the Parish.

The history of the Hospital was for the most part uneventful, though there were occasional excitements. There was such an episode in 1293 when Master William de Hikkeholte had just died, and before his successor could be instituted some people (they are just called 'sons of iniquity' in the document, which leaves a good deal to the imagination) had got hold of the Hospital's seals and tried to forge some deeds. The Archdeacon was ordered down by the Bishop, to go with a suitably impressive array of officials and find out what was going on and to excommunicate anybody who he thought deserved it.

The brothers occasionally got into trouble. Probably no more often than the common people, though since they came under the eyes of the archdeacon and the Bishop their escapades were probably more likely to be noticed. There was occasional trouble, too, with the Hospital's property. Some time in the 1390's the King's Escheator for the district (the local official whose duty it was to collect any dues the King was entitled to receive when his tenants-in-chief died) rode over to Aynho. This was Sir John Cope of Deneshanger, who probably thought the brothers would be a soft touch, and he proceeded to make off with £40-worth of their livestock. He had only the flimsiest of excuses, in that a remote relation of the Mandevilles had recently died, and the de Mandevilles (in spite of their sale to the Claverings, and the Claverings passing the manor on to the Arundels) were still feudal overlords. Sir John obviously did not think much of his own rights, though it had been worth trying his luck at the time: he made a death-bed repentance, but for all that his executors seem never to have returned the brothers their property.

The Hospital was never particularly rich. Roger and his son Robert were fairly generous, and their descendant John Clavering gave the Hospital his walled fishpond which lay just beyond the Hospital's courtyard, a mill, and the miller to go with it — in the middle ages one could give one's bondsmen (or at least the duties that they owed) just like any other piece of property. The Hospital had the right, too, to hold a fair at the feast of St. James the Apostle towards the end of July. It owned a few cottages in the village which brought in rent, and a small share in Croughton Meadow. But it was not rich, and in the late fifteenth century it had been many years since any poor travellers had been received there. Probably the income that had been sufficient in the twelfth century was now no more than enough to support the brothers themselves.

Bishop Wayneflete of Winchester had recently founded Magdalen College in Oxford, was touting around for endowments for it, probably among all his rich friends, and Aynho Hospital must have seemed just the sort of thing he was after. Not much, it is true, but a nice little property of 160 acres, and intended to support charitable activities which it apparently could no longer do. It was a matter not just of persuading the Lord of the Manor that it would be a good use for the Hospital property but the Bishop and sundry lawyers as well, but to a great man like Wayneflete that cannot have presented much difficulty. It will not have cost Lord Arundel anything, in any case, and in return he was to have an altar in the College Chapel, to be called the Arundel Altar, where a Mass would be said for his soul annually for ever. (At Aynho they had said Masses for the Claverings'; one hopes that in future the Claverings got by without them.) And as another quid pro quo the College agreed to let Arundel's servant Roger Hanslope have 'the farm of the Spital', the renting of the Hospital's land or what was very soon to be called College Farm, and Roger Hanslope is the first recorded member of a family that was to be prominent in Aynho for the next two hundred years.

That was in 1485. In 1479 there had died the only one of the Arundels whom we know to have lived at Aynho — Elizabeth, widow of Sir John Arundel, who is buried in the church and has a small brass to her memory on which she is called 'Lady of Aynho'. But it is likely that the Arundels used the Manor House in the village at best as a dower house or as a home for poor relations. It was seldom that they showed any interest in the village other than a financial one, and they were happy to let or lease it if the price was right. Early in the fifteenth century, for instance, the Manor was leased to a group of the villagers themselves, including the parson and William Brudnell. When that happened, the village must have been virtually self-governing, or at least ruled by an aristocracy of the villagers.

So it was probably not too much of a wrench for the Arundels to dispose of it when they finally had to. The fifteenth and sixteenth centuries were bad times for many of the old aristocracy, and the tenth Earl's eldest son, Lord Matravers, had been getting into debt. There are always plenty of people willing to accommodate aristocratic young men with rich fathers, and no doubt the young heir found himself deeply grateful to Mr. Rowland Shakerley, the London mercer who kept him in funds 'to his great Commoditie and Pleasure' — until the time came to pay him back. When that time came, having a title that went back to the twelfth century gave no protection from the just claims of the rising class, and something had to be done.

The sum involved was £465, and in 1540 Rowland Shakerley agreed to take the manor of Aynho rent free for twenty years and to pay himself back out of the profits. Lord Matravers then succeeded his father as twelfth Earl, and in order to raise yet more money to support his new eminence he offered to sell Shakerley the manor outright. Shakerley agreed, paid the Earl another £1,060 for the manor and all its 'escriptes and mynyments' (most of which he or his immediate successors, to our very great loss, seem to have thrown away) and faced the prospect of setting himself up as a country gentleman. There was probably some sort of public ceremony: there usually was on these occasions, when the Earl or his representative would present the new purchaser with some visible symbol of possession such as a handful of the earth of the place. And the villagers, no doubt wondering how their new lord would turn out, implored him in what are probably much the same terms as those in which Aynho villeins had sworn fealty to their Lords for centuries,

> We be seche yor wrshippe to be good land Lorde to us and by the
> trothe that we have in the most blessed trynytie that we will lyve
> & dye at yor fyet in Right and Trothe.

Chapter 3

Villagers and Squires

To describe Tudor Aynho is like beginning a novel in the middle, with only the barest outline of the story so far and with all the characters well launched on their parts in the plot. But from now on the documents are increasingly numerous and useful, and from a little later there is the tangible evidence of the houses of the village itself. With the Shakerley lordship the villagers and the Lord of the Manor begin to come alive.

There were probably some 200 or 250 people in the village when Rowland Shakerley bought the manor, and for the first time we know about them in some detail because they made wills (which very few ordinary people did before the sixteenth century), because a good many of them paid rent to the Lord of the Manor (there are no rent-rolls from Aynho from earlier than 1544) and because Henry VIII taxed them (and more people are listed in the tax return than ever before). There is a list of as many of them as we know on page 293, with the wealth they were taxed on, the land they held and the rent they paid.

The richest man in Tudor Aynho after Shakerley himself was Edward Love, tenant of the College Farm. At a time when titles counted for more than they do now, and when the correct designation of social grades was considered of importance, Edward Love was described as a Gentleman. He left legacies of from £40 to £100 to each of a large family. He had some handsome family plate including silver spoons, some plain, some 'with knobbes on the endes', and some of silver gilt and weighing an ounce and a half each and with the letters C and L on the handles. He had two silver gilt salts, one of which stood each 'hollyday' on his table, and a number of silver and gilt goblets, some of which were ancestral plate with initials on them. The rest of his possessions were on an equally lavish scale, and many years later, in 1608, the tax gatherers assessed his son Edward (who was still at the College Farm) for more even than the Lord of the Manor himself.

Joan Boughton was another farmer on a large scale in mid-sixteenth century Aynho — in fact, even larger, for whereas Edward Love probably only farmed the 170 acres of the College Farm, Mistress Boughton farmed 300 acres of the Lord's demesne to-

gether with another 100 acres that she held in her own name. Her
husband Henry had died in 1538, leaving 60 sheep apiece to each
of three sons. Her daughter seems to have married Nicholas Hanslope, an up-and-coming man whose father or grandfather had been
Roger Hanslope, servant of Lord Arundel's, and whose descendants
were to live in Aynho and be called Gentleman for another hundred and fifty years.

Next richest of these village aristocrats was Richard Cowley,
who farmed some 75 acres and was assessed for taxes in 1544 on
land worth £15 a year. He too left a good many sheep to his family
and friends, with instructions that they were to be 'neither of the
best of my flock nor of the worst but as Thomas Ball and William
Wyet . . . shall think convenient'. A farmer of his standing apparently did business at quite a distance: 'goodman Stele a baker of
Woodstock' owed him 36s for wheat, and 'John Botcher of Brackley', 26s 8d for a number of sheep.

But though it is likely that as many as half the families in
Aynho were farming when Shakerley acquired the Lordship, it is
clear from the wills of those lower down the scale that tradesmen,
and even servants, were not necessarily badly off. William Herbert,
one of eight men taxed on £2, was probably a stone mason and
held no land put paid 3s a year rent for his cottage. He had been
an ale-taster — one of the officials appointed at the Manor Court
to check the quality of the beer in the village ale-houses — and he
also kept bees. He seems to have had no son to follow him, and his
possessions were divided between his widow and his daughter Joan.
Joan was left a bed 'with a ceiling of timber painted' and the bedding for it; a big bright pan, a little pot, a window sheet, the best
candlestick and other things beside. John Burton was left tools
that included the best of three grindstones. William Herbert also
had clothes that were worth leaving to friends in the village: his
best violet coat with cut sleeves, a white kersey doublet, a jerkin
and a couple of jackets, a shirt and a pair of hose, and a silver clasp
that he left to the curate. It looks as though one could be com-
fortably off as a mason in a three-shilling-a-year cottage.

From a little later in the century there is a will made by
Robert Pryse, servant to Richard Howse, that gives some idea of
the intimacy of relations between villagers and shows that even a
servant might have some property of his own. Robert had been ill,
and Howse was to look after him in return for a bequest of all
Pryse's possessions. He left a cow, four sheep, some scanty household stuff, and some moneys owed him: 15s due from Richard

Bewley for a brass pot, 13s 4d owed by Roger Hutton in wages, another 13s 4d from Roger's brother John who lived in Adderbury, a legacy of 7s 6d from a man in Syresham, and 7s due from Richard Queeny for the use of Robert's cow.

The arrival of a new Lord of the Manor was an occasion for stock taking: for finding out who was who, what were the ancient customs of the manor, and who owned what and under what tenure. This last was particularly important to the new Lord since his income and his powers in part depended on the outcome: his rents, heriots and other dues. Most land in Aynho was still held by copyhold: that is to say, a house and farmland were granted to a tenant for his own, his wife's and sometimes for his son's lives at a fixed rent that had been set for that particular land generations before. The term derived from the fact that the grant was recorded in the Court Rolls, and a copy of the entry was given to the tenant. There was a small amount of land in Aynho that was freehold: its owners were still liable to pay a rent to the Lord of the Manor, but could sell or bequeath it without his permission (which copyholders could not do).

It was at the Manor Court that enquiries were made about such matters, in order that all relevant facts should be formally set down by the Lord's Steward:-

> Boughton holdeth ii tenements and maketh undertenants in them and showeth no copies how she holdeth them. How be it she saith she hath under seal of Arms of the late Earl of Arundel
> Ric. Cowley saith he hath a copy but he showeth none. It is said that Mr. Hanslope hath let the land to him who has no authority to do so. Enquire further.
> John Brignell saith he hath paid a fine for his house and land and as yet has no copy made. He was provided one by the Steward

At the Manor Court there were new grants to be made:-

> To this Court came Henry Leche and Margaret his wife and John his son received from the Lord one messuage and a yardland and a half [i.e. about 45 acres] with the appertenancies, to hold . . . according to the custom of this manor, paying for them 26s a year in equal portions at the usual dates. And because the said messuage is in ruins, and the aforesaid Henry Margaret and John agree to rebuild it at their own expense, they are excused an entry fine . . .

and there were old grants to be confirmed to those who had their documents in order:-

> Richard Burbery came to Court with a charter for 1 messuage &
> 1 virgate granted by John Clavering to Jordan son of Richard son
> of Roger of Aynho, for 16s a year . . . In the 22nd year of King
> Edward son of King Henry [i.e. 1294] . . .

(It is interesting that the rent paid by Richard Burbery and which
had been set 250 years before was much the same as that still asked
from new copyholders. It suggests what one knows from other
sources: that the rents paid by farmers to their lords, under customary tenures, established long ago, were increasingly unrelated
to the real value of their lands. We shall see in due course the consequences of this, for they were far-reaching.)

There were other things to be enquired into as well as tenures,
at Rowland Shakerley's first Courts:-

> William Evans dwelleth in the Inn and as all the tenants say he is
> an honest man (and so it should appear) he desireth him to set up
> a sign which should please the Lord.
> There are iii or iiii beggarly ale houses and often times ill rule
> kept in them and better it were to have a couple of honest ale
> houses who will pay honest fines for licence to brew and bake.

and there were doubtful points to be cleared up by reference to
the oldest inhabitants, for whatever was declared to be ancient
custom could not be set aside:-

> Memorandum that Thomas Baker being of the age of iiii score
> years old dwelt in the tenement that Thomas Baker his son
> dwelleth in now: showeth him that Wainmore Hook lay to the
> Lord's tenements as the other meads do
> John Grene being of the same age showed Henry Leche that the
> same hook lay to his house as the other meadows do
> And also that the lays at Spichwell lie to the tenants as the other
> lands do & hath been in the time of their grandfathers and in
> their fathers' time that dwelt in the same tenements

The particular point at issue seems to have been whether the Lord's
tenants could claim a share in the hay and the grazing in certain
meadows. But evidence such as this shows the strength and continuity of village tradition and the continuity of village families
from the middle ages. Much in Aynho was still medieval when
Shakerley bought the Manor, though the next two hundred and
fifty years would see changes for which Revolution is too mild a
word.

The Court concerned itself with every aspect of village life.
Many of the orders made were clearly for everyone's benefit:-

> Every man shall carry for his yardland ii loads of stone to the
> highway at the time appointed in the week of Pentecost
> Every man shall cleanse the brook from Stanford to the Mill mead
> for to keep the water in the right course

and there were constantly new orders and amendments to old ones
made for the management of the common fields, to regulate the
complexities of communal farming: we shall discuss these, too,
later on. Similarly with the charges that the Court brought against
individual villagers: many of these were clearly for the common
good:-

> We do present Richard Butler for a hog stye that annoys people
> in the church way
> We do present John Whyte Margaret Greene and Robert Crackloe
> for laying their dunghills in the street before their doors

and in all these orders and charges the interest of the community
is very clear. In any case, there was probably little stigma attached
to many of these offences: everyone did such things from time to
time, everyone sometimes found the rules too onerous, and for
many people these infringements were probably calculated: against
the opportunity, say, of buying a load of manure at a bargain price
had to be weighed the likelyhood of a fine if one left the heap on
the roadside until one was ready to use it.

There was often petty crime of one sort or another to be
taken notice of:-

> Agnes Merevale for coming into Thomas Reve's garden there
> taking away onions and other herbage
> John Merevale for coming into Thomas Reve's meadow there
> taking away his hay
> Thomas Bratford for an affray made upon the Constable and
> drew his dagger at him
> Richard Queeny for beating goodwife Perry

while some of these offences might seem now to have been breaches of private morality rather than of public order:-

> William Baudwen lay with a whore   fine 4d.

It is not always easy for us now to appreciate the peculiar mix of
priorities that was accepted at the time: of concern for community
interest together with a respect for individuals' property; concern
for the preservation of ancient rights and acceptance of inquisi-
torial powers of the Lord's court. Ultimately, under new pressures
this ancient balance of interests would collapse, but for the moment it was still fully accepted even by those who fell foul of the
Court.

The making of rules and regulations was not wholy onesided. The Lord's servants might take more than their dues: his miller (at his mill where all villagers were obliged to grind their corn, for a fee) was frequently presented at the Court for taking excessive toll, the village butchers for selling short weight and the village ale-house keepers for selling short measures. And it seems that the villagers had for years been paying a small sum of money rather than sending their bread to the Lord's bakehouse (where, legally, he might insist on his tenants baking it) and were reluctant to start sending their bread out again:-

> We do agree to bake at the common bakehouse so that we may have an honest keeper otherwise we desire our Lord to stand to our old custom which is 2d a yardland

Occasionally the Court concerned itself with implementing new legislation, for instance (in the reign of Elizabeth) with a law to encourage English-made headgear:-

> To present all those which wear not English caps to the Church on the Sabbath Day & other Festival days according to the Statute

and with another to ensure that the villagers kept up their archery:-

> To present the particular names of all those which have able bodies and have not within three weeks last past any bows or arrows . . . and have not within the same time shot

but local issues took up almost all the Court's attention, and the reason why archery was falling out of practice was that even in the 1540's alternatives had reached Aynho:-

> George Smith doth keep a greyhound bitch and a handgun and hunteth with the bitch and Smith shoots with the gun at rabbitts pigeons and woodculies| [sic] .

That particular entry in the Court Rolls continues:-

> And Mr. Hanslope's servants keep a trammel

i.e., a fishing net, and several entries refer to poaching in the river Cherwell.

Many of the enquiries, the orders and the charges made in the early years of Rowland Shakerley's lordship suggest that he was anxious to re-assert rights that after generations of absentee land-lords were becoming laxly administered by the steward and allowed by the villagers to be quietly forgotton. Shakerley, a rich City merchant, must have been a man of character, and the villagers may well have been apprehensive about his intentions. The Arundels had administered the village through salaried officials who had probably been content to let things take their time-honoured courses, but the villagers of Aynho already knew, from evidence within walking distance and experience within their own lifetimes, that new men could make trouble.

For centuries the hamlet of Walton had stood astride the Port Way north of the village, between Aynho and King's Sutton where Walton Grounds Farm stands now. It was smaller than either place, and had often been lumped together with one or the other for taxation purposes and the like, but it had survived the plagues and the general fifteenth century fall in population until, late in the century, it was acquired by a certain John Goylyn. Goylyn laid the old fields of the hamlet down to sheep walks and (so it was reported) turned eighty people out of their houses and lands. By 1537 the place had been bought by a rich London grocer and wool merchant, Richard Fermor (an ancestor of Lord Hesketh of Easton Neston) who had done nothing to restore the land to cultivation nor to repair the ruined houses. The evidence of these men's depredations was still there for all to see, for when John Leland, the first antiquarian traveller in England, was passing by in the late 1530's he described the ruins of the chapel as still standing. The villagers of Aynho must have welcomed their new Lord with decidedly mixed feelings.

In 1561 Nicholas Hanslope was in trouble at the Manor Court for having petitioned the Northamptonshire justices against an enclosure that Rowland Shakerley was undertaking. We know no details: the record of Hanslope's misconduct is the only evidence we have that enclosure was taking place. It seems possible, though, that Shakerley was consolidating the lands of his demesne. Enclosure (of which we shall hear very much more) normally involved the grouping together of scattered strips of land to facilitate their cultivation. A few large, enclosed fields are easier to plough than many narrow strips, and much more satisfactory for grazing stock. An enclosed field could be farmed in any way its owner chose rather than being subjected to the communal decisions of the Manor Court.

An air photograph taken in 1946 of the area of the Park south of the great house, when it had certainly been un-ploughed for 350 years, shows it entirely covered with ridge-and-furrow: it had once, in fact, been part of the open fields of the village. But this area was already enclosed and the property of the Lord of the Manor at the beginning of the next century, and scarcely any of

the demesne lands then lay, as once they must have done, inter-
mingled among the other scattered strips of the village farmers.
Though we do not know for certain that it was Rowland Shakerley
who brought about this change, it seems likely. The villagers may
have lost little by the consolidation of the demesne lands (if this is
what happened) and others who had initially supported Nicholas
Hanslope in his petition, subsequently backed down. There were
by then Acts on the Statute Book limiting enclosure and depopulation that had not been there in the 1480's, and Shakerley had
less freedom of action than Goylyn had had at Walton. But with
their knowledge of the effects of enclosure, not just at Walton but
elsewhere as well, it would not have been surprising that villagers
should have been concerned when they first heard of Shakerley's
intentions.

Rowland Shakerley is an obscure figure to us, however
strongly he may have impinged on the villagers in the sixteenth
century. Like many other self-made men he no doubt hoped to
found a dynasty of country gentlemen and by purchasing an estate
to buy his way into the aristocracy, and had he succeeded we might
have known more about him. But fate was against him. He and his
wife had five daughters but only a single son, who died before his
father leaving only a son, young Rowland, and a daughter, Anne.
Old Rowland who had bought the estate died in the late 1560's,
and young Rowland his grandson only five years later, leaving the
estate to be divided among females: old Rowland's five daughters
and young Rowland's sister Anne. Though such a situation was no
longer as fraught with difficulties and dangers as it had been in the
middle ages, it was still not an easy one (it would not be even now).
Young Anne inherited a third part of the estate, and each of her
aunts a fifth part of the remainder. In the event, Mary, one of the
aunts, and her husband Thomas Marmion came to live at Aynho,
and Thomas Marmion proceeded to buy out his sisters-in-laws'
interests so that when he died he was able to leave two thirds of
the estate — all except Anne's share — to his son Shakerley Marmion. In commemorating his wife's family by calling their son
Shakerley, Thomas Marmion probably hoped to preserve the family
line, and by buying out his relations, he must have hoped to preserve the Aynho estate intact for his descendants.

But it cannot have been very satisfactory. A third of the
Manor was Anne's, while her aunts had two fifteenths each until
they were bought out. It must have caused confusion both for
landlords and tenants, and when he died, Thomas Marmion left his

son £1,500 in debt. Born in 1568, this son Shakerley Marmion only made matters worse when he made a marriage that may have been meant to get him out of his difficulties. His wife was Mary Lukin, a daughter of another rich London merchant, who may have been glad for her to marry into a County family. But the £600 she brought with her was nothing, and Shakerley's debts went on mounting up. He or his father had probably rebuilt the great house, and that cannot have been a light undertaking. He borrowed money at 10 per cent; he borrowed another £2,000 from his father-in-law, and in 1611 he raised a further £1,995 by selling their freeholds to eleven of the village's copyholders.

It may have been anticipation of the possible results of Shakerley Marmion's improvidence that prompted the Aynho farmers to buy their freeholds. They may well have foreseen the possibility of his having ultimately to sell the Manor, and had some foreboding about the likely consequences for them. They must have known that the customary rents they paid and the customary successions to copyholds were less and less related to the economics of modern life, and already other, more forceful landlords than Shakerley Marmion were terminating such ancient tenures and uneconomic rents.

Indeed it is only by assuming such fears that one can explain the very large sums that Aynho farmers paid for their freeholds. Peter Parker, for instance, paid £100 for the freehold to one yard-land (a virgate) for which his copyhold rent would have been 16s or 18s a year. For 1½ yardlands, John Loe paid £150 and William Howes, £200. Their rents would have been around £1.4s. The highest price was paid by Richard Stanton, £350 for 2 yardlands, and Stanton was the first among these newly-enfranchised yeomen to die which suggests that their objectives (and Stanton's willingness to pay such a price) were to secure an inheritance to their children. Free inheritance prevented the Lord of the Manor from reclaiming the land when a man's widow died, and provided the freeholder with greater (indeed almost total) liberty to bestow his property where he wished. The fact, too, that these yeomen were able to find such large amounts of money goes a long way to confirming a landlord's view of the situation: that their rents were by now absurdly small in relation to the money they were making by farming.

The long term results for Aynho were the creation of a class of freeholders that would try to maintain its economic independence of the squire for another two hundred years. It put off the day when every villager would be the squire's man, and must have done much to support their defiance of him when — as under a new Lord of the Manor they would do — their dissensions from his authority were to grow.

But to allow so many of his tenants to buy their land, must have seemed even to Shakerley Marmion a desperate expedient, losing the Lordship over a third of the land which the Lords of the Manor had exercised at least since the Norman Conquest. Yet still it was not enough. Finally, in 1615, with the agreement of his creditors and of his father-in-law's widow and son, he agreed to sell his lands and to put what money was left in trust for his family. The purchaser was the younger son of a Cheshire squire, Richard Cartwright, who had made a fortune at the Bar and who bought Shakerley Marmion's two-thirds share of the Manor for £5,250. The next year, in 1616, he completed negotiations with Anne's husband, Sir Paul Tracy, and bought the remaining one-third for a further £3,000.

Marmion left Aynho and is lost to sight, but there is a foot-note to the Marmions' story in that his son, another Shakerley, born in 1603, was among the few people born in Aynho ever to have achieved anything in the world. He killed a man in a duel and became a soldier of fortune, but is remembered as a playwright. He died young, in 1639, but his plays (in spite of their not being very good) did achieve quite a success, and one in particular is of interest to us, *The Antiquary*, in which are a spendthrift heir, a disinherited brother, a moneylender with a foolish son and a grasping daughter. Young Shakerley may have been too carefree a young man for his family's misfortunes to have oppressed him very much, but one feels that, thinly disguised and with the generations of the characters transposed, the ruin of his family is all there.

Richard Cartwright bought Aynho at Michaelmas, 1615, moved his family down at Easter, 1616, and at Whitsun moved to Aynho himself. He was 51, and though more or less retired from the law, his energies were very far from exhausted as the people of Aynho were to discover. His family was not an old one; to judge by the return he made to a Heralds' visitation, he did not know who his great grandmother was. But it was a time when large for-tunes were to be made in trade or at the law, and when many new families were rising to take the place of those nobility who (like the Arundels) had fallen on hard times. The Shakerleys had tried and failed; the Cartwrights were to be more successful.

In view of the impact that the Cartwrights were to have on

the village, it seems a good moment to describe what Aynho was like in the early seventeenth century when Richard Cartwright arrived. Of the physical fabric of the village before the late seventeenth century, we know very little. There are only fragments at best remaining now of any of the houses that were standing in 1615, and none of these preserves anything like its original appearance. It is likely that many of the villagers' houses were still partly of timber, and that only the richer villagers had houses of stone. But though the earliest surviving map of the village was not made until eighty years later, it probably shows well enough the location of the houses at the beginning of the century. The main road ran due east and west from Buckingham to Deddington and beyond, past a row of houses which probably already included an inn (the Red Lion, now the Cartwright Arms), past the church, the rectory and the manor house and a row of prosperous houses standing opposite on the street, and then on, due west, down the hill through what is now a part of the Park. The square at the centre of the village was already there with houses round it, there were more houses on both sides of the Banbury road where now they stand on the east side only, and there may have been another inn (the Bell) there. Further afield there was already a scatter of houses on Blacksmith's Hill, though others were built there in the seventeenth century on what were probably virgin sites. There were few houses away from the centre of the village. Since the farmers held their lands scattered throughout the fields to east and west, they chose to live in the village itself, centrally to all their numerous holdings. Save for the smallest of the village farmers, Lawrence Watts who lived in the Square, the others lived on the edge where they had room for yards and barns, and the Home Farm and the College Farm, at least, still stand where they have stood for four hundred years even though they do not preserve any individual buildings of that age.

The simplest houses probably had only two rooms, or maybe only one with a loft for sleeping in. But though the houses themselves have disappeared, we do know how some of them were lived in. These are the homes of people who had just died and of whose possessions inventories were made. This, in the seventeenth and early eighteenth centuries, was a standard practice: for almost everyone who had enough property for them to make a Will, or whose bequests were sufficiently complicated to require a precise valuation of their possessions, there was an inventory taken immediately after death, and very informative these are.

The actual valuations in these inventories should be taken with a pinch of salt. Much, clearly, depended on the skill and judgment of the 'praisers', those who carried out the appraisal and who were chosen, usually, from among the villagers themselves. They could not always write (though that in itself does not mean that they did not know the value of things) and there are sometimes discrepancies to show how subjective the business was. For instance in 1671, when John and Elizabeth Bett died within four months of each other and when two of the three appraisers were the same in each case, the goods in the Chamber ('one bedstead and bedding to it, one trucklebed and bedding to it, three pair of sheets, one boardcloth one warming pan one chair') were assessed at £1.10s the first time and only £1 the second.

And two other points are worth making. One, that the contents of houses seem to have differed very much less, between the fairly poor and the fairly rich, than did the value of their beasts and crops. It is clear that all the houses in the village were extremely scantily furnished by modern standards, and yet that people's needs in terms of physical possessions seem to have been easily satisfied. (The alternative explanation, that few people owned great quantities of goods because even the richest had no spare cash, is not born out by the facts.) The other point to make is that the low value of people's property, and the small amount of their cash in hand, did not prevent them from finding quite large sums of money when the need arose.

Lawrence Watts, who died in 1634, had been Richard Cartwright's shepherd. He was able to farm for himself, in a small way, as well, and he was one of those who had bought their freeholds from Shakerley Marmion — in his case, 20 acres for £70. His, however, was the smallest freehold in the village, and one would like to think it was carefulness rather than stinginess that made him insert a rather mean clause in his Will — that if his widow Elizabeth claimed her one-third share in his estate, 'as by lawe shee may have', then she was not to have her 40s marriage portion returned to her. Lawrence Watts's inventory ran:-

Clothes and money	£2 10 0
In the Hall:-	
One table, one form, stools & other implements	£0 10 0
In the room next the Hall:-	
One wool bed, two blankets	£0 10 0
One bolster, two pillow bears, one pillow,	
three pair sheets, three napkins, one table cloth	£1 8 0
In the chamber over the Hall:-	

One bedstead, one feather bed, one rug, one bolster, one coffer, with other trumpery	£1	15	0
In the kitchen:-			
Brass and pewter	£0	15	0
Malt mill salting trough, with other trumpery	£1	3	4
In Dairy house & Buttery:-			
3 barrels, one tub, & other lumber	£0	10	0
In the barn:-			
Corn thrashed & unthrashed	£1	0	8
Bacon	£0	6	0
Seven sheep	£2	6	8
Three cows & one bullock, with hay	£10	0	0
1 garner & three ladders	£0	10	0
Wood about the yard	£0	10	0
5 lands of corn sown	£2	0	0

A rather larger house, with more bedrooms, was Elizabeth Young's who died in 1639. She was a widow who had remarried. Her first husband had been Edward Letch, probably descended from Henry Letch who had farmed one-and-a-half yardlands in Rowland Shakerley's time. Her second husband was John Young of Thame, and the land she had been farming with her son, another Henry Letch, was probably the same land that the family had held a century before.

In the Hall:-			
One table and frame one cupboard one chair with other odd things	£0	23	4
In the chamber adjoining the hall:-			
One bedstead with bedding and other odd things there	£0	40	0
In the chamber over the buttery:-			
Two bedsteads with bedding & other things there	£0	20	0
In the buttery:-			
Certain barrels & other things there	£0	10	0
In the chamber over the hall & entry:-			
One bed with cheeses and cheese boards & other things there	£0	10	0
In the kitchen:-			
One malt mill & certain brewing vessels & other things there	£0	40	0
The brass & pewter:-	£0	50	0
The linen 12 pair of sheets & other linen	£4	0	0
The corn in the barn unthreshed, & corn & malt in the house:-	£6	0	0
The winter corn, barley, pease & oats found in the field being 59 ridges	£16	0	0
The carts ploughs & other instruments of husbandry	£0	30	0
The two hovels of wood, & other wood about the yard with ladders & sheepracks	£6	0	0

One sow & pigs & two stores	£0	40	0
One horse, 5 beasts & a yearling	£16	0	0
48 sheep & 12 lambs	£12	0	0
Her apparel	£3	0	0
The money in her purse	£0	20	0

It is likely that a good many of the poorer men of the village, even though they owned no land themselves, rented a few strips from those who did. It seems that until 1620, too, the landless poor had the right to graze a cow on the commons, while later the squire undertook to pasture a few of their beasts on his own land. Thomas Mott, who died in 1632 and who paid Richard Cartwright 4s a year rent for his cottage, owned no land but none the less left his wife a cow and a crop of corn on the ground; one of the farmers must have let him some land. He described himself in his will as a labourer, but he may have been a sawyer as well: he also left 200 boards valued at 20s. Thomas Swetnam was another man who worked at two callings at once: described in his will as a husbandman, and holding 28 acres from Richard Cartwright, he was clearly a blacksmith too. To his son Giles he left, inter alia, a pair of bellows, an anvil, a vice, a 'bicborne' (whatever that may be) 'with other tools belonging to the trade', while to his other son, Thomas, he bequeathed two horses with their harness, a cart, a plough, a harrow and a dung cart. Incidently, he had a shop next to one of the Inns, almost certainly where is now the public bar of the Cartwright Arms. We shall hear more of Giles Swetnam later.

By far the largest of the early seventeenth century inventories to have survived is that of Thomas Collins, who died in 1607 and who probably kept the Bell Inn, in the village on the Banbury road. Running an establishment like the Bell must have been a full time occupation, and the inventory is too long to quote in full. There were eight rooms, besides a mill house, two stables, and outbuildings in the yard. There were thirteen beds, besides six flock beds worth 40s and six feather beds valued at no less than £10. There were three and a half dozen napkins, fifteen bolsters, nineteen tablecloths and as many as 41 pair of sheets. The eating — and drinking — arrangements were on a comparable scale, with four vats, three hogsheads, four great barrels, two little barrels, five kettles, quantities of plates and dishes of wood and pewter, and eighteen cheeses. The roads through Aynho must have been busy, and the Bell was not the only inn in the place.

Beyond the village lay the fields, where in 1616 some 27 men had holdings. Scarcely any of the present field boundaries existed then, and the land of the manor must have looked as different from its present appearance as must the village itself. There are still some huge, ancient hedges running along the parish boundaries, particularly on the north where there are traces of banks and ditches that probably had their origins when Aynho was first divided off from King's Sutton and Walton. There are a few other old hedges elsewhere, where one can amuse oneself by testing (with only moderate success) the theory of hedgerow dating by counting the number of species they contain. But almost all the fields are now differently bounded, changed out of recognition by enclosure on the high ground and by the canal and the railways in the valley. Even the roads have been altered: the Charlton road used to be a continuation of Blacksmith's Hill, the Deddington road used to run straight down the hill where now it first twists northward towards Banbury, the Port Way was a highway rather than a dank ravine between park walls, and the Oxford and Bicester road took a different course from its present one. There were spinnies where today there are none, and open fields where now there are woods. Only the basic structure is unchanged: the village clustering round the spring on the edge of the hill, the arable on the higher ground and the pasture in the valley.

Rowland Shakerley's enclosure had probably done little to affect the balance of rich and poor. In 1616 there was still much the same number of farmers in the village as there had been in 1545 and still holding similar amounts of land, though probably better off now as the result of price rises that benefitted almost all farmers in the later sixteenth century. Most people still held multiples or fractions of the old virgate, now usually called a yardland, and this was still of about 30 acres, more or less. A man might hold 60 acres, 29, 45, 61 and so forth. Out of the 27 farmers in Aynho, nineteen held between 20 and 68 acres, four had less (two of them innkeepers, Richard Collins and Bridget Bell) and only four held more: the tenant of the College Farm, Mr. Drope the parson, Thomas Hanslope and the squire himself. Richard Cartwright held by far the most. He had 300 acres of meadow and pasture, mostly where the Park was to be made later on, 157 acres of arable, 228 acres in the Warren (where he probably pastured sheep as well as raising rabbits) and 100 more in enclosures round the great house. His great advantage as a farmer was that since Shakerley's enclosure most of the Lord's land had been in 'closes', enclosures where beasts could safely be left untethered and unattended without risk of their damaging crops and where, conversely, crops could be grown without danger from stray animals. Magdalen College owned some 161 acres, some in closes and some in open fields, and all the other farmers put together farmed some 1,200 acres. A few had closes, notably Mr. Drope the parson who had glebe land as well as freehold of his own, but most held their land scattered about the open fields.

Perhaps the most striking thing about these open fields was the number of strips (called 'lands') that these farmers worked. Thomas Hanslope's 109 acres were distributed in no less than 262 strips and closes, with far the greater part in strips. Elizabeth Young's 45 acres lay in 109 lands, and between them the farmers of the village — all, that is, except the College and the Squire — held their 1,120 acres in about 2,600 separate lands. One would think it would be almost impossible to remember whose was which, but disputes seem never to have arisen. (The fact that so complicated a system could work so smoothly is in part a witness to the intellectual emptiness of village life: these complexities absorbed the energies of intelligent men because there was so little else to occupy them.) But it must have been extraordinarily wasteful of time, just getting one's team from one land to the next, which might be a hundred yards away or right the other end of the parish. It must, too, have required constant policing by the fieldsmen to prevent inadvertent encroachments of other people's lands. When ploughing, a two foot balk was supposed to be left between adjacent strips to prevent this happening, but these balks must constantly have been whittled away to nothing.

These strips were arranged in 'furlongs', divisions of various sizes, of which some two thirds lay east of the village. Each furlong had its own name; a list of all those recorded at the beginning of the eighteenth century is at page 303 with a map to show where they lay. Already by that time some furlongs had been enclosed and their names lost: the point of the names was that everyone in the village knew them, and when many people were illiterate and there were no maps it was only by referring to these furlongs by their names that one could discuss the complexities of running the fields. Some of these names have obvious meanings: Raynsbury Furlong (next the Camp), Spetchill Leys (perhaps once a property of the Hospital), Middle Sands, or Six Acres. Some are evocative: Sparrow Hill, Deadlands, Crabtree, Elderbush. Others are obscure: Wensden, Buglow, Arslong, Norcott Hill. When enclosed, and no longer farmed by the villagers, these names could easily be forgotten (though some are still in use as names of the modern fields that lie roughly where these furlongs lay).

Villagers generally had their furlongs grouped in two or more large, common fields, of more or less equal size, to make possible a two-, three-, or four-course crop rotation. In Aynho the furlongs east of the village were called the Upper Fields, those to the West, the Lower, but since one group was almost twice the size of the other they cannot have been worked as a two-field system and divided like that. But since in all there were some 150 furlongs, varying in size from 160 acres down to 17, there was considerable scope for re-grouping them and varying the rotations when the villagers thought it desirable, for instance when they wanted to introduce new crops.

In 1639 a three-course rotation was introduced, which was to last with variations for a century, but we do not know what the rotation in Aynho was before that. Elizabeth Young was growing corn and pease when her inventory was taken in that year, and some of her land must have been lying fallow. The inventory was made in May, when as much as possible of her arable would have been under cultivation, yet of her 109 lands only a half – 59 – were sown. This rather indicates a two-course rotation, with half the land lying fallow each year. On the other hand, the Manor Court had agreed in 1574 to make a drift way – a temporary path for cattle – across a certain field every fourth year, and this suggests four courses. We shall probably never know: the trouble for us is that the villagers took so many things for granted without having to write them down.

Besides the arable fields, there were commons for grazing. On the pasture fields and in the meadows animals were allowed at times of year that were strictly controlled in order to ensure the growth of grass, while the number of animals that each farmer might graze was in strict proportion to the amount of his arable. Rights to cut hay in the meadows seem to have been allotted by ballot. A hundred years later – early in the eighteenth century – the rules were written down, and though they are now virtually incomprehensible they are worth quoting as a further reminder of the complexities of the system:-

> The meadows are divided into 17 setts And every Sett hath eight Hides as they are laid down in the Book.
> Again the meadman makes Subdivisions in every Hide which are changeable according to a Custom held in the Meadows every year.
> The first six Hides in every Sett are each of them divided into four Parts of Subdivisions which are changeable every Year
> The seventh Hide is divided into three Parts
> The eighth Hide is accounted to be five Parts which is College.

The names of meadows were as pictureque as those of the arable furlongs — Flaggy Doles, Pill Doles, Ripham Smatts, Truckingham Mead, Radford Hook and others.

There was rough grazing, too, at all times of year on the waste lands lying along the roadsides and by the stream, where the land was too marshy to cultivate or where arable would have been trampled by the passage of traffic. At other times the fallow was grazed: there were always weeds and grass to be eaten, the animals' dung fertilised the land, and later on the fallow was often sown with fodder crops between the courses of wheat or barley.

The rules for managing the fields were made at the Manor Court. When so many owners had adjacent holdings it is not surprising that the rules were complicated, extremely detailed, had frequently to be altered and absorbed much of the Court's time. The Court met twice a year, usually in March and October, and the Parish Clerk would announce forthcoming Courts in church the Sunday before. Where it met is not clear, though it may have been in the nave of the church, and it was generally presided over by the Lord of the Manor's steward who was often a lawyer. All the males in the village over the age of 12 were bound to attend the meetings of the court, and men were fined if they stayed away. The annual 'view of frankpledge', the review of all the adult male villagers who owed allegiance to the Lord of the Manor, generally took place at the October court, when a list would be made of them all and each would pay headsilver, a penny, as a token of their and their lord's obligations. Occasionally the villagers seem to have absented themselves en masse, and some twenty or thirty would be fined for non-attendance. This was usually on the occasion of some particular contention between the villagers and their lord, but it was a token protest at best, and an expensive one; in the last resort they were bound by the court's decisions, and bound to the lord's jurisdiction in all local affairs.

The manor court always had to give a good deal of time to the rules for farming the common fields. The times for putting beasts onto the commons had to be considered year by year according to the weather; it was not always possible to lay down rules that would hold for all conditions

> The meadows and cowpastures shall be hained upon Candlemass day next and no inhabitants shall put or keep any cattle in the said cowpastures after the same day until the 9th day of May next nor|in the meadowes until every mans hay be mowed and carried away

or again

> No inhabitant or tenant shall keep any sheep in the meadow or
> cowpasture at any time during this year next to come

On the other hand individualism had to be checked since otherwise the whole system would get out of hand: a free-for all with
everyone growing what he wanted on adjacent lands would mean
the contamination of all of them with other people's crops, and
unless animals were herded together they could easily get out of
control

> If any tenant of this Manor do refuse to ear, or do not plow his
> arable lands . . . according to the ancient custom, he shall forfeit
> iiis. ivd.

and

> It is ordered that no man shall suffer his beasts to be put forth
> before the hour of five of the clock At which time the herd shall
> blow his horn

And there were constantly points of detail to be made, many of
which had to be repeated year after year because people got slack
about them: such things as ensuring that everyone's pigs were
ringed, that gleaners did not go on the stubble before the last corn
had been carried, that men whose furlongs ran down to ditches
kept them scoured, that people preserved the balks between their
strips and so forth.

The policing of the fields was done by officials chosen at the
Manor Courts, or appointed in accordance with the Court's orders.
Some of these were quite lowly jobs

> It is ordered that there shall be a hog herd chosen before our
> ladyday next and a wont catcher provided before St. Andrew's
> day next.

More important were the fieldsmen, whose job seems to have been
primarily to see that animals were driven onto and off the appropriate commons at the right times of year, to check encroachments
and to maintain hedges and fences (spending, where necessary,
funds provided by fines for hedge-breaking and the like), and the
hayward, whose job was to impound stray beasts until their owners
came to reclaim them. Those appointed did not always match up
to the job

> We the inhabitants of Aynho whose names are here unto sub-
> scribed desire that John Collins our Hayward by reason he hath
> much neglected his office whereby we have been predged [sic]

> that Mary Hutchins or any other whom you please may be put to
> the office that may perform it better

But though his job was onerous, the hayward was not unrewarded

> His wage is to be a peck of millcorn, 8d in money, and two
> sheaves of maslin for every yard land, a penny pinlock of the in-
> habitants and 2d a pinlock of strangers, and a cock of hay of
> every inhabitant that hath hay of his own.

(i.e. a penny from a villager and 2d from a stranger when his beast
was impounded; maslin is a mixture of wheat or barley and rye.)

The most important officials were the jurymen, twelve of
them, recruited from the leading men in the village. Their appointment was not democratic; in the 1630's it was complained that the
squire was selecting jurymen from among the less well-off of the
inhabitants, and the implication was that the more prosperous villagers expected as of right to be chosen for the jury, at the same
time as their property and relative independence would provide a
guarantee for villagers' rights against the Lord of the Manor. (In a
great village lawsuit of the late 1630's, Thomas Swetnam the blacksmith's son was described by his opponents as a man 'of mean and
low estate' in contrast to Thomas Hanslope whose gentlemanly
property commanded respect and deference, and it was accepted
by everyone that a poor man could not carry much weight in village
councils.)

It was the jury's task to frame the orders that were sanctioned
by the Court, to enquire into any infringements of the customs of
the Manor and the orders they had made, and to present the offenders at the next court. It was no sinecure:-

> The jury is to meet together at the Common Fields upon or before
> St. Andrew's day next in the morning by eight of the clock to the
> end that they may view the encroachments and where one neigh-
> bour have ploughed upon another

and

> It is ordered that the whole jury shall meet together upon Tuesday
> next by eight of the clock in the forenoon at the Cross and there
> to take view of the copyholders' and other the lord's houses
> whether they be in sufficient repair

(Copyholders and tenants were obliged to maintain their buildings,
and were fined at the Manor Court if they did not. We shall return
to this matter of dilapidations later on, when Richard Cartwright
was tightening up on customs that may have been carelessly administered in the recent past.) And if they failed in their duties,

jurymen and other court officials could be fined by the Court

> We present Richard Stanton, one of the jury, for refusing to view
> the waste done to the Lord's houses.

Other officials, too, were appointed by the Court. There was
probably general agreement about the usefulness of the ale-tasters,
whose job was to test the beer in the village pubs for quality and
quantity:-

> Thomas Gardner and George Pemberton do continue in their
> office of aletastership, and do present Richard Collins and Bridget
> Bell for selling with unlawful measures before they be assized by
> the aletasters.

(Thomas Gardner was described a little later as 'a man of mean
estate and simple or silly understanding' but his father had farmed
60 acres a few years earlier, the job of aletaster was not a particularly demanding one, and the villagers may have thought that
Thomas Gardner was just the man for it.)

The official whose job it was to present at the Manor Court
all the village's petty criminals, and to bring the more serious ones
to justice elsewhere, was the Constable. It was his duty, too, to see
that strangers were moved on and did not secure permanent lodgings in the village. For one thing, there was the danger that they
might become burdens on the poor rates. For another, one might
not know a stranger's background; he might more easily commit
crimes than villagers whose lives were so well known to each other,
and then make his escape. Nor was he accountable to the Aynho
court for breaches of local orders and customs. Someone in the
village had to stand surety for him if he remained, and from time
to time villagers were presented for taking in 'unlawful inmates' as
they were called, lodgers whose behaviour had not been vouched
for.

> It is ordered that after All Hallows tide no man shall receive any
> person dwelling out of the town nor any that shall hereafter
> marry dwelling in the town . . . unless they first give security by
> bond in the sum of £10 to the church wardens and overseers of
> the poor . . . to discharge the town of any charge that shall hap-
> pen to the town by them or their children.

The provisions about marriage — though it is badly expressed, the
villagers knew what was meant — is probably a provision for an
Aynho girl marrying a man from elsewhere who then came to live
in the village. The job of Constable seems not to have been one of

the more popular offices. To be appointed to it was one of the liabilities of being one of the village's more prosperous inhabitants,
and to be fined for not undertaking it was probably seen as a legitimate way of buying oneself off

> We present Edward Jarvis constable for neglecting his office of
> constable and for not punishing of rogues and vagrants according
> to the Statute

which said that they were to be whipped before they were sent on
their way.

More serious offences than those that the Manor court could
deal with were referred to the King's courts, and from time to
time people from Aynho had to travel to the county assizes, at
Daventry, perhaps, or even further. These have seldom left any
records locally, though one can be sure that Aynho people did get
into serious trouble from time to time. But occasionally there are
still echoes of these affairs to be picked up, and one of them was
William Stanton's attempt on a young wife, Margaret Knott.

The full details are lost, and in any case they would probably
not be particularly edifying: how Stanton was alleged to have
attempted to rape Margaret Knott, and was only prevented through
her husband's appearing in the nick of time. (Stanton was a lusty
fellow: seven children survived him, all daughters, who proceeded
through their husbands to indulge in acrimonious suits about their
inheritances. Stanton's youngest daughter was called Silence.)
Stanton was a churchwarden, and Thomas Drope the parson's son
complained of his behaviour to the archdeacon, while someone
else, perhaps Thomas Hanslope, laid an information before the
magistrates and had him hauled up at the assizes.

The details of the affair are submerged in a morass of allega-
tions and counter-claims, largely intended to discredit witnesses:
how Thomas Hanslope, riding home from Banbury, did indeed fall
heavily from his horse, but not because he was drunk; 'Mr. Hanslope was then very sober, but his horse was so skittish and unruly
that no man can sit or hold him'. Giles Swetnam the Smith, however, was 'in this deponent's judgement, unfit to do this deponent's
work for that he did both stagger in his going and stammer in his
speech, and for the same the said Swetnam was often reprehended
by the wife of the said deponent'. Stanton, said one, 'is much employed about Mr. Cartwright's business, and he is often sent for by
many strangers and neighbours to Inns and Alehouses in Aynho
and elsewhere, and if it were not for Mr. Cartwright's business he
would not come there, at least not so often'. But someone else

claimed that Stanton 'has no occasion to go to alehouses on Mr. Cartwright's business, but rather on occasions of his own.' And there were plenty of questions that wanted answering. Who paid for Margaret Knott to go all the way to Wellingborough to complain to the Justices? And did not Edward Jarvis often call Mr. Hanslope a drunkard these last seven years?

And the documents preserve moments of daily life. Of a man pausing for a moment to speak to a neighbour on the way out of church; of three or four companions talking in a pub in Brackley, after market, 'merry, but not drunk'; of Mr. Hanslope standing in Richard Crackloe's shop and having a document delivered to him there, and turning sideways to read it in the light from the window. The village that Richard Cartwright bought in 1615 was a community, full of individuals and full of life.

Chapter 4

The New Broom

It should by now be obvious that the village that Richard Cartwright had acquired was (like all villages) a place of long established customs and vested interests, and of individuals and families whose pride and independence were considerable, even if their wealth was no match for his. If this is not yet apparent, it soon will be, for Richard Cartwright was an ambitious man and in the village he found some worthy opponents.

Some of what his ambition led him to do by way of making money and making his mark in County society, must have raised no objections from anyone. In 1621 he obtained a grant from the King, under the Great Seal, for a market each Tuesday and for a fair to be held at Michaelmas. (The medieval market had probably failed centuries before, and the fair may also have been a revival.) A market house was built, probably somewhere near the triangle of grass outside what is now the Cartwright Arms, and the first market to be held was announced by a proclamation, read out publicly in Northampton. (Before local newspapers, and before printed, public notices, this was the only way of having official announcements published.) The market was to be held between ten in the morning and sunset, and all transactions were to be written down in a toll book.

What happened to the market is not known; it probably did not outlast the troubled years of the Civil War. In the 1660's there was talk of using the market house to accomodate a new school, and in the 1680's one of the village's largest farmers, John Pruce, was keeping his old lumber in it. Richard Cartwright sold corn there for a year or two, generally barley in quite small lots to local people for malting. But even he sold larger lots at the markets in Deddington and Brackley, and the established competition was probably too stiff for the new market to withstand.

It was relatively easy to make headway of a sort with the County. Richard Cartwright was a man of substance, a man with land and authority, and naturally a man to appoint to local offices. Before long he was a magistrate, and soon a deputy lieutenant, but he seems to have found the easy-going ways of the country very irritating. On one occasion, for instance, he had been asked to make up the local muster book and the Muster certificates — the lists of local men liable for service in the militia, and the records of their attendance at drill. Nobody took the militia very seriously, and when he went with his carefully prepared documents to present them, by appointment, at a meeting in Northampton, he found that only one other person (Sir John Danvers) had bothered to turn up. The men of longer standing were probably only too glad for the pushy newcomer to do the thankless, routine jobs on which the running of the County depended. But it was a different matter altogether when it came to dealing with the village.

Richard Cartwright, it has already been suggested, was not a conciliatory man — though it has to be admitted that in Aynho he had some cantankerous neighbours to deal with. And while he, no doubt, saw his actions solely as the assertion of his legitimate rights as Lord of the Manor, the villagers must have regarded them very differently. What the villagers probably thought of as a wise regard for established customs on the part of the Marmions, Richard Cartwright probably regarded as mere fecklessness, and the many ways in which he tried to re-assert the Lord of the Manor's authority will be described later on. But in promoting a further enclosure of some of the common fields he made himself felt immediately, and built up a legacy of ill-feeling that lasted for a generation.

Rowland Shakerley, by his enclosure in 1561, had probably consolidated the demesne arable in the area south of the great house, where the park was to lie later. On the slopes of the hill, in two or more great fields, lay the common pasture for the village beasts. On this land the whole village had had grazing rights in proportion to their holdings of arable, rights for so many cows, horses and sheep in proportions strictly controlled. The Lord of the Manor shared these rights with the villagers. Richard Cartwright had spent a good deal of money in buying stock when he came to Aynho, and when he found his own animals and the villagers' were grazing the commons together, catching each others' diseases and his suffering with theirs from over-grazing and poor pasturage, he decided that a further enclosure, of the pasture, would solve the problem by separating his beasts from the rest.

There were other things that might be settled at the same time. One was that the village farmers had scarcely any enclosures — closes — at all, and might well be glad of the chance to acquire them. Another was that the rabbits in the Lord's warren roamed throughout the Manor, uncontrolled and unconfined and doing great damage; by an enclosure the Lord might obtain some worthwhile concession in return for walling-in his warren. The precise details of what was proposed and what was done are unclear among the masses of claim and counter-claim, but it appears that the squire gave up his grazing rights over the village pasture in return for being allowed to enclose a part of it for his own, while at the same time the village farmers enclosed the whole of the lower field arable — the whole area of common arable lying west of the village and which until then had lain in strips — for their own several use.

The squire had some initial encouragement, since when Marmion had sold some of the copyholders their freeholds in 1611, one of the inducements for them had been that they might be able to tidy up their scattered holdings by exchanges and enclosure. At the Michaelmas Court in 1617 Richard Cartwright told the freeholders that he proposed enclosing 300 acres of the common pasture, while he would give up rights for 1000 sheep, 100 cattle and 20 horses. And he added, rather provocatively, that if he liked he could have a good deal more. Apparently, so he claimed afterwards, everyone agreed except Mr. Drope the parson, while Edward Love, the old tenant of the College Farm, promised to use his best offices with the Warden and Fellows to go along with the scheme.

Edward Love died in 1618, but the next year the squire and the villagers agreed to name two people on each side to try and work out a division that would be fair all round, and they appointed a surveyor to calculate exactly how much land and what rights of common were held by everyone. The squire spent quite a lot of money in buying land from two freeholders so that he would have more leeway in arranging the necessary exchanges, and he wrote for the assessors a note that began:-

> How bountifully and well I deal with my Neighbours of Aynho
> in their intended Inclosure if the same take effect

But he congratulated himself too soon.

All would have been well, he complained afterwords, save for the opposition of Mr. Drope and of Richard Stanton, the latter of whom had paid £350 for his 58 acres of freehold in 1611 and felt entitled now to have some reservations about exchanging part of it with someone else. After all the other villagers had agreed to the distribution, these two, claimed Richard Cartwright, had talked them all into changing their minds and backing out. He appealed to the Court of Chancery. He said the enclosure benefitted Church and Commonwealth by increasing tithes, production and profits, and that it was against all equity that the wilful obstruction of one or two individuals, 'occasioned upon some private displeasure causelessly conceaved' should have prevented the enclosure that most people had originally favoured.

But by that time opposition had grown. The College and the parson said that they had no right to exchange their lands even had they wanted to, which they did not. Mr. Drope, the parson, said he was unhappy about the title to some of the land he was being asked to accept: William Howes's belonged to a minor, and Mr. Hanslope's was subject to a chief rent. (Later on Richard Cartwright tried to claim that Hanslope's was not freehold at all, so the parson was probably right to be careful.) The college said it was quite irrelevant that their former tenant had agreed to the exchanges, and that in any case the land could not be farmed more profitably than it was at present, being

> continually sown with some grain or other as far as the same will endure to be sown by the Common Course of Husbandry of the Country

William Stanton concurred

> The enclosure would make the lands far worse for Rotting of Sheep and for Tillage For that by all experience the straightning of Waste and Commons is the Chiefest Cause of staining the grounds and rotting of sheep And that open and common fields are most Commodious for Tillage

and he and Mr. Drope denied that they had

> either misled menaced or dissuaded any of the Tenants or Commoners otherways than by delivering his opinion freely concerning the said Enclosure

and denied, too, all responsibility for having had the land surveyed in the first place. If that was how Mr. Cartwright chose to spend his money, that was entirely up to him.

Another group of freeholders agreed with enclosure in principle, but objected to the land they had been allotted, claimed that the squire had overstated his rights of common and tried to deny them theirs. They continued to complain about the squire's rabbits, and wanted the enclosure to provide that cottagers should no longer have any grazing rights for cows. The only people who declared themselves whole-heartedly in favour of the enclosure were, as might have been expected, the squire's own tenants.

But the enclosure went through in the end, and created major changes in the Aynho landscape. After the enclosure there was no more common arable west of the village; the common fields there, lying in two long strips either side of the Hobrook that runs west from the College Farm, were all divided up into separate closes and awarded to one or another of the freeholders. A good deal of land that had formerly been common pasture now became the property of the squire. It is likely that with this further enclosure of ancient arable, new crop rotations had to be worked out for the land still remaining open east of the village. But the fact that the enclosure of as much as a quarter of the arable could take place and leave the rest a successful and viable system for nearly two hundred years more is good evidence of how adaptable and tenacious the old open field system was.

The enclosure left a nasty taste, both at the time and afterwards. It must have fomented the already bad relations between the squire and the parson, that Mr. Drope was dissatisfied with the sum he was offered to compound his tithes on the squire's land. Even when the amount had been increased to £48 by the commissioners appointed to arbitrate between them, Drope still thought it insufficient, and took the case to the Court of Chancery where the Lord Chancellor awarded him £60. Ten years later Mr. Hanslope was still complaining that the commons were less good since enclosure than they had been before it. In the 1630's John Cartwright, Richard's son, claimed in evidence to a Royal Commission on depopulation (when the effects of enclosure throughout the country were worrying the government) that his father had acted generously. The villagers themselves were not so sure; they felt on the whole that they had lost more than they had gained. The information is too scanty for us to make out the rights and wrongs of it. We do not have all the figures we should need to reconstruct the spread of the fields before the enclosure, and besides, the quality of land, good or bad, counted for as much as its area. To redistribute their holdings in a way that would have satisfied everybody would have tried the cunning of a Solomon. Richard Cartwright and the Aynho villagers would have argued with a Solomon anyway.

Richard Cartwright's tenants themselves were probably not all on his side, whatever they may have said to the Court of Chancery. Not all of the more substantial land-holders had bought their freeholds from Shakerley Marmion. Perhaps some could not have afforded to and others may have felt that their interests were safe enough in any case. It was usual for a copyhold to be granted to an heir on payment of a heriot, paid in money or in kind or both. But if they had hoped for the old ways to continue, it seems that they were wrong. Soon after his arrival, Richard Cartwright intro-

duced more up-to-date business methods: that is to say, he started
letting out copyhold land, after its owners died or had been bought
out, to tenants-at-will for much higher rents. He probably justified
this to himself by saying that the ancient rents received from copyholders and which had been fixed by immemorial custom, bore no
relation to the profits which farmers could make in the seventeenth
century. In this he was probably right, but it cannot have endeared
him to tenants who wished their children to succeed to their holdings.

But if in some ways Richard Cartwight's dealings with his
tenants were modern, in others they still echoed the middle ages.
It was a class-conscious age, in which men expected deference
from their inferiors and bore themselves more humbly towards
their betters, and the new squire clearly expected his principal
tenants to be more than mere payers of rent: they were to be his
retainers as well, his personal servants and to provide ploughs for
service on his demesne as his tenants had done from time immemorial. It is unlikely that anyone objected. Much is revealed in a
letter of 1616 from his agent in Aynho, Richard Grafton, written
to the squire in London about the letting of a 30-acre farm that
Richard Cartwright had lately bought in the village. (The purpose
of the purchase was to give him more land to exchange with other
freeholders to facilitate the enclosure, but that does not concern
us at the moment.)

> Mr. Wyatt, Collins and young Pemberton are suitors to my mis-
> tress [i.e. to Mrs. Cartwright] for the land at £18 per annum as
> may further appear by their letters sent already . . . According to
> my best understanding, all things duly and truly weighed and con-
> sidered, John Loe and John Knott will be quiet takers and your
> best tenants, at £17 per annum. The reasons that induce me are
> these, viz. they are reputed honest men, they are both favourable
> to ride or wait, at your command, and judicial husbands to manage
> it to the best advantage, and so that one tenant shall yield two
> ploughs at command, and one to keep house and all things in repair.
> . . . For Wyatt he is surly and will do little beyond bargain, Pem-
> berton's credit is tainted, Collins would be a broker, grazier, keep
> no plough but your Inn and consequently lose you more than the
> price of the tenement. I beseech you let my mistress have your
> answer by this bearer for the land lies quite unfallowed . . .

There were numerous ways in which the new squire tried to
exercise his authority, probably all of them quite legitimate from a
strictly legalistic point of view, and many of them irritating out of
all proportion. For instance at a Manor Court in 1617, eight of the
leading villagers were presented 'for keeping a malt quern contrary

to the custom'. They had probably been grinding their own malt
for years without anyone's bothering: they all brewed their own
beer. When the elder Thomas Hanslope and Richard Stanton died,
for all that they were freeholders Richard Cartwright claimed from
their heirs a heriot of a year's rent (both paid small chief rents
to the Lord of the Manor) and had to go back to a Court Roll of
seventy years before to find a precedent that entitled him to do
so. In the Michaelmas Court of 1617, the fieldsman wanted to
introduce a new Court Order, but had been over-ruled by Richard
Cartwright: he may have been within his rights, but Marmion, one
suspects, would have left the villagers to manage the fields as they
thought best.

Then there was the matter of dilapidations. Traditionally, the
Lord of the Manor had the right to summon to the Manor Court
those copyholders and tenants who had allowed their buildings to
fall out of repair, and to fine them if they did not repair them.
There was no disputing that, but it seems likely that by insisting
on it Richard Cartwright was again reviving an imposition that was
being quietly forgotten. It may have been only after years of coax-
ing and badgering that at the Ladyday Court in 1633, the Jury
were ordered to enquire into a host of breaches of manorial customs, including:-

> You shall enquire of such of the Lord's tenants as have let their
> houses and buildings go to decay. And for true presentment
> thereof you shall view every of the Lord's tenants' houses in
> particular and certify the particular decays and ruins of their
> houses, distinctly truly and without partiality one to another

The ensuing list was a long one

> We find that Mark Gardner's barn wanteth thatching
> We find that the widow Swetnam's barn wanteth thatching
> We find that Walter Bayliss's house wanteth thatching
> We find that John Loe's side wall of his house is in decay
> We find that widow Young's house wanteth thatching
> We find that the widow Gardners hath let fallen down one bay
> of building
> We find that William Borton's out houses want thatching
> We find that Deferill's out houses are decayed
> We find that Giles Swetnam's house wanteth thatching
> We find that Mellycome's houses in great decay and some of
> them are fallen down.

(Mellycome's buildings, at least, got worse and worse, however. In
1636 he was presented 'because he hath suffered his house to fall
down and refuseth to repair it.' In 1638 he was again 'letting his

houses fall down and refusing to build them up again'. He was
probably fined year after year, and probably thought it cheaper
to pay, say, 6s 8d annually than to be at the cost of repairs which
only got more expensive as time went on. He may have thought it
a matter of principle, too.)

The list of offenders in 1633 ends with a scrawl in Richard
Cartwright's own hand

> You must view the Red Lion

and it looks as though the poor jurors were trying, unsuccessfully,
to avoid a confrontation between the Lord of the Manor and the
landlady of the Inn where, no doubt, they spent many more agreeable evenings than they did at the Lord's Court. But they could
hardly have expected the state of the Red Lion to have been un-
noticed, if it was half as bad as Richard Cartwright claimed it was,
and he must have seen the place almost every time he went out of
his own house. He set down on paper exactly what she had done,
or what he claimed she had done, and he made two drafts from
which it is obvious that he was trying to get the phrasing right for
the time when he was going to present his case against her at the
Manor Court.

> The ruin & decay of the house wherein goody Bell dwells
> The upper room over the buttery the roof thereof is rotten &
> stands upon supporters ready to fall and the floor is rotten.
> The upper room over the hall is in the like ruin only the floor is
> something better
> The walls of all these are ready to fall both above and below
> The barn is ready to fall both walls and roof utterly decayed
> The roof over the kitchen and the walls on the backside utterly
> decayed

As a statement of facts, there was probably little argument about
it. His proposals, though, look like an attempt to conciliate opposition — to enlist a bit of sympathy which may have been largely
on the other side:-

> Notwithstanding all which ruin and decay which by law the said
> Bridget Davies alias Bell ought to repair, in regard she is a poor
> woman I make her these offers before you all:
> First, in regard it manifestly appears that I must presently be at
> an intollerable charge to put this decayed house thus ruinated by
> her into repair, which if it be not presently done will fall on her
> head, I therefore require her presently to avoid the house that I
> may go in hand with the repair thereof presently, which if she
> will willingly presently do and quit the town I will give her five
> pounds in ready money. And she shall have liberty to take and

carry away all her goods whatsoever except only such things as by law she cannot carry away. And to avoid all contention therein let her make choice of one man, I will choose another, and they two to judge what things she cannot lawfully remove and carry away.

If this will not please her then I am contented that she shall have the house which I hear she desires to go to called Stillgoe's house with the land & cow's commons belonging to it, paying me forty shillings a year rent for the same, which is a less rent than it now goes for, so as she may put me in surety to keep the same in sufficient repair, for I may not be put to any more losses by her in this kind, this being too heavy for me to bear that never raised her rent nor took fine off her.

If none of these offers will [illegible] her then I will take a course presently to recover my own by law, for I mean not to be foolishly charitable, especially to so unthankful a tenant.

Widow Bell chose the second — to take Stillgoe's house, and it was not very long before she was well in arrears with her rent. One's sympathy may be wasted on her. What happened to the Red Lion we do not know. In the 1680's a good deal of money was spent on modernising it, but little of it (the Cartwright Arms) looks any earlier than that now (if indeed that early) and perhaps Bridget Bell left it in so bad a state that it had to be pulled down.

Richard Cartwright's relations with the villagers were not helped by disagreements that seem to have become vendettas: the affair of Bridget Bell and the Red Lion appears almost to have become that. It was perhaps inevitable that he should have been on bad terms with those who, next to himself, were the leading gentlemen of the place. It was not to be expected that Thomas Hanslope, and Thomas Drope the parson would welcome the newcomer wholeheartedly. The relations of each with the squire seem to have been of more-or-less continuous friction interspersed with sharper crisis. Thomas Hanslope's reservations about Richard Cartwright's enclosure have been mentioned already, and ill-feeling about it continued for years afterwards. There was the matter of the status of Thomas Hanslope's freehold, which the squire tried to prove was not freehold at all but copyhold. Hanslope had the better of that argument, though only (according to Cartwright) because Hanslope had 'by casual or other means' (a nasty innuendo) 'gotten into his hands' various papers that Cartwright needed to prove his case.

To Richard Cartwright, away in London, John Loe, one of his tenants, gleefully wrote:-

> Hanslope hath undertaken as if he was a Lord in Aynho in your
> absence . . . and told William Wyatt he would stand to no orders
> for he did not care he would break them at his pleasure which all
> the neighbours much grieved at.

There was a dispute about commons, where Hanslope claimed
double rights. Hanslope had the better of that, too, when it came
to court, but had at the same time to admit that having

> cast some unjust and scandalous aspersions upon the plaintiff
> upon the Court Orders . . . upon better consideration he is very
> sorry that any such unjust occasion of offence was given by him,

a confession which probably cost his pride a good deal to make.
Little things, too, served to bring greater ones to a head: when
Hanslope's dog killed six of the squire's turkeys, worth 2s 6d each,
the squire sat down with the Court Rolls and wrote down all Hanslope's transgressions over the previous thirteen years and found
that he owed £7 in unpaid fines. But the squire's longest running
and bitterest dispute was with Mr. Drope the parson, and Mr. Drope
was a good match for him.

Not that Thomas Drope was a particularly agreeable man
himself. He probably came originally from Wainflete in Lincoln-
shire, had become a fellow of Magdalen College, Oxford in 1571,
and rose to be Vice-President. He was not exactly a model college
head: he gave his lectures at odd times so that nobody came to
them, he 'huddled up' in fifteen minutes the disputations he was
supposed to conduct, on several occasions his commons were
stopped because he had been neglecting his duties, and as Bursar
he had been accused of

> lending the college money to usury, suffering the bakers and
> brewers in the mean time to be unpaid.

He probably resigned when he married, came to Aynho where he
bought some land, and conducted his duties as parson in much the
same way. Richard Cartwright anyway complained of the lack of
sermons, and Thomas Drope seems to have left much of the day-
to-day work of the parish to young curates who were more enthusiastic than he was. (Though it was in any case a time of religious
enthusiasm: Thomas Drope was of perhaps too old a generation to
enter into it as younger clergymen could.)

Thomas Drope's quarrels with Richard Cartwright began
early, in the late Spring of 1616, and though we have only the
squire's account of them, the parson's conduct sounds so unspeak-
ably frightful that even allowing for a certain dramatic exaggeration,

he must have been, to put it mildly, a very difficult man. Perhaps Richard Cartwright's words sound almost too honeyed and his behaviour almost too reasonable, but it is he who has our sympathy none the less.

It started at the Spring lambing, when Richard Cartwright had arranged to meet Mr. Drope at the sheep pens for the latter to take his tithe of Mr. Cartwright's lambs. The squire greeted the parson in a friendly enough manner. "Mr. Drope", he said, "I am a stranger to you, yet I much desire your particular neighbourhood and inward acquaintance before any man else in the town for your coat's sake, for I am a man that loves the Church and churchmen. And for the business now in hand, I must confess my own weakness therein, having been otherwise bred. And therefore I desire to know what is your due in this and all other tithing businesses, and you shall have the same with a free and cheerful spirit."

Since they had only met once before, the squire was not a little surprised when the parson replied "Sir, I am as absolute a parson as you are a lord. I pay you neither pension nor portion, I owe you neither suit nor service. I am absolute." "At which most strange unoccasioned answer I was amazed" wrote Richard Cartwright when finally he was driven to complain to the Archbishop. It was not a good beginning.

Less than a month later, the parson came round to the great house to tell the squire that an acre of glebe lay within the boundaries of one of the squire's closes. It was not an unusual situation, with the involved sub-division of the fields of the village, and probably caused Richard Cartwright no surprise. But what was clearly excessive was that Drope then demanded as its produce two loads of hay and summer pasture for a nag. At least, a certain Mr. Wells said it was too much, who was standing by and who Richard Cartwright said understood such things better than he did.

> Whereupon Mr. Parson told him he was a base busy fellow with many other reviling uncivil terms unfitting his Coat

while the squire said that he would speak to his predecessor, Mr. Marmion, about it and try and discover what the previous practice had been, but added that he was sorry to see so great intemperance in the parson, upon no occasion.

Things went from bad to worse. Next it was sheep shearing time, at mid-summer, and as Richard Cartwright was away in London, the operations were being supervised by his wife. Down came the parson to the wool house to make sure of his tithe, and when she saw him fiddling about with the steelyard that was being used to weigh the wool, Mrs. Cartwright told him to sit down while the servants did the weighing out. But 'Mr. Parson told her he was not to be directed by her. She said, if he would hold his hands off the scales she would be contented. Whereupon in great bitterness he told her that she must learn the fashions of the town, and that if she would not then she should be taught them, and told her that she knew not how long she should enjoy that place. And after the weighing, Mr. Parson called for the Bellwether fleece. My wife told him she was informed that by the custom of the town, that did belong to her. Whereupon Mr. Parson said he was a rogue and a villain that told her so. Now, because it was his own servant, to free him of blame she caused it to be weighed out, and bade him take his tenth part which came not to a handful of wool. Yet for all that he persisted still in many bitter uncivil speeches towards her in such violent manner that he made her weep.' Mary Cartwright was a tough lady, and it must have taken a good deal to provoke her to tears.

Worse still was to follow. At the Michaelmas session of the Manor Court, Richard Moore, the Cartwright steward, was presiding — a lawyer, later a Master in Chancery and perhaps a man from Cartwright's chambers. Drope kept interrupting the proceedings so that Moore had to tell him that if he did not sit down and shut up, he would be fined £20 on the spot. This quietened Drope down somewhat, but at that point in the proceedings the jury left the Court, 'having their charge' — presumably to consider the various charges brought against offenders, and any fresh orders that had been proposed. When they seemed to be taking an extremely long time about it — all through dinner and beyond, while the men of the village presumably continued to sit around in mounting exasperation — Richard Moore sent for one of the jurors to find out what was happening. What was happening, apparently, was that Drope (who was not a juror) was in with them, telling them to stick to all the old Court Orders and not to agree to any new ones, and that Giles Southam the foreman was telling the parson that they did intend to make new Orders but would be glad of his help and advice. This of course, in 1616 as now, was tampering with a jury, and the steward was quite rightly annoyed.

So when eventually the jury returned to the Court, the steward was determined that they should all admit what had been going on. 'And he told the foreman Southam that he was to examine him something upon the oath which he had taken, whether any man other than they of the jury had come and confered with them or advised with them what to do. The said Southam answered upon his oath that no man had been with them nor confered with them.' The Steward then went on to ask another juror, Richard Bewdley, the same question, and was met with another denial. Then he called in the juror who had first reported the parson's being with them, who answered 'that he marvelled his fellow jurors should deny so apparent and manifest a truth upon their oaths, in regard it was true and could not be denied but that Mr. Parson had been with them and confered with some of them publicly and privately as the rest of the jury well knew. So Mr. Steward told them that he was very sorry to see such manifest bold perjury committed by them, and that if they should be questioned in the Star Chamber they should lose their ears.' And he told the parson that his behaviour was worse even than the jurors', because he at least ought to have known better.

It was scandalous, no doubt, but it is interesting to see that the jurors at least regarded the parson as an ally in maintaining the status quo against changes that were contemplated: it was of course when the new squire's intentions were being anxiously debated by everyone. At such a time it was not surprising that gossip and rumour should have been widespread, nor that some if it should be directed against the new squire.

In February, 1618, one of the Jarvis family (she is just called 'widow Jarvis') tried to commit suicide. 'She rose in the night out of her bed from her maid, and went out of the house and voluntarily threw herself down into the draw well with an evil intent, for the man who was let down with a rope to help her out, asked her what she meant by this. She answered "Oh, I have not done well", and though she lived about two months after, yet she was sick and weak till her death.' So Mr. Salter, the Coroner from Northampton, came over on his horse to hold an inquest: a matter of some importance, since if it was decided that her death ranked as suicide, not merely could she not be buried in the churchyard but all her possessions would be forfeit. Though not, as the rumour mongers put it about, to Richard Cartwright as Lord of the Manor, but to a much more remote individual, Lord Amner, Richard Cartwright's feudal overlord.

It was obviously not an open-and-shut case, and it would probably be difficult even now to establish whether her death was due to the poor woman's attempt at suicide. The coroner had little doubt about it, but the local jury felt differently. They must all have known her, must all have known whatever the circumstances were that had driven her so far, and of course they all knew the consequences of a suicide verdict. Richard Love, who was tenant of the College Farm and of course had nothing to fear from Mr. Cartwright, waited for them as they walked with the coroner from the Inn where the inquest was being held to widow Jarvis's house to view the body. 'As they passed by him, he told the coroner, that the business he was about was a most shameful business . . . and withal did openly advise the jury to remember their oath and that she was an ancient woman and died like a Christian.'

The coroner had other views. When the jury did bring in a verdict of natural death, he threatened to bind them over. When two of the jury were found not to have turned up at all, he fined them 40s each on the spot. Richard Cartwright, on the other hand, pleaded with the coroner to let them all off, and furthermore had already told him that if the jury brought in a verdict of suicide, he 'would become suitor to the Lord Amner for a reasonable composition, that his Lordship being satisfied the rest might be distributed among her children.' But the villagers knew nothing of these exchanges, and the result was that Richard Cartwright got no thanks from them — indeed, quite the reverse.

The following day, as the coroner was saddling up to ride off, Love and Drope came up to him and asked him, point blank, whether Mr. Cartwright had tried to bring any pressure on him, and accused the squire of having tried to nobble one of the jury who was a Cartwright tenant. 'My landlord is a strict man', the juror had complained, 'and hath charged us to find her [sc. a suicide] and we must find her'. The coroner replied by telling them what had actually passed between him and the squire, and no doubt told them, too, that since the case had been decided as they had wished, he would prefer that they did not bother him with tittle-tattle.

For the squire it was the last straw, and he wrote formally to the Archbishop to complain. What in turn the Archbishop did, we do not know, but Drope seems to have given the squire a good deal less trouble after that — at least, none that has been reported — and perhaps he was admonished so sternly that even he took it to heart. But there were still congenial quarrels to be had with other people.

On one occasion, for instance, in 1621, a horse that belonged to John Loe had broken loose and strayed into Mr. Drope's stubble field, whereupon the parson impounded him and demanded 18d from Mr. Loe. Drope, on the other hand, had pastured his bull in a field of John Loe's in which he claimed rights of common, which Loe denied and in turn impounded the bull. It is not unlikely that the poor animals would have lived out their lives in their respective captors' hands, if one of Drope's men had not gone along to Loe's house when John Loe himself was out, and persuaded Mrs. Loe to release the bull. John Loe knew that he would have a sympathetic ear with Richard Cartwright when he reported what the parson had done.

'I will plainly inform you how he did behave and demean himself the next Sabbath following, before the whole congregation. "The Peace of God", etc., scarce being ended, started out of his seat into the body of the church, & began in this furious manner before myself and divers others were rose upon their knees, to say "Neighbours, did you hear, or know, that the parson's bull of Aynho was pounded before ? Here is John Loe hath pounded him". Upon which I replied this answer "Give me my 18d. and you shall have your bull", which he refused to do.' There followed a good deal of further abuse from all sides, with Mrs. Drope, Peter Parker and others joining in. 'You would scarce believe unless you had seen him' Loe went on. It must indeed have been quite a scene. Nor was that all — in fact 'the parson hath forgotten his large protestation made unto you at your taking horse to London, thinking there is no Mr. Cartwright at Aynho.'

Then there was trouble, too, with Drope's curates, though that was less the parson's fault than the fault of the times, when religious controversy was rife and when there were plenty of young, enthusiastic clergymen around who were more concerned with the truth of their beliefs than with whether it was entirely tactful to preach them. But in any case Drope was a lazy man, even if he was an obstinate one, and he was probably glad enough for keen youngsters to do his preaching for him. Preaching was expected of parsons, and one did not have to be a Puritan to appreciate a sermon.

An early curate of Drope's was John Parry, who insisted on preaching though he was only licensed to read. Hauled up before the Lord of the Manor by the churchwardens, he made matters worse by accusing Mr. Cartwright of having called him 'chittie face and knave' behind his back. He repeated the charge two weeks later to Dr. Sibthorpe, vicar of St. Sepulchre's in Northampton and a chaplain to the King, who might be expected to take a serious view of insults to the clergy. In the event, Dr. Sibthorpe clearly took a still dimmer view of the over-enthusiastic, troublesome young man, and gave him a stern warning to behave in future. It

was probably only because Mr. Drope sent him packing soon afterwards that Richard Cartwright gave him a testimonial to his good
behaviour — on the strength of which Parry got a preaching certificate (to which he still was not entitled) and went off to make
more trouble elsewhere.

Another curate who made trouble was William Howse, though
Drope may have put him up to it. It was apparently still the custom
to make processions round the village on holidays — Holy Days —
and at Whitsun, 1620, William Howse, leading the troup of villagers
by the usual route, found Richard Cartwright's garden door nailed
up. Howse sent someone to ask Mrs. Cartwright whether it could
be opened for them. She, however, sent a servant to tell them to
go round another way, which they then found to be impassable,
blocked by hedges and ditches. The procession then refused to go
any further unless they went the way they always had, whereupon
Howse took off his surplice, gave it to the clerk to carry, and he
and the other parishioners all went home. The trouble with the
story is that we have — as so often — only one version of it, apparently written in reply to Richard Cartwright's previous complaints.
William Howse takes a good deal of space, too, denying that any
of them used bad language to the squire or behaved other than in
an exemplary fashion, and Richard Cartwright has peppered the
margins with comments like 'Not a true word', 'neither hedge nor
ditch', 'most untrue' and others to the same effect. In any case,
William Howse did not last much longer as a curate before he was
succeeded by yet another. It would not be surprising if all Drope's
curates felt stifled, between a squire who liked clergymen to know
their place and a parson who knew his own importance.

Not unnaturally, Richard Cartwright tried hard to buy the
presentation to the living of Aynho, so that at least his children
should not be disturbed by this kind of thing. But once again he
stumbled into a legal hornet's nest, because though the living had
belonged in the middle ages to the Claverings' abbey of Walden,
nobody was sure whose it had become after the Abbey was dissolved in 1538. It had unfortunately been omitted in all the Royal
grants of Abbey property. Drope had had considerable difficulty
in getting presented to it (though perhaps the Bishop knew his
Oxford reputation in advance) and had actually had to take the
Bishop to the Archbishop's court to prove his entitlement to the
living. That was before Richard Cartwright had bought the manor,
but when he did so he soon began to look around for those who
claimed to own the right of presentation in order to buy their in-

terests. Drope had meanwhile been doing the same so that his son should follow him as parson, and the argument and litigation that ensued was only ended after Thomas Drope's death by the intervention of the King himself on behalf of Richard Cartwright's protegé, Reginald Burdyn. Thomas Drope died in 1633, and a small brass tablet on the floor of the chancel in Aynho church says 'he fought the good fight.' So he did, but one does sometimes wonder whose.

Chapter 5

War

By the standards of the time, men in Aynho were probably not ill-informed about events in the outside world. The main road through the village brought travellers to the inns, and the squire's servants, returning with him from Town, would have brought the villagers the latest news. John Loe, when he wrote to Richard Cartwright to tell of the affair of Mr. Drope's bull, had told him that 'neighbours in London' could give him further details, so others as well must have come and gone between Aynho and the capital. It must have been a spasmodic way of keeping up to date: the latest news one day, then perhaps days to speculate on what might have happened next. But in any case it was less than once in a generation that high politics affected the villagers' daily lives. The last time must have been when the church services had all be changed in the 1540's; the villagers in the early seventeenth century would probably have said that getting used to the new squire was more than change enough for one lifetime. But none of them anticipated the events of the Civil War.

One of the provocations that led up to the Civil War was the King's imposition of a tax to pay for warships: Ship Money. Traditionally, it had been for seaports and for coastal counties to provide ships for the Royal Navy, but the King was increasingly short of money, realised that it was impossible for inland counties like Northamptonshire to provide ships since they naturally had none to provide, but saw no reason why they should not pay for them instead. And Richard Cartwright, along with the other propertied men of the county, was called to contribute.

The first year — 1635 — he paid his £3 without demur. The opposition on principle that was to make John Hampden the hero of Parliament was not for Richard Cartwright. But the following year was different. Sir Robert Banastre, the Sheriff of the County, sent a warrant to the constable of Aynho for the amounts due both from Mr. Cartwright and from Sir Thomas Pope, who owned the manor of Walton over the parish boundary into King's Sutton. The constable himself decided how the total amount should be divided — £30 from Sir Thomas, 45s 6d from Mr. Cartwright. No doubt the constable felt he was doing right by his own squire, but

the Sheriff had other views. He reduced Sir Thomas's assessment to
£22, increased Richard Cartwright's to £17, and Richard Cartwright
appealed to the Privy Council.

Richard Cartwright said he had only been taxed £3 the year
before, had always been 'forward and an encourager of all services'
to the king, got some of Aynho's leading villagers (Henry Letch,
John Bricknell, and Benjamin Watts, son of Lawrence Watts the
squire's old shepherd) to testify that Pope's land was worth twice
his own, and added for good measure that Sir Thomas Pope was a
close relation of the Sheriff's anyway. Sir Robert, however, was
ready with his answer. He had recently ridden through Aynho and
had been much impressed with the thriving condition of Mr. Cartwright's estates. Someone more responsible than a mere constable
should have made out the details of the assessment. Far from
furthering the King's interests, Mr. Cartwright only did so when it
suited his own, and his failure to turn up when his appeal was first
to be heard in Northampton had set back the collection for the
whole county. He might have addded, too, that even if Sir Thomas
Pope's estates were worth twice Mr. Cartwright's, that was hardly
the proportion between £30 and 45s 6d. So he had reduced Sir
Thomas's contribution, increased Mr. Cartwright's, and for good
measure transferred another £6 to Mr. Cartwright when the people
of Culworth had complained of being over-taxed.

At this point, when the affair looked like provoking a head-
on clash between Richard Cartwright and the royal officials, old
Richard Cartwright died. He was 74, still active and vigorous, and
not greatly mellowed by age so far as care for his own rights and
interests were concerned. And his son was worthy of him. John
Cartwright was only 23, but he had all his father's determination
with the vigour of a younger man. Perhaps he lacked some of the
restraint that his father's knowledge of the world had taught him,
learnt in long years as a London lawyer. And perhaps, too, he felt
that it was his duty as his father's son to pursue his father's quarrel
through to its end.

Richard Cartwright died in June, 1637. By August, when John
had only offered £6, Sir Robert may have felt that it was an opportunity of teaching the young man a short, sharp lesson — a stitch
in time, perhaps — and Sir Robert sent the bailiffs over. The new
squire refused a last demand for payment, so off went the bailiffs,
summoned the help of a few villagers, and made for one of the
squire's fields where they began to round up six or eight of his fat
cattle. By that time news had flown round the village, and opposi-

tion had gathered on the squire's behalf. Thomas Swetnam, John Howes and others had assembled, and William Stanton stood in the gate with a pitchfork. They had their master's orders, they said, and the bailiffs would get none of his cattle until they came with a stronger force than the squire's.

Three days later, Sir Robert Banastre came himself, with the under sheriffs and with their servants. Men working in the fields saw them coming, and ran to rouse the village. Someone told Sir Robert that an ox team coming down the road was the squire's, and he called on the driver, Thomas Davis, to stop. Davis refused and drove the oxen forward, and Sir Robert would have been 'trodden down in the dirt by the oxen, to the great danger of his life, had he not been rescued by his servants.' By that time more villagers had run up, and fighting broke out. Thomas Davis would have been killed, save for the intervention of the curate, but the sheriffs' men, probably better armed and prepared for just such an affray as this, won in the end. The oxen were driven off, Davis and 'a poor smith' (probably Swetnam) were marched off, tied like felons, to Northampton jail, and a few days later Sir Robert sent out warrants for the arrest of William Stanton and two other Aynho men who had joined him in first opposing the bailiffs.

John Cartwright and Sir Robert both complained forthwith to the Privy Council. John complained about the arrest of his servants, 'poor creatures lying miserably in prison', and complained too of the way his mother had been treated, 'a poor desolate widow'. If the bailiffs had had her to deal with, they would have found her a doughty opponent, disconsolate widow or no. The Privy Council, however, sent on Sir Robert's complaint to the Attorney General, telling him to gather all the information he could about this deplorable case so that Mr. Cartwright should be made an example of. The King himself was displeased with his 'refractory and insolent carriage', and the Council wished to consider what action they should take against his servants who had opposed Sir Robert's men. There was too great opposition to the tax throughout the country, and stern action was required.

William Stanton and the two men arrested with him seem actually to have been summoned before the Board of the Council — perhaps they were sent all the way to London to appear, and one wonders whether they found the experience daunting. Stanton at least was a prosperous man with land of his own, but faced by the formality and the power of the King's courts, all three must have been fairly overawed. In the end, John Cartwright submitted and asked for pardon. No doubt he felt that there was only so much that he should endure for his principles, and perhaps too that there was only so much that he should ask his retainers to endure. Sir Robert wrote on his behalf, saying that he had acted with a young man's passion rather than from want of loyalty, so John Cartwright was pardoned and his servants released. But for all Sir Robert Banstre's testimonial, it must have rankled with John Cartwright to have had to give in, and the episode may well have decided him — if his mind wanted deciding — as to which side he was going to be on when disputes between the King and his opponents reached the stage where compromise was no longer possible.

That John Cartwright was to be a Parliament man is perhaps the more surprising in view of his marriage to the daughter of Sir William Noy, the King's late Attorney General and whose idea Ship Money had originally been. Sir William had died in 1634, but he and old Richard Cartwright had certainly been acquainted: Richard Cartwright had sought Sir William's opinion over his Enclosure, and perhaps young John was marrying the daughter of a family friend. But if so, he did not allow his marriage to touch his principles, and if he had married with the same impetuosity that he showed on other occasions, he had more leisure to repent. His marriage was a disaster.

Katherine Noy had brought him £3,000 in money, and another £1,000 in jewels and plate. This, however, did not prevent John's sending her packing as soon as their son was born, taking away the young child and shutting up his wife in a friend's house thirty miles away and then giving out that 'want of means of housekeeping' prevented him from making a home for her. It was an implausible excuse at best, and when he came into his inheritance, Katherine threatened to sue him for cohabitation. John in return had her still more closely confined in a farmhouse of his own, 'strangely and sordidly attended' (said Katherine: we only have her side of the story), staved off her threats with vague promises, and so terrified her neighbours that none of them dared come near her. John, meanwhile, continued to live with his old mother, with whom he obviously had a much closer relationship than he had with his poor wife. It was three months before Katherine was able to make any contact with her friends so that a warrant could be had from the Archbishop (marital cases were for the Church courts) to compel John Churchill to set her free.

(There may have been faults on both sides. Katherine's father besides being a distinguished lawyer, was an entertaining fellow, 'full of humours and froliques' said John Aubrey, and once the first excitement of marriage was over she may have found the Cart-wrights a trifle dour. Her behaviour may have been provocative; her husband may have been young, handsome and a man of charac-ter, but it is unlikely that he cared for humours and froliques.)

In the end, to avoid the publicity of a Court hearing, Katherine appealed to the King himself for justice. Things may in the end have been patched up between John Cartwright and his wife, since it was at Barn Elms, his London house, that the poor lady died in 1644, but a reconciliation was some time in coming about. Nor can the King's intervention on behalf of the daughter of his old servant have endeared John Cartwright to the Royal cause in the war that was approaching. But by then, anyway family quarrels were increasingly becoming swallowed up in national ones, and if it was unusual for husbands and wives to find themselves on opposite sides, it was nothing unusual for close relations, for fathers, sons and brothers to be divided against each other.

For many of the common people, loyalty to local leaders was as powerful a force as loyalty to the King or to Parliament. But all such loyalties were increasingly coming in question, and not only in the towns where ancient overlords scarcely existed and where greater opportunities for the exchange of ideas made for a greater independence of thought. The Civil War can be seen as a war about authority: about whether old systems of government would sur-vive in an age when increasing literacy, new money and new ideas were making people question established authorities and time-honoured institutions. Old forms were collapsing, and uncertainty about what would replace them made people anxious and disputa-tious. In Aynho the squire had tried to preserve his ancient powers and at the same time to make innovations: the villagers may well have felt confused, and we know they were angry. The contentions in the village since Richard Cartwright's arrival seem a foretaste of those of the war itself.

Puritanism was well supported in the country round Aynho. Banbury was a hot-bed of it, and the destruction of the old Ban-bury crosses by Puritan iconoclasts in 1600 was already notorious. Puritanism was favoured by the Copes at Hanwell Castle. The town of Northampton was puritanical too, and the 'Orders and Dealings in the Churches of Northampton' that had been established in the sixteenth century with the support of the Bishop of Peterborough, found plenty of time for Bible readings, lectures and Calvin's catechism. Such things spread into the county round, and when the puritanical bishop Scambler died, his successors did not suppress

Puritanism with the same vigour as he had promoted it. Many of the newcomers to the county, like the Cartwrights, were lawyers or merchants who had made money in London, men who had been trained to think for themselves and who had been exposed to the latest political and religious ideas. And puritanism had already reached down to the grass roots: there were meetings at Bloxham and Hanwell, and 'troops of Christians' came from miles around to attend them. Even in Aynho, there had been a scandal when one poor villager refused to take his hat off in church.

As to the leading families of the neighbourhood, some were for Parliament, some for the King. John Mordaunt, Earl of Peterborough and Lord Lieutenant of Northamptonshire, was a Parliament man for all that his father had been a Catholic who had been implicated in the Gunpowder Plot. Sir Edward Montagu of Boughton was a staunch Royalist. Yet the Earl's son Henry went over to the King within a year of his being given command of a troop of horse by his father, while Montagu's son Edward became a supporter of Parliament as soon as he inherited from his father. Sir Edward's younger brother, Henry, was a lawyer and one of the King's most trusted advisers, yet Henry's eldest son was the leader of the popular, puritan party in the House of Lords, and went on as Earl of Manchester to be a Parliament general. A younger brother of his, on the other hand, became a Catholic and a close friend of the Queen's. These were only two families, and even among these the instances of conflicting loyalties could be multiplied.

Throughout the area, the picture was the same. The Earl of Northampton at Compton Winyates and all his family were for the King, while Lord Saye and Sele and all the Fiennesses at Broughton were for Parliament. So it went on, and as the aristocracy and the gentry decided, each for himself, so for the most part the country followed. Sometimes, of course, personal antipathies counted for as much as loyalties: it was enough that John Cartwright was a Parliament man for Thomas Hanslope and Thomas Drope, son of the old parson of Aynho, to support the King. But in any event, there were numerous small centres of loyalty and of disaffection and numerous skirmishes between one little band and another, and not all the battles were fought by the great armies of each side. For anyone who lived in a place like Aynho, where each side was well supported in the neighbourhood, things could be very uncomfortable.

In the summer of 1642, even before hostilities had formally begun with the King raising his standard at Nottingham in August, there was the making of a conflagration at Banbury. Lord Brooke had been granted some cannon by Parliament, in order to fortify Warwick Castle. They had reached Banbury safely, and there Lord Brooke arrived on July 29th with a hundred men to collect them. At 9 o'clock the next morning, he and his men set out with the guns from the town, only to be met after four miles by the Earl of Northampton with a superior force of horsemen and musketeers. The two parties faced one another during long hours of tension, each alert and ready to open fire, but neither willing to shoot first. The leaders parleyed, the Earl made various rather wild suggestions including an invitation to single combat, while the news that had spread fast through the neighbourhood brought crowds of locals to the support of either side. Men came with harrows as a defence against the Earl's cavalry, while women came with an abundance of victuals and beer. (They would be a good deal less ready before long to share their supplies with the soldiery.) And nothing happened.

At the end of the day it was agreed that the guns should be returned to Banbury, and not moved by either side without three days' notice. But news had by now spread into Northamptonshire, and a force reputed to be 1,500 strong now arrived in Banbury in support of Lord Brooke and were feasted by Lord Saye and Sele's son, Colonel Fiennes. To Banbury, too, flocked hoards of people from the country round with their possessions, their wives and their children for safety. Then, as rumour succeeded rumour and as the Northamptonshire men heard that Royalist marauders threatening their homes, 'home they must, to defend their own country, wives, children etc.', and panic followed as all those who had sought refuge in Banbury as precipitately left it again, rushing out into the night with what they could carry, seeking safety in the darkened countryside. The royal forces reached Banbury again a few days later, placed guns on Crouch Hill to command the town, and took Lord Brooke's guns off to Compton Winyates. But for the time being, Banbury remained in Parliament hands.

Some among the Northamptonshire men may have been from Aynho, and a few weeks later there was excitement nearer home when news came of a Royalist force under Sir John Byron, riding south from Daventry. Local forces had pursued Byron's troops as far as Brackley, where the Cavaliers took a brief rest to bait their horses and to snatch some supper. But not for long: an outpost sounded the alarm and hastily they saddled up and sped away. Byron intended to give the Parliament forces the slip if he could, but for safety he gave a packet of 'writings' and other valuables to a servant, with instructions to make for Oxford. The servant, however, lost his way somewhere near Croughton, hid the packet in a field of standing corn, asked for lodgings in the village and was at once taken up as a suspicious character.

Meanwhile, word had reached Banbury of Sir John Byron's move. 'Men . . did rise in Arms, and raised the country, and came to Aynho that night, a great Company, Horse and Foot armed, and raised the Town.' They swept on to Croughton, where they arrived just as Byron's servant had been taken into custody, and where they immediately made him 'discover all'. A man called Old Burburough, probably from Aynho itself, rode off and found the things that had been hidden — a Commission, some letters, money and some rich clothes. Old Burborough took charge of them, took Byron's servant up behind him, rode back in triumph through Aynho to Banbury. In the meantime others of the Banbury men had captured the trumpeter and three other soldiers of Byron's troop, and they too returned to Banbury in the morning, riding through Aynho with their prisoners.

The first real battle of the Civil War was Edgehill, fought at the end of October. It was an indecisive battle, and the royal armies marched on to Banbury where the King gave orders for the taking of the castle. The King then rode on to Aynho to spend the night. Banbury castle fell without much resistance — some accounts say without any — and the Earl of Northampton's son, Sir William Compton, was placed in command of the garrison. At Aynho the scene must have been one of splendour, of bustle and business, for not only was it the headquarters of the royal army, but for that night Aynho was the capital of half the kingdom. 'From our Court at Aynho' the King issued a proclamation to the Cities of London and Westminster before riding on to Oxford.

There was one of the King's subjects, though, who was conspicuous by his absence: John Cartwright. John Dormer, who rode over from Rousham to pay his humble duty to his sovereign, wrote to John Cartwright to say that he had heard 'much murmuring' because

> you were not present to entertain him, many threatened your person, others your goods, and some your estate. I was sorry to hear so many and such words uttered.

But John Dormer was a friend of poor Katherine Cartwright as well, and he wrote to her too, urging her to post to Court and lay her case before his majesty. She in return asked Dormer to plead for her with the King's advisers, and for her husband no less than for herself since John Cartwright and his mother had been indicted for High Treason.

Dormer continued to do what he could. John Cartwright was probably in London, Katherine in Oxford, and she too was apparently doing what she could for him. John Dormer, who must have been a true friend, had a regard for both of them, and wrote to tell John Cartwright that he had found Katherine

> full of grief for your losses. She hath got such cattle and other goods of yours as she could into her protection, which are safe here, and she hath a warrant from his Majesty for other left behind, which she . . . will presently send for, and so preserve something which otherwise would have been lost.

Dormer went on to ask John Cartwright to forgive him for interfering between him and his wife, but that he knew Katherine's

> zeal and fervency, to beg your pardon for what is past, as I am able to testify by her former passage and tears. Though nothing could move you formerly be pleased yet to look back, and to know that she is still your wife, and what solemn protestations you made in your marriage. Though now she hath many friends, yet still know that she desireth your love and that you would not ruinate yourself your child and her, with such evil council, but please to post hither where she is pleased to use her . . friends to assist you and bring you into favour. If you come not suddenly it will be too late, and then not to be helped.

The matter was urgent, for there was a proclamation of pardon being drawn up and Dormer had heard that Cartwright's name was not on it. But whether because he felt that it would be humiliating to owe a return favour to his wife, or whether because of his belief in the rightness of the Parliament cause, John Cartwright did not look back. At his London house, Barn Elms, he took the Solemn League and Covenant, and so proclaimed his allegiance to the enemies of the King.

Meanwhile Mary Cartwright his old mother was living at Astrop, beyond King's Sutton. It was a dangerously exposed place for so notorious an opponent of the crown, and sometime after the capture of Banbury Castle by the Royalists, a troop of them rode over and treated the old lady with great brutality. They stuck burning matches (the pieces of wick that musketeers used for firing their guns) between her fingers, ran a sword through her gown, narrowly missing her body, and carried her off to Banbury leaving the house a wreck behind them.

The Royal garrison made frequent sorties that summer of

1643, molesting travellers and pillaging the country in their almost daily quests of supplies. In September there was action by larger bodies of troops, when the Earl of Essex was marching to Gloucester with a Parliament army, and Henry Wilmot was determined to intercept him. The Parliament forces gathered at Baynard's Green, beyond Souldern, where they hailed their general 'with great shouting and triumph', after which the Earl moved on to Aynho to establish his headquarters. The royalists, however, were near Banbury in strength, with outposts at Deddington. All next day the cavalry skirmished around Deddington, inconclusively (but no doubt damagingly) surging to and fro through the unfortunate town, while the Parliament foot advanced to Souldern where they spent the night 'much scanted of victualls'. Next day they marched to Hook Norton, shielded by the cavalry from the Royalists forces at Banbury, and if they had wanted to cross the Cherwell dryshod they may have marched through Aynho.

The next year, 1644, saw the King's army in the district once more. At the end of June, he trounced the Parliament forces under Sir William Waller at Cropredy Bridge, north of Banbury, and he then marched unopposed through the country, with 'drums beating, colors flying, and trumpets sounding' and with an artillery train that probably included the guns — the five Drakes, the Minion and the 'two little leather guns' which his troops had captured from the enemy. Early in the morning they marched through Middleton Cheney and Farthingho, and then turned towards Aynho where quarters were found for the foot while the King rode on to Deddington to lie there the night. After two years of war, the great house was probably in no condition to receive him.

That was the last time that substantial bodies of troops appeared in the area, but the war was not yet by any means over for the village. There was a Royalist outpost at King's Sutton, but after they had been surprised by a raiding party of the Parliament forces, out from Northampton, they shifted their garrison to the great house at Aynho. There were two troops, 60 men in all, under the command of Major Compton at Banbury. It was not a strongly held position, even though they built a drawbridge from the village into the front court of the house, and at any sign of real danger they retreated to Nell Bridge or even to Twyford to secure their retreat to Banbury. They were reported as spending most of the day drinking in the village, keeping a careless watch, and shutting themselves into the great house at ten at night.

(There is a little mound, projecting into the Park a few yards

south west of the great house, which according to tradition in the
Cartwright family represents the remains of earthworks thrown up
to defend the place. There was, moreover, another story handed
down that some soldiers were buried there. Around 1950 the daughter of the family, then a girl of 11, set out to test the story by digging there, and found bones identified as human. The tradition of
the burial of Civil War soldiers seems improbable: why should they
not have been buried in the churchyard if any of them had in truth
been killed? It is perhaps more likely that the mound where these
bones were turned up was a much eroded prehistoric barrow, though
again it is odd that it should have survived at all for so long, so close
to the house. The truth of these traditions cannot now be confirmed or denied, but they deserve to be recorded for what they
are worth.)

There was the odd skirmish. Once, a troop of Parliament
horse out from Newport Pagnell, where Sir Samuel Luke had a
sizeable garrison, caught up with some Royalists between Brackley
and Aynho, seized them and carried off some oxen that they had
taken. It may have been one of them who a little later wrote to Sir
Charles Compton from Newport jail

> Right Worship-full It was our hard chance . . to be taken pri-
> soner . . between Aynho and Brackley, a coast where I little
> dreamed of danger, which came unlooked for, And since Fate hath
> brought us into durance at Newport I hope your Worship will
> afford us exchange from Banbury or be pleased to send us some
> monyes for our subsistence untill a happy exchange may bee sent.

In a second letter he asked Corporal Bayley, if the exchange was
not agreed to,

> to acquaint ye Troop with our condition which I know will
> afford us some monyes for our present maintenance

and asked him, too, to send on their washing.

But the end was coming. July 1645 saw the battle of Naseby,
up near Market Harborough, and with it the end of the King's
hopes. Banbury Castle was fiercely besieged for fourteen weeks in
the late summer of the previous year, and though a relieving force
under the Earl of Northampton had|raised the siege in September,
the castle was again invested early in 1646. The defenders were
well provisioned, and the attackers themselves had to secure their
rear with an earthwork around the town, but when news came of
the King's surrender to the Scottish army at Newark, Sir William
Compton and his garrison saw that further resistance was useless.

The terms of surrender were honourable indeed, the officers
allowed their servants, arms and horses, and the common soldiers
given free passes to wherever they wished to go. The Royal garrison
at Aynho had ridden away for the last time before that, leaving
the great house in flames behind them.

For four years the people of the village had endured the war,
and it must have been a bad time. Much had happened since the
country people had first brought food and drink for the soldiers
of Lord Brooke and Lord Northampton, facing each other outside
Banbury. Their crops had been trampled down, their animals made
off with, and their corn requisitioned. On one 'voyage' alone,
Major Ennis's troop from Newport had taken horse worth £300.
When Banbury Castle was first besieged in 1644, the defenders'
provisions were down to two horses before relief came, but at the
time of the surrender in 1646 there were in the castle 200 quarters
of wheat and malt, many hogsheads of salt beef, several tons of
biscuit, 20 live oxen and 60 live sheep, all of which must have been
supplied by the country round. Sometimes a poor man's only
horse would be taken, sometimes half a rich man's team. Draught
animals and waggons that were borrowed would never be seen
again, and woe betide a farmer who had been provisioning the
wrong side when the enemy came riding through.

When demands for supplies were made, it was often with a
threat that if the local constables should

> fail therein or delay it there will be a party of horse sent to fetch
> you to Justice, and a great fine laid upon your town.

and then anyone might be unlucky enough to be taken prisoner,
held until exchanged, 'quality for quality', and given poor treatment meanwhile unless he could pay for better. Travelling around
the country was highly dangerous; disaffected soldiers, desperate
for want of pay, turned to highway robbery; at Adderbury, for
instance, in the spring of 1645 there were 'diverse scattered soldiers
lurkeing for people going to the Fayre'. Staying at home was scarcely any safer; men were pressed for service by either side, and if
they ran away were pressed again. If not as soldiers, then as labourers: the siege works at Banbury castle must have called for a
great deal of hard labour on either side.

Not surprisingly, the affairs of the village were in a state of
some confusion. No Manor Court was held for six years. It was reported in 1644 that

> all the Country about Clifton, Aynho . . and those, are well
> affected and willing to take up armes for the service of the king
> and parliament [i.e. Parliament]

but this was certainly not true of Aynho itself, where by no means
everyone was a supporter of Parliament or of the squire. Mr. Hanslope, in John Cartwright's absence the leading gentleman of the
place, appointed himself some kind of steward, collected rents and
paid them to a quartermaster of the King's forces. (It may have
been under duress: there were 60 soldiers in the great house, and
in any case the Lord of the Manor had been attainted for treason
and could be held to have forfeited his rights.) Then Thomas Drope
the son of Richard Cartwright's old enemy, Henry Letch and
Thomas Southam, all substantial yeomen, had none of them ever
lent a penny to Parliament, 'though well able so to do', and the
rector, Reginald Burdyn, for all that he had been Richard Cartwright's nominee, seems to have been a royalist.

Some evidence of the effects of the war can be had from the
parish registers. There was an unusual number of deaths in 1640–
42, though an unusual number of those who died were people
from elsewhere. 1643 was worse, the worst year for deaths since
the registers had first been kept 73 years before. There had been a
wet spring and a broiling summer, and the armies had spread disease,
particularly typhus, as they went through the country. Some of
Essex's army had been quartered in the village in September, and
they may have brought fresh infection with them. The vicar himself died in that month, and for some time afterwards the registers
were not properly kept up: people had other things to care about.

After the fighting was over, it was time to take stock. John
Cartwright had probably not been at Aynho since the war began:
as a rebel, he would have found it a great deal safer to remain in
London rather than to risk capture and imprisonment, or worse,
by venturing down to view the ruin of his estates. Not that he was
personally ruined, by any means, for all the losses that he cata-
logued in a petition that he sent to Parliament when the war was
done:

> Your petitioner having in an eminent manner showed his good
> affection to the Parliament the King's forces took the rents and
> profits both of those lands and all other your petitioners estate in
> those parts during all the late war: Imprison'd his dear mother nine
> months in Banbury town and Castle to the utter hazard of her
> life And demolished your petitioners house at Astrop and burned
> the chief mansion house at Aynho with all the outhouses down to

the ground being a goodly Seat to his damage near twenty thousand
pounds

A draft of his petition adds 'losse of 1000 shepe and other cattel'.
For all that, he was still able to find over two thousand pounds to
make other purchases over the next ten years, and to rebuild the
great house early in the 1660's.

Old Mrs. Cartwright, his mother, had probably gone to Barn
Elms after her release from captivity: the house at Aynho must
have been uninhabitable, even though there is good reason to believe that it was not all, by any means, burnt down to the ground
and that the wings at least remained. Perhaps from there she and
her son returned to Aynho together, and there, once accommodation had been found for her, she stayed with John's son William,
born in 1634. She had had the rearing of him after he had been
taken from his mother as a child; when she died she charged him
in her Will to 'demeane himselfe as an obedient tractable and love-
inge sonne to his Father' which would be 'A recompence to mee
for all that true care and pains I bestowed upon him in his infancy
and upwards.'

But he was not yet grown up, and in her letters to her son
John in London she refers to young William's needs from Town —
she sends John a note from him, 'by which you will see what lute
strings and other thinges hee wants'; she tells John that 'Those
stockings you sent your sonne will doe him noe good at all', and
a note from William told his grandmother that 'If you make me a
red scarlett Jackett it would be warme and hansome'. William was
old enough to think for himself; a letter to his father, written 'ex
aedibus Wottoniensibus' (perhaps William was away somewhere at
school ?) seems at first to be simply a Latin exercise, full of the most
correct filial sentiments, but in the middle of it William, the son
of a former Parliament man, writes of the horror they all feel at
the King's impending execution, at the barbarous and inhuman
cruelty being used 'in Patrem Patriae' and how slender their hope
that the evil will be warded off.

But Mrs. Cartwright had work to do while John was in London.
She writes that she is hoping to get the rubbish cleared from the
orchard since she had had some help from neighbours with their
teams; and there were numerous tenancy matters to be re-estab-
lished: Cosby had promised to pay his arrears of rent at the next
rent day; Freeman had promised 'if hee bee alive he will pay his
money within this fortnight';

Pruce desireth to have Rich: White's cotage & Underwood desires
that wch. Knot lives in & Knot is willing to go to the Warren & I
think convenient so to dispose of them & settle Rich: White in
Howes house when he removeth for Swetnams if he have stones &
build a good chimney below as he promiseth

There was more to mend than the family fortunes, and more
to sort out than tenancies: there was order and authority to restore
as well. Old Richard Cartwright had had trouble enough. Back in
1633, not in the best of health and perhaps feeling that at three
score and ten he should be tidying things up and leaving his affairs
in order for his son's trouble-free succession, he had ordered the
Jury at the Lady-day Court to enquire into a list of uses and abuses
that, if they had done all that was asked of them, would have taken
all their time until the next Court. The list of dilapidations, quoted
already, was one fruit of these injunctions, but that had been easy
to produce. Other things they were to enquire into had been the
customs for holding freehold and copyhold estates; heriots; a list
of freeholders', copyholders' and tenants' names with full details
of all their holdings; all other customs, when instituted and how;
the exact boundaries of the Lord's demesne and how many trees
of each kind there were growing upon it; who was liable to pay
headsilver; all damages done on the waste and all customary fines
due to the Lord; undertenants, dilapidations, rents unpaid, merestones moved and lands enlarged and paths and ways altered. And
this formidable list ends 'There are 3 or 4 enquiries more to be
given to the Jurie besides these.'

It would have been a stupefying task, even for men who knew
the village as well as they did, and before the war the villagers must
often have felt the hand of the Lord of the Manor lying heavily
upon them. Now, for all the recent troubles, the villagers had for
a time been free of his authority, and probably exposed too to
some of the more radical and subversive ideas current at the time,
spread about by travellers and the Parliamentary armies: the
notions of the Diggers, of the Ranters, and others which were more
revolutionary than any they would ever have heard.

The last Manor Court before the war had been held in 1641,
the next in 1647, but by 1650 there was still clearly much to be
done by way of restoring the Lord of the Manor's authority. It
was in the spring of that year that John drew up notes for his
steward, who was to take great pains in all matters about the
Court, 'being very materiall'. All the old presentments were to

be made — nuisances, encroachments, blocked ditches, moved merestones, tenants who did not grind at the Lord's mill, all breaches of former Court orders, alehouses, inmates, new buildings, hedge breakers, leases, whipping post, stocks, cucking stool, dilapidations and arrears of rent in money and kind. It was a matter of stock taking as well as of re-asserting his position.

That year more than 21 people were fined for not appearing at that Lady-day Court, and fined 3s 4d each. 3d or 6d would have been traditional. Some would not pay, and the bailiffs distrained — '6 pannes 2 dishes'; 'on yron Pott'; 'a ketell & a pott' are written against names on the list, and some people, clearly, would rather go without the necessities of life than pay such monstrous fines. For building cottages without sufficient land attached to them, an offense that in Richard Cartwright's day had cost 10s, John Crackloe and William Baldwin were each amerced £22, which must have been fully as much as the cottages were worth, and John Crackloe was fined another £5 'for receiving a dangerous pson sevall tymes into his house formerly convicted of Fellony'.

In 1651 things had not improved. Thomas Swetnam and Henry Letch, and both their wives, were presented for forcibly resisting the bailiffs, and Henry Letch was fined £20 for not giving security to the overseers of the poor for his tenant in a newly built cottage. The following year, John Cartwright seems to have tried moderation instead; perhaps he realised that it would be better to exercise authority by having small fines accepted rather than to have large ones defied, and the fine for non-attendance at the Court was down to 6d. Thomas Parker was fined a mere 10s for building an illegal cottage, and John Crackloe only 3s 4d for his unlawful tenant. But tensions had been growing, and some may have seen these concessions as being signs of weakness. The year ended with John Cartwright's agents being physically attacked.

In August, the bailiffs tried to distrain a horse from Henry Letch and a sow from Thomas Williams, and one of the poor villagers, James Watts, swore an affidavit to what had happened.

> James Watts saith . . that John Jenkyns & Robert Elyot took a horse of Henry Letch of Aynho standing near the gate of the said Henry in Aynho aforsaid. And that thereupon Elizabeth the wife of John Jeffes & daughter of the said Henry flung a stone so big as his fist at the said Jenkins, standing then very near to the said Jenkins. There were present at this action Ann Williams the wife of Thomas Williams and also the wife of Faulke Gardner, the wife of Faulke Gardner said, hang him, stone him to death . . and the

other women .. all raised a great hubbub against the said bailiffs.

But the bailiffs persisted, though they knew by now that it was going to be a dangerous job:

> Anne Williams Elizabeth Leach [sic] [wife of Henry Letch].
> Elizabeth Jeffes [wife of John Jeffes] on the 29th day of September in the year of our lord God 1652 .. with force and Arms (that is to say) with Swords Knives daggers and other weapons as well as offensive as defensive riotously routously & unlawfully did make an Assault & affray him the sayd Robt Elyot then and there in the Execution of his Office of Bailiff aforesaid & then and there did beat & wound & evil entreat, so that of his life it was despaired

At the bottom of the document there is a scrawl, perhaps a note by the magistrate, which seems to read

> threw stones & severally tried to knock him on the head

which is, after all, a good deal more likely than the picture of these heavily armed Amazons that their accusers was presenting.

What the outcome was, we do not know. The culprits may have been brought for trial to Northampton: it was a serious offence to obstruct the Lord's officials, as was an assault on anyone. The fact that James Watts made a sworn statement shows at least that action was contemplated. But Henry Letch was still around ten years later, and still showing his independence, when in 1665 he was fined £5 for refusing to serve as Constable — and in view of all that had passed, it is surprising both that he was chosen and that he should have refused. Eighteen months later he still owed the £5, and in 1670 he was presented once more, this time for building no less than two cottages and for taking in an undertenant as well.

He was old by then, and a good deal had happened since Henry Letch first appears in this story, farming the land of his widowed mother, Elizabeth Young in the 1630's. John Cartwright died in 1676, and his son William a few months before him. The new squire was a child of five when his father died, and it would be many years before there were again squires of the character and force of John and Richard Cartwright. Nor would the villagers' lives ever again be disturbed by events such as those of the Civil War. It was time to settle down and to rebuild village life.

Chapter 6

Three Parsons

The rectors of Aynho do not readily fit into the history of the village, and they are therefore, perhaps, better given a chapter to themselves. This is not because they took no part in village life: far from it. The rector was the one person in the village whom almost every villager could be sure of both seeing and hearing every week. The farmers probably had more trouble with the parson over his tithes than they had with the squire and his steward over their rents. But though he was in the village, the rector was most decidedly not of it. He came from far away, and left no family behind. After the passing of the Dropes and the Hanslopes, he was the only gentleman in the village beside the squire, and in his education he left the villagers far behind. He dined with the squire, and no villager ever did. The rector was a man apart.

All this would have been true of most parsons of the seventeenth and (particularly) the eighteenth centuries, but there were three rectors in Aynho who were a cut above even their contemporaries, men who made a name in the world and were known, or known of, in Oxford, in London and even abroad. These were Robert Wilde, Matthew Hutton and Joseph Wasse, and if some parts of their stories go rather beyond the confines of the village, it is well to remember that given talents, and opportunities such as ordinary villagers seldom had, one need not be cut off by living in a corner of Northamptonshire.

Robert Wilde, perhaps the most attractive of all the three, got the living in the most inauspicious circumstances. Reginald Burdyn, Thomas Drope's successor, died in 1643. It was a most difficult time, when the Royalists were in Banbury and garrisoning the great house at Aynho, and when John Cartwright, named a traitor and living in London, was in no position to make a presentation to the living. John Cartwright's incapacity, however, was no trouble to the Royalists: quite the reverse, in fact, since here was a rich living fallen vacant and in a troublesome area where the ministrations of a loyal parson might well help the Cause. The candidate chosen by the Royalists, James Longman, was chaplain to Sir Christopher Hatton who was a friend of the governor of Banbury Castle. And though the squire's signature to the presentation could not easily be had, his mother — old Mary Cartwright — was already in Royalist hands in Banbury and might be made use of.

They first tried gentle persuasion, while a certain Dr. Tailor kept pestering her to sign a document on Longman's behalf. This failing, the governor of the castle, Sir William Compton himself, came

> to her bedside in her Chamber where she was imprisoned, and told her that she and such as she, were the cause of all this bloodshed, and bid her get up, saying that a Castle was fitter for her than a Bed, and that she must to the Castle, whereupon she being up and ready, a soldier left there to watch her carried her forcibly away to the Castle, she having been all or most part of the night very sick and was then ready to swoon, upon this violent carrying of her away by the said soldier. And she saith, that she being brought to the Castle she was put into an exceeding cold room (it then being winter time) ill boarded unglazed open roofed and without any bedding, with three or four doors locked upon her, to which room there was no passage but through other rooms where nasty soldiers lay, and so strict was her imprisonment that none were admitted to go in unto her from five in the afternoon till eight or nine in the morning, in which hard imprisonment she was continued seven days and nights or thereabouts, insomuch as she being very weak and aged, was in great danger of perishing there. During which imprisonment in the Castle the said Dr. Tailor and one Willoughby servant to the Earl of Northampton did prosecute the business on the said Longman's behalf telling her there was now no law in force but the sword, and if fair means would not do it, foul means should . . .

It must have been very frightening, and being January, bitterly cold; another contemporary account describes how the old lady had to stuff handfuls of straw between the cracks of floorboards and ceiling to try and stop the snow blowing in. It may in the end have been the weather as much as Sir William's threats and the nasty soldiers that made her capitulate, write to her son and urge him to present Longman to the living. He did so for her sake, but it was an unfortunate beginning to Longman's incumbency.

Longman found the presence of a Royalist garrison in the big house no great help in caring for the place. He would ride out from Oxford to take services, riding back again when he was done to the comparative safety of that centre of Royalist sentiment. During the times of services he would place a sentry on top of the tower, to watch for marauding Roundheads. He took his last service at Aynho (for the time being) the day after the Royalists finally abandoned the big house, and afterwards there were plenty to give evidence to the Parliamentary Commissioners about his neglect: that he had lived in Oxford for two-and-a-half years, seldom venturing out and then only to fill his sermons with dire warnings of what would happen to those who resisted the King's authority. (Not surprisingly, there were also those like Mr. Hanslope who were prepared to give evidence on the other side.) It was not surprising, either, that the Commissioners should recommend his expropriation, and his replacement by a 'godlie and orthodox Divine'.

One might have expected that such a man, appointed by Parliament in 1646, would have been some grim and long-faced Puritan. Puritan of a sort, Robert Wilde certainly was, but grim and long-faced, not at all. The story is that he and another man preached sermons in competition for the living, and when a friend asked him how he had fared in preaching for the living of Ayno (as it was often called) he answered 'We have divided it. He got the No, I got the Ay.'

Wilde was the son of a shoemaker in St. Ives in Huntingdon, went to Cambridge and subsequently to Oxford, and took a Bachelor of Divinity's degree there in 1642. He was probably working as a schoolmaster before he got the Aynho benefice. There were in the seventeenth century more earnest and well-educated clergy than jobs to be found for them — one remembers Drope's over-enthusiastic curates — and Wilde must have been glad to get a living. There is no doubt that he took his duties at Aynho seriously. Richard Baxter, the great puritan divine, was once on his way to London, and having heard stories that made him suspect that Wilde was not leading quite so earnest a life as a puritan minister should, he decided to stop off at Aynho and remonstrate with him. It was a fast day, and Wilde was preaching. Baxter slipped into the back of the church to hear the sermon, and afterwards came to to Wilde and humbly apologised for having believed such tales of him.

There is a charming letter, written by Wilde to a friend who had sent him a copy of a work by a favourite Puritan writer, Edward Reynolds. When the book arrived, Wilde must have been sitting in his study in the rectory at Aynho, surrounded by his books and trying to prepare his sermon for Sunday:

Generous Sir

On Saturday last (the day and weather being as sad and dumpish as old Saturn himself) whilst I was in my study (my books and myself musty and melancholy) and my provisions for the next day being as poor as ever were made by a country Curate, sometimes scratching that which goes for my Head, and then to biting

my Nails for offending my Noddle; in comes your Friendly Letter
(the welcomest Quartermaster that ever came to my House) to
take up Quarters for that gallant Mans Works Dr. Reynolds . . .
You cannot imagine what fear, shame, confusion and envy my
poor Shelves discovered; some poor Authors stood gaping, others
tumbled down, and others burst their Bindings, making to break
Prison, rather than stand before such a Judge of Learning. Those
few Fathers (which I had) seemed to meet in a Council, what
they should do, whether to stay or depart. Old Origen began, but
was so full of Allegories, and Whimseys, they could not tell what
to say to him. Justin thought that he should again be a martyr,
and be burnt to light Tobacco . . .

   Thus Sir, it was for my Study. But for myself, oh how I was
raised and ravished! No sooner did that Book big with Christ,
enter and salute me (pardon the allusion) but my Heart . . leap'd
for Joy . . .

Wilde's religion was presbyterian, unwilling to accept anything
of ritual or church government that was not warranted by scripture, and it was for that that he was turned out of his living in
1662. But for all that, he was a monarchist. When Charles I was on
trial for his life, he had the courage with some other ministers of
the neighbourhood to sign 'The Humble Advice and Earnest Desires
of certain well-affected Ministers' to the Council of War, expressing
their 'utter dissent' from the proceedings against the King, and when
eleven years later Charles II was restored to the throne through
the actions of General Monck, he published in celebration a long
poem in rhyming couplets, 'Iter Boreale', celebrating both Monck's
march south on London and the King's return to his country. It
had a huge success; Dryden wrote of City merchants being so
taken up reading it that they neglected their business; Samuel
Pepys, only catching up with it three years later (and probably
piqued at having missed out on it when it was the latest thing) wrote

So home to my wife; and with her read 'Iter Boreale', a poem,
made just at the King's coming home; but I never read it before,
and now like it pretty well, but not so well as it was first cried
up.

Though this did not stop him thoroughly enjoying himself when a
friend came to share their Christmas dinner in 1667 and read
Wilde's poems to them afterwards. It is not great poetry, and many
of the topical allusions are now lost on all but specialists in the
period. But a few lines of 'Iter Boreale', speaking of the King's
voyage from France, show how entertaining his verses still can be —

The joyful Ship shall dance, the Sea shall laugh,
And loyal Fish their Master's health shall quaff;

> See how the Dolphins crowd around their large
> And scaly shoulders to assist the Barge;
> The peaceful Kingfishers are met together
> Around the Decks and Prophesie calm weather;
> Poor Crabs and Lobsters are gone down to creep
> And search for Pearls and Jewels in the deep;
> And when they have their booty, crawl before
> To leave them for his welcome on the Shore'.

After that, it is sad that Wilde was deprived of the benefice in 1662, and Longman reinstated. The reasons were the same as those that led to the deprivation of some two thousand ministers appointed under the Commonwealth: their refusal to subscribe to the 39 Articles of the Church of England with all that they had to say about Sacraments, Bishops and much else that Wilde must have considered superfluous to the practice and beliefs of Christianity. Wilde may have lived on in Aynho for a year or two after that, and apparently Dr. Longman gave him some help; probably the squire did too. And when Sir John Baber, the King's physician, sent him money, he answered in verse. He began facetiously —

> Ten Crowns at Once! and now at such a time
> When love to such as I am is a crime . . .
> What, now to help a Non-Conformist! Now
> When Ministers are broke that will not bow!

but continued, suddenly serious

> It was because you knew I loved the King.

But he was probably not entirely without resources. His poems enjoyed an enormous vogue in restoration London, to the extent that when some witty, anonymous verse appeared it was likely to be attributed to him. Some plays have been ascribed to him as well, though since Puritans were so much opposed to playhouses this seems rather unlikely. He died at Oundle in 1679, and his Will was as characteristic a mixture of Christianity and worldly humour as his life had been: he left money for six Bibles to be diced for annually by twelve children on the altar in Oundle church. It is still done.

Longman may have been a good enough rector once he no longer had to contend with the troubles of the War, though his position cannot have been easy given the history of the last years. His successor, Matthew Hutton, though not the delightful man that Wilde had been, was another rector who was known beyond the confines of the parish. He was a cousin of William Cartwright's wife, Ursula Fairfax, and came from a Yorkshire family where his grandfather had been Archbishop. So, unlike Wilde, he was well-connected. But at Aynho he was a fish out of water, and one might guess that he took the living partly in order to be near Oxford and its libraries. At Oxford in the 1650's and 1660's, as a student, he had been one of a group of antiquarian-minded young men, collecting books and documents, walking out to see ruins in the neighbourhood, and amusing themselves in the evenings with music — Hutton had a good voice and played the viol. But then as now one could not live for ever as a student, and he was probably grateful for the living offered him by his cousin's father-in-law.

Poor Hutton.

> Had I a place in or near a Cathedrall, I would have ransack'd all the dark corners of it, and have rescued old papers from dust and cobwebs, and been ready to serve any worthy person in transcribing faithfully what I thought would be of use

he wrote, and though Oxford and its libraries must have been some consolation, most of his researches were into histories of monasteries and bishoprics, and particularly those of the north of England. It is more likely that he spent a good deal of time away from Aynho. His Oxford friends mention him occasionally in their letters, but it is obvious that he was one of those people with all the inclinations of a University don without having quite the brilliance to be one. After his death his papers were bought by the Earl of Oxford, and they are now in the British Museum. But they tell us nothing of the man, and only a few of his personal letters survive to suggest that Hutton must have been a nice, quiet, rather anxious man, pleased to tell his friends the scraps of gossip that came his way and which he thought might amuse them but obviously not someone to make much of a mark in the world. Hutton may have been a conscientious parson, enjoying dining with Dame Ursula in the big house and sending his correspondents extracts from his notes on ancient manuscripts from his study in the rectory. But his heart was elsewhere.

His successor, however, the third of this trio of eminent rectors, was a very different character. He was Joseph Wasse, who succeeded Hutton in 1711. Wasse too was a Yorkshireman, and had already achieved some distinction as Chaplain to the Duke of York and as editor of an edition of Sallust (in 1707) which achieved some reputation. He was enthusiastic, clever, good company and almost certainly a good parson, and, though one does suspect him of being a trifle pleased with himself, he is entertaining enough to be forgiven.

His reputation had preceded him to Oxford on the strength of his Sallust, and when one day he presented himself at the Bodleian to read an obscure Greek manuscript, Thomas Hearne the deputy keeper of the library knew him at once.

> This morning there came to the Publick Library a Clergyman, who asked me to show him Vettius Valens, which is a Greek MS in Selden's archives not yet published . . . I found him to be Mr. J. Wasse of Cambridge, who is now rector of Aynhoe on the Hill . . . I had no discourse with him, but Dr. Hudson had a great deal. He told the Dr. that he could easily and quickly translate this Author. Which was spoke with the same Confidence with which he uses to speak upon other occasions. Now the subject of this Book is Astrology, there is a vast deal of ancient abstruse Learning in it, & I do not think there is hardly one Man now living in England that understands the Book . . . But 'tis no wonder that Wasse should speak with so much Confidence upon this Point, when he talks with the same Confidence on all other Subjects. He pretends to every thing, and thinks that he is a compleat General Scholar, whereas he is not a master in one branch of Learning . . .

Hearne's opinion of him went from bad

'So very conceited as to make him despised by abundance'

to worse

'This Mr. Wasse is a craz'd man.'

But Thomas Hearne was a querulous old woman who would not have appreciated anyone with the drive of Joseph Wasse. Wasse was interested in everything. He reported to the Royal Society in London on a slight earthquake that had shaken windows in Aynho, Bloxham and Adderbury. He attempted to observe an eclipse of the sun from the rectory garden, with a 6′ Meridian set on a 20″ oak post set 5 feet into the ground to minimise vibration: unfortunately, it rained, but 'the birds were a good deal affected, and some Martins in my house came home to their Nests.' He excavated 'a pretty nest of 5 Urns' and reported on an earthwork the other side of Astrop. He travelled in the wilds of Scotland, and corresponded with learned men in Amsterdam. And according to a friend of both men, the great Dr. Richard Bentley, Master of Trinity College, Cambridge and by general account the most erudite man of his age, said 'when I am dead, Wasse will be the most learned man in England.' So much for the snide remarks of Thomas Hearne.

He also reported to the Royal Society on a smallpox outbreak in Aynho (of which more later) and on a freak thunderstorm, on July 3rd, 1725.

> Two persons at Aynho were a little hurt, and one of them struck down to the Ground, and says, he thought he was felled with a

Beetle [i.e. a sledge-hammer] . I myself heard the Hiss of a Ball of
fire almost as big as the Moon, which flew over my Garden from
South East to North West.

James Marshall of this Town . . . received a Blow upon his Hat,
which rattled like Shot through the Branches of a Tree; it beat in
the Crown a little without penetrating it; He staggered & was
giddy for two Days afterwards. Two of his Sons were at the same
Instant, both knock'd to the Ground, and stunn'd a little.

Others of Wasse's experiments concerned his observation that
people shrank three quarters of an inch in half a day, and only re-
gained their height after a night's sleep. This he put down to the
compression of the cartilige between the vertebrae while people
were upright, and by measuring himself, Mr. Cartwright, and
several villagers he found it to be equally true of those whose lives
were active or sedentary.

Mr. Hutton of Somerset House himself, who is the greatest Pro-
ficient in the Art of Sitting Still now living, cannot contrive a
Chair in which he will keep to his morning Elevation for 14 Hours

He measured himself before and after an hour's exercise with a
garden roller on the rectory lawn, and found that he shrunk by
half an inch. He mentioned the fact to the Secretary of the Royal
Society, whereupon the Fellows seem to have spent a happy time
measuring each other and everyone else they could find to prove
the truth of Wasse's assertion. He mentioned it to an officer after
some soldiers had been discharged for being slightly under height,
'and thereby kept several Persons from being disappointed'.

It was thanks to him, too, that (until the writing of this book)
people have known what they did about Aynho's history. When
John Bridges was collecting material for the history of Northamptonshire that was published after his death, he depended largely on
local correspondents and it was Wasse who sent him the Aynho
account that is printed almost verbatim in his great work. Wasse
had earlier taken Bridges to show him Rainsborough camp. He
took a lively interest in local affairs. When Mr. Asplin, the vicar of
Banbury, wrote a tract against turning to the East in prayer, Wasse
sided with Asplin's opponents, and when Asplin threw one of these
opponents over the churchyard wall, Wasse described Asplin as
'truly of the Church Militant'. He preached rousing sermons —

I have broke several pulpit desks and put the Church Wardens to
the Charge of frequent Repairs but cannot as yet avoid the Im-
portunity

and he wrote and published a book of private prayers for the use of the Cartwright family.

A biographer was able to write of him

> Here [sc. at Aynho] he lived a very agreeable and Christian life much esteemed by that worthy family, and his parishioners; he esteeming them equally, and would never seek after any other preferment.

He died in 1738

> Aged about 60, of an Apoplexy, & left most of his fortune & library to his nephew, a clergyman, who sold most of the library, loving hunting better than Greek or Hebrew. He was a facetious man in conversation, but a heavy preacher. A very deserving charitable man, and universally esteemed.

Chapter 7

The Eighteenth Century:Rich and Poor

In 1676 the squire was dead. Everyone must have known that it was the end of an era. For sixty years the villagers had lived with two most forceful personalities, Richard Cartwright and his son John, and now there was no squire at all and the heir was a child of five. Old John, squire for forty years, died in October; his only son William had died in the previous April. Richard Watts, the village blacksmith, had agreed to cover the coffin in lead for 25s., and 'to put Mr. William Cartwright's name and the daye when he dyed upon the leaden coffin & if he do all the work very well according to the mind of John Cartwright Esq he desires Mr. Cartwright will give him a crown more for it.' It was not a moment when the squire would| carp over a few shillings. The survival of the family itself must have seemed in doubt at that moment. Four infant sons of William Cartwright had died already; Thomas, aged five, was the only male descendant. If Thomas too had died as a child the Aynho estate must have been divided among his sisters, Richard Cartwright's attempt to found a county family would have been brought to nothing and the whole of the village's later history would have been different (It is doubtful that this book could have been written either.) But Thomas was to live, and to rule as squire until the middle of the next century. In the meantime the estate would be administered by William's widow and the steward until Thomas came into his inheritance.

The seventeenth century had been Aynho's heroic age. If Richard and John Cartwright had been strong characters, it was only by virtue of their authority that they had triumphed over the Dropes, Letches, Hanslopes and others who had from time to time crossed their path. In the village they had found worthy opponents, and if in the next century there seem fewer men of the same calibre, it was partly for want of any challenge to bring them out. But it was partly, too, because many of the old families of yeomen farmers were dying out. There was such a high proportion of daughters to sons born to villagers in the seventeenth century that one begins to wonder whether there was something in Aynho that acted against the conception of male children. The leaders of eighteenth century Aynho are tradesmen, innkeepers and tenant farmers,

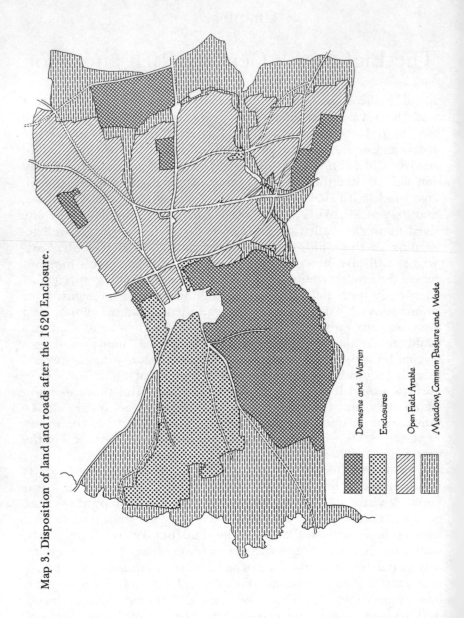

Map 3. Disposition of land and roads after the 1620 Enclosure.

Demesne and Warren

Enclosures

Open Field Arable

Meadow, Common Pasture and Waste

1. The Aynho landscape in the eighteenth century,
with the Fermor brothers hunting

Attributed to Francis Sartorius, 1764. The view is taken from the south east
corner of the parish, south of the Cuttle Brook and east of the Bicester road.
The windmill on Old Down is clearly visible; not visible in the reproduction is
a house that may represent the present Upper Grounds farm house, but which
seems not quite correctly placed if it is. The great house can be seen on the
skyline, Adderbury and King's Sutton churches in the distance. The nature of
the open field landscape shows very clearly: the division of the land into furlongs and strips can be made out in the right hand background.

2. Aynho from the air, c.1950

Seen from the south, with the great house standing between the park and the
village. The Park, unploughed for four hundred years, preserves the ridge-and-
furrow of the medieval open fields.

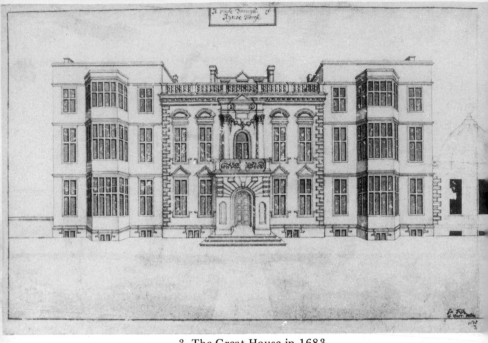

3. The Great House in 1683

The facade to the park. The centrepiece as built by William Marshall in the 1660's; the flanking wings remain from a late sixteenth century house. Though much altered, the centrepiece and wings still stand to form the basic structure of the existing building.

4. The old church in 1721

Seen from the south, drawn by Peter Tillemans. The extension of the south aisle, partly overlapping the chancel, is probably the Shakerley chapel of 1565.

5. The Grammar School: an engraving from an 1823 drawing by J.C. Buckler.

6. Edward Jarvis's house in 1949
The best of the early houses in the village, probably built c.1635. Its sophisticated masonry details were probably beyond the capacity of village masons. The arrangement of windows on the front reflects the staircase arrangements within.

8. John Cartwright (?), by Sir Peter Lely (?)

7. Richard Cartwright (?) in 1606, by Paul van Somer

worthy men enough but inevitably lacking the independence of the yeomen of the century before.

William Drope, grandson of the great parson Drope who had been such a thorn in Richard Cartwright's side, died in 1693, leaving just three daughters who all married outside the village — though it was a century before all his 99 acres reached the squire. Benjamin Watts, who had inherited the 20 acres that belonged to Lawrence Watts, Richard Cartwright's old shepherd, also left only three daughters, Anne, Sarah and Lydia. William Stanton, who had stood up for Richard Cartwright against Sir Robert Banastre, left seven daughters. So did William Wyatt, who died in 1663. He left his house and 54 acres to be divided equally among his children, and these acres

> The said copartners did agree should be put into seven scrolls in writing and Shuffled together in a hat by an indifferent person chosen among themselves, and out of the said hat he should at an adventure take and did take first one of the said scrolls alone and delivered the same unto the the the said Mary . . .

and so forth until all was done. In the absence of male heirs, it was normal for property to be divided equally among daughters, but the holdings that resulted were often too small to subsist upon, and too large for a garden, so they would be let to some farmer until there came a rainy day when they would be mortgaged or sold.

When Thomas Cartwright came of age, he bought 94 acres of the Hanslope property, which included some valuable meadow and an old but substantial house; he bought probably from Hanslope's son-in-law another 30 acres for £302. Edward Jarvis's grandson, another Edward, was bankrupt in 1713 with an only daughter; Thomas Cartwright first took a mortgage on their 30 acres and finally bought it for £400. Other owners moved away, like the Southams who went to Croughton, keeping their Aynho property for a generation or two but finally, when the time and the price were right, disposing of it to the squire. Others again, like the Hobcrafts, dissipated their property by making provision for younger sons, which had the same effect, ultimately, as providing for daughters did: it would produce small, fragmented holdings that were uneconomic to keep.

But the decline of the yeomen farmers was not solely due to the extinction of their families. The squires did not buy all land that came onto the market; Thomas Cartwright in particular seems to have been quite willing not to compete with villagers for land that they wanted, and villagers did acquire land when it was offered. What is significant is that so few did, and this can only be because few were in a position to do so. It must be significant too that the squire's own tenants were gradually becoming fewer and their farms larger. It was Richard Cartwright's translation of copyholds into tenancies that facilitated this consolidation of farms, but the old, smaller units could still have continued if there had been an economic incentive for maintaining them.

Inevitably, one result of the decline of the old families was a sort of power vacuum as land was increasingly concentrated in the hands of the squire, though until the end of the eighteenth century the squires were seldom concerned to buy cottages and a busy market in houses and their gardens continued among the trades- men and the craftsmen of the village. (It is arguable that the squire's powers only became absolute, so to speak, when he owned the cottages in the village as well as the land, and could thus con- trol who should be allowed to rent a house in the village and who should not. Such powers, as total in their way as had been those of medieval Lords of the Manor, were only fully established in the nineteenth century; Squire Thomas on occasions sold cottages off, perhaps considering a few shillings' rent a year not worth the collection.) But the loss of freehold land must have contributed to a decline in the villagers' status vis-a-vis the squire, as fewer indepen- dent farmers remained and more became tenants of the Cartwrights. Independence now meant owning a cottage and following one's trade rather than ploughing one's acres. In the eighteenth century the tenant farmers may have been more professional than their predecessors had been, since increasingly they farmed from choice rather than because of an accident of inheritance. In the nineteenth century this tendency towards a greater professionalism was com- plete, and tenancies on the Cartwright estate were sometimes sought by farmers from far away. But there was not a man in the village by then who did not owe his house or his very livelihood to the squire.

A few figures will make clear the extent of the change. In 1618, the thirteen freeholders between them owned some 700 acres, and these thirteen were leading figures among some 56 house- holds of farmers, tradesmen and labourers. By 1790, 40 freeholders owned a mere 196 acres, and there were by then about 140 house- holds in the village. The seventeenth century yeomen ploughed their own lands and came of families that had been in Aynho long before squire Cartwright's arrival, and from what we know of their behaviour it is hard not to think that some of them felt themselves his equals in all but wealth. The tenant farmers of 1790 were farming larger farms than their freeholding predecessors had done, and were enjoying larger incomes, but there was by then scarcely anyone in the village who actually farmed land of his own or who for one moment could have entertained thoughts of equality with the squire.

So the history of Aynho in the eighteenth century is not a dramatic one. There are no great feuds and quarrels, and the clash of powerful personalities is replaced by the endeavours of tradesmen to make a living, by the slow dispersal of ancient land-holdings, by the efforts of the Overseers of the Poor to provide for a number of paupers that would steadily increase, and by the tentative experiments of farmers with new rotations and crops. The next great upheaval for Aynho would be the enclosure of the remaining open fields in 1792, and the hundred years that followed the death of John Cartwright in 1676 was a long calm between storms.

The squire's steady acquisition of land did not alter the pattern of farming. Among the tenant farmers, some rented more land and others less, but almost all the farms, rented or freehold, included lands in the open fields, and though the squire might own adjoining strips, one might be let to one man, the next to another. It was not until the enclosure that the inconveniences that this gave rise to were finally remedied. Farms were still often divided as the land had been when the squire bought it: in 1704, for instance, the squire let to John Lawley a lease of 'Gardner's bigger yardland' and 'Gardner's lesser yardland', yet this must have been land that Richard Cartwright had bought from Mark Gardner in 1619. Thomas Cartwright had bought most of the Hanslope land in 1697, yet 80 years later the Cartwright estate was still being separately assessed for poor rates on 'Hanslap's land' and it was still being let on its own. It was partly conservatism, but it was partly also a matter of convenience: agreements did not all terminate at the same time, and existing tenancies and long-recognised holdings would have been upset if lands were re-arranged. The enclosure of 1792 would show how much work that involved.

The squires' buying substantial holdings when they came on the market might keep these ancient units of arable intact, but since Richard Cartwright's enclosure there had been more closes — separate fields — than before, and it was therefore easier for a farmer who wished to specialise to take on more or less enclosed land. Thomas Bower, butcher in the 1740's, rented closes and commons for twelve cows, but no arable at all. Furthermore, while the squire's farms might, so to speak, fossilise old holdings, the divisions consequent upon the deaths of freeholders gradually led to people holding amounts of land that no longer bore any close relation to the old 30-acre yardland, and some of these amounts were by now very small. By 1740, for instance, William Wyatt's lands had been so split up that one villager held no more than three strips that had been a part of Wyatt's whole 2 yardlands only 80 years before.

In any case the squire was often not concerned to buy all the tiny amounts of land that increasingly came on the market, and left them to be acquired by other people. Consequently, when the squire bought the lands of the last two yeomen, John Bricknell's in 1764 and John Letch's in 1787, their inherited holdings had been augmented by a rag-bag of purchase over the years. The process had been going on for a long time already, many of the squire's earlier purchases had been similarly added-to before he bought them, and the nominal yardlands of the eighteenth century were very approximate indeed.

In 1740 the rector made a list of all the households in the village, with the number of people in each. By good fortune this roughly coincides with the dates of other lists that we have, of rents, rates and tithes, and all appear together in the list of farmers on page 299. While the number of men farming is somewhat reduced from 1618 (page 296) it is a far smaller proportion of the total population of the village. In 1618, out of 56 households, 30 had an acre or more of land (as freeholders or tenants) in the open fields. In the 1740's, out of 127 'families' counted by the parson, only 21 seem to have farmed any land. At the same time, the range of farm sizes had been increasing, with some farms getting quite large. A reason for this must have been the growing population. In former times, when the number of landless labourers was not large, there was a limit to the amount of land that a man could farm since he relied primarily on the labour of his own immediate family. With a larger labour force, the ambitious farmer could increase his holdings.

It is likely too that there was another factor making for an increase in the size of rented farms, and that was in the economics of farming. From the later years of the seventeenth century the

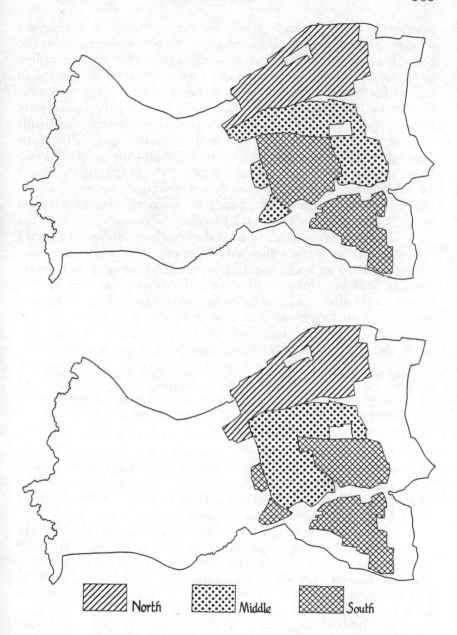

Map 4. Open Field arable. Boundaries of North, Middle and South fields in 1680 (top) and 1696 (bottom).

prices that farmers were getting for their produce were stagnant
or even tending to fall; their expenses, however, were increasing.
Biggest of these burdens was the land tax, levied on landowners
and amounting to an income tax of 4s in the pound. The squire
paid it for his tenants, but owner occupiers would have to find it
for themselves. On top of that, farmers had to pay gradually increasing poor rates, the fieldsmen's rate (though that was small)
and the rector's tithes. One must not overstate these difficulties:
other people in the eighteenth century besides the squire did buy
land, and Edward Letch was able to buy 1¾ yardlands that came
on the market in 1736. But such a transaction was exceptional,
and most land that changed hands between villagers in the eighteenth century was in very small parcels.

Though we do not know what the crop rotation was in Richard
Cartwright's time, the village's farmers practiced a 3-course rotation from 1639 and continued to do so until the middle of the next
century. But the grouping of strips into furlongs made it possible
to re-arrange them to form different fields when the need was felt,
and such re-arrangement was frequently done: in 1680, between
then and 1696, some time before 1763, and again in that year,
when the farmers introduced a rotation of four courses:-

Buglow Field -	Wheat Pease Barley Fallow
Middle -	Pease Barley Fallow Wheat
Conigree -	Barley Fallow Wheat Pease
South -	Fallow Wheat Pease Barley

and there was a certain amount of latitude allowed: a farmer might,
for instance, grow oats on his barley land, and a court order that
plough teams must not turn on growing crops suggests that operations in one field were not simultaneous: in fact if one man was
ploughing while his|neighbour's land was cropping there must have
been quite a discrepancy between work on adjacent strips.

Besides the re-arrangement of furlongs, there was some experi-
ment with alternative crops. From at least as early as 1702, and
probably before that, the squire had been given leave to grow san-
foin on an outlying area of common. In the 1740's the village
farmers tried sowing the barley fallow with turnips to be eaten off
by sheep (fattening the sheep and manuring the fallow at the same
time) though this was apparently not a success and was discon-
tinued four years later. In 1737 they tried undersowing the wheat
with clover, and in 1744 the barley, though it is not recorded how
successful this was. In 1751 eight farmers, presumably on account
of some need for additional pasture, agreed not to crop one furlong
at all but to lay it down for grass, 'to be eaten or otherwise made

use of for our benefit as shall be agreed upon from year to year by the majority of us'. On another occasion when the pressure was for more arable, they agreed to enclose and to plough one of the commons, Old Down.

But though the spirit of improvement may have been about, there were still ancient customs that survived. In a lease of 1704 from Thomas Cartwright to John Spencer, Spencer undertakes to pay with the rent of his farm two couple of pullets each New Year — a survival of the render of chickens that the peasants had been paying to the Lord of the Manor at least as early as the fourteenth century. He also agreed to deliver a load of coal from Warwick to the great house every year — another survival of medieval customs, even though the burning of coal at Aynho must have been something fairly new. When the church was being rebuilt (which we shall come to) in the eighteenth century, the squire was able to call on those farmers who owed him a service of gift-cart, as they had done since the middle ages, to carry stone from the pits at Fritwell. Farmers might still be required to keep hounds for the squire's hunting. And the old customs for dividing the meadows on the Cherwell, quoted already on page 49, were still followed in all their arcane complexity.

Another ancient survival that was still kept up was the payment of tithes to the rector. Tithes were supposed to be a tax of ten per cent on a farmer's gross income, and for as long as they were taken in kind — as in the middle ages they had been, and for many years after — they were a source of irritation to everyone. To the farmer, who resented (though accepting) their constant toll on his produce; to the rector, who would long since have preferred his tithes in money; and to both sides in that there were perpetual opportunities for argument and for litigation. Their collection could be relatively straightforward, though troublesome: milk, for instance, was the rector's every tenth morning and evening from Holy Rood day at the beginning of May until St. Luke's in the middle of October. Every seventh calf, pig or lamb was his, with money payments instead if a farmer did not have exactly seven. (The payment was equivalent to a value of 5d for a calf — probably some indication of how long ago these customs had been established.) But real complications arose from the fact that the tithes on the demesne lands had been commuted in 1620. This meant that beasts were liable to tithe when they were pastured on other land but not when they were on the demesne, and since the squire's tenant farmers were constantly moving them from one to the other there were endless occasions for dispute.

Livestock was grazed and hay was cut on the pastures and in the meadows. But livestock played an important part in the management of the arable, too, both for grazing and for manuring the fields. Horses were tethered on a part of the fallow that had been sown with vetches; at Lammas the horses were taken off and sheep took their place. After the corn was cut on the arable and the gleaners were done, the sheep were turned on to the stubble and fed off the weeds and the grass and trod in their dung. Later in the year they were turned for a few weeks on to the winter wheat, and in March on to the spring barley. Yet farmers preferred to keep their animals off land where they were liable to tithe if they could, and around 1700 the steward recorded that there would be very few sheep kept on the 'titheable' if it were not for the necessity of dunging the land. At some time during the course of the eighteenth century the bulk of the tithes were commuted for cash; the circumstances are not recorded, though (being Aynho) the negotiations were no doubt spirited, but the result must have been a relief for everyone concerned.

The farming year seems to have consisted largely in moving animals from one set of furlongs to another. Each farmer tended his own flocks with his own shepherd, but the village cows (such as were not pastured on enclosed land) went in a common herd to whichever part of the commons was to be grazed. In the seventeenth century the herdsman used to blow his horn at five in the morning, for the cows to come shambling out of the yards and byres where they had spent the night and troop off to pasture; in the eighteenth century the hours were half past four in summer and half past five in winter. People rose and went to bed with the sun. Those who refused to let their cows go with the rest were fined, and one can quite see why: with so complicated a system of landholding and with such care being necessary to graze the right fields at the right time, there would have been instant chaos and perhaps long-term damage if farmers had grazed their beasts independently.

The number of animals that the village farmers were allowed to graze was strictly controlled in order not to overstock the available grazing, and over the years it tended to diminish. In 1616 the allocation for each yardland of arable was 4 horses, 4 cows and 40 sheep; in 1620, after Richard Cartwright's enclosure, the numbers were increased to 5, 5 and 50, but they were soon reduced again. In 1657 the number of sheep was reduced still further to

36, and by the eighteenth century the allowance was 2 horses, 4 cows and 28 sheep. Practical experience no doubt proved that a smaller number of well-fed animals were more profitable than a larger number of poorer ones. Winter feed could be a problem as well. Early in the eighteenth century farmers would often sell their calves to the butcher and then buy in-calf heifers in the autumn, to over-winter them on straw that would not support large cows.

In the eighteenth century the total number of cows' commons, as they were called, was 202 or 204, a large herd to drive and manage, though perhaps some of the larger farmers (like Edward Homan who in 1740 had 21 cows' commons, or Mrs. Pruce with 27) may have given some help with men or boys of their own. In any case most farmers had closes where their beasts would be grazed from time to time, and it was probably seldom that all the village cattle were pastured together. By then the number of commons that each farmer owned was no longer always strictly proportional to his land holding. It was less easy to divide common rights than to divide acres, and as ancient holdings became dispersed, so commons became detached from land and came to be inherited, bought and sold on their own. It might thus be possible for a poor villager to keep a cow or two even if he had little land.

In the sixteenth century, landless cottagers had the right to keep a cow and a few sheep on the common land. But whatever rights the cottager may have had, they were gradually whittled away. In 1565 cottagers had been forbidden to raise more than one calf in the year. In 1574 this was changed to one calf in three years. In the next century, cottagers were forbidden to keep cows on the Commons at all, and so a poor man's only hope of doing so was by acquiring a cow's common, by renting arable from a richer neighbour or by availing himself of the generosity of the Squire. The orders for managing the fields and the village livestock were made, of course, by the jury at the Manor Court, but the jury was chosen by the Lord of the Manor (or his steward) and certainly did not represent the interests of all the villagers. Through the jury, the villagers ran their own affairs, but there was nothing democratic about their selection: we have already seen how they expected to be chosen from among the leading men of the village, and they were unhesitating in running the village in their own interests. It was probably accepted by everybody that they should.

In the eighteenth century, if not before, the fieldsmen had a system whereby people without horse commons could rent one. Anyone entitled to a horse common and who did not need it could let it to the fieldsmen, who could then let it again to a farmer who wanted extra commons to support a plough team, or to someone like John Merry the miller or Mr. Boxall the excise man who needed a horse for their business. Individuals seem not to have been allowed to rent out their horse commons themselves, though it is hard to see why not unless it was due simply to the weight of the tradition of communal farming. The fieldsmen made a small amount of money this way, but made more by collecting a rate on cows' commons, and sometimes on horses' and sheep's. This went on mole catching, ditching, gunpowder and shot, bird scaring, placing merestones at the bounds of a man's lands, and mending bridges.

> Pd. James Nelson for ching 15 dosen of moles
> Pd. for 3 men to days a Making the Banck at the River
> Pd. the Crokeeper
> Pd. Thomas Secull & James Ansty for Doing up Lanford Bridge

But the largest single item of expenditure was a bull to service the village cows. In the seventeenth century, the parson had usually provided the bull: it will be remembered how John Loe had pounded Mr. Drope's bull in 1618. In 1675 Dr. Longman had been fined by the Court for failing to provide one. But by the eighteenth century the fieldsmen may have felt that gentlemen of the refinement of Dr. Hutton or Mr. Wasse were not to be relied on to provide a 'serviceable' beast, and the parson had come to pay the fieldsmen some of his tithe money (called the 'overplus of the tithe') and they bought the bull for themselves. This was usually in April, and they would either sell him in October or (perhaps if he was a particularly fine animal) would keep him over the following winter. One year William Butler at the College Farm undertook to keep him from November to May, charging 6d a week for straw and 1s for hay. Later in the century, keeping the bull in hay and straw went up to 2s 10d.

In the eighteenth century the bull usually cost around £3, and there were extras:-

> Pd for spent when the boles sold   1s

which would have sealed the bargain with about eight pints of beer. And if it had been bought at a distance, say at Banbury or Brackley markets, there might be toll gates to pass and something for the man who drove him all the way home. Sometimes the bull needed treatment, and Edward Knott the blacksmith might be called in to drench him. Once he was paid for

> Dressin the Bulls futt

but not, apparently, successfully; a few weeks later Samuel Mayo
the butcher had to shoot the poor beast, and the fieldsmen had to
pay 2s 6d for

Bering of the Bool

and later the squire himself paid the fieldsmen £1. 15s to compensate them for the village's loss.

The leading farmers of the village were prosperous men, even
when they did not themselves own the land they farmed. Peter
Pruce, who died in 1682 and had been landlord of the Bell, rented
a good deal of land from the squire and at his death owned property worth £246. He had a dozen cows, 60 lambs worth £21 and
101 ewes worth £55. 11s, and his implements included a waggon,
two dung carts, a 'long cart', four ploughs and some harrows. It is
true that like many a business man with a fast turnover his debts
almost equalled his assets (in fact they came to only 7s 6d less)
but the appraisers' assessment of his estate was almost certainly
too low. Henry Borton, who died in the following year and who
probably derived all his income from farming, left £115: his livestock comprised 80 sheep, ten cows and a calf, a bull (perhaps the
village bull was a poor one, though it was only a few years since
the parson had been fined for not keeping one), four horses and a
sow and four pigs.

It is interesting to see how values had changed a hundred years
later. John Letch, probably the great-great-grandson of the Henry
Letch who had been such a thorn in the flesh for John Cartwright,
died while still young in 1787. (His wife lived on into the 1840's.)
John Letch was the last of the village's independent, yeoman farmers with land of his own, exactly the same land, probably, that
Henry Letch had farmed a century and a half before. Whereas
Henry Borton's ten cows were valued in 1682 at £10, John Letch's
fifteen were assessed at £75. While Henry Borton's and Peter Pruce's
sheep had been their most valuable property, John Letch's flock
was only worth £45. It is interesting, too, to see how much capital
one needed to farm, and how much equipment: John Letch's
farmed about 90 acres of arable and pasture with three waggons,
four horses, two muck carts, one plough, one harrow, and a quantity of sheep racks, hurdles and harness. Counting his livestock but
excluding the value of his crops in his fields and barns, what auctioneers would call his 'live and dead farming stock' was worth
£190.

Most of the village farmers carried on a mixed kind of farming; it was difficult not to, since the number of beasts that could be pastured on the commons was related to the amount of arable cultivated, and since in the days before artificial fertilisers the dung from the beasts was all there was to keep the land in good heart. Such an arrangement had obviously made more sense in the middle ages, when most villagers farmed for their own subsistence rather than for the market as farmers did by now. But there were specialists, John Lawley for instance, who at the end of the seventeenth century was a grazier. He concentrated on livestock, probably fattening oxen, dairying and raising a few sheep. In 1678 his wife had agreed

> to serve the Ho'ble Mrs. Cartwright with the best Cream and Butter when & as oft as she hath occasion In Consideration whereof she is to have four pence three farthings a pound for the same . . . She is to send it to the house & if she send any cream she is to have 4d a quart for it And for new milk cheese two pence three farthings a pound

John Lawley owned no land of his own, and rented closes from the squire or from anyone else who had enclosed land to let. Lawley, incidently, had a long and bitter dispute with the rector over tithes. The rector complained that Lawley sold his sheep a week before shearing and thus deprived the rector of his tithe wool; and that he moved his cattle from the commons where they were titheable to the demesne where they were not, a few days before they calved and thus escaped paying tithe calves as well. (Lawley said he only moved his cattle off the commons when the grazing was bad, which it probably often was.)

Next to the farmers, the elite of Aynho were the inn-keepers, and for most of the villagers they probably cut a more important figure than the farmers did. Late in the seventeenth century, when there was a general shortage of small change, Peter Pruce at the Bell and Thomas Norris at the Red Lion both issued halfpenny tokens, and for these to have passed as currency in the neighbourhood can only mean that these men were well respected and that their credit was known to be good. Both inns, though, belonged to the squire, who might be asked for help when improvements were required:-

> A desire of Thomas Norris about repairs at the Red Lion Inn.
> That end of the house next Will Swetman to be reared higher and slatted and floored and partitions to be mended and floors and ceilings to be mended and stairs and the roof reared higher and a cellar to be made under the parlour and a stable in the yard to be made and a pump and gates . . .
> Since the writing hereof Thomas Norris condescends to be at all

charges about the cellar except the floor for which he will be at
half charge.
John Jameson agrees to paint the sign of a Bell for the Inn at
Aynho in Peter Pruce's tenure (John Cartwright finding a board
for the purpose).

The Norris family gave up the Red Lion in 1700 when Mary
Norris, Thomas's widow, died early in the spring, and John Pruce,
who had followed his father at the Bell, took over the Red Lion.
There he remained for twenty years until he finally decided to concentrate on his farming: he was getting on in years by then, and
probably found it increasingly difficult to run two businesses at
once. Edward Homan, who had originally followed him at the Bell,
now took over the Red Lion and the Bell was pulled down.

Later in the century there appeared another Inn, the White
Hart, originally kept by Thomas Bygrave who had come to the village in the 1740's as Thomas Cartwright's footman. He was evi-
dently no business man, for in 1775 his affairs were in such a tangle
that he made over his entire property to his two sons, Thomas
who was a victualler and Edward, a maltster. Edward stayed at the
White Hart, Thomas the younger moved to the Red Lion, and the
family were still in the innkeeping business a century later.

Below the farmers and the innkeepers in the village hierarchy
came the tradesmen, the craftsmen and the shopkeepers, some
relatively prosperous, some slowly declining towards bankruptcy.
Aynho was a village of fair size — there were 567 people in the
place in 1740 — and provided employment for a good many of the
normal country trades besides a few that one might not expect to
find. And as with the innkeepers, a good many of the tradesmen
handed down their businesses and their crafts to their sons, their
sons-in-law or to other relatives for generations.

For instance, the Burberows. A Richard Burberow had owned
a yardland and a house in Rowland Shakerley's time; it had been
'Old Burberow' who had caught the Royalist messenger near
Croughton in the Civil War. It may have been his grandson who
was a baker, and who built the house in the Square that is next to
the present shop and which bears the initials of Timothy Burberow
and his wife with the date, 1696. He also owned the house beyond
it, now standing well back from the road and which has been much
rebuilt since, and when he died in 1719 he rather perversely left
half of each house to each of his daughters, Mary and Anne, who
naturally did an exchange as soon as they decently could. Both
daughters married into the business, so to speak; Anne married

Benjamin Coates, another baker, and Mary married William
Banbury who kept a shop.

It was the Banburys' second son, Erasmus, who in 1760
added the wing at the back of the 1696 house that has his initials,
E.B. Their eldest son, William, had been left only a shilling in his
father's will — perhaps cut off with it, since the family were
Quakers and William may have committed some dire offence such
as 'marrying out'. Erasmus himself married a Mary Smith whom he
may have met through his business: her father was a Quaker linen
draper from Reading. Erasmus did business as a mercer, but he
sold other things as well: for many years he sold the fieldsmen the
powder and shot for their gun. His cousin Timothy Coates, who
had inherited the house next door and who was also a Quaker, did
'marry out' and apparently got away with it.

The Burberows had been in Aynho from time immemorial.
Another Aynho family, which in years to come probably forgot
that its ancestors had ever lived anywhere else, was the Seculls, but
we know that the first of the Aynho Seculls — spelling his name
Seacole, or the rector so spelling it for him — was Arthur, who
came to the village in the 1690's. He was a young mason, perhaps
apprenticed to a mason in the village or perhaps as a young jour-
neyman having heard of the work that was going forward at the
squire's house. In Aynho he first rented a cottage from the last of
the Dropes, and in 1697 he married Joyce Hobcraft, daughter of
one of the village's old yeoman families, and ultimately he inherited
from his father-in-law the house that is now no. |79. Perhaps as an
advertisement for his skills, he may have put a new front onto it:
the windows with their stone heads are clearly different from those
of any other house in the village, and the inside, with a semi-
circular stone stair at the back, is more old-fashioned than the outside. But his skills must have been fairly modest: when the old
church was rebuilt in the 1720's, Arthur Secull did no more than
rebuild the churchyard wall.

He died in 1758, probably over 80 years old, and in his Will
he left £20 to his son William

> in case he shall have taught my grandson Thomas the son of
> Thomas Secull the Art and Trade of a Mason lawfully apprenticed
> for seven years

and he had some particular treasures to bequeath as well

> I give to my grandson Thomas the son of Thomas Secull a great
> looking glass and my largest gold ring and I give unto my grand-

daughter Elizabeth Secull the daughter of Thomas Secull my lesser
gold ring

but at the end of the Will his executors, Benjamin Coates the Quaker and Edward Burbidge, have written

all the personal effects of the Testator did not at the time of his
death amount to the sum of twenty pounds

and some time before that he had received occasional help from
the Overseers of the Poor. He had mortgaged his house to Francis
Burton, the squire's agent, in 1753 for £10, and raised another
£10 on it a year later. But even if his provision for his grandson's
apprenticeship could not be complied with, the family remained
the village masons until well into the twentieth century, constantly
on call for repairs to walls and farm buildings, and sometimes
undertaking quite substantial works like building the walls of cottages.

Edward Burbidge, the other executor of Arthur Secull's Will
with Ben Coates, was an apothecary. His father had been Master
of the Grammar School (of which more later) and had made provision in his Will that if his eldest son was 'bred a scholar' he should
have a double share of the inheritance. But his eldest son died aged
only 20, his next son was already apprenticed to a coachmaker in
London, and so the third son, Edward, benefitted from the provision. Edward must have been the village apothecary — chemist and
doctor combined — for almost half a century. He dealt in all sorts
of things — Boluses, Saffron, Electuaries, Syrup of Diocodium,
Laudanum, Purging Draughts, Pomatum, Hartshorn Shavings, and
a wonderful specific called Opoldedoc, which was apparently
equally effective whether taken by man or by 'that noble animal,
the Horse.' His daughter Sarah married John Martin Watson, surgeon and apothcary from Steeple Aston, when she was 34, and inherited her father's house, now no. 13, which has an elegant little
parlour at the back which looks as though Edward Burbidge may
have added it when he was married in 1760.

(In the 1820's trouble arose over that provision in John Burbidge's Will that his son be 'bred a scholar'. Sarah and John Martin
Watson had died intestate and childless, so the question arose of
who was to inherit? Ultimately, a descendant of the coachmaker
was found, an ironmonger living in Southwark, and of course he
and his lawyers contested whether or not a coachmaker might not
be described as having been 'bred a scholar'? It was probably a
try-on, and probably nobody benefitted from the attempt except

the lawyers. In any event, the ironmonger in London was not interested in property in a village that perhaps none of them had ever seen, and they sold the house and the cottage at the rear (probably now the kitchen of the present house) to the Squire; a nice windfall for them of £300.)

Erasmus Banbury was not the only shopkeeper in eighteenth century Aynho. There was another shop as well, for twenty years after the middle of the century kept by William Burton (or Borton) who sold almost everything imaginable. He sold haberdashery: stays, yarn, stockings, apron strings, thread, binding, flannel, and crepe for mourners. He sold hardware: candles, rushlights, 'stone blue', penny dishes, pitchers at 2½d and 5d, and chamber pots. He sold groceries: salt, sugar, nutmegs, butter, oatmeal, bacon, brimstone, cloves, mace and ginger nuts. It must have been a marvellous shop, the atmosphere thick with the mixed smells of all kinds of goods and gear.

Nor was Ben Coates the only baker. There was Robert French, who in the 1750's was supplying the Overseers with bread for the poor; and Timothy Hulbird who was a consumptive, who lived at number 17 and who has provided us with one insoluble problem. In 1738 the fieldsmen

Pd. Timnity hulberd for a top of a plomp   4s 6d

and we may never know what the top of a plomp was. Later in the century there was George Whetton, who had a prolonged row with the fieldsmen about grazing his horse, and poor Elias Simpson who went bankrupt and had his goods sold by auction, and who later earned a little money by doing odd jobs such as weeding about the newly enclosed fields.

And other trades were supplied as well. In 1663 John Turbet from King's Sutton was doing slating and plastering; by the middle of the eighteenth century the Turbets were living in Aynho, and one of them bought Arthur Secull's old house; there were still Turbets, slaters and plasterers, in Aynho a hundred years later. There were generations of the Knott family who were blacksmiths, and after them generations of Wattses, who had a smithy and owned one or two cottages in the alley that now leads up to the school from the square: the cottages were swept away in the 1830's, but in the eighteenth century they had been secured to the Watts family by complexities of legal documents worthy of the estate of a Duke. There was a dynasty of Wrightons who were weavers, while the Jeffs family was perhaps remarkable more for their versatility:

in the eighteenth century one was a tailor, one a carrier, one a blacksmith and one a wheelwright. There were always several carpenters; William Burton (not the same man as the shopkeeper) had a timber yard in the angle of Blacksmith's Hill and Skittle Alley. There was Thomas Walker, whose father-in-law had set him up as a wheelwright at number 10 (a key position on the main road — a wheelwright's shop might be compared to a garage) in 1778 and where the same business was still being carried on by the Baughan family early in the twentieth century. There were butchers for such of the villagers as could afford butcher's meat; around the middle of the century Samuel Mayo and John Bower charged twopence ha'penny or twopence three farthings for beef, and threepence a pound for mutton, but most of the poorer villagers would have eaten only bacon and cheese save on special occasions. And there were the Merries, for several generations the millers at the Mill off the Bicester road and at a windmill that stood on Old Down towards the eastern bounds of the parish, and who were by the end of the eighteenth century among the richest families in the village.

The village farmers, innkeepers and tradesmen formed an elite in eighteenth century Aynho. The Squire's retainers formed an elite of a different kind. He kept a sizeable staff — out of 27 people counted by the Rector living in the big house in 1740, 24 were servants. Top of the hierarchy below stairs in the 1740's (as much of a hierarchy as that in the village) was Mrs. Councer the housekeeper, earning £12 a year, and the Butler with the unlikely name of Simper Carvell. Mr. Carvell was paid £20, was able to invest money in village property and was described in his will as 'gentleman'. Equal with the housekeeper on £12 was the cook. Below them were the coachman on £10 a year, the groom on £8, Thomas Bygrave the footman (and probably another footman as well) on £7, and an under-groom on £5. There were numbers of maid servants of all descriptions. Elizabeth Goodman the laundrymaid was paid £7, housemaids £3. 15s, and kitchen maids £3. 10s.

These wages must seem extremely low, though they are higher than those paid at the beginning of the century when the coachman was getting £6 a year, a dairymaid £3. But for the servants who lived in, these wages were 'all found', including such things as washing, shoe repairs and the cost of livery and any other special clothes that were needed, such as mourning for when one of the family died or leather breeches for the groom (6s. in 1710). There were perks and free cottages for those of the upper servants who lived out. There were legacies when the family died: Thomas

Cartwright left the equivalent of six months' wages to each of his
servants who had been with him for any length of time. There were
tips, too, from visitors.

In the seventeenth century the squire's servants had often
been recruited from within the village, and a few contracts of
employment from Thomas Cartwright's minority in the 1680's
survive. They show that servants then, at least, were expected to
be versatile: to perform both everyday jobs and more ceremonious
ones as the occasion arose:

> Henry Knott agrees to serve the hoble. Mrs. Cartwright as Gar-
> diner under Thomas Harold & to do any other business she shall
> appoint & serve the Hogs & roll the Walks & in consideration
> whereof she is to give him £5 a year & his diet & lodging in the
> house but he is to provide his own washing himself & provide
> himself decent clothing to wait at table at Dinner & he to be
> guided by Thomas Harold about weeding the garden

Another reads:-

> Ed. Goodier agrees to serve Mrs. Cartwright as Groom & go along-
> side Jo. Collins constantly with the team to plow and cart & ride
> postillion when occasion shall be & do any business Mrs. C. shall
> appoint in consideration whereof he is to have £3 in money & a
> livery suit & to have his diet & lodging but not washing.

The Knotts and the Goodiers were village families, and Henry and
Edward must have been expected to send their laundry home.
Another of these contracts is with a maid servant, and though her
wages are higher than either of the men's, it sounds as though she
earned them:-

> Elizabeth Birds agrees to serve the Hoble. Mrs Ursula Cartwright
> for a yeare to begin from Lady Day 1679 in the employ she is now
> in & besides to sift the Coals & Cinders, Make the fires in the
> Kitchen, Keep the Chimney clean on the backside of the Kitchen,
> Clean up the vessells & help about the Beds in the afternoon, spin or
> do such other work when the Cooking is done. And if all be per-
> formed accordingly she is to have six pounds standing wages from
> Lady Day last.

Squire Thomas was still a child when these arrangements
were made by his mother, and some of them suggest a certain in-
formality that would probably be less acceptable when he came
into his inheritance and demanded the establishment that his station called for. Latterly, at least, the servants in the great house
came mostly from outside the village, and there were few like
Thomas Bygrave who settled in Aynho in after years. The upper

servants did not serve as village officials, and the lower servants did not appear annually at the meetings of the Manor Court. It is unlikely that they took much part in the life of the village. They may have visited the Red Lion in their spare time, but village gossip would have been of little interest to the occupants of the big house, while retailing some of the big house gossip might well have got them the sack.

One may feel that there is plenty of information about the inhabitants of Aynho in the eighteenth century. So, up to a point, there is, but it is confined to the top third or so of the villagers. We know about those whose lives required something to be written down — farmers who paid rates and rented land, tradesmen who sent bills, people rich enough to buy and to sell their houses and to make Wills. The majority of Aynho's villagers did none of these things. They were the poor. They neither owned houses nor worked at a trade; they worked as servants or labourers or doing odd jobs for anyone who would pay them, and since they had few possessions to bequeath it hardly mattered that they could not have afforded the lawyers' fees to make a Will.

The decline in the old yeoman families and the multiplication of small freeholds was a trend of Aynho's history that affected the farmers and tradesmen. For the poor, who owned no property and almost certainly never would, what mattered was the prospect of a job and a cottage and the availability of help when they needed it. And what made jobs gradually harder to get, and gradually increased the call for help, was the steady growth of population. Once again, a few figures will make the situation clear. From time to time, over three hundred years, figures can be found that indicate this growth of numbers, even though it is not until 1740 that we have an exact count of the men, women and children in the village. Figures in italics are no more than estimates, though the basis for them is sound

Year	Households	Population	Houses
1540	*45*		
1620	56	*275*	*56*
1675			*80*
1720			*100*
1740	124	567	
1801	144	623	124
1821	160	719	141
1841		662	135

These figures are clear enough, and so are their implications, but they tell us nothing of individuals among the poor. Almost the only generalisations that can be made are that on the whole conditions for the poor tended to worsen, and that most of them, working all their lives, never earned more than enough to ensure that they could still work the next day.

We generally hear of them only when they had dealings with the Establishment, so to speak — when they were born, when they married and when they died, when their poverty called for some assistance from the Overseers of the Poor, and if a chance record of their employment should survive. In 1743 Thomas Cartwright's agent, Francis Burton, put an asterisk * against the names of 8 out of 23 cottagers on his rent roll, and a star at the bottom of the page read

*insolvent

These were people from whom there was no point in trying to collect rent, but also no point in trying to dispossess since the overseers of the poor would then have to house them and to pay their rent for them — which would have to come out of the rates paid by the squire's tenants. But for most of the labouring population of the village, help from the Overseers would have been the exception rather than the rule, something to be resorted to in a crisis but neither needed nor sought for as long as they were in work. It is of this mass of the labouring poor that we know the least.

We have little information about how much they earned or what their living expenses were. At the beginning of the century a craftsman, a carpenter, say, or a mason, could earn 1s 2d a day, and a labourer 8d or 9d. By the end of the eighteenth century the labourer's wages had risen to a shilling, a craftsman's to 12s a week. It was almost unknown for a labourer to own his cottage unless he had inherited it, and even then it would probably be mortgaged. Rents varied, of course, with the size of the cottage. The Squire's cottages at the mid century were being let for 10s to £1. 15s a year, and the more expensive ones were taken by craftsmen or else by farmers for specialists like shepherds.

Though wages rose during the century, prices rose also, and the increasing population of Aynho (and of everywhere else) meant both increasing under-employment and declining real wages. In 1740 it seems likely that many of Aynho's farmers had labourers living in: the rector's census in that year gives the number of servants in each family, and many of the farmers' 'servants' were probably farm workers. A few years later the list of men eligible for the militia described 27 men as 'servants' against 30 as 'labourers', and while some of these servants were probably apprentices, cellarmen at the Inns, ostlers and so on, farm workers probably comprise the bulk of them. For as long as bachelor labourers lived on the farm, they were probably reasonably housed and fed. But to pay wages to a man living out was probably cheaper than to keep him living in, and by the end of the century there were probably few labourers who still lodged with their masters.

While low wages meant that once a family was poor they generally remained poor, there were many more reasons for poverty than that simple one. There were many whose families had been in Aynho for generations, gradually declining from a prosperity of generations before, yet continuing to live in Aynho because of ancient attachment, family ties, some scrap of property still retained or from mere want of any alternative. Walter Baldwin, for instance, descended from William Wyatt, a freeholder with 54 acres when Richard Cartwright had come. In 1740 he lived in a cottage behind the Red Lion, an old family property but which he now only rented from the squire to whom he had been compelled to sell it in 1728; he had got £52 for it, but he already owed £21 on a mortgage. There were the many branches of the Borton family — seven of them by 1740, probably descended from Burtons who were yeomen in the 1540's. One remained a substantial farmer, though he no longer owned land and was in arrears with his rent; another was a shepherd, another a carpenter, two more were labourers, and two — Sarah and 'widow Borton' — were women living on their own. There were two households of Baylises — William, aged 79 and unable to find 10s a year for his rent, and John, aged 52, a tenant of farmer Letch. There were only two in each household, and their children were probably grown up and gone. These two may have been descended from Thomas Bele, who farmed 45 acres in 1540. Coming down in the world was easy, indeed often unavoidable. Improving one's lot within the village was so hard that instances are very difficult to find. It must have been some windfall of inheritance that enabled John Gregory, a labourer, to buy his cottage next to the Red Lion in 1749, and made it possible for his grandson to work in the village as a breeches-maker when to train for any kind of trade meant finding money to pay for indentures.

Numbers of children might be another cause of real poverty. James Smith had eight between 1728 and 1740, and the Overseers had to pay 15s rent (though they did not support him otherwise; presumably he was in work, earning enough to feed them all but insufficient for his rent.) His fathering so many children on small means may have been regarded as feckless by the authorities, but this is unlikely: children were thought of as the natural consequence of marriage, and marriage as an adult's natural state. Single people were unusual, and there may have been good reasons in particular cases: Joyce Hobcraft, another of those marked 'insolvent', was related to several families in the village and was only 50, so there was no clear reason why she need have been unemployed or unsupported by relations. The rector marked her as 'single woman' when she died, and she may have been a particularly difficult old spinster.

The consequences of age, of large families and of inability to provide for one's descendants were all clearly foreseeable and must have been accepted as stages in the ordained course of life. What could not be foreseen were accidents that carried off breadwinners. The rector's census included 'widow Peckover' for instance. Jane Peckover was 47 and had been widowed nine years; her husband's death from an unsuccessful amputation had left her with two small children and another to be born posthumously. Then there was in William Grant's household in 1740 himself, his wife whom he had married the previous year, and their new-born baby. Four years later he was killed by the kick of a horse, and in 1751 his widow was sharing a house with two other families. There were the orphan children of Thomas and Mary Hall who had died of smallpox in the summer of 1734 leaving John and Mary, babies of 2 and 3, to be brought up at the ratepayers' expense until they were old enough to be put out as apprentices or to service.

Families who were the victims of accidents like these were unlikely to remain in the village in the long run. It is clear that numbers of poor families settled in Aynho for a few years only and then moved on. There are many surnames that appear in the Registers for a generation or less, and scarcely any of these names occur among property owners recorded in deeds. Precise figures are impossible to calculate — the exact proportion of the families living in Aynho for less than twenty years, say, to those who settled for more than a generation, and in any case the ratio would vary over time: it seems| probable that in the crisis years of the late eighteenth and of the earlier nineteenth century, before emigration and the policies of squires tended to re-establish a close community in later years, the poor in Aynho were considerably more mobile than the better-off.

Families that had ever possessed property in Aynho tended, naturally, to be longer resident than those that never had; there were sound reasons for staying that might still obtain a generation after the family had lost any property it might have owned. Some freeholders' families kept possession of their houses for generations. The Letches lived at No. 92 from 1648 when Henry Letch bought it until 1840 when the widow of the last of the family died. The Wattses, blacksmiths, occupied the same house for eighty years after 1740. No. 74 was not sold between 1658 and 1793, though twice inherited through daughters. The Burbidges' house was in their occupation for a century before 1827. William Baldwin inherited property from his father-in-law, William Wyatt, in 1663, and his descendants continued to live there until the early nineteenth century, though latterly as tenants. Freeholders had an economic and an emotional attachment to a house and to Aynho itself that most tenants did not have, even though freeholds were often bought and sold as we have tried to show.

Indeed, mobility was almost a rule rather than the exception. There were always more children in the village than there were jobs or houses for grown-ups. Aynho must have been teeming with children, and a far higher proportion than if all children had remained as adults. This can be shown statistically: the annual View of Frankpledge, the inventory of all the men in the village over 12 years old who owed suit to the Manor Court, shows gradually increasing numbers from the early seventeenth century to the middle of the eighteenth, when the record ceased to be kept, but this increase in no way keeps up with the rise in the birth rate (see page 127). The explanation must be that, increasingly, once they were old enough to earn their own living, children moved away. A high proportion of those born in the village are not recorded again, and except for a few Quakers there is virtually no evidence for any of Aynho's villagers being dissenters who were not married or buried in church. Thomas Swift, for instance, a labourer, had eight children between 1718 and 1737, of whom seven seem to have survived childhood. Only one of them is recorded as marrying in the village, and only one — Anne, the youngest daughter — died within it, unmarried. Out of those families mentioned already whose breadwinners died young — the Grants, the Peckovers and the Halls, only one person among all the wives and children, Jane Peckover, died in Aynho (and she, as we shall see, had found a particular usefulness in her widowhood). The children must all have gone away, and their mothers gone too. Indeed, to judge by the number of

couples where the registers record the death of one partner only, it
must have been common for the survivor to have gone away to
spend their last years with grown-up children who had established
themselves elsewhere.

The better-off apprenticed their children, like John Burbidge's
son, put out to a London coach-maker. Prosperity might follow,
with luck and hard work; in the 1760's, for instance, John Castle,
son of an Aynho tailor, was in business in Oxford and Buckingham
as a tailor, mercer and cooper. It is likely, though, that the great
majority of Aynho's villagers lacked the resources to apprentice
their children to a trade: one remembers the frustrated provisions
of Arthur Secull's Will. The young men for the most part went to
work on farms, the young women went into service, and it is the
equivalents of both, from other places, who are described as 'servants' in eighteenth century Aynho lists. As a result of this mobility,
marriage to outsiders was not uncommon and brought a small
but steady stream of 'foreigners' into the village. Then, as now, it
was the custom for brides to be married in their own church, and
the map on page 131 shows where Aynho girls' husbands came from
(other than from Aynho itself) over 150 years. It may seem remarkable that so few are from immediately nearby villages, but
there is little reason why they should have been. The long hours
of work meant that walking to King's Sutton or even to Croughton
of an evening was something not lightly undertaken save on a
Sunday, but living in the same village or on the same farm made
courting easy. And it cannot be said whether these are marriages
between Aynho girls who met their future husbands when out in
service, or whether their husbands themselves were working in
Aynho and afterwards took their wives away. Probably both,
though since few of the husbands' names occur subsequently in
th village perhaps the former was more common and the girl working away from home, after re-visiting Aynho for the last time so
as to be married in her old church, then returned with her husband
to make a new home elsewhere. But there must have been many
young men working in Aynho, too, who married village girls and
took them back to their home village or to seek better fortune elsewhere.

But the fact that most people spent their whole lives in the
village meant that family life was close and that most people had
relations living in Aynho. If one was able to draw a map, with lines
linking all houses lived in by second cousins or closer, the result
would be a dense, black spider's-web through which one could

hardly make out the shape of the place. Some households included elderly relations, and in the early seventeenth century the laws against 'inmates' — lodgers — were clearly not meant to apply in respect of members of the same family. Richard Cartwright's list of families drawn up in about 1620 seems to include five (out of 56) where elderly parents were living with grown-up children, and one where two widows were living together. (The 1544 tax list reproduced in Appendix 1 on page 293 seems to include a number of families in which the head was taxed on land, a relation on property, so it is possible that some of these relations may have been members of the same household). In 1740, when the rector listed the village families, fourteen of them (more than ten per cent) were probably living alone, or else lodging with families to which they were not closely related. Several more were elderly couples without children. No doubt this was partly from convenience or from choice, but it may have been from poverty as well: poor families could probably not often afford to rent a house with an extra room for grandparents, while if the old people lived on their own they might more easily get help from the Overseers.

It is easy to calculate the average size of families, for instance, from the parson's 1740 census, and to appreciate through a simple comparison of numbers that resources adequate to support the village population in 1620 were scarcely likely to be able to support numbers 2½ times larger, two centuries later. But of course there are no average families, and there are degrees of poverty among the poor. There are large families and small, families of adults and families with many children, lucky families and unfortunate.

It is, in fact, more difficult to generalise about household size and composition in the eighteenth century than about almost anything else, for all the information there is available. Some families in 1740 may have been unusual, like John Smith's. Smith was a farmer, born in 1704, who married late in life. The eight (plus a servant) in his household must have included at least one of his four sisters, none of whose marriages is recorded. There were old people like another John Smith, over 80 but owning one cow's common to give him a little milk and butter and a little occupation. There was Mary Mayo, 55 in 1740, related to several village families but living alone and apparently unable to pay her rent.

Some families can easily be reconstructed. Henry Golder had three in his household in 1740: he and his wife had had five children between 1703 and 1715, four of them had died, and the last and precious survivor may still have been at home, looking after them as they grew towards old age. Richard Forde, called a 'poor shepherd' and the tenant of another shepherd, John Borton, had four in his household in 1740. These were probably himself, his wife, and the two youngest of his four children born between 1719 and 1731. But other families are impossible to reconstruct with any certainty. Francis Stutchbury married in 1714. There were six in his household in 1740; were all his four children still with him? There is no record of them in Aynho other than their baptisms. Robert French the baker had six children born in the village by 1740, yet his household was the largest in the place after the squire's: eleven plus a servant. Who were the others? Farmer Tomkins had a household of four and three servants, yet he was probably childless in 1740 as was Edward Letch, five and three.

There are very many households where the numbers are too high, or too low, to include all the children who might be expected still to be with their parents. Was the rector careless in keeping his registers? Were children boarded out to neighbours who had larger houses, did people take in lodgers, were many households accomodating elderly relations, particularly those of the better-off? Probably all these things, and it is almost certain that the composition of the typical Aynho family was more complex and possibly more fluid than it is today and that close family ties between households made for a flexibility in meeting contingencies that was not dependant on wealth.

There must in consequence have been a great many *ad hoc* arrangements made by people for their relations when they had need, and to these, whose details we can never know, one can add others that came to be recorded in legal form. Sometimes it was a matter of providing for the old. Thomas Bricknell in 1614 had left provision that his father-in-law, who outlived him, should have 'his diet washing and lodging here in my house in Aynho with my wife and the keeping of six sheep for as long as he is able to stir abroad' — a few sheep, in fact, to look after as a hobby and to bring him a bit of spending money. A hundred years later, when John Bricknell took over his old father's house (probably the same house) he agreed that in return for the older man's 'household goods and chattles personal cattle (sic) of whatever nature soever store of grain corn and hay utensils of household and husbandry and all his other personal cattles' John would provide his old parents 'and the longer lived of them good necessary and sufficient diet meat and drink washing lodging house room and all other necessities

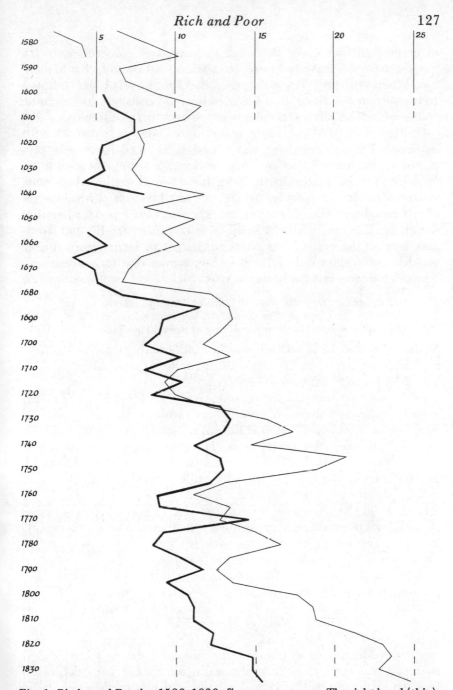

Fig. 1. Births and Deaths, 1580–1830; five-year averages. The right hand (thin) line shows births, the left hand (thick), deaths. Peaks in the thick line represent epidemics of small-pox in 1723, and of 'sore throat' (diphtheria?) in 1769.

meet and sufficient for their age and quality.' Sometimes, too, a husband would leave a house to a widow to provide for her old age. When William Jeffs, tailor, died in 1730, he left his own house to his son on condition that his widow could continue to live there; to his widow he left a second house for her own maintenance.

More often, of course, it was children who were provided for in people's Wills, and there was occasionally need for special provision to be made for them. Arthur Secull's arrangements for his grandson's apprenticeship in 1752 have been mentioned already. When Alice Wyatt died in 1663, she left her best clothes to her eldest daughter, Alice Goodyer, but she was concerned for her next daughter, Hannah, 'she not being able to guide herself', and therefore left all the rest of her household stuff to Henry Borton if he would take responsibility for her. Sometimes one senses tensions. Samuel Baldwin left his house in trust for

> my daughter Mary the wife of Timothy Mayo to receive and take
> the rents fines and profits thereof to her sole and separate use . . .
> without the control or intermeddling of her said husband

William Jeffs in 1768 left a house in Souldern for two years to John Marsh as a trustee, in order that out of the income Marsh should pay £5 a piece to his two daughters.

It was not unusual for parents to give children a start in their own lifetime, and there are several deeds which record the provision of a house to newly-married children, sometimes specially built. In the mid seventeenth century, John Hobcroft owned a house where No. 84 now stands. Half of this he gave to his daughter Elizabeth in 1658, while for his son John he built a new house at the other end of the plot — now the oldest house on the Charlton road, No. 74. In 1708 the then new-built house No. 17 was divided between its builder Thomas Wrighton and his son Abraham who was getting married. The origin of the wheelwright's business that was carried on for over 150 years by successive occupiers of No. 10 was when Stephen Cox, a baker in Woodstock, bought it in 1778 on behalf of his daughter Sarah who was about to marry a young wheelwright, Thomas Walker. And the better-off villager might provide for servants, as did William Winkles the squire's old gardener, who in about 1780 left his house to 'his faithful servant and friend, Susannah Merriman, in consideration of her great care and tenderness towards me during several painful illnesses that it has pleased God to afflict me with.' He added the sensible provision that she should sell it, 'that she may know what she has to depend on, which I think will be to her advantage.'

There must have been many young men obliged to fend for themselves elsewhere. This might mean trying their luck at one of the annual hiring fairs in the towns round about, or else chancing the uncertainty of a city like Oxford or London against the attraction of living there. Some few lads may have defied popular prejudice and enlisted for soldiers, but it is not likely that many did. Once, all able-bodied men had been liable for service in the militia and to muster once a year under officers recruited from the county aristocracy, but the system had been unpopular with all classes (remember Richard Cartwright's experience when taking the muster roll to Northampton). For foreign service, word would be sent to each village constable that he was to provide two or three men, but that happened rarely and then there were usually vagabonds to be found whose choice would save discommoding a hard-working villager. Later on, a system of balloting was introduced for which all the able-bodied between the ages of 18 and 45 were liable, but some reason for exemption on grounds of health or family commitments could usually be found, or if one was rich a substitute could be found and paid to serve in one's stead. In any case service in the militia did not generally take one far from home.

But some men went further. In the eighteenth century young James Priest, son of a carpenter, went off to the East Indies (it is not clear how) and years later, when there was some property to be divided, had to be presumed dead. James Wycherley, son of a village Quaker, was lost track of for some time in America around 1800, though he was eventually found working as a Maltster in New Jersey. Some other Quakers had gone to America years before: John Borton in 1674, who it was said had been given a tract of land by the King of the Indians, and Richard Haynes in 1682 who obtained 100 acres in New Jersey.

With travel taking as long as it did, with letters to foreign parts taking months, and with people's writing ability, if they could write at all, being such that sitting down and writing a letter was a major undertaking, it was easy to lose touch with friends and relations who had travelled far away. But perhaps not everyone who travelled to distant lands was lost as James Priest was, or settled permanently like the Quakers. Perhaps an occasional villager returned with sea-shells for cottage mantlepieces and tales to fire others' imaginations. Nobody, so far as we know, ever left Aynho and found a fortune, but they cannot have failed to find experiences beyond anything imaginable in a small Northamptonshire village.

It is not always easy, in writing about people's standards of living (which is what this chapter has been, basicly, all about) to invest them with life when all that may be known are the rents they paid, the size of their families and when they were born or died. In such a manner a picture of villagers as a class may be built up, yet when by doing so one dwells on the uniformity of their lives, one is soon struck by the many instancies of diversity. It is tempting to concentrate on the individuals about whom more is known, and to hope that they are representative of the mass of villagers who are no more than names. To treat villagers as so many economic units, as in this chapter, while necessary in order to understand how the village community worked, denies to them their individuality. Fortunately we can approach it in other ways: through the houses they lived in and which still survive, and through some of the things they did apart from earning their livings. These are the subjects of the next two chapters.

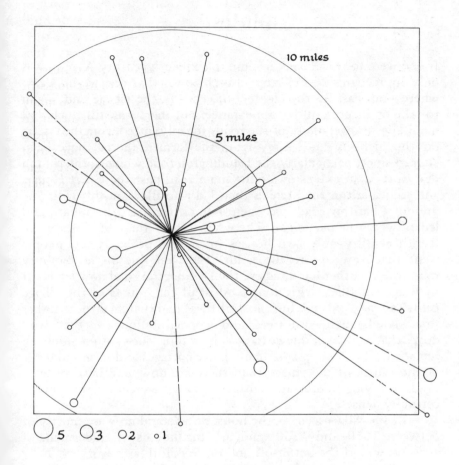

Fig. 2. Provenance (other than Aynho) of men marrying in Aynho church,
1650–1800.

Chapter 8

Buildings

If one were to travel back in time to sixteenth century Aynho, it is only by recognising the same church tower that one would know where one was. By the eighteenth century, the village had begun to take on its present-day appearance. But there was still much that would be strange. Many of the roads (deeply rutted from the traffic on the highway and mirey from the farmers' herds) have been altered since, particularly the Deddington road which formerly ran due west as an extension of the main road past the Great House, and the Charlton road which then led into Blacksmith's Hill. The present Charlton road was then a track through a farmyard and led nowhere in particular. There were until the end of the eighteenth century only two houses on it, and probably few people went that way save to the fields. The west side of the Banbury road, on the other hand, where the Deddington road now leads off it, was then thick with houses. Most of the houses of the village centre already existed, but most of these had thatched roofs rather than slated, outside shutters, and wooden mullions to their windows that — save in one cottage — have long since rotted and been replaced. There were, too, many more cottages and farm buildings in the centre of the village than there are now, and if there were fewer outlying houses and cottages, the village centre was almost certainly denser.

In the village centre, the houses that stand now are mostly of between 1650 and 1750, and are the houses of tradesmen, of artisans, and of the better-off and more skilful farm workers. They have survived because in the nineteenth century they were still not too old to be economically maintained, the larger ones still of sufficient quality for the class that built them, and the smaller well suited to farm labourers. Most of the houses of this level — better, originally, than many labourers' cottages and poorer than the houses of the yeomen farmers — were either built by the squire for his own upper servants or by their owners for their own occupation on freehold sites.

There was some difference in the character of different parts of the village. On the main road, opposite the big house, lived villagers of substance. Here in the eighteenth century lived Mr.

Burbidge the apothecary, the squire's butler when he had a family and lived out, Mrs. Markham whose husband had farmed a sizeable acreage at Walton, and one of the larger of the village farmers. Further east, on the main road beyond the Red Lion, lived lesser retainers of the squire's. Shopkeepers and bakers and the White Hart inn were in the Square, and a number of tight little groups of cottages just off it, pulled down in the nineteenth century. There was a varied assortment of tradesmen and craftsmen along Blacksmith's Hill, many of them connected in one way or another with the building trades: here in the eighteenth century lived at one time or another the Seculls, the Fathers and Henry Hobcraft, all masons, and the Turbets, slaters and plasterers, while John Borton, carpenter, had a wood yard in the angle between Blacksmith's Hill and Skittle Alley. All were tradesmen and artisans of sufficient standing to have been able to acquire cottages worth £20–£50, and the area remained an enclave of owner-occupying, cottage freeholders until the end of the eighteenth century.

On Blacksmith's Hill one can show graphically the steady break-up of properties that has already been remarked on. The maps on page 135 show what seem to have been the property boundaries in about 1690, and what had happened to these holdings a century later. The plots that were being built on in the seventeenth century have the long, slight reversed-S curve that one associates with consolidated and enclosed strips, and it is certain that two, at least, of these plots had been virgin sites. By 1790 the original holdings had been split up into a large number of separate, tiny freeholds. It was a process that was taking place all over the village as the result of sales, the separation of houses from land, and partition among heirs and heiresses, and again figures express it best:-

	1618	1790
The squire's houses, let :	27	46
Other landlord's houses, let :	15	52
Owner occupied houses :	12	26
Number of landlords :	4	20

Few people lived far from the heart of the village; security was still an important consideration. In the early seventeenth century, however, the yeomen farmers lived on the edge of the village, since they needed space for their barns, ricks and yards, and only the smallest of those who had bought their freeholds in 1611, Lawrence Watts (who had a mere 20 acres) seems to have lived in the village centre.

But for as long as they farmed closes and strips that were scattered throughout the parish, it made sense to live at the middle of them, and there were in consequence no farmsteads out in the fields: that was a development that came with the enclosure of the last of the open fields in 1792.

We know how rich the farmers of Aynho had once been from the amounts they had been able to find to buy their freeholds from Shakerley Marmion in 1611. But of all their houses, only three survive in recognisable form, and these provide both evidence for their wealth and, implicitly, of their decline. Best of the early houses in the village is Edward Jarvis's, No. 86, built probably at some time after 1630. Jarvis only owned some 30 acres, but he described himself as an 'engineer' as well (whatever that may mean) so he may have had some further source of income. (The only engineering he is recorded as doing was digging a well in the public road outside his house, for which he was presented at the Manor Court and fined.) His house has a sophisticated plan for its date (fig. 3) with fine stone fireplaces on the first floor and originally an ingenious staircase layout that is reflected in the odd window arrangement on the front. Henry Letch's house, next door (No. 53) may have been built either by him or by his predecessor Peter Parker; it has a handsome parlour on the ground floor with finely moulded ceiling beams. The third of these survivors is John Bricknell's, No. 92, and it may be significant that the Letches and the Bricknells were the last families in Aynho to farm and own their own land.

All others of these yeomen's houses have either been demolished or so altered by later generations as to have lost almost every trace of their original layout. The destruction of the other houses of these prosperous villagers must be due to one of two things — one, that these houses were already old, and second, that as time went on, as population grew and as the number of independent farmers fell, there was less demand for larger houses. The squire's own tenant farmers, of course, always needed farm houses, and old houses might survive for a while. As farms grew in size, however, and as their numbers fell, so fewer farm houses were needed. And when after the 1792 enclosure new farms and farmhouses were created in the newly enclosed fields, the need for large houses in the village itself fell still further.

Apart from the great house, the two largest private houses of seventeenth century Aynho have both disappeared. One was the Hanslope's, already old; the (admittedly unreliable) map of the

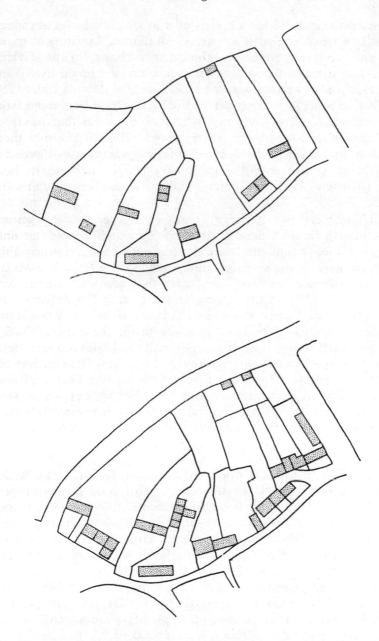

Map 5. The area north of Blacksmith's Hill and south of the Charlton Road in c.1690 (top) and c.1790 (bottom), to show the progressive subdivision of properties in the 18th century.

village drawn in 1696 has a sketch of it in which it looks as though it was late medieval, with a central hall flanked by wings at either end, one for family rooms and the other, perhaps, for the services. In the late eighteenth century the house was occupied by Robert Weston, the Cartwright agent, and it was pulled down around 1795 in order to enlarge that corner of the Park. The other large house, by contrast, was relatively new when the map was drawn, and it had been built either by parson Drope (who died in 1636) or more probably by his son William. It was a four-square house of two-and-a-half storeys with a central gable over the front door. It stood close to where the Home Farm stands now, and nothing of it remains.

These were two houses that were too large for later generations, houses fit for village gentry and for which it would be hard to find suitable occupants after the passing of the Dropes and the Hanslopes late in the seventeenth century. One was quite new, the other already old, and one may infer that many of the farmer's houses were old from the returns to the Hearth Tax in the 1660's and 1670's. The Hearth Tax was a crude sort of property tax, levied on the occupants of houses and assessed on the number of fireplaces in each house. The Hanslopes' and the Dropes' houses were rated on seven hearths apiece. Edward Jarvis's, with four, was one of the ten largest, but this ten included the College Farm, the Rectory, the School House and the two Inns. Yet Edward Jarvis was a good way from being the largest farmer earlier in the century when his house was built, and the reason why many of the larger farmers' houses had fewer hearths is almost certainly because they were older.

The Hearth Tax was levied two full generations after Shakerley Marmion had enfranchised the leading copyhold farmers of the village, and not all their houses are identifiable in these returns. This is partly because of changes in ownership and tenancy, but it is also because the larger houses were already being subdivided. The 1673 Hearth Tax lists 81 households, of which no less than 51 have only one hearth. This number of households is an increase of 25 per cent over the number of families 50 years before, and many must have been occupying parts of older, larger houses that had been split up. This splitting-up of property among children has been mentioned often already, and typical of what occurred was what happened when Benjamin Watts died in 1663. He was the son of the smallest of the freeholders earlier in the century, Lawrence Watts who owned some 20 acres, and his house and barns stood on the west side of the Square. When he died, he left his farm to be divided between his three daugthers. To Lydia he left the Hall, the Dwelling House (sic) and buttery and rooms over them, one third of his barn and part of the yard. To Anne he left the parlour next the Hall and the chamber over it, the butt house and other out-buildings, a second third of the barn and a further area of yard. To Sarah he left his kilnhouse, malthouse, the rest of the barn and the rest of the yard. By the early eighteenth century Lydia's portion was in the possession of a Souldern man, who let it (the house at the corner of the Square and Little Lane) to a mason, Henry Hob-craft; Anne's and Sarah's portions came ultimately, and separately, into the hands of Timothy Burberow the baker who built his new house in 1696 at the north end of the old Watts property. It is scarcely surprising that hardly a trace of earlier seventeenth century building now remains there, even though the corner house does retain a blocked doorway that might be of Lawrence Watt's time. A further illustration of what might happen is provided by the later history of Edward Jarvis's house, number 86. When the last of the family was bankrupt early in the eighteenth century, the squire bought his land but the house was bought by a village tailor, pre-sumably as an investment: it was in multiple occupation through-out the rest of the century, split up between several tenants, and the fabric retains traces of extra doors and fireplaces inserted to serve its various occupants.

But though it is therefore certain that some of the poor in the seventeenth and eighteenth centuries were living in parts of larger houses that had been broken up, it is most unlikely that there were enough of such houses to accommodate more than a fraction of the poorer villagers. Such people must have lived in cottages of only one or two rooms that had been built as such. There is now only one two-roomed house in the village that is known to have survived from the mid-seventeenth century, but even this, number 74, probably had two hearths (one up and one down) and it was built for his son by a farmer with perhaps fifteen acres of land. There must have been many poorer cottages for poorer men.

Cottagers were never rich enough to build for themselves. There were in the past, however, a number of close-built groups of small cottages in the village, cottages of one room to a floor and crowded into the smallest possible sites. It is almost certain that these must have been built for tenants by the squire or else as speculations by private landlords in order to capitalise on the growing population. The map on the back end papers, of the village

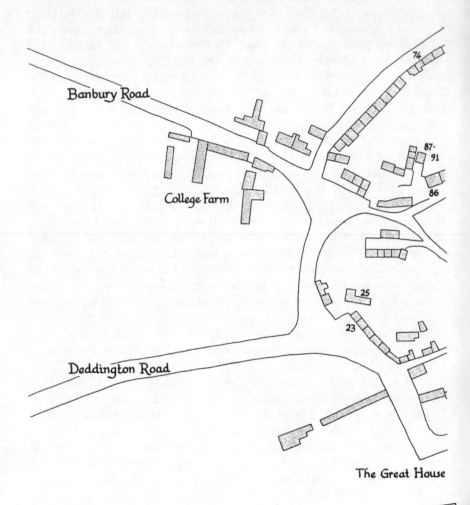

Banbury Road

74

College Farm

87-
91

86

25

23

Deddington Road

The Great House

Map 6. The village centre, c.1950. The numbers given
to the houses (and used in the text) are those given by
the Cartwright Estate, probably between 1900 and 1918,
and employed until recently.

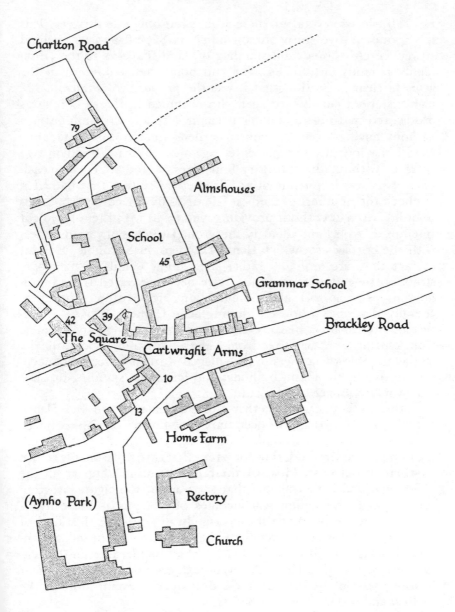

in 1790, shows several of these groups but only one survives. This is a group of five (now three), numbers 87, 90 and 91, behind Henry Letch's house and standing on land that was in the Letch family's hands until 1784. The end house has a dovecot in the gable, a clear indication that it was the property of someone of a higher status than the cottager who occupied it. Henry Letch was prosecuted in 1654 for taking a tenant into a newly-built cottage without having given the churchwardens security for his tenant's good behaviour; he was presented again in 1670 for building two cottages without the statutory four acres of land attached to each one. (This was in pursuit of an Elizabethan statute that had tried to check the numbers of landless labourers by forbidding landlords to build cottages without providing land to go with them.) While it is tempting to try and identify this group (which is of various dates) with the cottages for which Henry Letch got into trouble, in point of fact they are probably rather later. Some details of their construction suggest that they may have been converted from a farm building of some sort, and more than one eighteenth century deed actually describes a house as having been formerly a barn — converted, presumably, because there was more money to be made from renting a cottage than from using a barn, and because the declining number of farmers in the village led to an increased concentration of working farm buildings and left some standing on sites that were no longer convenient.

But in any case, whether this particular group was Henry Letch's or not, they are certainly one-down, one-up cottages which someone of his family built cheaply in order to let, providing minimal accommodation for a rent that gave a reasonable return on their initial cost. Most of these groups do not appear on the 1696 map and it is probable that they are of the eighteenth century, though the falling real incomes of villagers as the century wore on must have made it increasingly difficult for this kind of investment to pay. The overall number of houses in the village continued to rise, but it is likely that the chief builder later in the century was the squire. He built seven cottages east of the Grammar School early in the century (now destroyed), several more in the 1780's, and probably others besides.

Building by the squire must have done much to prevent housing conditions in the eighteenth and early nineteenth centuries from deteriorating as fast as unemployment was growing as the result of the growth of population. The average number of people to a household, for the period over which one can estimate it,

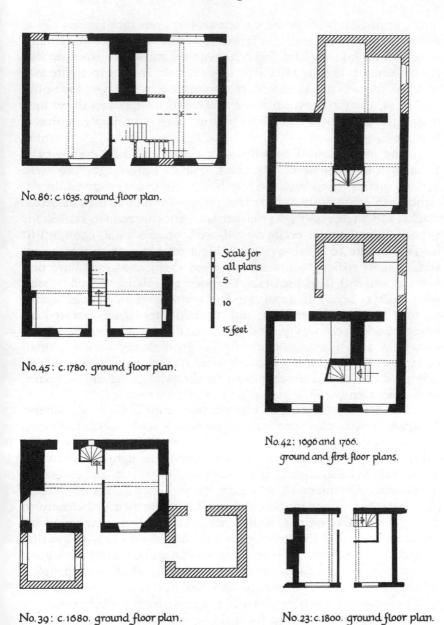

No. 86 : c.1635. ground floor plan.

No. 45 : c.1780. ground floor plan.

Scale for
all plans
5
10
15 feet

No. 42 : 1696 and 1766.
ground and first floor plans.

No. 39 : c.1680. ground floor plan.

No. 23 : c.1800. ground floor plan.

Fig. 3. Representative house plans.

seems surprisingly constant at about 4½, even though this figure does not mean very much in terms of overcrowding (or the lack of it) unless we know something of the size of houses themselves. But if (as seems probable) the late seventeenth and early eighteenth century houses in Aynho were an improvement over their predecessors, then at least until the middle of the eighteenth century housing conditions for the bulk of the villagers probably gradually improved.

One indication of how difficult things could be even for the tradesmen and craftsmen was the number of mortgages they took out on their houses, and the few that were ever redeemed. In the eighteenth century there were few outlets for a small man's savings; stocks and shares and government securities were inaccessible for anyone living in the country and with only a small capital. But lawyers in the town always knew local people with money to invest, and of other people who needed cash, and must have performed a useful (and profitable) service in putting them in touch with each other. The usual rate for a mortgage in the eighteenth century was 4½–5 per cent, and when the mortgagee wanted his money back there was generally someone else with funds available to whom the mortgage could be assigned. Many of these small mortgages carried on for years. And even if the mortgage was foreclosed, it did not necessarily lead to the eviction of the occupant, who was often only the tenant of the first owner.

Houses were seldom mortgaged to anyone living in the village. This was not because no one in the village had capital to invest: village tradesmen did buy houses that they did not live in so as to enjoy an income from rent, and two surviving eighteenth century Wills from Aynho specifically mention money out on mortgages. A villager's reluctance to mortgage his property to his neighbours may have been because he did not wish to be tied too closely to them by legal obligations: a villager might well feel some reserve to the man who held the deeds of his house. More likely still is that villagers did not want their financial circumstances to be too widely known: when tradesmen sent bills annually, when most people's children married in the village and did not want their prospects spoilt by their parents' misfortunes, and when apparent prosperity was the chief qualification for holding one of the village's offices, then people took care to preserve the appearance of wealth. But few who took out mortgages redeemed them unless they came into money, and this is itself an indication of a decline in the villagers' fortunes. People would generally take out a mortgage to

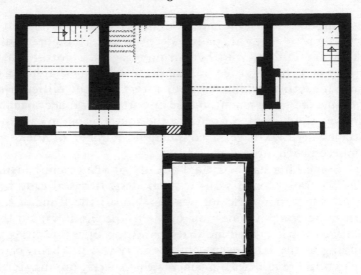

Nos. 87-91: formerly farm building. ground floor plan.

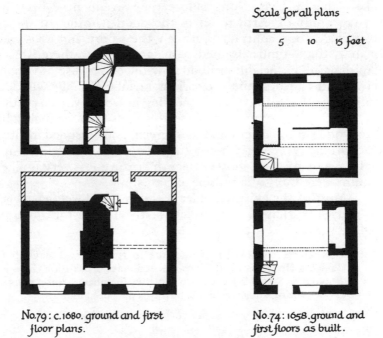

Scale for all plans

5 10 15 feet

No.79 : c.1680. ground and first
floor plans.

No.74 : 1658. ground and
first floors as built.

Fig. 4. Representative house plans.

raise money for some business opportunity that might enable them soon to repay it, or to tide over some temporary difficulty (like John Turbet, who had to mortgage the cottage that he inherited in 1784 in order to raise the £40 legacy that he was bound under his father's will to find for sister). But the difficulties all too often become permanent, or the opportunities failed to materialise. When at the end of the century the squire began in earnest to buy cottages in the village, a considerable number of them were encumbered with mortgages.

Something has been said already of village craftsmen. In the building trades, their skills were modest. It has already been suggested what Arthur Secull was capable of: the front of his house with quite roughly cut stone heads to the windows; but there was plenty of work to be done that was within their capacities. Humble building in the late seventeenth century was still being carried out in earth: there are two agreements that specify building in 'mortar', and rammed earth must be what is intended. One of them is for building yard walls, and the other for an outdoor privy for one of the squire's tenant farmers, the latter on stone foundations. It is likely that not very long before they would have been building cottages out of earth to let to the poor. Another of these seventeenth century contracts between the squire and a village craftsman is for a timber-framed barn, and though there is no timber building in the neighbourhood now the expert use of various technical terms to describe the various members of the wooden structure show that a tradition of building in wood was very much alive. Incidently, it is clear from these contracts that for timber building the wood was to be cut and used green, and seasoned in situ. There had probably been timber cottages in Aynho built until not long before, but by the late seventeenth century it is very unlikely that houses were built of anything except stone.

Most of the existing, older cottages could well have been built by village workmen. A contract for the 1670's for a house in the village runs:-

> Matthew Borton & Jo. Wing agree to floor over 2 Bays in Ed Hanley's House saw out Transoms and make 2 partitions below & 2 above & 3 two-light windows in the Chambers a Shop window & one pair of doortrees . . . & put up a pair of stairs . . .

Wing and Borton were carpenters, but a building craftsman could be competent in other skills than his own:-

> Jo. Wing agrees to build 2 bays of new building in old Goody

> Baker's house & repair the rest so much as shall be needful in Consideration whereof . . . he is to have 2 years rent allowed him which is £3 . . . J. Wing is allowed 6 old Ashes which may be worth 4s & is to have 2 loads of stone at Aynho pitts paying for the digging.

Superior work, however, called for specialists. John Neal, the best of the village masons in the late seventeenth century, was quite versatile:-

> John Neal agrees to build a substantial stone bridge over the ditch on the north side of Turner's Plank Mead for a coach or cart to go safe over . . . and to hang the furnace that was lately brought from Bloxham in the chimney of Bower's house in the best manner he can for saving fuel and to make a chimney back in the kitchen at Mr. Cartwright's house with brick substantial and workmanlike.

and he could do stone carving as well:-

> John Neale agrees to make a new Scrole out of the freestone now lying in Mr. Cartwright's yard & to make it answerable to the other over the garden doors . . .

Perhaps some of the seventeenth century tombstones now so unhappily propped against the churchyard wall, with their fat swags and podgy cherubs, are John Neal's.

But for the best craftsmanship one had to go further afield. The two principal building works of the later seventeenth century in Aynho were the rebuilding of the great house after its damage in the Civil War, and the new Grammar School. There is more to say about the school in the next chapter — about how it was established and run — but a number of agreements survive from the 1660's and 1670's for its building and fitting up which make it fairly clear how the work was organised (with separate contracts between the Cartwright estate and various workmen) and from which it is clear, too, that building of this quality was beyond the skill of village craftsmen.

At least one drawing must have been made. Thus Thomas Freeman and Peter Fletcher 'agree to undertake the carpenters' work about the new school according to a draught subscribed by Thomas Freeman.' Neither of these two men were villagers. And where there were no drawings, other patterns were specified: thus Nicholas Harris of Ardington agreed to make windows for the school 'as well wrought as the casements in Mr. Cartwright's drawing room.' The plastering was done by Thomas Turbit of King's Sutton, whose family came to live in Aynho later on. Glazing was done by another King's Sutton man, with best Worcestershire glass. Two more King's Sutton men did most of the walling, John Neal doing only the low wall between the school building and the street.

But the most interesting of the schoolhouse contracts are those for the masonry details. These were ordered, ready cut, from masons in Adderbury and Banbury

> John Kenning of Banbury agrees to serve Mr. Cartwright with freestone from Hornton quarries ready hewed and worked for the making of the jambs of the little gate at the school house next to the street . . . the door is to be six feet high and three feet wide and a half in the clear, with the jambs moulded on the foreside

The contract strongly suggests that the gateway in question (which is still there) was something of a standard item, only the dimensions requiring detailed specifications. At the same time, Thomas Wyatt of Adderbury agreed for windows

> the window stuff to be wrought in the same mouldings as the windows in the parlour in the new buildings at Aynho, and the ground table to be wrought as the ground table in the said new building is

The stone was to be from Adderbury and Milton, two miles further off. Here again the pattern to be followed is clearly indicated, and this time it is to resemble work recently undertaken at the squire's own house for which he had had designs from the King's own mason from London, William Marshall.

Detailed accounts for the house do not survive, but there are a number of agreements for small jobs about the house and grounds that provide further evidence of the levels of local skills. For ornamental columns for his garden, the squire contracted with Christopher Kempster of Burford, a master mason who worked for Sir Christopher Wren and was well up in fashionable architecture. When William Marshall sent down a drawing for garden gates, these were entrusted to a joiner in Banbury, but with instructions to leave out the decoration. And when Thomas Turbet was engaged to do some plastering in the great house,

> and to do all as well as the withdrawing room now is or as the best country workman can do

it is clear that his limitations were recognised.

Of all the villagers' houses now standing, only Edward Jarvis's (described previously) must have been built, in part or in whole, by craftsmen from outside the village. Most of those that survive are unpretentious houses of the later seventeenth and early eighteenth centuries, of the middling sort and of a variety of forms.

Some have chimneys in the end walls (like numbers 23, 39 and 45), others in the centre (like Jarvis's, Arthur Secull's and Timothy Burberow's, 86, 79 and 42). Front doors either lead into a lobby against the stack, or into the main room. The main living room was generally called the hall, sometimes the hall house; it had a large fireplace where most of the cooking was done and from it ascended the stair to one or more rooms above, either rising beside the stack or|housed in a slight projection at the rear. In the better houses there was a parlour as well or a ground floor chamber, often with a slightly smaller fireplace. Smaller houses had only one room on the ground floor (like the group that the Letch family built as a speculation in the seventeenth or early eighteenth century, numbers 87–91, or the house built in 1658 by Thomas Hobcraft, number 74) but the upper floor even of a small house was probably partitioned into two.

We know nothing of the furnishing of the poorer houses in the seventeenth and eighteenth centuries, but we know rather more about houses of the sort just described, the houses of tradesmen, craftsmen and farmers. The practice of making inventories of dead people's goods gradually fell out of use after the first decades of the eighteenth century, but the houses even of the richer villages were then still sparsely furnished, and what furniture there was was far from luxurious. In the hall one would find a table, stools, benches, a chair or two for the head of the|house, probably a cupboard for crockery and food, and fire irons, bellows and cooking pots. By the early eighteenth century the benches and stools were disappearing from the better houses (Timothy Burberow, who died in 1729, had banished his four old forms to the brewhouse). But chairs were longer in finding their way into bedrooms: inventories of 1723 and 1729 mention them, but none do before that except for Peter Pruce's in 1683, and at an inn (the Bell) furniture would often be pushed into unlikely places. But bedrooms nearly always had a chest or a coffer for keeping clothes and spare bed linen, and all the better-off villagers had sheets, woven in the village from hemp grown on the hemp piece at the beginning of the Charlton road. Pewter sometimes turns up in bedrooms, too, where people may have felt it was safer than in the living room that opened off the street. It was probably only brought out on special occasions, while most of the time people would have eaten off platters of earthenware or wood. The richest villagers in the sixteenth and seventeenth century might have had hangings of painted stuff on their walls — a sort of poor-man's tapestry — but the normal wall and ceiling treatment of village houses was a white lime-wash. Ceiling beams were certainly not blackened, even though they must gradually have discoloured from smokey fires. Nor were they normally left in their natural oak or elm. Lime wash, renewed each year, was an excellent preservative and made even a small-windowed room bright and cheerful. In one house in the village this white wash still exists, and the effect is lovely.

People cooked and warmed themselves on wood fires, by great open fireplaces that the nineteenth century largely blocked up in order to insert coal grates and which the twentieth century has mostly opened up again. Coal was being burnt at the Bell in Peter Pruce's time: in the hall was 'a bar or iron to burn coals on'. It was burnt in the great house too in the late seventeenth century, but these were exceptions. Most people did their cooking in an iron or brass pot hung over the wood fire or else by grilling in front of it. Fuel was always a problem; its shortage was remarked in the mid-seventeenth century when a fire was specifically called for as a necessity in the new school, lest in winter the pupils should be too cold to work. Edward Jarvis's house has a bread oven, and later they were fairly common. But as late as the early years of the twentieth century the poorer villagers, if they had anything to bake (roast meat included) would send it to the baker to be done in his oven, and the number of bakers in the village in the eighteenth century shows how few villagers baked for themselves. Shortage of firing must have been a principal reason for this.

Kitchens are mentioned occasionally in the inventories, but there is seldom much equipment in them apart from a few pots. They usually seem to have existed only in the larger houses, where there was room enough to avoid cooking in the common living room, the hall. Butteries feature in many houses, their furniture mostly barrels, and their function was probably a combination of larder and beer cellar. Many people brewed their own beer, and separate brewhouses feature from time to time. On the whole the impression one has of these yeomen's and tradesmen's houses is that they were far from luxuriously furnished, but adequately, and that though people's standards of comfort were very far from what they are today, the better-off villagers did not live too badly. But the poorer villagers' cottages are unrecorded, and one can only guess at how far they fell below these basic comforts.

Chapter 9

Some Village Institutions

If village life was not always easy, there were comforts and distractions to be had. Chief among these for most people must have been the inns, and with wages low and with some of the better-off brewing at home, it is obvious that the purpose of visiting a pub was for most people social rather than alcoholic — though no doubt the quality of the beer was important: the ale-tasters saw to it that standards were maintained. It was the natural place for meetings. The Churchwardens, the Overseers of the Poor, the Constables and the Fieldsmen all had their annual meetings there, the first two in the Spring, the last two in the Autumn —

> Payde at John Pruces when neberes meett in tacking Gioles Sooutham Acountes Laste Constabell November the 12 daye   1s 8d
> Whcn Nebours meat at Edward Homans A Bout toune Conserns and Bisnest   6s
> Spent at the Red Lion when we received the money for the Bull Stag   6d
> Pd. at Mr. Homans at giving the Fieldsmens Accounts and settling the order of the Horse Hitch & sowing the clover in the barly field   4s
> Spent at Ed Honas when the Counts was given up For Bread and Bear   3s

In the middle of the eighteenth century, beer was about 1½d a pint, and the village inns sold cider as well which was probably cheaper. The village statesmen must have consumed a good deal. The inn was the place for all sorts of business: old Mrs. Jarvis's body was lying at the Red Lion when the coroner's jury had to view it during the inquest on her possible suicide; they met there for the inquest on little John Merry, the 4-year-old son of the miller at the College Mill, who was drowned; when an orphan was put out to nurse or to apprenticeship; and when meetings were held with Overseers or the Constables of neighbouring villages to discuss matters of common concern.

As to other entertainments, we know all too little. The villagers' own treats and holidays are not the kind of things of which records remain, though it was the custom for there to be a Wake on the Monday after Michaelmas and possibly some kind of a holiday on Whit Monday and Shrove Tuesday, besides Christmas and Easter. Perhaps there were sports; there was almost certainly dancing. On three occasions in the 1720's, John Jeffs the tailor was paid by the squire for playing when there was impromptu dancing at the great house; if he played for money for the squire, he probably played for nothing for the village. What instrument he played is not recorded; perhaps a pipe and tabor is the most likely. Dr. Hutton the rector had played the viol when he was young with his Oxford cronies, and though it is unlikely that he would have contributed much to village jollities, he might have encouraged the formation of a group of village musicians to make music in church: there was no organ then. There were Morris dancers at Syresham and Brackley to whom Thomas Cartwright paid half-a-guinea a team in 1725, and it is certainly more likely that they came to Aynho than that the squire went to them. He had paid for music lessons in the 1690's:

Pd. Mr. Purcell the Spinet master   £2

and Purcell had dedicated a group of sonatas for his sister, but he obviously did not think himself above encouraging rustic talent.

The subject of Inns leads one to another reason why people drank beer — the badness of the village water supply. Aynho's water, until twentieth century, came from the same spring that had probably brought the village into existence, close to the point at which the street presently called the Causeway leads into the Banbury road, and where in the eighteenth century and later there was a pump to drive a water supply up the west side of the village to provide for the great house. There were, in the eighteenth and nineteenth centuries, a few public pumps that drew water either from this conduit or, more generally from the level of the watertable up the hill. There were rather more private pumps, and eighteenth century deeds are full of clauses reserving rights of way to pumps in other people's yards, and of arrangements to share the cost of maintaining them.

The Manor Court did its best to ensure that the water supply was no worse than it need be. In 1721, for instance, the Jury were ordered to

> Have care that the town pump be paved around to keep any filthiness from running into the well. If anybody attempts to wash guts . . . without a Tub or Bucket to carry off the filthiness so that it does not run into the well again . . .   3s 4d.

The supply seldom failed, but it was said to have become distinctly murky from time to time: not surprisingly, since it was difficult to keep wells clean, and the rubbish that inevitably fell in would be more in evidence when the water-level was low. A few wells survive, their upper courses beautifully stone lined with coursed rubble, laid without mortar and so as to make, as it were, horizontal arches. Occasionally, when a well needed cleaning out or a rope broke, someone would have to climb down. It was not dangerous: placing one's feet against the rough stone lining and bracing one's back against the opposite side, one could climb up and down quite easily, but it is tiring to climb like that and no doubt wells became pretty foul before people felt ready to clean them. No wonder so much beer was drunk.

It is, of course, impossible to know to what extent the water supply contributed to people's ill-health. Probably not greatly, since the death rate in Aynho in the seventeenth and eighteenth centuries was probably no worse than that of other villages round, though that is not saying much. To calculate people's life expectancy in those centuries is almost impossible, but it is easy to show that child deaths were commonplace. The close correlation between the graphs of births and deaths on page 127 can only be explained by a constantly high rate of infant mortality, with only occasional divergences when an epidemic of some kind produced more deaths than usual among all age-groups.

Joseph Wasse, with his enquiring mind, wrote in the registers during the time of his incumbency what people died of, and the chief obstacle to using these as a record of the illnesses that country people were prone to in the eighteenth century is the difficulty of recognising some of them from his diagnoses:-

Hesther Underwood a distracted person
John Bricknell infant of a swelling in his body
John Goodyer of a deep consumption aged about 55
Prudence Wing an infant of Fits
Sarah Baldwin suddenly: wasted with the Cholick
Edward Higman of Hamstead Joiner of a Pleurisie
Susanna Turpin dropp'd down in the street & died of an Impos-
thume in her Lungs
William Righton anabaptist of a pleuretic Feaver
Ann Norwood of Fitts Palsey & Consumption
Thomas Taylor of a Sort of Leprosie
John Harris a crooked Man of a universal Decay
Mary Turpin aged about 30 of a Dropsie after Tapping
Abraham Righton very fat was taken speechless of a sudden at
Tingewick of an Apoplexy

And there are plenty of records of deaths after the usual sorts of country accidents:-

> Henry Hobcroft a Mason killed by the Fall of Earth in a Quarry
> Mary Hobcroft infant supposed to be overlaid
> Thomas Tomkins by being too freely bled after a long illness occasioned by a broken Leg
> Samuel Peckover of a Mortification after his Arm had been cut off near the Shoulder

When people were ill, they probably relied heavily on the prescriptions of Mr. Burbidge, though one may be allowed some scepticism as to the efficacy of some of his nostrums, whatever the claims of Opoldedoc. Those more seriously ill sent for physicians from some distance: Mr. Griffin of Bicester, Mr. Wisdom of Shipton who amputated Samuel Peckover's arm for £4. 1s 6d (but who did not save his life), and 'Sourgin Lukas' or 'Mr. Luckars'. And there were practitioners closer to home, like Edward Knott the blacksmith whose unsuccessful ministrations to the parish bull have already been mentioned and who was equally on call for blooding a poor woman or one of the Cartwright servants. Not suprisingly, some people considered themselves better off without such ministrations. Mr. Wasse registers include

> John Makepeace bruis'd by a Fall & would not be blooded
> Alice Wrighton of a Feaver she would take no Bark etc.
> Henry Borton shepherd of ye Feaver he would not be blooded nor take anything

And besides those who died of their illnesses, there were always some in the village whose troubles were chronic, such as those who were disqualified from serving in the militia: Thomas Marsh the shoemaker and schoolmaster who was ruptured — always a common complaint among men who had done heavy work; William Smith who had 'one eye and one child', and others who were deaf, nearsighted or simple.

But the most serious of common diseases was smallpox, and again we are fortunate in that Mr. Wasse, perhaps considering that the account of an epidemic in a small and relatively closed community would interest the members of the Royal Society in London, sent the Secretary a summary record of the outbreak that lasted from September 1723 till December the next year.

It began on 18th September, when William Priour, a thin dark young man of 20 from Catherine Hall in Cambridge came over to see the squire and the rector. There had been an outbreak of smallpox at Cambridge, though this does not seem to have deterred Priour from his visit, as it well might have done. In spite of bad weather William went to Brackley races and spent several hours there without any sign of anything wrong. That night he felt ill, got out of bed and drank a large quantity of cold water. Next day he felt worse, with violent pains in his head and back, and with some difficulty he managed to mount his horse and ride a few hundred yards to where his old nurse lived. The signs of smallpox appeared on his body later that day, and though the squire gave orders for all possible care to be taken of him, on 8th October he was dead.

The story was circulating in Oxford soon afterwards that at the funeral the coffin-bearers were drunk and dropped the coffin, which burst. It is not unlikely, but one can hardly blame them for needing a bit of Dutch courage. Smallpox was a frightful disease, and what is more surprising is that during the next fifteen months village life went on so much as usual, with the Manor Court meeting, the Fieldsmen, Constables and Overseers going about their business and the new church being built, all under the shadow of a long-drawn-out epidemic that afflicted 133 of the inhabitants — over a quarter — before the outbreak was over. And of these 133, 25 people died. The strain, as one after another of one's friends and family caught the disease, must have been appalling.

Before William Priour was dead, three people in the village were already down with it: Sarah Lamprey, a large, fat women in her forties; William Addington, a thin, fair boy in his teens and Joseph Wagstaffe, a weaver, a lean, swarthy, black-haired man of 40. Sarah and Joseph were both dead within ten days. Early in October another man from outside the village, William Hatley who had caught the disease on his way from London to his home in Warwick, had reached Aynho before he could travel no further. Four days later Sarah Miller, a young girl of 21 and an older woman, Frances Howes, caught it, and by the end of the month nine villagers had smallpox and four were dead. So it dragged on, with as many as 29 new cases in December alone, until by the end of February eighty people had had the disease of whom seventeen had died.

Towards the end of February there was a spell of continuous and heavy rain, and the epidemic slackened slightly; Wasse no doubt, like many of his contemporaries, would have put it down to the change in the weather, which shows how little disease was understood. In the second week of April, however, young James Priest the carpenter went down with the 'good sort' of smallpox, and with the coming of warmer weather the number of cases rose again. June, July and August were the worst months, but it was December before the last case occurred, fortunately a mild attack sustained by a little girl of 2, Elizabeth Swift. But even of those recovered, many were probably disfigured, and some worse: William Smith, for instance, one of those who died, had lost an eye. And there were dangers, too, in affecting to take the disease lightly: William Hobcroft, a day labourer in his twenties, thought he was better and went out too soon; he died a week later.

The disease struck some households worse than others — which is hardly surprising, considering the close quarters in which many villagers must have lived. Seven members of the Priest family caught it, though only one died, old Roger who was 80 and already weakened by fever. Three of the Castle family died, while John, Anne, Thomas and Elizabeth Swift all fell ill on the same day. Nor were they all the poor: Arthur Secull the mason caught it, and William Merry the miller, a young fat man in his twenties. In the circumstances, with whole families falling sick, it is not surprising that Wasse records some of the victims as being 'not well attended'. Considering the fear that the disease must have inspired, some people's behaviour on their neighbours' behalf must have been little short of heroic.

It is clear from the Overseers' accounts that there had already been some attempt to set up an isolation hospital of a kind in a building called the Dog Kennel in the Warren. When Henry|Golder had smallpox in 1719, he was nursed at the house of Mary Hobcroft (who had presumably already had it) but three years later Thomas Aries's family were carried to the 'dog kenly' and back to the village when they had recovered. Many people were sent there by the Overseers in 1723-4 (the poor, presumably, though other people may have gone there too), and the Overseers paid for supplies, including quantities of beer from Edward Homan, and nursing.

From then on it features quite often in the accounts. In the 1740's a good deal of work was done at the 'Dodgkenill' — it was re-glazed and slated and a drain and cesspool were made. Later in the century it was usually called Fairslade House or the Pest House, and though there is no proof that this was the building previously called the Dog Kennel, it probably was.

It was quite often needed, though never again for an epidemic of the proportions of the 1723-4 one. The Overseers did not flinch from sending people there when necessary — a stitch in time saves nine — but it could be an expensive business. In 1753, in addition to the usual rate, about a dozen Aynho people contributed to a special 'Collection as was gather'd towards John Grant's having the Small Pox' in suitably graded contributions from Francis Burton the Cartwright steward and Mr. Prowett a farmer, who gave 5s each, through Mr. Banbury the shopkeeper, Mr. Burbidge the apothecary and James Priest the carpenter who gave 3s., Thomas Bygrave the innkeeper who gave 2s 6d, Timothy Coates the baker, 1s 6d, down to Mrs Arrowsmith who may have been the widow of a former schooolmaster and who gave 6d. The whole Grant family were there for eight weeks, and payments to John Baker, Elizabeth Secull and to another woman for looking after them came to over £7.

Even for single people the expenses could be considerable. Thomas Betts was at the Pest House from September, 1755 till early November, and William Borton's bill for cheese, bacon, oatmeal, sugar, salt, nutmeg, cloves, candles, rushlights, hard soap and several other items (including brimstone and treacle) came to 12s 8d; Mr. Burbidge's bill for physick came to 7s 2d; the landlord of the Red Lion supplied wine, beer and brandy to the tune of 14s 8d; Timothy Coates sent bread and flour, while other bills were for firing and nursing — £1. 14s 9d for three weeks and four days at 10s a week. In all his illness had cost the ratepayers some £3. 15s.

When there were no patients, one of the village women looked after the place. Elizabeth Secull was paid for several years for keeping it swept and the beds aired, and from time to time the Overseers had the chimneys swept. Later on the building ceased to be a Pest house. It was occupied as a cottage in the 1860's, but by the beginning of the twentieth century it was derelict and the village children would play in the ruins. Its stones were used in building the present village hall in 1929.

Care for the sick when there were epidemics was one of the more unpredictable and arduous of the Overseers' responsibilities. Totally predictable and slowly increasing was their responsibility for the unemployed, the chronically infirm and the old. Only those born in Aynho or who had 'acquired a settlement' by reason of long settlement or employment were eligible for relief by the Aynho overseers, who went to considerable trouble to ensure that no-one came on the Aynho rates who might be found to be the responsibility of another village. In the 1720's they went to almost incredible expense over one couple, Thomas Edmonds and his wife from Ashendon, about whose right to a settlement there was room for doubt. The overseers' bill came to £44. 5s, which included, besides the cost of maintaining the Edmondses for a considerable time in Aynho, more than £29 in lawyers' fees. £44. 5s was three times as much as a labouring man might earn in a year, and it was more than three times the overseers' annual income. It was twenty years before they went to law again, and then only with the prior agreement of the Vestry, the little caucus of villagers (probably most of the ratepayers, in fact) who supervised the overseers' work. But the cost of the Edmonds episode shows how important the principle of supporting only the villagers' own poor must have seemed. When, late in the eighteenth century, the canal company (which we shall come to) built a pub by the Wharf and placed George Herbert from Bladon in it as landlord, the overseers made a formal agreement with their opposite numbers in Bladon by which they hoped to avoid ever having to support him or his family.

For those who had a genuine claim on the parish, the overseers did a great deal. Thomas Hall's orphaned children, John and Mary, were placed in the care of Jane Peckover who must have brought them up with her own children. John seems to have gone through shoes, stockings and breeches at an alarming rate, and the overseers were constantly buying him new clothes at William Banbury's shop, or paying village women to make shirts and stockings and to do the children's mending. Occasionally — perhaps when they were ill — they paid for little luxuries such as eggs and milk. Another orphan who for a time lodged with widow Peckover was Bet Fathers, to whom again the overseers seem to have behaved very responsibly. She was heir to a small property in King's Sutton, and when the overseers learnt that there was a mortgage on this which was about to be foreclosed, they bought out the mortgagee for £27, managed the cottage on the girl's behalf and mortgaged it, to pay themselves back, to the squire — who would not be likely to act to the girl's detriment.

The overseers went to equal trouble for the old. Old William Polton was 70 in 1743, and in that year they were paying him 1s 6d a week, paid Jane Peckover 1s for making him two shirts, and bought him a cap to comfort his old head. For old widow Haines they bought a 2 lb. pewter pot that year, for 10d, and later agreed for Jane Peckover to house, clothe and feed the old woman for 3s a week. The year before they had been to some expense about Joyce Hobcraft's house — 13s 6d for mending her chamber ceiling, 1s 6d for glazing her windows, and over £2 to William Borton, the carpenter, for 'stuff and work about Joyce Hobcraft's house' and to Joyce herself they gave 6d a week from 1740 on.

And there were other crises. In 1742 there was trouble when Nathan Spires's wife was brought to bed: one does not know why, since there is no record of his death. Perhaps he had absconded. They paid 9s to two village women plus another 2s for beer during Abigail Spires's lying-in, found lodging for her and the baby for several months in the village, and in 1744 removed them both, at the ratepayers' expense, to South Newington (where perhaps Abigail had relations). The generally subsistence level of living for the poor meant that people had no reserves to fall back on when they were ill; those in genuine need found that the overseers stood between them and destitution.

It was obviously good sense to employ one pauper — Jane Peckover — to look after others, but she appears so frequently in the overseers' accounts that one feels she must have had a real talent for caring for people. Other people too earned a little by nursing the old, washing or sewing. For some the overseers provided hemp, and they could earn a little by spinning it; the yarn would then be woven by one of the village weavers, the cloth whitened by John March the fuller, and when finished the lengths of cloth were either given by the overseers to the poor or sold to bring in a little more money. In the same way, when times were bad, Thomas Baldwin the shoemaker was given leather to work. More than once the overseers considered setting up a workhouse, but nothing ever came of the idea.

Even the removals were not done too brutally: when the Edmondses were sent off to Ashenden, the Overseers paid Mr. Homan at the Red Lion 15s for food and drink for the couple, they were mounted on John March's horse, hired for the occasion, and the two overseers rode with them. On the road they paid expenses at Brill and when they reached their destination, and afterwards gave Goody Hobcraft 5s for a hood 'which Goody Edmonds had away.'

But there was a price to be paid for the overseers' benevolence. Those who were receiving regular parish relief had to wear an armband with the letters P (for pauper), A (for Aynho), which must have been humiliating even though probably everyone in the village knew who was 'on the rates'. And though the overseers spent a good deal of money, they recouped themselves when they could. In 1722, when Thomas Aries died and the overseers had latterly been supporting him and paid for his funeral, they made a profit of £5. 5s 5d on it: their expenses had been £7. 5s 7d, but they sold his corn for £3. 17s, his pigs for £2, and his household goods for £7. 15s, and appear to have kept the proceeds. But perhaps he had no heirs and in any case they were doing the right thing by the ratepayers.

And as time went on, it was to become increasingly important to try and keep down the costs of poor relief. At the beginning of the eighteenth century the overseers were as a rule spending less than £20 a year on poor relief, but this had doubled by the 1750's while in 1790 they spent over £200. Population was growing, while incomes and jobs were not. The resources of the village were not expanding. The amount of land, of course, remained what it had been, and the farmers' tentative experiments with improved agriculture failed to increase their productiveness as fast as population was growing. In any case it meant no more jobs than before. To some extent, of course, more villagers meant more need for what one might call service occupations — carpenters, tailors and the like — but it was probably easy to lose money in jobs like that. We have seen one of the bakers go bankrupt, and old Arthur Secull dying in something near poverty. John Rymill was another local tradesman who failed in the 1780's, owing money as a carrier and butterman to half the grocers in Banbury and being sold up at the Red Lion. These were not the only men whose affairs went wrong in the late eighteenth century, and the solution that now seems to be obvious, to seek one's fortune elsewhere, was not so readily available to the eighteenth century villager. The labourer without skills was hardly more likely to find work away from Aynho than at home.

Something has already been said about the school in discussing the buildings of the place. In the seventeenth and eighteenth centuries almost all the better-off villagers could probably read and write after a fashion. There are not many who sign legal documents with a cross only, though a higher proportion of these are women than men. On the other hand, of those who would seldom have occasion to sign deeds, fieldsmen's accounts and so forth, probably many fewer were literate: they had little occasion to learn their letters, and their parents would probably rather have had them scaring crows at 6d a week than wasting their time in school. But there were certain men whose talents were in request:-

Pd. John Baker for Writin the Counts   1s

and John Baker and William Priest, carpenter, were also paid by the fieldsmen for making a survey of Old Down when the farmers who had commons there agreed among themselves to plough it.

Against this, there was James Anstey, described in a document of 1701 as 'architect', who only signed with a cross. But though it is difficult to imagine an illiterate architect, his name occurs nowhere else and one can only guess at what he may have meant by calling himself one.

That village children were receiving some sort of education in the seventeenth century is obvious, then, from the results, though it is quite uncertain where or how. Some had books: Giles Southam, who died in 1645, left his to his third son, Thomas, 'except the Bible which I usually carry to church.' But the education of the villagers took a turn for the better with the foundation of a grammar school under the terms of Mary Cartwright's will.

Mary Cartwright herself, incidently, could only write very badly. Her surviving letters were obviously written by a secretary, and she has occasionally added crabbed and ill-spelt postscripts. But education was regarded then as something required of men rather than of women, and Mary Cartwright would probably not have felt ashamed of herself on that account. One may be sure that it was not self-consciousness that prompted her to leave £700 to found a school, but the consideration she mentions — namely, that it should be

> A means to raise unto God A great number of faithful servants
> And to the Commonwealth [i.e. to the nation] many useful and
> good Members.

Part of the £700 was to be invested so as to bring in £20 a year to pay a schoolmaster and £10 a year to put poor boys out as apprentices. The balance of the capital was to pay for the new building.

John Cartwright was not entirely happy about this bequest, which had been left to him as sole executor and trustee to put into effect. He seems to have taken legal advice, since he was afraid that after an investment had been bought to bring in £30 a year the balance would hardly be enough to build a school and a house for the master. There was already the old market house standing in the village, built by his father; the market had lapsed with the Civil War (or at least by 1660) and the market house had a good sized room on each floor and would do (thought John Cartwright) admirably. But there was no land for a school yard, and no house for the master, and in the end the lawyers told him that he was indeed bound to build a school specially, under the terms of his mother's will. So after a delay of almost ten years work began on building the school that still, after considerable alterations, stands as the Grammar House at the eastern end of the village.

Some details of its building have been discussed already since the accounts and contracts for its erection are the best record we have of how the grander buildings of the village were put up. Work began in about 1663, and we can follow much of the course of its building, through the building of walls and the ordering of windows, through the plastering of the walls to its final equipment with a desk for the master and a broom cupboard

> William Borton agrees to make a desk in the schoolmaster's seat for books and a place at the lower end of the school for besomes and a thing to carry out dust in

The schoolmaster's house had two rooms on the ground floor, two on the first, and three small attics, and the school end had a main schoolroom on the ground floor with another above it.

John Cartwright had already begun to take advice on how his school should be organised and what the rules should be; it would be odd if those he consulted did not include Robert Wilde, who had probably been a schoolmaster before becoming rector of Aynho. And he wrote down the advice he had had 'from diverse' and much of it was not only good in itself but is now an interesting record of the practical and the theoretical notions on teaching that were current at the time.

It was envisaged from the start that the school should be for the benefit of the poor, 'who are not able to give this education to their children'. It was important that the master

> be not intangled with works not well consistent nor much below an ingenious well bred man, and that he be not oppressed with too much toil through the number of scholars.
>
> Therefore first I hold it necessary that there be provision of two to instruct the poor children in Aynho; the one for such as are very small, and learn English only, and the place of their teaching is to be in the town, near home, and remoter from the other school, that higher thought than English learning may be nourished in the higher school: That the higher school be not clogged with too many, and the schoolmaster not debased to much mean offices which any one of the meanest education may perform, for this will break his heart . . .
>
> A person of meaner quality may teach these poor English scholars, and at a small rate until they learn Latin only; and to write and cast account are to be done in the higher school . . .
>
> The number of the scholars learning English only in the first school to be as many of the poor as are pleased to come . . . and others to pay for their instruction if they please to come thither . . .

In the main school, the grammar school, there should be twenty free places, but more could come as fee-paying pupils.

> The schoolmaster's house to be at one end of the school, of that capacity that for his incouragement and inlarging of his allowance he may receive boarders into his house
> The school to be of good & large capacity, with a well boarded Floor that here where is but little Fuel for the fire the children suffer not by the cold . . .
> The books to be read by the grammar-scholars, Grammar, Castalion Dialogues, Aesop's Fables

and various other excercises.

> Then Caesar's Commentaries, Talens Rhetoricke or the like, Virgil, Horace, Juvenal, Julius and the Greek Grammar. Cambden for brevity, and beside the Greek testament (viz) Luke and the Acts of the Apostles, some part of Isocrates, Lucian's dialogues, Hesiod, Homer and somewhat of Theocritus, or other according to the schoolmaster's discretions. Theames & Orations, and for Hebrew as the schoolmaster pleases.

Plenty of good sense about the building of the school and the separation of the older pupils from the younger (for the masters' sakes, not theirs) but a programme of classical learning that seems, to say the least of it, ambitious.

A good deal of this advice (which has not been given in full) was incorporated into the rules, and these were — inevitably — both more detailed and often more practical than the preliminary advice had been. After saying that the school should provide free education for 25 pupils, the very next rule said that no boy should be admitted who had 'any noisome or infectious disease' — there speaks the sound sense of someone who knows all the epidemics that schools are prone to. The rules went on to lay down the hours: six till five in the summer, with three hours off in the middle of the day; half past seven till four in the shortest months of winter. Holidays: three weeks at Christmas, and a fortnight each at Easter and Whitsun, with half holidays on Thursday and after the boys had said their catechism on Saturday afternoons. Extra holidays could be given at the special request of any important visitor who gave 12d to buy books with, and parents could have their boys home for additional holidays of up to six days every three months, 'the time of harvest only excepted' when presumably any boy who was needed was free to go and help in the fields. Some things had priority.

There was a good deal about church going — twice a Sunday,

with the boys examined on the Sermon on Monday morning. (In the 1670's the Squire had a west gallery put up in the church, where the schoolboys could sit away from the congregation yet under the eye of the master.) And discipline:

> That no Scholar shall at any time with Knife or otherwise howsoever cut notch deface or break the windows forms Seats Tables Desks Table of Orders . . . but shall have exemplary punishment given him by the Master for deterring of others . . .
>
> The Master shall have especial care of the decent department of the Scholars and shall exemplarily punish misdemeanors especially swearing Cursing Lying Stealing filthy or obscene talking or acting Gaming for anything of a price and foul or uncivil Language to any person and in especial manner Shall diligently endeavour to see the Lord's day kept free from any prophanation as much as in him lieth . . .
>
> That if any Boy of the said School Shall be disobedient Stubborn vitious or exemplarily bad after several admonitions and due Correction or shall after a fair time of trial prove unteachable . . . shall afterwards be dismissed from the School.

Another draft of the rules sensibly adds

> That they abstain . . . from fighting quarrelling & bargaining & from lying swearing or stealing, from climbing trees or any high places for nests, apples &c from fishing or washing [i.e. bathing] except 5 or 6 more be present if under ye age of 14 . . .

There was less about the actual curriculum, and it seems likely that John Cartwright realised how few boys' parents would want them to go through the full course of a classical education since he provided merely

> that the Master apply himself diligently to teach all the Boys admitted to read write and take account well and afterwards if they be not removed to teach them the knowledge of the Latin and Greek tongues.

The master could supplement his stipend by taking paying pupils as well, though if the total numbers in the school rose above 50 he was expected to pay an assistant — an usher — out of his profits. In practice, it is hard to see how one man could teach even half that number single-handed, when their ages ran from 8 (the minimum age at entry) to 15 (free scholars could stay for up to seven years) so that boys of all ages might be at any stage in any subject. But that is what the rules said.

Those who advised John Cartwright about the new school clearly envisaged that before moving on to the Grammar School the children should have already been grounded in reading. Throughout the eighteenth century there was always someone who was being paid a few pounds for teaching 'the poor children'. As often as not, this person did some other job as well; Thomas Marsh, who lived on the Banbury Road, was a cobbler as well as schoolmaster in the middle of the century, and cobblers were often among the more educated and thoughtful men: sitting at a last all day and able to go on working while talking to visitors or workmates, one had more opportunities for improving oneself (and others) than by working in the fields. Eighty years before, while a Mr. Harris had received £5 a quarter for teaching in the Grammar School, Elizabeth Goodyer received 8s 2d a month 'for teaching poor children'. Probably all the schooling they got was enough to enable them to pick their way through the Bible, the Creed and the Catechism, but even that was something. Of the later history of the Grammar School we know very little, and it must have continued throughout the eighteenth and early nineteenth centuries an existence of humdrum obscurity. But the payments by the squire for the basic, primary education of the village children were to be the foundations on which, in the nineteenth century, a properly organised village school was to be built.

By the eighteenth century, the school was already a village institution. The church, of course, had been one for centuries longer than that, and there must have been few villagers who did not attend it each Sunday, many of them probably twice. Some probably relished the sermons, particularly when they were preached by someone as good as Wilde or Wasse; anyone of intelligence in the village must have felt at times a lack of intellectual stimulus, and a good sermon, well delivered, was thought-provoking and a matter of entertainment at the same time. Most villagers probably attended church as a matter of course; it was staying away that would have cost them a positive decision, not (as in these days) going. But it can scarcely have escaped the notice of any of them that the parish church, by the early eighteenth century, was in a deplorable condition.

Things had been bad when Thomas Drope died. The archdeacon, soon afterwards, sent one of his officials to examine the building and his report is of six, densely-written pages that (apart from providing an excellent account of how the old church was furnished and fitted up) were a damning catalogue of neglect. There were the purely superficial deficiencies to begin with — half the necessary books of prayers were missing, the old clock was past repair, there was no poor-box, windows were broken or stopped up with boards, pews and seats were shoddy and shabby, and the general effect was clearly one of dilapidation and decay. But there were more serious things than that, and phrases like 'dangerously out of repair', 'in need of a butteris', 'wants paving', 'wants slating' are freely scattered about. The archdeacon's man did add that the chancel was not in so bad a state, because Mr. Burdyn the rector had a note of what was needed and had begun work. But there is no doubt that the church was in need of major repairs, and the year 1637, when the report was made, was scarcely an auspicious time to start putting things to rights.

Things seems to have dragged on through the seventeenth century and into the eighteenth, the chancel perhaps better maintained than the nave (since the maintenance of the chancel was the parson's responsibility, the nave the parish's) and with matters not helped by a long standing dispute between the squire and the church-wardens about responsibility for the gutter between the nave and the Shakerley chapel: the squire said the gutter was the village's, the church wardens said it was the Lord of the Manor's, with the result that it remained neglected, the water pouring in, for years. By 1720 the fabric of the church was clearly in a very bad state indeed.

It probably required a parson with the dynamism of Joseph Wasse to get something done about it, and what Wasse did — or rather, what the squire, a contractor from Brackley and Edward Wing of Aynho did, in their capacities as paymaster, builder and architect — was to pull down the church and rebuild it. It was almost certainly a decision that was forced on them. From 1720 onwards Edward Wing, whose normal employment was as a carpenter, was spending more and more time 'propin of the church', culminating in three and a half days' work in November, 1722. Though the decision to rebuild was not formally taken until August 1723, it seems likely from the amount of stone that was carried that it had been anticipated some time before. The churchwardens, too, had bought a new book in 1720 specially to record the building work that was going on, so they must have anticipated a major operation.

The accounts begin with the purchase of quantities of timber, and 9s 6d to William Knott the blacksmith

> for mending the woorke men tooles that digd stone for y^e use of y^e church

Those farmers who had waggons to spare drew stone from the

THOMAS SON TO WILLIAM
CARTWRIGHT BY URSULA
DAUGHTER TO FERDINANDO
LORD FAIREAX

9. Thomas Cartwright in 1720–25
Traditionally attributed to Thomas Hudson, but (unless Thomas Cartwright
was unusually conservative in his costume) probably by another painter.

AYNHO

1 View of the house &c
The Cartwright Esq taken
the further [...] of the [...]

10. T[...]
By Peter Tillemans. The Park w[...]
1700, and the elm walks may ha[...]
very large, and the last of them s[...]
remodelled by Thomas Archer f[...]
it. One of the horsemen in the f[...]
hounds fo[...]

21

by Thomas Cartwright around
:d by him: the trees are not yet
the 1950's. The house has been
rtwright, and a storey added to
ıy be intended for him, and the
beagles.

11. William Ralph Cartwright as a boy
By Gainsborough, c.1785, when William Ralph Cartwright would have been
about 14.

quarries at Fritwell; Edward Homan was paid 2s 4d a load; George Bower was paid variously, 2s 4d or 6d a day; and James Marshall, who carried stone by 'gift cart' — a feudal survival somewhat similar to that agreement whereby John Spencer had undertaken to fetch coal from Warwick — was compensated 3s 6d when the axletree of his cart broke under the load. And there were numerous smaller payments for all the little jobs incidental to major building operations

> Peter Jeffs 0-7-6 for 3 whellbarrow whells
> John Borton & John Baylis 0-13-2 for digging a saw pit
> Thomas Jennens 0-7-6 for a grind ston for ye use of ye church

Indeed it seems as though it was already a foregone conclusion that the old church was to come down. For when the Commission appointed by the Bishop to consider the local proposals met in the old church, on Monday and Tuesday, 20th and 21st August, Edward Wing was ready with his drawings to show the Commissioners, and with the expert evidence to show that

> The Parish Church of Aynho is a very antient building and that notwithstanding the Great Charge and expense the parishioners have been at in repairing the same through length of time the same became so much decayed and ruinous that to repair it and render it a place for the Exercise of Religious Worship would be a burthen too heavy for the parishioners to bear.

The Commissioners consisted of various diocesan officials, a few local gentlemen and clergy, of two masons, Francis Blencowe and Joshua Wigson, and of two carpenters, William Bennet and Edward Wing. Wing opened the proceedings — pre-empted them, in fact — by describing in detail the new church he had designed. How large it was, how many it would seat, and the provision he had made for the Cartwright tombs in the south chancel aisle. Then the masons spoke up, testifying that they had

> viewed the parish church of Aynhoe and examined into the ruins and decaye thereof and that they verily believe it cannot be repaired but must be pulled down . . . If a church be built according to the said Modells or Draughts the same will be very beautyfull convenient & sufficient to hold all the inhabitants of the Parish.

After that there cannot have been any doubt about the outcome. The gentlemen of the Commission were unanimous: provided that the inscriptions and monuments from the old church were kept, the building might be demolished and the new one built. Only the old tower was to be preserved, whose condition was less parlous than the rest of the fabric. Edward Wing himself went slightly further, and, either for himself or for a record for Mr. Wasse or the Squire, he drew a plan of the old building before it went, a most unusual piece of antiquarianism for the period and one for which we must be thankful.

This is a good point at which to say something more about Edward Wing, since he is probably only one among many villagers who were prevented by the circumstances of their birth from achieving all that they might have been capable of. The wonder is that he got as far as he did. His grandfather was a shepherd, and his father, John Wing, was the leading carpenter in the village from about 1665 to the early eighteenth century, and capable of modest work in stone as well. Edward was John Wing's eldest son, born in 1683, and in the mid 1690's there are already payments to John Wing 'and his boy' for work about the estate. There is a stone set in the park wall on which Edward Wing has cut his name in careful, firm Roman capitals, and the date Jany 20, 1702. The wall itself was built by the same Francis Blencowe, contractor of Brackley, who later on sat as one of the church commissioners and who thereafter built the new church, and perhaps Edward Wing had been working for him. Or perhaps, because he would have been 18 or 19, he was celebrating coming out of his apprenticeship. Whatever prompted him, he was a young man of talent, and one wonders what sort of a future he saw for himself.

It is impossible to discover where he learnt the quite competent draughtmanship that he showed in his designs for the new church, and it is indeed conceivable that these drawings are not by his hand. He may have profited from the work that was going on at the big house in the early years of the new century, where Blencowe was making additions and alterations to the designs of Thomas Archer. Edward Wing visited London at least once during the months before the Commissioners met, and in London his brother John had been apprenticed as a bricklayer. It is almost certain that Edward's visits must have been for advice in his great undertaking, and one would very much like to know whose he sought.

Aynho church was Wing's great opportunity — an opportunity when he was already 40. It has been described quite adequately as 'a rustic attempt to build something after the style of the churches erected in London under the "Fifty New Churches" Act of 1711.' So it is, a pleasant building in a sort of bumpkin Baroque, and it is likely that Edward Wing was working at the limits of his talent.

For one thing, there is no record of any earlier building by him, and nothing else in the village that seems likely to be (unless he built any of the ordinary village houses). And for another, on his next, and last known, building he came badly unstuck.

His second building was at Fenny Stratford, where he designed another church, this time for the antiquarian Browne Willis. There were two reasons why he got the job. First, it must be no coincidence that the vicar of Newbottle, who was also a member of the Aynho church Commission, was a Mr. Willis — though he seems not to have been a very close relation of Browne Willis's. In any case Browne Willis was a friend of Joseph Wasse's, and had been coming through Aynho for years — in 1707 he was at Astrop, a little rural spa next door to Newbottle, taking the waters. Through one or another of these men, Edward Wing must have been introduced to the antiquary. And what may have also appealed to Browne Willis was that Wing had made a plan of the old church at Aynho before its destruction.

Edward Wing provided the drawings for the new church at Fenny Stratford, and he and a partner called Round carried out the carpentry while a bricklayer called Daniel Eastmont was responsible for the masonry — Fenny Stratford church is of brick, with stone dressings. But three years after it was started, Wing got the sack. The accusations against him, from his fellow contractors, from the townsmen of Fenny Stratford and ultimately from Willis himself, were such that if only half were true he could hardly have carried on. His workmen spent all day getting drunk. The woodwork was severely defective, and the classical detail incorporated in the panelling at the chancel end, completely illiterate. He left unpaid bills on all the tradesmen of the town, and vastly overcharged Willis who had to submit his accounts to arbitration. And what makes one suspect, slightly, that perhaps the Aynho drawings are not Wing's unaided work is that a signed drawing by him for Fenny Stratford is a cruder drawing altogether. It is conceivable that in the design for Aynho he may have had assistance, and certainly one has Blencowe to thank for the fine quality of the masonry. It is a pity, having sown seeds of doubt about Wing's competence, that the original woodwork at Aynho, by which one might have judged him more fairly, has almost all been destroyed in Victorian alterations.

The rest of the story is rather sad. Wing continued to be employed locally; two successive entries in the Squire's accounts for

1729 are payments of 12s 6d to him for making a plan of a house in Bloxham, and 6d for making a case to carry plate up to London. He had married twice, his first wife dying a year after marriage, and of his five children by his second wife, four predeceased him. He appears from time to time in the ordinary, day-to-day life of the village. In 1744 he was fined 3s 4d for keeping a tippling-house, though that did not prevent his serving as parish clerk, and he held other village offices as well; whatever his shortcomings, his clearly superior education marked him out as a useful member of the village community. He seems never to have owned any property, nor to have made a Will, and he died in 1755 of a cancer of the throat. It is an unhappy story, and it must have been all too typical of villagers who for lack of training and opportunity did not achieve what their talents might otherwise have gained for them.

But to return to the church. With the Faculty for the new building issued in September 1723, work could begin in earnest. Demolition did not take Blencowe and his men long, though there were some operations to be done with more care: slates to be removed from the porches and saved, woodwork to be taken out and sold, and bones to be re-buried with as much reverence as circumstances allowed. The work of demolition probably went on through the winter (and through the smallpox epidemic); by the spring of 1724 scaffolding was up and masons and carpenters were hard at work, while by the autumn work had gone so far that ironwork for the windows could be fetched from Towcester and a load of wainscot for the interior from Oxford. That winter the windows were stuffed with straw: the glass, from Stratford, had already arrived but was not placed in the frames until the following spring. By September 1725 the plastering was finished and the pews were being painted, Thomas Hobcroft was paid 2s 3d for three days 'a Clening the Church' and all was done.

It was fast work: two years from the issue of the faculty to the completion. All told, the cost had been some £1,600, apparently advanced by the Squire. An inscription on a tie-beam records the church's rebuilding by Thomas Cartwright, 'The Pios Patron and Generours Benefactor.' Certainly he must have given a good deal, though he was able to recoup some of it by the Manor Court's permitting the ploughing up of parts of the Commons and the letting of this as arable for four years to various of the village farmers in order to raise funds for the building.

The inside of the church has been much altered since then. Later generations have treated it badly, often disapproving of it because it is not gothic, which some people (particularly the Victorians) have considered the only true style for a Christian church. They ignore those splendid churches in London, built by Wren, Hawksmoor and others in the sixty years after the Great Fire, and it is as a country cousin of these that Aynho church may best be appreciated. It is not a distinguished building, but it is decent and respectable, well suited to the kind of worship of the Church of England in the eighteenth century. It is the more remarkable when one considers the background of Edward Wing, its architect, and it is satisfactory that after so long one villager, anyway, has so permanent a memorial.

The rebuilding of the church may have been partly the result of a new feeling of unity among Aynho's villagers. It probably also did something to create such a feeling. Such sentiments were certainly necessary, since for sixty years past there had been in Aynho a sizeable community of Quakers whose growth was probably as much the result of pastoral neglect by Dr. Longman and Mr. Hutton as the fruit of their own efforts. But whatever the reasons, from the 1650's onwards there was a thriving body of Friends in Aynho, and the authorities regarded them with the gravest suspicion. Nor is it difficult to see why.

To some extent they asked for trouble. They went into the 'steeple houses' and denounced ministers they disapproved of. They did not have their children baptised. They threw legal proceedings into confusion by refusing to take the oaths prescribed by law. They refused to pay tithes to the parson, to serve in the militia, or to take their hats off to the squire. The authoritarian government of the Commonwealth, and the Restoration government anxious to suppress all possible causes of public disorder, must both have regarded the Quakers' antics as thoroughly subversive. Even the excellent Robert Wilde, in his encomium on General Monck, brackets Quakers and rebels together

> He took Rebellion rampant by the throat
> And made the canting Quaker change his note

For thirty years after 1659 the Quakers of Aynho were persecuted with vigour, and the persecution only served to strengthen their convictions.

In 1659 a labourer, John Brett, spent some months in Northampton gaol for refusing to pay a small tithe. Next year he was seized again, this time by soldiers, and he and John Borton were marched off to a Justice to take the Oath of Allegiance. They refused: taking oaths was against their consience, and once more they were packed off to prison. Soon they were in fresh trouble, together with Edward Hawley, a shepherd, and John Hobcroft, labourer, when each was fined 1s a time for staying away from church. The churchwardens, Peter Tims and old Henry Letch, had to come to their houses and distrain their possessions. Nor were women treated better: Margaret Parker, a widow with three children, was kept in prison for over two years for refusing to pay tithes,

> amongst thieves murderers and whorish women and some accounted witches

and during all this time she was not allowed to see her friends, only to speak to them through the prison door.

In 1673, a meeting at Edward Hawley's house gave the authorities the chance to bag the whole set of them who owed tithes — all those who had been in trouble already, together with Timothy Burberow, Roger Priest, Thomas Mercer a hempdresser and several others. Acting on a Justice's warrant, the constable and his men came in force. From Timothy Burberow they discharged a cow and a calf; from Thomas Mercer they took 8s-worth of hemp which he had been dressing for other people. The fines came to less than the value of the goods seized, and were paid in the end, the richer Friends paying for the poorer: Timothy Burberow paid Roger Priest's and Margaret Parker's as well as his own; John Borton paid for three other people.

Yet the Friends were irrepressible. In 1683 and 1684 the ecclesiastical authorities found that the Burberows, the Mercers, John and Mary Hobcroft and a number of other people had refused to take Communion at Easter. Richard Lyne had kept his hat on during service and had had to be told several times to behave reverently; he was also accused of having withheld an acre of land belonging to Dr. Hutton's glebe, charged with neglect of his office as churchwarden and with failing to hand over his accounts, and to add insult to injury a brief note described him as 'lewd'. Whether he was or not, the authorities easily equated Quakerism with vice. William Goodyer and Edward Letch had also behaved badly during a service, and Edward Letch was excommunicated by the Bishop and had to ask for Absolution. Three others had been carried off once more to Northampton gaol, including Timothy Burberow, this time for not 'sprinkling his children'.

The situation must have been extremely difficult. The village officials, the constables, tithing men (the constables' assistants), and churchwardens were all close neighbours of the village Quakers, and they must have disliked their position as much as the Friends did. Perhaps more: at least the Friends derived a moral satisfaction from following their principles, whereas the village officials probably obtained none whatever from administering the law. Thomas Norris, one of the churchwardens in 1684, was seriously admonished for not presenting the offenders. The Quakers must have appeared to their neighbours as both thoroughly good and thoroughly perverse, and attitudes must have ranged from admiration to exasperation. On the other hand there were probably some conforming villagers who shared the authorities' view of the Quakers as a body subversive of authority, and maybe more who paid their tithes and resented the Quakers' high-minded refusal to do so.

Relief came in the 1680's, when James II (in part as an excuse for relieving Catholics, who suffered worse persecution than the Quakers did) issued a Declaration of Indulgence, releasing from the effects of the various penal laws all those dissenters, Catholics and Quakers included, who could produce proof of their loyalty, and ordering the release from prison of all those who had been put in gaol by the Bishops for such church offences as not taking Communion. The Declaration was generally unpopular: Nonconformists themselves generally hated Catholics even more than they resented their own disabilities, and it was some time before anyone in Aynho took any action about the local Quakers. But news probably travelled fairly slowly, and it may have taken time to get legal advice on how those Friends who were still in prison were to be got out of it.

Eight months later a certificate was signed by the churchwardens and overseers, the constable and almost a score of village people 'Inhabitants of Aynho . . . and Neighbours Antient' on behalf of Burberow, Mercer and Fowler, three who were still in prison, whose offences they thought were 'pardonable' under the Royal Warrant. The Friends were still at risk; they could still be sued for debt, and Timothy Burberow was soon in trouble again when Dr. Hutton demanded nine years' arrears of tithe with triple damages. The damages alone seem to have amounted to £50, and the squire's bailiffs were at the same time on to him for back rent. For the rest, however, the tithe collectors came each year and took whatever they thought was right of shop goods, corn or hay to the amount that was due. Even as late as 1813 they took a mare worth £20 from Mary Wycherley for tithe of £13. 6s, and later returned with

£6. 14s which they left on her table.

Several things contributed to the decline of the Quakers. In part it was probably the advent of a better rector and the forging of a better relationship between the parson and his flock. In part it was probably the very decline of persecution that made the Quakers cease to appear as martyrs and rather to be accepted as just another group of villagers, less attractive in their way of life for being less dramatised. In part it was the more even tenor of life of the eighteenth century: the ferment of the seventeenth that had thrown up the Friends was giving place to a greater acceptance of the established order. In later years nonconformists do occasionally appear in the village — an anabaptist in the eighteenth century, a 'methody' in the nineteenth, and well into that century there were Quakers, the Wycherleys, running the village shop. But for the most part the villagers seem quietly to have accepted the established church.

The difficulties that the authorities had with the Friends lead on naturally to one last topic that needs to be discussed: law and order. The job of maintaining the law was the duty of the Constables and their officers. The Constables, unlike the other village officials, were not strictly speaking village officers, though they served for the village: they were appointed not by the Lord of the Manor nor by the Manor Court nor by the Parson but by the Justices of the Peace, and though they were responsible for bringing to justice those that had offended against the Orders of the Manor Court, their larger responsibilities were to see that the Laws of the Land were properly administered and obeyed. And they had plenty to do, not generally with large crimes (of which there were very few) but with strangers passing through the village.

There were always numbers of travellers on the roads, and though the inns provided accommodation for the respectable, who had a few pence to share a bed or a shilling or so for a bed of their own, there were wayfarers besides these. As early as the 1630's the archdeacon's official, reporting on the state of the church, had said

> The North porch wants paving. And there is a very convenient place wherein a door might well be hung and kept shut on nights to keep out Rogues and Vagrants from lodging there and from prophaning that holy place, which they are accustomed often to do by reason that the Town stands in a great thoroughfair and upon an out skirts of the Shire, so that they can quickly from thence escape out of the reach of any Justice of the County.

These the Constable was obliged to see on their way. They were a nuisance, and were to be got rid of as soon as possible, though he had to give them help of a penny or two for their maintenance. The numbers of these poor travellers were often extremely high. In 1681, for instance, there were never fewer than six in a month, and that in August when all available hands could find work in the harvest. The total for that year was no less than 185, and that was probably not in any way exceptional. In the eighteenth century the numbers are not recorded — we have only one Constables' Book for Aynho, and that stops at 1709 — but they probably continued high. There were soldiers, too, to be assisted on their way to join their Companies or travelling home after their discharge, and since people were not expected to travel on the Sabbath, if they arrived late on a Saturday night they would have to be kept until Monday morning. Soldiers were about more at some times than at others: in the late 1680's, with James II's throne tottering and with half the country fearing another Civil War, there were numbers of them passing through:

> Paid for the releef of a Soulder that had Orders had lodged al night
> Pd for the Reeleef of 7 soulderes that had Orders & lodged from
>   Saturday till Munday
> Paid for ye taking of 10 horses and that i was warnd to pres when
>   ye dragons com up

Many of the travellers that the Constable assisted were people with passes — people with a piece of paper from the Constable of the previous village saying that they were on their way to their own places of settlement. Others were vagrants, people without passes, perhaps without any settlement even and thus with nobody who could be held responsible for them. Others again possibly did have passes, but found it more congenial to traipse from one village to another, picking up a bit of casual work when and wherever the season and their inclinations suited them to it, rather than having to return as paupers to the daily grind of their legal homes. Vagrants were to be despatched even faster than those who had passes, and for good measure were supposed to be whipped before they were sent on. It was all very well for the gentlemen in Parliament, whose ideal of Society was one where everyone was in his place and there was a place for everyone, to make such laws as these, but in practice the Constables must often have had qualms. People might have been turned out of employment far from home, they might be genuine wayfarers with no idea of where they were born, they might have been travelling tinkers or packmen, used to a life on the road and fallen on bad times, or labourers driven to the road by desperation at the difficulty of finding work in their own home parishes. We have seen Edward Jarvis hauled before the Manor Court for neglecting to punish vagrants. Strictly speaking, the Manor Court was exceeding its powers in so acting, but the Chief Constable of King's Sutton Hundred could and did present the Aynho Constables before the Justices at Quarter Sessions since

> These Constables have had warning sufisent from mee and likewise they are very negligent in punishing vagrants according to the statute made in that behalfe

They did, however, occasionally do their duty

> Pd for whiping fore vagerents   1s

and one hopes that when they did, the recipients deserved it.

There were stocks to be maintained, thanks to which they still stand close to the turn of the Deddington road

> Paid to Willi: Knott for one work about the Stocks   0 : 0 : 4d
> Willi: Borton for mending the Stocks
> Willi: Swetnam for mending the ironwork   0 : 3 : 0d

and they were put to use

> Spent upon the tithing men & myself when I set Philip East in the
>   stocks   0 : 1 : 4d

It is not recorded what Philip East was set in the stocks for, and the fact that two blacksmiths and a carpenter had first to be paid for putting the stocks in order suggests that they were not used very much.

There was little serious crime, though there were occasional disturbances

> Pd for sum men for ading and assistin when the Soulder broke the
>   windows at Norises   0 : 1 : 4d

and occasionally offenders to take to the Justices when some more serious offense was suspected

> Paid in Expenses for the Caring of a Man that was taken upon
>   Suspicion of Felloney to ye Justice   0 : 2 : 0d

while more rarely still there were excitements that were probably spoken of for years afterwards

> Pd when wee tane the too hiee wayemen

when the expenses came to over £2. 10s. On occasions when a crime had been committed, such as a theft, and the culprit could not immediately be taken or was thought to have fled the village, there was the expense of Hue and Cry — an ancient practice that still carried on, whereby men would be sent, on foot or horseback, at speed to warn neighbouring villages that dangerous criminals were at large.

It was probably only towards the end of the eighteenth century that the authorities began to be seriously concerned about what must have been the commonest of all the village crimes — poaching. A law of 1670 had laid down that only gentlemen or substantial landowners might hunt game, and Thomas Cartwright, at least when he was a young man in the years around 1700, had kept a pack of beagles. The dog-kennel at the Warren, later used as an isolation hospital, may have been where the pack had lived. The keener the squire was on game himself, the severer he was likely to be on poachers, and he was not prepared to rely on the law alone to suppress them. In 1732 he caused John Buckingham of Croughton to be bound over in the sum of £15 not to keep 'guns nets dogs or other instruments for destroying conies', and in 1726 Richard Holyfield of King's Sutton had been similarly bound not to poach the fish in the Cherwell, 'whereas he has catched great quantities contrary to the law.' It is likely that there was a good deal more poaching later in the century, when living standards among the poor were falling and there was a growing need to supplement larders by whatever means might be found. The great age of poaching, so to speak, was the nineteenth century, and we shall come to that.

Little has been said so far of the squire's involvement with the village. The farmers and tradesmen did their business with the steward, and the squire was probably often absent: Thomas Cartwright, squire for seventy years, was one of the Members of Parliament for the County for almost fifty of those years, and his own inclinations as well as his parliamentary duties must have taken him frequently to Town. (The occasional formality of an election, incidentally, will have given him no trouble for Aynho, where scarcely anyone had a vote and where anyone who did would be certain to vote for him.) But he would greet familiar figures as he rode or drove through the village, and the villagers would stand aside for him as he walked from the church. Nor was what squire Thomas did by way of charity by any means negligible; in a typical year towards the end of his life — 1743 — the annual charity account came to £67. 19s, no small amount for the times, and includes entries for activities whose usefulness one can only applaud —

Thos. Smith for 5 weeks schooling for the boys	8s 3d
Thos. Marsh a bill for the boys shoes	15s 1d
Will. Baldwin for Boots	19s 6d
To put out Sam Peckover Apprentice	£12 0s 0d
The poor people for beer for 21 weeks	£1 1s 0d
Mr. Watkins to tend Ned Wing	£6 16s 6d

Squire Thomas is one of the family one feels one would like, hunting his beagles in his youth and a patron of the great Henry Purcell himself, in his mature age carefully nurturing the family property but liberally supporting people and customs worthy of support.

On his death in 1748 he was succeeded by his son William, already middle aged, who was squire for twenty years. His son, another Thomas, died a mere four years later in 1772, leaving as his heir a child of only a year old. This son, William Ralph Cartwright, was to live into the 1840's, to rule as squire for as long as his great-grandfather had, and to transform the village more radically than had any of his forebears. But it is at Eton we may meet him, just entering the Sixth, with his life before him, and his stepfather writing to him

> May School Honours be a Prelude to those of the University, and may these be followed by the Just Distinctions due to an Honest and Good Man upon the greater Stage of the World.

Chapter 10

Enclosure

The enclosure that William Ralph Cartwright undertook in the 1790's (or rather that his faithful and indefatigable agent, Robert Weston, undertook on his behalf) amounted to a revolution. It utterly changed the face of the fields, changed the course of most of the roads in the parish and led to the destruction of some thirty buildings. It was the prelude to everyone in the village becoming, in one way or another, the squire's man.

While we know every detail of the negotiations and the precise allocations of land made to everyone, in no surviving document did anyone write down why they were doing all this, and why between them the landowners of Aynho (chief among them the squire) should have agreed to spend nearly £2,000 in lawyers' fees, surveys, fencing and new roads, and to abandon the ancient strips that men had farmed for a thousand years in favour of a brand new landscape of enclosed fields — the fields of the present village. But though it is a pity that we do not have William Ralph Cartwright's thoughts on the matter or those of his agent Robert Weston, it is not difficult to guess at their motives.

Enclosure was taking place throughout the country, and was prompted almost everywhere by similar considerations. For farmers, these were to have fenced fields where they could graze what beasts or sow what crops they wished, to have their lands grouped conveniently together rather than scattered throughout the parish, and to have fields large enough to plough continuously rather than constantly to be moving from one strip to another. For landowners there was the obvious advantage of the higher rents to be had from such improved farms. For a squire like William Ralph Cartwright, there was also the kudos of being seen to be the owner of an improved, prosperous and up-to-date village.

Parts of the parish had been enclosed by Rowland Shakerley and by Richard Cartwright, but all the fields to the east still remained open. This is not because enclosure had not been thought of in the succeeding years. When Francis Burton had been the Cartwright steward in 1760 the idea had been floated, and it may only have been because of the deaths of three squires within thirty years that nothing was done. There may, though, have been some lack of drive in Burton himself. He seems to have been a melancholy man, readier to see difficulties than possibilities and, writing to squire William Cartwright about the obstacles he saw in his way, he concluded by hoping that Mr. Cartwright would not 'suffer any Inconvenience by the Death of such a poor miserable Cripple as I am become.' (In fairness to him, his life may not have been a happy one: his Will ran in a similar vein; in which he asked to be buried next to his Father and Mother and children, 'whose separation from me has been the great Affliction of a painfull Life, and a deserved Punishment for my Sins.') In practice, he foresaw problems cropping up over the Rector's tithes and the glebe; with Magdalen College; opposition from John Letch and the remaining freeholders; and he recalled unfortunate experiences in a recent enclosure at Hinton in the Hedges. In the event, the 'Miserable Cripple' was to outlive both Squires William and the second Thomas Cartwright and to remain as steward into William Ralph's minority. But that minority put an end to any possibility of enclosing for a good many years. Nothing more happened until 1791, and by that time Robert Weston had been the steward for fourteen years already.

Though we have to take on trust the motives of those concerned, no doubt there had already been considerable discussion between Weston and the young squire's mother, his step father Sir Stephen Cotterel and his other trustees. The trustees had been fortunate in any case in having been able to buy substantial amounts of village property during the minority. The last of the village yeomen, John Letch, died young in 1787, leaving his property 'for the benefit of his wife and children' on whose behalf his executors sold his land, the same land that his ancestors had farmed in the sixteenth century, to the young squire for £1,500. John Letch's younger brother had inherited other land that his family had bought more recently, and this he had sold to the Squire's trustees in 1784 when bankruptcy threatened him. Part of the Drope estate had passed to a young man in Fritwell, Drope Gough, who to judge by the speed at which he ran through his inheritance, thought himself a finer fellow than perhaps he was; in debt in 1786 for £1,600, this gave the Cartwright trustees the chance to buy yet more acres in Aynho on behalf of the young squire. By 1790 the squire owned 1,780 acres out of the 2,240 in the parish. Of these 268 belonged to the College and to the Parson's glebe, and since the squire was unlikely to be able to acquire these, there remained only 190 acres of farm land, belonging to fifteen different owners, that could hinder his becoming as complete a master of the village as he could hope to be.

But enclosure was a complicated business, not to be done overnight. Indeed, it could only be done at the right time of year, and then only after every care had been taken to ensure that everyone received his rights in the complex recasting of property that enclosure involved. The actual procedure was laborious, time consuming and expensive. It involved gaining the agreement in principle of those chiefly concerned; appointing Commissioners to oversee the survey and the subsequent redistribution of plots; assessing not only who owned what but putting a value on every holding, good land or bad; valuing each man's interest in the Commons; getting a Bill through Parliament to make possible the exchanges of freehold that would be necessary; apportioning the land to be enclosed in the fairest way between all those who had an interest in it; and finally (but not the least) the actual, physical business of grubbing up old hedges and planting new ones, and digging out old roads and re-aligning them. It was expensive as well as protracted: besides fees to Commissioners, surveyors and Parliamentary agents there was the cost of hedging and of fencing the new enclosures until the hedges were grown, and compensation to be paid to tenants for broken leases. These costs were divided in proportion between all the landowners of the village, and while the squire bore most of them he could probably better afford a few hundreds than the small freeholders could afford the few pounds that fell to their share.

Weston had been making preparations for some time before negotiations were begun in earnest with other owners. He had had the parish suveyed by a Mr. Russell of Brackley, and had been laying in quantities of timber for fencing. The College's tenant, Mr. Watkins, probably already knew what was in the wind when he received a letter from Weston, running in part:-

> 'The Inclosure of Aynho being now the wish of Mr. Cartwright and his friends, I am desired by Mrs. Cotterel [the squire's mother] to write to you upon that subject and to state what appears to them the best method to be adopted, if it meets with your approbation . . . It is proposed that three referees be appointed, the division made, and then apply to Parliament for an Act to confirm . . . One of the referees is left for your nomination, or with the College and you jointly, if they want to take any trouble in the business . . .

Watkins himself lived near Tamworth, and farmed the College Farm through Mr. Tibbetts, an under-tenant. His nominee as Commissioner was a Mr. Wyatt who lived even further off, near Burton on Trent, but Wyatt turned out to be a brisk and bustling person whose activity made up in part for the difficulties of distance. The next thing that would normally be done would have been to value the freeholders' lands, but there were to be delays before further progress could be made.

For one thing, Wyatt could not be got hold of at short notice: he was a busy man and booked up for months to come. For another, Weston himself was in need of a rest, and on Mrs. Cotterel's advice set off for a few weeks to Bath. And another problem was to require settlement before negotiations on the enclosure could begin.

In 1791 a Turnpike Act for improving the road between Aynho and Bicester had been passed. Improvement entailed re-alignment, and it had been intended originally that re-routing should coincide with the redistribution of lands at enclosure. Now, with Weston's illness, enclosure was to be delayed, the road was to go ahead, and the first that Watkins knew of his land's being affected was when Tibbetts his tenant wrote to tell him about it. He wrote to Weston

> Understanding from my tenant Tibbetts that a new road is now making from Aynho to Bicester & that by some alteration being made in the plan with a view to enable Mr. Cartwright to enlarge his Park, it will now go over a considerable portion of my land, I cannot help thinking it somewhat extraordinary that I have never been informed of it before.

Weston was most apologetic. He had been under the impression that the Turnpike Trustees' lawyers had already told Watkins all about it, it was he who had asked Tibbetts to write, and in any case only a quarter of an acre of the College Farm was involved. He continued, sincerely if ungrammatically,

> The smallness of the Injury done, the multiplicity of other concerns which occupy my attention, & the rectitude of my Intentions in doing Right by you and all others; and altho' I have failed in point of Propriety, be assured that nothing has or will be done to your Injury . . .

With Watkins mollified, Weston himself restored by his weeks in Bath, he felt able to tackle the next difficulty: that of the Rector's tithes. Here it was a question of whether the enclosure could be used as the occasion for ridding the squire's demesne lands of tithe payments once and for all, either by giving the Rector land in lieu, or by paying a lump sum. When Richard Cartwright had carried out the enclosure of 1619 the tithes on the demesne had been set at £60 a year (after parson Drope had succeeded in having them raised) and the point at issue now was whether the church could be given land of this value or whether with the redistribution of the land the value of the tithes had to be worked out all over again. This involved Weston in prolonged correspondence with the Bishop of Peterborough and at least one meeting with him; it was important for both sides to be satisfied with the outcome for, as a friend of Weston's put it,

> Do but consider how very disagreeable the Rector may not make himself in demanding Tithes in future times especially if Patron and Rector should fall out upon the quality of a Bottle of Wine or some more trivial circumstances.

Yet another problem was what share of expenses should be borne by old Mrs. Cartwright, William Ralph's grandmother, who had land in the village that had been settled on her on marriage as her jointure, and whether William Ralph could legally take the land and pay her an annuity instead.

What with these discussions and the delays that had already taken place it was the winter of 1791-2 before further progress could be made. But then Weston decided to move fast. The only time of the year that the Enclosure could be made and new allotments entered on was after harvest, when the fields were empty and before winter ploughing began. There was just time between midwinter and Michaelmas 1792 for getting the necessary Bill through Parliament, for making the redistribution and for getting the new plots set out on the ground. Weston had originally planned to get the distribution made and then the Bill passed to confirm it; now he resolved to do things the other way round. Parliament would rise before Easter, and there was still a good deal to do.

In the middle of January in the new year a notice was pinned to the church door formally announcing that the squire's trustees intended to apply for an enclosure act and summoning all landowners to a meeting at the Red Lion on the last Wednesday in the month. It is unlikely that anyone present expressed opposition. John Baker, the owner of the largest freehold apart from the squire and the College — a mere 79 acres — lived in Oxford and wrote to apologise for his absence, but added that he had perfect confidence that justice would be done him. 'I do not doubt but that you will do everything in your power to have matters adjusted right.' Watkins was probably also unable to attend; travel from Tamworth at that time of the year was not pleasant, and he was not the only man deterred by the weather; a day or two earlier Mr. Mabletoft the Rector had sent a note to Weston, apologising for not calling on him 'on account of the bad walking', though he lived only a couple of hundred yards away (admittedly Weston's daughter feared that poor Mr. Mabletoft was showing symptons of dropsy.) It is unlikely that the small owners who attended did more than nod their agreement to what the squire was proposing: to proceed as quickly as possible with the Enclosure.

The preparation of the Parliamentary Bill itself was by no means a simple matter, and however competent a land agent Robert Weston may have been he was out of his depth in his understanding of what could and what could not be incorporated in an Act of Parliament. Here he was entirely in the hands of parliamentary agents, a Mr. Walker and a Mr. Barwell. February and March were filled with correspondence between London and Aynho about tithes, turnpikes, old Mrs. Cartwright's jointure and other minutiae that tried Robert Weston's patience sorely. By parliamentary rules some things could be included in an enclosure act and others could not, but it was all very exasperating. 'There may be many things' he wrote 'which require great attention to place them in a form agreeable to the Rules of Parliament, but if the Substance is not in large measure preserved, the Bill will not answer the ends proposed.' Weston clearly found it hard to restrain his impatience with quibbling Parliamentary draughtsmen.

But all was ready at last, and by comparison with the difficulties in this century of getting a private Bill through Parliament one is amazed by the ease with which matters proceeded. On Monday, March 19th, the Bill received its first reading, and Barwell wrote to Weston to say that he hoped for its second reading on the Friday. A day or two later he wrote again to say that there was not a quorum, but this was not a serious set back: next week the Bill had its second reading and was sent to Committee. Here witnesses were called to testify that enough of the freeholders concerned had given their consent to the Bill and that the facts contained in it (the preamble saying who owned what) were correct. The Committee made a few amendments, the Commons gave it a third reading, and sent it to the Lords. Here it rapidly received two readings, went to Committee where Weston was called to give evidence, and on April 30th, only six weeks after its introduction, it received the Royal Assent. 'Soit fait comme il est desiree'. The next day the printer was ordered to send a hundred copies down to Aynho on the coach.

As had been agreed beforehand, the Act named three Commissioners: Wyatt, John Horseman the rector of Souldern (representing the church's interests; he had served on other enclosure commissions before), and Weston himself. Their powers were absolute. They were to be responsible for the preliminary survey, for the valuation of the land and for the subsequent allocation of holdings. They were to decide how much fencing was needed and who was to pay for it. They could fix the routes of all new roads and footpaths. They were to assess the compensation payable for broken leases, and who was to pay for what share of the legal expenses of the enclosure. They were to calculate the amount of tithes to be paid by each freeholder, using a complex formula involving the average price of wheat over the last fourteen years and the separate values of each man's holdings of meadow, pasture and arable. Unless they broke the law, there was no appeal from their decisions.

With the Bill passed, there was no further time to be lost. Within a week Weston wrote to Wyatt suggesting that the Commissioners should begin their work as soon as possible. Wyatt replied that he was busy until late June, but that there was plenty that Weston could get on with in the meantime and that there was still no reason why the new enclosures should not be entered upon at Michaelmas. The Commissioners held their first meeting on the last Tuesday in that month, and at Weston's invitation they made a good beginning by having dinner together at the Red Lion. Dinner over, each took his formal, solemn oath to deal fairly and honestly with all business relating to the enclosure, and they then adjourned until the next morning when their hard work began. A week later they could report great progress. They were already in a position to give Russell, the surveyor, the lines of the new roads to be staked out, and when they adjourned on the Wednesday Wyatt had enough confidence in the local men to absent himself from the next two meetings: affairs were in good hands.

On the last Sunday in August they pinned a notice to the church door. This contained a list of each freeholder's lands, and any mistakes were to be notified to the Commissioners. (This one may assume was a purely formal matter: the Commissioners must already have been in constant consultation with them all to ensure the accuracy of Russell's survey.) Each owner was asked to submit a written statement of where he wished his new allotment to be, and all were told that common rights were to cease forthwith, leases at rack rents on October 10th. And a notice was placed in the Oxford and Northampton papers about the new roads: that anyone who wanted to see a plan of their new line could see it at the Red Lion, while if anyone had any complaints they could make them to the Commissioners at their next meeting on 11th September.

Either Russell and the Commissioners had done their work well, or else those small owners who might have wanted to object were too overawed to do so. Probably a bit of both: there is no reason to suppose that the Commissioners were other than scrupulously fair, and any villager who might have preferred the old order to the new probably had no reason for complaint save his private sentiment. If indeed there were any who had such an attachment to the old way of doing things: we know absolutely nothing about how the villagers felt about the enclosure, and though the absence of any recorded objections cannot be taken as demonstrating their support for it, the fact that the undertaking was being done on behalf of the principal landowner cannot be taken as proving that it was to the villagers' disadvantages. Only one objection was voiced at the Commissioners' September meeting, and that was from a Mr. Porter, not even a villager, who pointed out the value of a bridle path along the eastern boundary of the village, past the Warren and Old Down, and which had been left out of the road map. This the Commissioners ordered to be reinstated.

At the end of the following week they could give Russell the first of the boundaries of the new allotments and begin calculating the amounts of fencing to be put up by each owner. (These boundaries are now hedges, of course, but initially there had to be double fences between the new fields since the hedges, of quickthorn, would take a few years to thicken up. And the apportionment of fencing costs was very necessary to avoid argument about responsibility for boundaries between adjoining owners.) On September 23rd another notice was placed on the church door: all rights in the open fields would cease on 10th October when the new fields were to be entered on.

That winter of 1792–93, the fields must have presented to the villagers an extraordinary appearance. Lines of stark fences dividing neat, rectangular fields where previously the old irregular furlongs had been separated by grass balks, tracks and the piled up earth of the headlands where ploughs had turned for a thousand years. Great areas were being ploughed by one farmer in one operation rather than as a dozen different operations by a dozen different men — whole, uniform stretches of brown earth turned up together rather than the corduroy-stripe appearance of the open field furlongs. Ancient trees and hedgerows were torn up; ancient footpaths no longer ran, and new roads cut across ancient fields. And what the villagers, Robert Weston or the young squire thought about it all we cannot ever know.

For a year or two, at least, it meant plenty of work, and this at a time when village unemployment was rising fast. In November Sir Stephen Cotterel, William Ralph Cartwright's step-father, wrote to him at Oxford —

> Now for the chapter of Aynho, where we spent almost a fort-night, and where I think I made considerable advances in the science of Inclosing — Everything I have to impart to you from there is good and pleasureable. The Inclosure goes on rapidly, and we have had the fairest Season, and have made the best use of our time for planting quicks, etc. Not less than 100 men (as I under-stand from Weston) are in your employment, and I had great pleasure several mornings in going out with him to see them digg-ing etc. — the scene was perfectly new to me and pleasing. Perhaps the idea that the labour was to tend ultimately to the advantage and comfort of my friend presented itself at the same time to my imagination. Further particulars I leave to him to explain, who means to write to you shortly, especially if he bring to conclusion a Treaty which is on foot for the purchase of Mr. Watkins' estate at Aynho: in which case you will have nothing but small and trifling proprietors to interfere with you in that quarter.

The reference to Mr. Watkins' estate was to Weston's attempt to buy out Watkins' interest in the College Farm on his master's behalf, and in the end, after protracted correspondence, they failed to agree a price. But it was scarcely a serious flaw in William Ralph Cartwright's ownership of the village, though it was the largest holding — some 208 acres — that was not his own. After that came John Baker's 79, the parson's glebe which amounted to 60, and then 40 owners who had 110 acres between them. For most of these their holdings comprised no more than a few perches of gar-den ground around their cottages, and over the next 25 years the squire was to buy up nearly all of them.

At the enclosure itself he had been able, by exchanges of land with other owners, to enlarge his park. In the east he was able to acquire the furlongs beyond the Port Way and up to the line of the Bicester Road: the Portway now runs in a dank ravine between high walls (screening the passers-by from the gaze of people in the squire's garden) and the building of these walls was probably among the improvements done by the men Sir Stephen had watched. On the west the changes were very much more radical since they entailed the demolition of a good many houses and other buildings

Map 7. Disposition of roads and lands after the 1792 Enclosure.

Cartwright Demesne and Enclosures

Magdalen College Enclosures (College Farm)

Glebe

Other Proprietors' Enclosures

as the map on page 186 shows. Before Enclosure the Deddington road ran due west as a continuation of Mansion Street, passing on the left the old house where the Hanslopes had lived and which was now occupied by Robert Weston. Now its line was shifted to the present one, over the site of houses and cottages that had once formed an additional village green, and where these and other houses stood the land was taken into the Park. As for the villagers who had rented houses here, they were mostly re-housed in new cottages along the Charlton road (numbers 64–71), along the main road itself (20–24) and above the Causeway (47–50). Nice new houses, but smaller than some of the ones that had been demolished, and it is an open question whether the inhabitants felt themselves any better off.

The greatest single object in enclosing had been the re-arrangement of the squire's farms into economic and conveniently run units. A secondary result was that it now became worthwhile to build new farm houses and farm buildings in the fields themselves. Previously, any farmer whose strips lay haphazard throughout the open fields (as all farmers' strips did) found it most convenient to live at the centre of them in the village itself. Now, to serve the new, compact farms set out in the newly enclosed land there were new farm houses built where there were already farm buildings (as at the Warren), new farm buildings where there already stood suitable houses (as at Upper Grounds Farm) and both buildings and farm houses built where fields lay in a convenient block with no buildings to serve them (as at Nell Bridge Farm). And though in detail the leases of the new farms varied with the land that was leased, all had certain points in common that no doubt reflected both the best current practice and some elements of continiung local tradition. Meadows were not to be moved twice in a year on penalty of £2 an acre, nor ploughed except at a £10 an acre penalty. All dung and straw were to be laid or consumed on the farm. And a six-course, convertible rotation was required for the arable: turnips, barley, two years of clover and ryegrass, winter wheat and spring wheat. The present forms of the village farms are broadly those set out at this time, though some few fields have been added to one farm and taken away from another.

One of the most important questions for the historian of Aynho to answer is at the same time one of the more difficult. It is: what was the long term effect of the enclosure on the prosperity of farmers and villagers? Did it make it more difficult for a villager to own or to rent land? And how did it affect villagers' jobs? Many people, both at the time and later, had no doubts. Writing in general terms about enclosure in Northamptonshire in 1794, two years after the enclosure of Aynho, one widely-read commentator said as though it was a well-established fact:-

> Though several of those who occupy small farms must necessarily be removed, in order to enable the proprietor to class the land into farms of proper size, yet it is equally clear that a new set of people must be introduced, such as hedgers, ditchers, road-makers and labourers of every description.

It is likely, though, that in Aynho the change in villagers' conditions was a good deal less dramatic than these remarks suggest, and that the enclosure did no more than confirm changes that had been taking place over very many years.

The number of farms had been falling, and their size increasing, long before the enclosure. The table below summarises the changes over four centuries:-

Year	House-holds	Farms over 300 acres	100–300 acres	20–100 acres	Under 20 acres
1544	45?	1	1	19	6
1619	56		3	18	9
1744	127?		6	7	7
1794	140?		8	4	4
1822	160	1	5	3	3
1871	139	3	3	2	1

These figures speak for themselves. By the middle of the eighteenth century the number of households had doubled since Richard Cartwright's time, yet the overall number of farmers had already fallen sharply. The continuing growth of large farms at the expense of small and of smallholders seem not to have been affected dramatically by the enclosure. It may be that the 1794 farms (immediately after the enclosure) had been laid out without realising the full potential for reorganisation that the enclosure had offered, but it is likely that it was only in the nineteenth century that improved agricultural techniques and the need to invest in up-to-date machinery, buildings, and in the bulk purchase of artificial fertilisers, justified economically the further consolidation and growth of farms. When this happened, it happened at the expense of the medium sized farms; the numbers and size of the smallest were already negligible.

Not since the seventeenth century had any large proportion of villagers been farming. It is the decline of the yeomen that is illustrated in these figures, and their decline occurred long before

enclosure and for reasons unconnected with it. Those who cultivated a few strips for barley to feed a pig, or who had acquired a
cow's or a few sheep's commons for a hobby and to raise just a
little their standards of living, did not do so after the enclosure,
but there were never, for over a century before, more than a handful of such households as these.

The enclosure did nothing to accelerate the loss of the last
freeholders' few acres, though the factors that had long operated
to diminish the size and number of these holdings would continue.
Newly enclosed holdings were inherited and mortgaged as land
had always been, and small acreages were more often rented out
than farmed by their owners. The boom in farm incomes during
the wars will have helped small owners as well as large, and the
fact that difficult times followed, conditions that made it hard for
men to keep up mortgage payments and may have compelled them
to sell, had little to do with enclosure.

It is more difficult to say to what extent the enclosure was
responsible for a situation when – in the long run – there were no
longer any families of local origin farming Aynho land. One might
have expected that the Aynho farmers who were accustomed to
the old methods might not take kindly to the new. Two old tenants
of the squire's, Timothy Burberow and Susannah Prowett, did cease
farming, but Burberow was old and Mrs. Prowett was a dairy farmer, largely on old enclosed land of the squire's which was little
affected by the new Enclosure. Another, Thomas Wagstaff, died
about the time of the Enclosure, but his son, another Thomas,
took one of the new farms. Mary Letch gave up; she had rented
her dead husband's land after its purchase by the squire, and perhaps after the Enclosure she had no interest in taking a different
farm. Matthew Borton, Edward Dunn, Thomas Smith, Samuel
Mayo and Thomas Bygrave, the rest of the squire's principal
tenants, took newly enclosed farms at higher rents than before.
James Tibbetts, the tenant of the College farm, gave up some
additional land that he had formerly rented from the squire, but
continued farming the College lands after their enclosure.

Of these farmers, some were of old Aynho families, some
already 'foreign'. The Bortons, the Burberows and the Mayos had
been in Aynho for centuries, the Smiths and the Wagstaffs at least
since the early eighteenth century, the Bygraves and the Prowetts
since its middle years. Dunn and Tibbetts were relative newcomers.
By 1822, however, only Samuel Mayo still appears as an old village
name among the squire's tenants. Immediately after the enclosure,

two farms (the Warren and Lower Grounds) were let at higher rents than Cartwright farms had ever fetched before, and these were let to John Aris from Weedon Lois and to Edward Dunn, another outsider. It is not unlikely that the old farmers found it difficult to raise the capital that the new farms required; Matthew Borton, for instance, carried arrears of rent of £200 for thirty years, only gradually reducing the debt during the boom years after 1800.

In short, it does thus seem likely that Enclosure may have accelerated the letting of land to outsiders who could command capital that local resources could not. But one cannot prove this without knowing the exact circumstances of each farmer: there are many things that might lead a man to give up farming, age and the lack of an heir being but two. Even before 1792 so small a proportion of old Aynho families were farming that their decline can scarcely be called significant. Save for the village innkeepers, it had hardly been possible at any time in the last two centuries for an ordinary man to accumulate the capital needed to stock a farm.

The cottagers seem to have lost little by enclosure. Whatever common rights they may have enjoyed had apparently been extinguished long ago. Richard Cartwright, when he had enclosed land in 1620, seems to have agreed that in return for their loss of common grazing he would pasture twenty of the cottagers' cows on his own demesne. Long before the Enclosure the Cottage Cows' Commons, as they were called, were being let out by him to his tenant farmers. The cottagers may have received some compensation, perhaps by way of allotments, but whatever common rights cottagers still had were too insignificant to be noticed in the Enclosure award. They may have had the right to gather firing on the waste, but even that is not recorded. And despite the increasing employment, the balance of occupations was little altered. The number of heads of households recorded in the 1841 census as farm labourers is a little under half the total for the village — 66 out of 141 — and it seems that this represents very little change from the proportion a century before.

Enclosure, however, has for so long had such a bad name that it is natural to seek in it for the causes of the very real distress that prevailed in the village in the first decades of the new century. Certainly the newly enclosed farms could be worked with fewer labourers than could the old. Far less time was wasted on nonproductive tasks — in merely getting about from one strip to the next. But this economy of labour occurred simultaneously with a rapid growth in the village population, and while it was natural to blame the clearly identifiable, revolutionary event — the Enclosure — for the increasing distress, the growth of population which was its real root cause was less dramatic and so less clearly visible. The charge quoted at the beginning of this discussion, that enclosure led to the transformation of small farmers into labourers, seems to have little support in Aynho, and the partial contribution of Enclosure to unemployment is probably all that can be said against it from the villagers' point of view.

Chief among the positive results of the enclosure were the increased productivity of the enclosed farms and the higher rents paid for enclosed land. This was primarily of benefit to the squire, of course, though it must have helped every other owner. The same contemporary quoted already thought 8s. 6d. an acre a reasonable increase in rent for enclosed land, which amounted in some cases to a doubling. There was no advantage in this to landless labourers, but nothing to their disadvantage either. Lower rents would not have induced farmers to employ more men than they needed. The hard times of the new century were largely due to other factors, and these will be spoken of in the next chapter.

There was a loss by enclosure, though an intangible one: the loss occasioned when there was no longer the need for farmers to co-operate in framing orders for their mutual advantage and individual restraint, to discuss together their common needs and to make general concessions to the common good. The mixture of individualism and common purpose that had bound the village farmers together for their mutual benefit was now a thing of the past. Henceforth rules for farming were made by landlords and enforced by leases, and the only agreements a farmer need make were with the squire on one hand and with his labourers on the other.

Yet it would be wrong to stress this aspect of things, attractive though it is. The number of farmers had been steadily falling. It was many generations since the farmers had made up the majority of the village, and it is clear that they had always been active in preserving their own interests as a class even while they accepted the necessity of co-operating with their peers. Latterly, the whole traditional system of village government had been in decline. The entries in the Court Rolls (a book by now) cease in the 1760's; there are occasional later records of the Court's meeting, but one has the impression that the life had gone out of it. There had long been a slow falling-off in the number of new orders made and the number of villagers presented for the old, trivial, communal offences. Either the smaller number of farmers did not require such elaborate control, or enthusiasm for the old institutions was dying: probably both. Enclosure ended the need for communal farming and for the apparatus of its control, but one feels that in Aynho the ancient ways were being gradually forgotten and that few people cared.

This is not to say that elsewhere enclosure could not have a very much more dramatic effect on the village community. Where there were more small tenant farmers than in Aynho, or where the cottagers retained common rights that in Aynho they had long lost, enclosure could be a catastrophe, deserving all that contemporaries and later historians have written against it. In Aynho, however, a growing population and the policies followed by squires and farmers for two centuries past had achieved, gradually, the social revolution that elsewhere enclosure accomplished overnight. If (and it is a big If) a true village community had ever existed, one may mourn its loss, but in Aynho it had passed before the earliest record.

Chapter 11

Good Living and Hard Times

It seems probable (though such things are hard to measure) that in the course of the eighteenth century the rich of Aynho had been getting richer while the poor were getting poorer. Certainly, by 1800, while the birth rate and the poor rates were both increasing all over England by leaps and bounds, the farmers were making more money than ever before. The price inflation of the Napoleonic Wars suited them very well, and in numerous places besides Aynho, enclosure was enabling them to grow more to supply the increasing demand. And, of course, what was good for farmers was good for their landlords.

The squire himself, early in the new century, was putting the finishing touches to his inheritance by remodelling the great house. It was old when he came of age: basically it remained the house that William Marshall had designed to replace the building burnt in the Civil War, and though modernised by Thomas Archer fifty years later it was by now hopelessly old fashioned: the formality of seventeenth and early eighteenth century houses was quite out of tune with the easier, far less rigid way of life of the early nineteenth. A new drawing room, dining room and library were wanted, together with better bedrooms and stairs, and for the work the young squire engaged Sir John Soane, the most brilliant architect of the day, then at the height of his powers.

Soane called on William Ralph Cartwright in London in 1795, and at first the squire, probably ignorant of the ways of distinguished architects, thought Soane would merely produce some plans which the squire could then get carried out by someone else. This notion brought a slightly frosty letter from Soane, politely pointing out that he expected personally to supervise the execution of any work designed by him — and it was, presumably, on this basis that the house was remodelled between 1800 and 1805. The shell of Marshall's central block, with its upper floor by Archer, survived and still survives; the wings which Archer added were wholly remodelled by Soane, and none of Marshall's and little of Archer's work remains inside. Soane himself produced alternative designs for grander building than that actually carried out, yet what the house may thus have lost in grandeur it certainly gained

in liveable-ness: a delightful house for a rich young man and his
newly-married wife.

The squire and his family must have led a charming life. His
stepfather in 1810 wrote a long poem describing the joys of staying at Aynho. (Sir Stephen Cotterel must have been a charming
man himself; his letters to the young squire, two of which have
been quoted from already, are full of anecdote and endearments,
and one only wishes they contained more about Aynho so that
more might be quoted from them.) The squire's first wife had died
two years before and he had just remarried; Sir Stephen was clearly
delighted to see such happiness again at the great house —

> . . . The Breakfast o'er, each forms his plan
> As inclinations lead.
> Some at Old Down the fish trepan,
> Some walk, some ride, some read.
> At two we lunch — Behold the tray,
> Cold beef, cold ham, cold veal,
> No countryman in Bessy's day
> Made heartier breakfast meal.
> Then with slow, sauntering steps we tread
> And visit home plantations . . .
>
> We dress, we dine. What need describe
> Things so well understood.
> *Jordan*, thou Prince of cookery tribe
> Thou'rt plenteous, choice and good . . .
>
> And though no longer toasts are given
> One health I'll drink by stealth,
> A bumper now I'll fill, by Heaven!
> William and Julia's health!
> But now the folding doors expand,
> The Fair again we see,
> 'Your servant, Charmer! Your commands?'
> 'Sit down and drink your tea' . . .

Other visitors also enjoyed themselves. Lord Manvers, visiting
Aynho after staying at Stowe (with the Marquess of Buckingham)
and at Middleton (with Lord Jersey) found the solution to a difficult rhyme —

> Middleton is flat and dull,
> Stowe is ostentatious, full.
> Would you know where Comforts reign O
> Traveller, pray stop at Aynho.

And the family lived well. A bill for meat and poultry over Christmas week a few years later, when there were 14 in the family, 22
below stairs runs in part —

Sheep 58 lbs @ 6d	£1 9	6
Sheep 39 lbs @ 7d	£1 2	9
Pork etc 54 lbs @ 6½d	£1 9	3
3 roasting pigs		
Beef 338 lbs @ 6d	£8 9	0
Smith 2 turkeys	£1 5	6
One goose of Smith	6	6
Eggs for kitchen use	8	0
Eggs for house	3	0
Tripe	1	0

The quantities are astonishing. Nor are the vast amounts to be taken as any indication of lavish seasonal entertainments for villagers and tenants: similar amounts seem to have been consumed throughout the year.

It is relatively easy to imagine what the great house looked like in squire William Ralph's day. It was probably not very different from its appearance under the last squire: the taste of the first decades of the nineteenth century had something in common with that of the 1930's and '40's, though the fact that furniture then was new would have made the house seem brighter and fresher than do houses furnished with antiques today. We are all familiar with such houses from visiting them.

Though nobody in the village approached the Squire in his standard of living, there were some who did not do too badly. Robert Weston's income at the turn of the century was between £300 and £400 a year, less than a tenth of the squire's but more than ten times that of a labourer. The farmers paid rents of £200–£300 a year for farms of 150–250 acres. Mr. Watkins, the tenant of the College Farm, farmed it by an under-tenant (Mr. Tibbetts, who was mentioned in the last chapter; 'I have a great respect for the old man' Watkins told Weston) while an aunt of his lived in the farmhouse. She left in 1792, when Watkins wrote to Weston asking if he knew of a suitable tenant, adding 'the furniture that is now in the house may remain, which tho' but indifferent is better than none'. But when eighteen months later that same indifferent furniture was put up for auction at the Red Lion, it turned out to include a four poster bed of mahogany, bedsteads with hangings of silk damask, goose feather beds, mahogany chests of drawers, dining tables and chairs, a pier glass, a pair of globes and two clocks.

It is unlikely that Mr. Watkins's aunt's home was any better furnished than that of Mr. Mabletoft the rector, who when he came to Aynho in 1778 bought from his predecessor four chests of drawers, three tables, a curtained bedstead, a featherbed, a mahogany bedside table, walnut chairs and an elbow chair, a mahogany firescreen, the bookshelves in the study and a pair of library steps. In the next thirty years he must have enlarged his establishment further: on his death the rectory comprised hall and lobby, drawing room, dining parlour, breakfast room, study, several bedrooms, besides butler's pantry, kitchen, pantry, brewhouse and beer cellar. And out in the newly enclosed fields the new farmhouses were no doubt as clean and as well furnished as the farmers' wives could make them.

We know far less about the furnishing of the lesser houses of the village. The period is over when as a matter of routine an inventory was made of the possessions of the dead, and the latest (a surprisingly late one, incidentally) is that of William Wrighton who died in 1780. His cottage was of only two rooms, and if it seems well furnished for such a cottage, this is probably because he came of a relatively prosperous artisan family. The cottage contained

Dwelling house	A corner cupboard
	A warming pan & a looking glass
	An oval table
	Five chairs & a pair of buckets
	A brass pot & three kettles
	A frying pan & a square table
	A lantern
In the Chamber	Four pewter dishes
	Ten pewter plates
	Two beds & all bedding
	Two boxes & a chest
	Two chairs

But the furnishing of many villagers' houses will have been scantier than this. Many villagers lived in a poverty that will be hinted at in due course — hinted at because it is difficult adequately to describe the overcrowding, the meagre diet and the shortage of work. But before going on to describe how bad things were, it is worth mentioning some of the things that did a little to relieve the gloom.

William Ralph's new building at the great house has been described already. When he laid the foundation stone there was a guinea to the workmen for bread and cheese, and when the new work was 'topped out' there were two guineas more. There were annual treats such as rent dinners and harvest homes: the bill for harvest home at the Red Lion in 1812, for the Home Farm, read —

| 33 suppers | £3 6 9 |
| 6 gallons Ale | 19 6 |

12. The Square in 1815: by J.C. Nattes. The White Hart is at the centre of the picture, the shop on the left where it remains, though at this date having only a name board over the door rather than a shop window. A line of bollards keep livestock off the pavement in front of it.

13. Looking up the Hollow Way in 1815. In several of these views by Nattes the cottages appear surprisingly dilapidated, and it is possible that William Ralph Cartwright did not spend money lavishly on repairs, though on the other hand Nattes may have exaggerated this for picturesque effect.

14. Cottages on Blacksmith's Hill in 1815. The building on the left seems to have been intended as a cottage at some date, to judge by its chimney and its glazed first floor windows, though it may not have been occupied as such at the time this picture was drawn. A barn door opens on the right centre, and a line of stone piers suggests a former cart shed or byre.

15. Cottages on the Lower Green, 1815

16. The same cottages on Blacksmith's Hill in 1949
The buildings converted into cottages. The lintel of the cart entrance remains with a window tucked beneath it; other altered doors and windows can be compared to the 1815 picture. The group is discussed on page 140.

17. The same cottages on Lower Green, c.1910

18. Looking down Blacksmith's Hill, 1815

Jarvis's house (plate 6) is on the right, with its front door altered from its original position (to which it has now returned). It was then occupied by the cutler, Jethro Eely (page 199). An open stream appears to flow down the hill and beneath a grating on the left, and a pump stands outside Jarvis's house.

19. Lace-making in Watson's Yard, 1815 behind number 13. Much of the building shown has been pulled down. A family are outside the door of their cottage, mother and daughter sitting making lace in the sun.

and the other farmers will have entertained their harvesters in a like fashion. There were the Friendly Societies' annual feasts, to be described later on. And there were other amusements too. Most of these have probably gone unrecorded (or at least undiscovered) but a report in the *Banbury Guardian*, years later, records what cannot have been an isolated occasion —

> On the 29th ult (July) the cricket match, Adderbury vs. Aynho, was played at the latter place. The scene of action was a sweetly sequestered portion of the Park, kindly permitted by W.R. Cartwright, Esq., who honoured the meeting with his presence during the greater part of the day . . .
> W.R. Cartwright, Esq., with his wonted courtesy, ordered a sumptuous collation to be spread in the marquee, and in the evening the players and their friends dined at the White Hart (Mr. E. Holloway in the chair) when the imaginary distinctions of victor and vanquished were at once amalgamated in one flood of right feeling and cricketers' jokes.

(Aynho won, by 9 wickets.)

During the war there was a further relief available — one that must have helped many of the villagers financially and provided entertainment as well. This was service in the Volunteers. For many years, villagers had been liable to serve in the militia unless they were old, infirm or had large families. Call-up was by a lottery, but if a man was picked he might (if he was rich) buy himself off or (if he was poor) perhaps prevail on some adventurous lad to serve in his place. It was not taken very seriously, and the chance of having to serve was probably regarded much as small-pox or an accident in the fields: such misfortunes were accepted as a part of life, and one just hoped that when these mishaps occurred they happened to someone else.

But with the outbreak of war in 1794 a new enthusiasm and a new patriotism began to grip the country. Many people, and not only the authorities, began to see the militia as no longer a sufficient bulwark against a whole nation in arms. The French, Britain's traditional enemies, were mobilising *en masse*, and it was the Briton's patriotic duty to meet the threat. In the spring of 1794 a meeting was held at Northampton and subscriptions opened to support a force of yeomanry cavalry.

The yeomanry were to provide their own horses, 14½ hands at the least (except the drill sergeant's, which was to be 15 hands). Once a week, save for hay time and harvest, they were to meet for drill. Their uniforms were to be paid for out of the subscription money raised, but the yeomanry would only themselves receive wages when on active service quelling riots or facing an invasion. And since it was assumed — rightly, with these conditions — that the yeomanry would be recruited from the more substantial men of the county, it was provided that none should serve without the approval of the rest of the Troop, thus 'effectively secured against the Admission of any Person with whome they may not wish to associate.'

The volunteers in the Brackley division were formed into a troop by the end of May. The recruits from Aynho included the young squire (enrolled as a major), Mr. Leonard the schoolmaster, Samuel Merry (one of the miller's family), George Spiers, probably a carpenter (an interesting name to find, suggesting both that the yeomanry were not as exclusive as their constitution might have one believe, and also that a village carpenter may have been rich enough to own a horse) and two others. Their uniform was green, with black collars and cuffs; they wore buff waistcoats and buff leather breeches and bearskins with a feather and cockade. The new troop met on 4th June for 'military evolutions', and since it was their first time out as well as being the King's birthday, officers and men then adjourned to the Crown in Brackley, where 'many loyal and constitutional toasts were drank, and the day was spent in the most convivial and harmonious manner.' Thereafter there were occasional field days to vary the routine of the weekly drills, and no doubt every occasion was taken of ending the day's work enjoyably. The numbers in the yeomanry grew after war was renewed in 1803, and most of the Aynho farmers had joined by then, no doubt attracted as much by its being a congenial club as an outlet for their patriotic sentiments.

But the yeomanry was limited to those who owned or could borrow a horse, and who had a little time and money to spare. After 1803 the threat of invasion grew greater than ever, and hatred of the French probably stronger. For those who were keen to do their bit but who lacked the resources necessary for service in the yeomanry, a volunteer infantry was formed at Brackley.

The Brackley Volunteers were divided into six companies, of which the Aynho company was the fifth. They were uniformed in red, and were expected to parade with any firearms they might possess and for which ammunition would be provided by the authorities. Not that many villagers — if any — will have owned guns; under the Game Laws none but landowners were allowed firearms, and shortly the authorities were to provide 121 firelock muskets, drums and drumsticks, spears for sergeants and pikes 'to any extent for accepted men not otherwise armed.' And as these and more equipment came in, armouries were built at Brackley, King's Sutton, Byfield and Aynho. The Armoury at Aynho was a simple, wooden building with a table to clean pieces on, a stove to warm the room in winter, and pegs on which to hang caps and belts.

The men could earn 20s a year if they turned out to every drill, and later they were paid a shilling for each inspection. After the drill they were given bread and cheese and beer, with beef and a leg of mutton for the sergeants. There were extra 'encouragements', too: rewards for men who showed particular enthusiasm, and 2s 6d as a prize for marksmanship. Fifers and drummers were found and trained — though some who volunteered were discharged after just one practice. But one of the Aynho Company's two fifers, Jethro Eely (one of the village's artisans: a cutler, treasurer of the Red Lion Friendly Society, and one of the few villagers who still owned their own cottages) proved good enough to be sent over several times to train the King's Sutton fifers, two would-be drummer boys from Aynho were given three weeks board and lodging in Brackley while they learnt to play, and another villager was paid 9s a week for two whole months while training. The Aynho band must have been surprisingly good. It was further improved in 1807 when a serpent and a pair of cymbals were bought, and new uniforms with laced caps and sashes acquired for the musicians, a turban cap for the cymbal player, and a pair of fringed epaulets for the Band Master.

Much was supplied from private sources; indeed, it is hard to see the military authorities stumping up to buy a serpent. Mr. Mabletoft the Rector subscribed £40 and Robert Weston £50; Mr. Burbidge the old apothecary and Mr. Watson his son-in-law also subscribed, while the landlord of the Alfred's Head, the pub on the canal, gave not only money but offered the use of his barges if need should arise. Farmers were asked to make carts and waggons available in case of emergency: carts for equipment, and waggons (with seats which were to be made to fit across them) for the transport of the men themselves. If ordered to march, the Volunteers were to take food for three days; they were not to trespass or pilfer, they would be supplied with all that they needed, but they were warned that 'when they were cantoned and pressed forward, they must be satisfied with the most crowded and slightest accommodation, and a rigorous Discipline must prevent them from requiring more than the Country and circumstances can allow.'

They were kept at a high state of readiness: drilling, pipe-

claying and (inevitably) having their hair cut (at a penny a time).
They drilled outdoors and in ('paid for a new cord for the chan-
delier at Astrop Ballroom — broke by the men when at drill'). The
administration was sometimes a trifle carefree: the adjutant accompanied a return by a letter reading 'I enclose you a Monthly Return:
I think it is nearly right', while certain proprieties were still to be
observed, war or no war: on another occasion he wrote to his
Commanding Officer 'The Weather have been unfavourable we
have not yet been out, I have fixt on Monday 25th . . . but if it is
more convenient to Major Blencowe to defer it until Thursday 28th
as he have company at his house . . . I hope you will let me know.'
And whatever the enthusiasm of the Aynho Company, their state
of military efficiency may not have been of the highest. When
there was need for a new officer, and it was proposed to promote
a serjeant, Tippets, the same adjutant wrote of him that 'he always
attend the drill and is tolerably well discipline.' Not much of a re-
commendation, one would have thought, but apparently it was
sufficient. The accounts included

> June 1807 Paid in part for new officers Coat for Ensign Tibbetts
> appointed to the Anyho [sic] Company   £2 : 12s : 6

One would like to have seen them at drill and watched the discipline of those who were not officer material. But service in the
Volunteers must have been great fun, even the drills, with a band to
march to, while the occasional field day must have been thoroughly
enjoyable, marching about the countryside, showing off one's
smart red uniform, practising manoeuvres, and facing imaginary
enemies with whom one would a little later spend a jolly evening
over pints of free beer.

There must have been much regret when in 1809 the Volunteers were disbanded. But by then the threat of invasion was long
past — past for good since Trafalgar, though it was some time before the government realised it. By now the call was for regular soldiers, soldiers prepared to serve abroad. But good fellowship and
good service were not to pass away unrecognised —

> By the order of Colo¹. Cartwright Paid to 401 men at 2/6 each on
> the Committee Acct. when Disbanded   £50 : 2 : 6
> Paid 401 men one shilling each Allowd by Government
>   £20 : 1 : 0
> Give to each Man one Quart of Ale Bread and Cheese on the same
> day   £16 : 17 : 3
> For the Officers cold collation at Byfield   £1 : 1 : 0

and many Aynho men must have been sorry when waggons came

round to take away the arms from the armoury and carry them off to the depot at Daventry. One wonders what became of the serpent.

Though the authorities never resorted to any sort of general call-up of the twentieth century kind, the meet the changed circumstances they increased six fold the number of men to be ballotted for the militia. When a man was serving, the Parish made an allowance to his family. When a man served as substitute for another village, there were elaborate provisions for the one parish to pay the other's expenses, and the bureaucratic wheels ground slower, if possible, than they do today. It was three years before the Aynho overseers were paid for the family of Joseph Norman who served as a substitute for a Warwick man, while the Aynho overseers themselves did their best to avoid payment for a Hanslope man who served as a substitute for James Pottinger of Aynho. The village did not always find it easy to meet its quota, and on one occasion advertised 'a handsome bounty' to anyone who should volunteer. The ratepayers were liable for a considerable fine if they failed to meet with numbers raised (many villages did fail, and were fined) and with the rates what they were, any effort was worth making to avoid extra charges.

We do not know how many Aynho men did fight in the war, but for the moment soldiers were popular (they were not usually so) and probably more than one adventurous lad without ties joined the colours. Sergeant Pollard, of the Aynho volunteers, ran into trouble for recruiting a young man for the Infantry without having the authority to act as a recruiting sergeant, though the squre intervened to put things right and obtained for Pollard the necessary powers. And the squire's own second son, William, born in 1797, joined the army when he was only 15, fought under Wellington in the Peninsular and was a veteran of 18 at Waterloo.

But all of these were occasional moments of relief for lives that were in general extremely hard. The problem was at bottom one of chronic underemployment and overpopulation. The reasons for the rising birthrate in the late eighteenth and early nineteenth century are not properly understood, but the evidence for it is conclusive. The population of the village had been 567 in 1740; by 1801 it had risen to 623, and to 719 by 1821. To some extent this was relieved by emigration to the towns, whose populations were increasing more rapidly than can be accounted for by their own birthrates. (The village population, fast though it was rising, was not increasing as fast as it would have done if everyone born in the place had stayed at home, as the graph on page 127 shows.)

Occasional apprenticeship indentures survive to show how Aynho boys continued to be 'put out' to masters elsewhere – in the 1790's, for instance, George Boxold to a plane maker in Stratford, and George Spiers, son of an Aynho carpenter, to a joiner in Banbury. The emigration of the unskilled is almost impossible to trace. There was, basicly, simply not enough work in Aynho for the able-bodied to do, even with the labour-intensive agriculture of the time, and after Enclosure, with fields easier to manage, the amount of work available almost certainly diminished.

Work on the enclosure, for all that in involved so many men, did nothing to raise wages: there were clearly too many men wanting work in Aynho and in the surrounding villages for that. For grubbing up old hedges, levelling ridges and the like – heavy, manual|work – a man could earn 1s 4d a day, 8s a week. A skilled man could earn more: Thomas Fathers the mason earned 1s 8d a day for building plain walls, and his boy 9d. Labourers' wages rose very little during the Napoleonic Wars, and not by enough to offset the rise in the price of provisions.

What family budgets were in Aynho we do not know, but in Deddington in the 1790's a man and wife with three small children was reported as spending £17 a year on bread out of an annual income (when he was in full employment) of £23. At Roade, between Towcester and Northampton, the same reporter instanced the case of a labourer with five children who was able to supplement his annual wage of £20 by bellringing, grave-digging and cutting his fellows' hair, while his wife and children earned a little by lacemaking to bring the combined family income up to £26. 8s a year. Half of this sum went on bread, £5. 4s on meat, 17s 4d on beer (a gallon a week), a very little on butter, cheese, tea and sugar, and about £2. 10s on clothes and the same on fuel. With rent and other expenses this left him some £4 a year in deficit, and he was a man who was able to add to his basic wage in other ways while 'his neighbours, who know him to be industrious and careful, give him old clothes, etc. He has sometimes been assisted by his landlord'.

Low wages meant that a man out of work had no resources to fall back on: that he was bound at once to appeal to the Overseers for help. And shortage of work, even as far back as 1780, had led to the Overseers employing the poor as roundsmen. This meant that labourers who lacked regular employment were taken on by each farmer in turn to work for a number of days depending on the size of the farm. The farmer would pay the man 10d a day, and the Overseers would make up their wages to whatever sum was considered necessary for subsistence — at first adding 2d a day to make the wage a shilling. It was a bad system in almost every way, that of supplementing wages from the rates, and the fact that it was followed by innumerable parishes besides Aynho did nothing to redeem it. It kept wages down, it spread the cost of farm labour beyond the farmers and onto all the ratepayers of the village, it discouraged farmers from giving men long-term employment, and it discouraged the labourer from looking ahead beyond the next few days. Coupled with the old laws that made a man eligible for relief only in the village where he had his settlement, it led directly to his demoralisation. It kept him in his home village, and kept him there in a state of increasing degradation.

On the other hand it is understandable that the authorities should have behaved as they did. If there was poverty, it was presumably because wages were too low, and if farmers could not afford to raise them then the authorities must supplement them. If there was unemployment, it was better (they will have argued) to find work for the unemployed, even at a subsidised wage, than for assistance to be given to men who remained idle. As to the matter of settlements, while the Overseers elsewhere refused to give settlements to men born in Aynho (or anywhere else) so the Aynho Overseers were equally adamant against giving settlements to strangers in Aynho. (When the Aynho Overseers put out poor boys from the village as apprentices, they had to indemnify the Overseers of the towns concerned against the boys' becoming chargeable to their new homes.) Around 1807 the Squire and the farmers drew up a formal agreement binding them all to give nobody from elsewhere a job on terms that would entitle him to a settlement in Aynho, terms such as a formal contract of employment for more than a year.

With small fluctuations, the amount of poor rates throughout the Napoleonic wars remained very high. The year 1813 was particularly bad, and in October a meeting of the Vestry was held at the Red Lion to consider the problem. There were in that year 81 men and boys in need of regular work. (There had been 89 families 'engaged in agriculture' recorded in the 1811 census, out of 142 families in the village. Many of these agricultural families will have included more than one farm worker, but the best of them were probably assured of regular employment, and the 81 in need of it must represent well over half the labouring population.) Their great need was guaranteed work, to ensure that a man and his family would not become a charge on the ratepayers unless they were actually ill. The squire, the farmers, the landlord of the Alfred's Head, Mrs. Bygrave of the White Hart, Edward Holloway of the Red Lion, the Turnpike Trustees, the Canal Company, Samuel Hughes, baker, and James Wycherley, shopkeeper, all agreed to take on men for one or more of the next three years. Some labourers stayed with their masters, others chopped and changed. It must have been an unsatisfactory arrangement for the employer, virtually compelled to employ men for whom they may have had insufficient work and of whom some in any case will have been the less desirable village characters. It must have been humiliating for the men, directed to certain work as the condition of receiving a subsistence wage, though it is difficult to know what else the authorities could have done. The rates did fall over the next few years — from £748 in 1813 to £555 in 1821 and £458 in 1831 — but rather as the result of national trends than because of any local remedies.

The situation may have improved slightly with the end of the war in that the prices of farm produce — of food — fell after 1815. But equally, that meant that farmers were not prepared to maintain the level of wages that had been paid during the war, and it is unlikely that the poor and unemployed found themselves better off. The allowances that might be paid by the Overseers were set by the local J.P.'s. William Ralph Cartwright sat as a Justice for the Brackley Division, and the sums allowed to the unemployed by him and by his fellow magistrates in the early 1820's were:-

For a man and wife with one child	8s per week
For each child after the first	1s
For a widow with two children under 10	5s
For an old couple	5s
For a single old man	3s 6d
For a single old woman	2s 6d

But the problem was a national one rather than local, and in 1833 the government felt — however belatedly — that something should be done: that the existing system of poor relief, in essence and Elizabethan one, was now quite incapable of coping with a population six times the size it had been in the sixteenth century. (Even in Aynho the population was more than twice what it was in 1600.) By |way of preparing the ground, a national enquiry was to collect information on the whole range of local problems, local solutions, and the views of those who had to administer the existing law. Out of a dozen parishes responding in Northamptonshire,

Aynho was one.

It is not clear whether the practice of supplementing wages out of the rates still continued in Aynho. William Ralph Cartwright told the enquiry that there was no unemployment in Aynho, yet the rates remained very high. In the previous week, he said, 41 people had been helped out of the rates (about one person out of every twelve). A farm labourer could earn some 11s a week at hay time, 16s at harvest, and 9s in winter when the days were short. It was the practice for the farmers to pay single men, without families to support, 2s a week less, while the Overseers paid fathers of large families 1s a week for each child after the third. A labourer could probably earn about £27 a year; enough to live on, thought the squire, but not enough to enable him to put anything by against sickness or old age. Diet was bread, potatoes and a little bacon, with occasional meat on Sundays. There was cottage rent to pay, of course, 6d a week without a garden, 1s with one, and there were allotments to be rented too if a man had the time and the money, one to five chains at 4s a chain per year. Elsewhere villagers kept a pig, but the squire makes no mention of cottage pigs in Aynho.

There were some additional sources of income for families. Women could earn 5s at haymaking and 7s at harvest, and at these busy times even children could earn something, 2s 6d and 4s. Otherwise there was a little lacemaking and a very little spinning. There was no regular work for children, the squire reported, yet a boy of 11 could earn £3. 18s a year — he was clearly no longer regarded as a child. Farmers were urged to pay by the piece rather than day wages, and in this way, thought the squire, a good man could earn rather more.

When against this background the squire reported that he found 'no indisposition to work or industry' (in contrast to the responses from the majority of other villages) one wonders what he is really describing. Was it the unlikely fact (if fact it was) that after 50 years of pauperisation the villagers still worked with a will? Or his own lack of observation? Or his understandable desire not to run down the village that he almost wholly owned? Though it seems that in circumstances such as these the villagers must have been degraded and demoralised, working with a dull resignation at jobs that were unrewarding in almost every sense, early nineteenth century villagers did not necessarily feel as we do.

Yet if we cannot enter the mind of the farm labourer, we are entitled also to be sceptical of the sanguine attitude of the squire.

At least one of his friends, writing to him a few years earlier, expressed his doubts:-

> I entirely concur that it is not wise to add to the alarm which has
> gone forth on the subject of Scarcity, but I confess that I cannot
> from thence draw the conclusion that no measure should be
> taken to guard against the apprehended evil; much less that the
> distress which is not in speculation but in daily experience, from
> the present high prices, should be passed over without an attempt
> to alleviate it.'

But William Ralph Cartwright was not inhumane by the standards of his age and class, and it would be asking too much to require him to be an unusually imaginative one. Few people, rich or poor, questioned the inevitability of their respective stations, and provided that the rich dispensed charity and the poor were diligent and frugal, few will have thought there was anything else that should, or could, be done. A letter from William Ralph Cartwright's mother to Robert Weston, surviving by chance among his business correspondence, must be read with this in mind.

> I enclose the letter from Turvey — a more miserable family sure
> never existed, if it would please God to take one or two of the
> sick ones, which from your account is most probable, the rest
> with your kind assistance may experience a degree of comfort
> they have long been strangers to.

Her concern for the poor family is patent, and her writing that it would be easier if a few of the sick children would die is not really callous. Child deaths were daily occurences, and few doubted that the children of the poor were better off hereafter.

But villagers were not entirely without resources: self-help on an individual or an organised basis was widespread. Though there were disincentives to leave the village, many did so. Bright children continued to be put out as apprentices, though it was often the Overseers who had to find the £15–£20 premium. There were many men who must have gone off on their own: in 1833 the squire reported a labour force of 88 men over 21 and 40 lads, and such a high proportion of boys to men can only mean that a great many men left the village. (The census of 1831 records men and women in more or less equal numbers, so that either men left with their wives, or as many single girls left as single men.) Occasionally we hear of them: George Nichols, for instance, who went to the Hiring Fair at Buckingham one Michaelmas and was taken on for two years running by a man at Eydon. Or Catherine Smith who went to the Buckingham fair and was taken on by a Mr. Hedges from Stukely for £5 a year, with a shilling earnest to seal the bargain. Next year she was asked to stay, for £6, and was given a week's holiday to go home and see her family and friends.

By way of organised self-help, there was the Red Lion Friendly Society, set up in 1801. Its rules stated that

> The Society is established for the purpose of raising by means of Contribution of its Members, or by voluntary donation, a fund for the relief of its members in sickness and debility, for the decent and respectful interment of their remains when dead, and to enable each of them to bequeath a sum of money at his pleasure . . . and to promote and encourage peace, love and unity.

The Society was to have a maximum of 121 members, run by a Committee of fourteen who were to include the members 'of the best eduation'. There were two classes of members — the ordinary members who paid 6d a week and received 6s a week if they were too ill to work, and first class members ('tradesmen and others') who paid 10d and received 9s. If a member died, the Society paid £2 towards the funeral while each member was to contribute a shilling towards the dead member's estate to provide some help for his wife and family. There were certain exclusions: people lost benefit if they enlisted in the militia or ran into danger, if they had themselves innoculated for smallpox, and when they were in prison unless imprisoned for debt. The society prospered: in 1811 they lent £20 at 5 per cent interest to John Watson, carpenter of King's Sutton, and £70 to Thomas Wagstaffe, an Aynho farmer; in 1819 they had £119 deposited with the Northampton savings bank and a few years later £120 with a lawyer in Deddington.

But the Society was a social club as well as for the insurance of its members. Members met every four weeks, on Monday evenings at the Red Lion, at seven in summer and six in winter after the day's work was done. The stewards and the clerk seated themselves at a table while the members came up one by one and paid their contributions, with another 2d from each member for spending during the evening. Members then retired to their seats while announcements were made and any necessary business transacted. After an hour the books were closed, beer was bought to the value of the night's contributions, and the social part of the evening began. Members were expected to behave: they were fined 2d if they should 'give the lie, curse, swear, or propose any wager, or any kind of gaming, or use vile expressions, as damn it, rot it, etc.' And the fine was 6d for 'using the name of God as a vain expression ' or if a member 'give scurrilous language, reflects on a brother member's character or strikes or seizes him by the collar or makes use of any threatening expressions.' It is highly unlikely that anyone got drunk, and significant that the rules did not mention it: at 2d a head nobody could have bought enough beer for that.

It was only on Whit Monday that the rules envisaged that possibility, for that was the day of the Society's annùal Feast. Members all met at the club room at ten in the morning and formed up in procession. Thence they walked two and two to Church, where the Rector preached them a special sermon for which he was paid half a guinea by the Society. After church the members filed back to the Red Lion, held their annual meeting to elect officers, and were then free to enjoy the Feast. Each member paid 2s 6d towards it; the jollifications went on well into the evening, and there were severe penalties against drunkenness, fighting and quarrelling that day. The stewards might send out food and beer to a sick member, but families were strictly excluded from the Society's entertainment. Things were equally strictly organised when a member died. Unless the funeral took place more than two miles from Aynho, or death was from smallpox, all members were expected to attend with funeral hatbands and gloves which they were to provide at their own expense (and recommended to buy from shopkeeper members if possible). Part of the funeral allowance of £2 was spent on a pint of beer for every member, who was to pay his shilling to the dead man's heirs at the next following meeting.

There was another, similar society formed at the White Hart in 1811, limited to 101 members and with benefits and a scale of subscription similar to those of the first class of the Red Lion society. Members met quarterly on Saturday nights and held their Feast on Easter Monday. Towards the end of the century the society still existed, as the Cherwell Valley Lodge of the Manchester Unity of Oddfellows, and they held their dinners at the Great Western Arms by the railway station. These societies must have been a real help for many villagers, even though there must have been some too poor to join: the annual 2s 6d for the Feast represented only a ½d a week, which it must have been possible to save if they were in regular employment. But the occasional shilling due on a member's death must have been a nasty shock, a large slice out of a subsistence wage, and if one was out of work the weekly 6d must have been impossible to find, while the Society paid no benefit for unemployment. Nevertheless the existence of two, apparently prosperous, Friendly Societies shows how many villagers there must have been who were willing to provide against misfortune in a responsible manner.

But neither the actions of the authorities nor the providence of villagers could really affect the underlying problem, the effects of over-population. After 1815 the poor rates never fell to anything like pre-war levels; they fell, but only to a plateau below which no measures seemed able to reduce them. Even for those villagers prepared to leave the village there was no guarantee of work in the growing towns. From the 1820's onwards it seemed to more and more people that the only chance of a secure future for able-bodied, enterprising men might be abroad, in the broad, new acres of Canada and America.

The first to leave, in the summer of 1829, were two men and a single girl. Over the next few years a trickle grew to a flood as adults and children — often whole families — left for the New World. The Parish borrowed money to help them, and the squire, answering one of the questions asked by the Commisioners into the Poor Laws in 1833, reported that up to a hundred people had already gone and that the benefit to the Parish had been 'great and immediate'. The flow continued: another 37 sailed in the spring of 1836 including nine single people and a widow, in search of a brighter future. The same family names occur again and again. In some cases one member of a family might go first to prepare the way for others; in other cases friends and relations would be attracted by the favourable reports sent back by predecessors. Some at least prospered: a letter from an Aynho emigrant was published in the Northampton Mercury in 1834 [sic] as an encouragement to others who might follow

                                                Richland.
                                            Sept. 22, 1833.

Dear Father and Mother,
    We received your letter August 24th and was glad to hear you was all in good health, as, Thank God, it leaves us. We like this country very well. We have purchased two cows for thirty-five dollars. We never was so well off before as we are now. We intend to have a farm as soon as you come. We are now living two miles from Pulaski, by the side road towards Oswego, and it is very pleasant indeed. Our house is built with trees about a foot thick, laid one on top of another, and let in at the corners, chopt smooth on the inside; it is about 20 feet long, 18 feet wide, 2 storey high, the gable ends are boarded up; the roof is made secure with boards, for board is cheap in this country. We have board for the floors. Our chimney is made with brick and stopt, which makes it as comfortable as it is in England. I can get plenty of work at ditching, and well sinking, and cellar sinking, so bring your tools with you and small drills, and your stocking axes. Augers, broad-axes, saws, sickles and scythes are as cheap here, and household

furniture is as cheap here. Wheat one dollar a bushel, rye 5 shillings, oats 2 shillings, barley 5 shillings; superfine flour 3 dollars a cwt; potatoes 2 shillings a bushel, apples one shilling, pork ten cents a pound butter ten cents a pound, whiskey three shillings a gallon, rum, brandy and wine one dollar a gallon. Wages is high in this country, and I get my living where I work. Bring plenty of garden seeds, a few field beans and vetches with you. Dear mother, bring plenty of sewing cotton and threadneedles and pins. Father bring your measuring tape and one for me. Please to bring a pocket knife for me of Thomas's make, Banbury. Dear brother Thomas, if you was here you would make a fortune. I wish we had all come to this country when we was first married. I wish you had come when we did, if you had we should have had a farm by now. Thomas does reckon of his grandpap's coming. John is seven months old. Give my best respects to all my neighbours, enemys and friends. Father has sold his farm, he finds that he can get land cheaper, which he intends to have another soon. They are all well at present. Jane is with them. Henry Elly and his family is all well, so I must conclude with my kind love to you all.
                    John and Ann George.

More villagers followed over the next few years, until in 1845 there left the largest single contingent of all, seven complete families and four single people, 51 people in all. They went by waggon to Liverpool, and the two churchwardens, William Scott and Edward Holloway, went with them to see them off. Even the journey to Liverpool must have taken most of them further from Aynho than they had ever been before, and the slow waggon must have taken several days on the road. In Liverpool they were held up by contrary winds, but that must have given them a welcome day or two longer to get accustomed to the boat and to the sea: few can have seen either. They sailed at last, at seven in the evening on 1st April. A steam tug took them down the Mersey and the churchwardens spent the night on board with the emigrants and had breakfast with them in the morning. Out in the Irish Sea the tug cast off and Scott and Holloway returned in her when Scott sat down to write to the squire of the success of the expedition. As they left, the party was 'in good health and spirits and hearts full of gratitude for the kindness shown them and there was not an individual . . . either sick or sorry when I left home.' As he wrote, he looked back to see the emigrant ship in full sail and the Welsh mountains far off, covered in snow.

Some of those who emigrated can have been no loss. In a list of those who emigrated in 1842 were four men, Spires, Robbins, Watts and Anstell. Against Spire's name the old squire wrote 'a very good riddance', 'ditto' against Robbins' and Watts', and 'ditto ditto ditto' against Anstell's. Others, like the Tebby family, had frequently come to the Overseers for help, and now never would again. But other emigrants were men of enterprise, and the village was probably the poorer by their departure. Abraham Howes, for instance, who left with his family in 1845, was able finally to settle as a farmer on a hundred acres of his own land near Winnipeg. It was not until the second world war that his ancestors re-visited the village, and very many villagers must have wished to make as clean a break as possible with their old homes — of which their memories cannot have been wholly happy.

The loss of over 150 people by emigration must have eased the pressure on population to some extent, but un- and under-employment continued for many years to come. A report in the *Banbury Guardian* of a case before the Brackley magistrates in 1846, after the great emigration was over, shows that for some people the problem was by no means solved —

> The overseers of Aynho charged — Watts with having neglected to provide for three children who are now in the Brackley work-house. It appeared that the children had been chargeable for nearly twelve months; that till now the father had not been asked to pay for their support; that Watts lived with his mother, an elderly women, who was not willing to have his children with her; that he had had about three months work in that time, and had given his earnings to his mother . . .
> Mr. Litchfield censured the parish officers for not having brought the defendant's neglect before the magistrates earlier. Watts was willing to take the children and do the best for them that he could. The Bench decided on committing. Mr. Gilbert, the reliev-ing officer, spoke in mitigation of imprisonment. Mr. Litchfield said it was the duty of the magistrates to check such conduct. *Watts was sentenced to 14 days imprisonment.* [*Banbury Guardian*'s italics.]

Considered in every detail, carefully, it is an appalling story, and the magistrate, Francis Litchfield, the rector of Farthinghoe, appears inhuman. Only the Aynho officials come out of it with any credit — as in the seventeenth century the local constable was reprimanded for not flogging vagrants, here in the nineteenth the village officers were being hauled up for trying to turn a blind eye, in the cause of humanity, to a situation which in human terms the law could do nothing to remedy. It is hard to know what good was to be had by putting Watts in prison for a fortnight and giving him a bad character for the rest of his life. But that was the system; the *Banbury Guardian* (which was a Liberal paper) probably disapproved of Litchfield more because he was a Tory than because he seems in this case to have been a heartless brute.

Faced with such conditions as these, it is scarcely surprising that a few turned to self-help of another kind: crime. The astonishing thing is that there is so little of it. Probably some of those caught pilfering were merely given a warning the first time by the squire or the farmer who caught them: they would be marked men thereafter, but probably only the more notorious bad characters were prosecuted. Apart from anything else, imprisonment of a wage-earner meant the parish having to support his family. Among Aynho men who got into trouble with the law in the early years of the century were William Westbury, arrested in 1807 for having run away from his wife and family five years before and leaving them destitute and a charge on the parish. John Turner stole an elm plank, the property of the squire and worth one shilling and nine pence, and was set to six months' hard labour. Timothy Watts had got Hannah Dark into trouble and was put in jail in Northampton until he agreed to support the child. John Borton had a fight with Valentine Willifer and was imprisoned for refusing to find sureties to keep the peace towards Willifer in future. Edward Tuckey and Thomas Foxley were jailed for stealing a truss of hay.

These were scarcely major crimes, and were presented before the Justices at petty sessions. More serious crimes were reserved to Assizes. Among the papers in the Aynho parish chest is the following document, probably from the years immediately after 1815. Lovell and Staunton, the men in question, may have been from Aynho; the fact that the paper was kept by the rector of Aynho suggests that at least one of them was, and the events described all took place in next door villages. Staunton could have been hung for his share in them, and he may have hoped to buy himself off by peaching on his accomplice.

Gaol — Northampton

The Voluntary Examination of William Staunton
taken the 28th day of April —

I & George Lovell in Novr. last stole Mr. T |Hopcrofts Ferretts — on Croton Feast Sunday — We were at the Blackbird together and went from there to Hopcrofts — Lovell cut the heads and buried the carcases in a pit in Lovells hovel — about a spit deep — this was done just before they searched
George Lovell & I stole Mr. Welch's sheep of Kings Sutton — it is the Mr. Welch who came last to Kings Sutton — about 6 weeks after Mich[s] — Lovell killed it & we took it home in a bag — Lovell skinned it & put the skin into Mr. Smith's long pond at Charlton

under the wall ab^t 6 yards from the sluice — some stones in the bag to sink it — it is the lower pond on the right hand of the road as you go from Charlton to Croton — George Wilkins of Kings Sutton met us in Mr. Clerkes close called Galley Hill when Lovell had the sheep on his back — Wilkins deals in coals — Lovell dropped the bag & we both went the other side the hedge — Wilkins looked at it & said go on boys I shall not take any notice of you we had the sheep from Mr. Welch's clover ground the front of Mr. Willes' house —

Lovell stole Mr. Pirkins of Charlton — Pincers. Two years ago — he has them in his house now — in a little box opposite the fireplace —

Lovell stole Mr Taylors bacon of Charlton in December last I was with him — He and I were drinking together at the Crown at Charlton that evening till about 10 o'clock —

Lovell & William Byles stole Mr. Scotts of Hinton great coat & boots in Novr as Lovell told me — they had been at the Leathern Bottle at Brackley good part of the night — and in going hence stole the things — about 5 o'clock in the morning.

Lovel & James Billington of Charlton make a practice of Milking Mr. Pirkins Cows when they lay in West field — I have been with them doing that —

James Billington stole 3 sacks of Potatoes last year from Mr. Pirkins when I was digging them up for him, we were to have had them between us but Billington gave me two Bushel of Barley, which he told me he stole from Mr Haddons barn, for my share — Billington has some pick-lock keys & can get into any barn he wishes — there are 20 or 30

Lovell & I Wm Byles went about Mich^s to Mr Richd Mumford of Astrop and stole abt 15 couple of Fowls.

It is a sordid and depressing account. These were bad characters, one and all, and probably deserve no pity, but it is an unpleasant picture: the frightened man in the cell, trying to save his own neck by telling on his neighbours. And the crimes are squalid and petty, fruit of a wretched and degraded life. It is better to change the subject.

Self-help — of whatever sort — was all very well so far as it went; so were the actions of the authorities, and neither of these went far enough. Old Richard Cartwright had set up a bread charity and this was maintained by his descendants, to give poor widows a share in 2s worth of bread each Sunday: they would collect it from church after mattins. Five pounds a year of the income from this charity was kept back by William Ralph and the same amount by his wife for their own personal distribution in the course of the year as they thought fit — and no doubt they added sums of their own from time to time. Occasionally some body such as the

Northamptonshire Agricultural Society would make small awards
which would be a windfall to some poor family —

> William Galloway, Aynho, 45 years member of the Adderbury
>   Friendly Society   £3 3 0
> Awards to Labourers in Husbandry for bringing up large families:
>   John Buckinham, Aynho, 8 children   £4 4 0

And this dreary time has left one memorial which forms a more
cheerful note on which to end a depressing chapter: the almshouses.

    These were put up in accordance with the Will of John Baker,
who died in 1816. Baker was a prosperous glazier of Oxford, and
is a slightly mysterious figure. He has been mentioned already in
connection with the Enclosure as owning 79 acres in the village,
and these he had probably inherited from an uncle of the same
living in Aynho; it was land that had probably once been Thomas
Drope's. But this is really of academic interest; what mattered to
Aynho was that on his death the younger Baker left his property
for annuities to be paid to an equal number of old men and old
women of the village and, if it was legally possible, to build almshouses for them.

    In the event, after various viscissitudes (including his execu-
tors' having to buy off someone who claimed to be Baker's heir)
Baker's trustees were able to begin work on the almshouses in the
summer of 1821, with an 'entertainment' at the Red Lion of beer
for the builders and wine for themselves. Most of the stone was
local, from pits on land belonging to the College Farm, but slates,
Hornton stone and timber came from further afield, arriving by
canal at Aynho wharf. Labour, of course, was almost entirely
local, and the same old families occur yet again: Thomas Secull
the mason, Francis Turbit the slater and plasterer, William Watts
the blacksmith and John Spiers the carpenter. John Cauldrey,
however, who did the plumbing and glazing, came from elsewhere
and had to be lodged at the Red Lion — shortly to be re-named
the Cartwright Arms.

    The first occupants were admitted at Michaelmas, 1823.
Their ages ranged from the 50's to the 80's. John Borton at
number 1 was 64, but he was clearly the fittest of them all: he
lived for another 20 years, and supplemented his allowance by
earning 6d a week as caretaker and 2s 6d a year for tending John
Baker's tomb in the churchyard. The weekly allowance for the
inmates varied from time to time with the state of the Trustees'
funds, but was generally around 8s a week for men and 7s for

women. Compared to the scale of allowances granted by the Justices to the old this was almost princely, and the cottages were warm and dry. The almshouses have been a blessing ever since, one good to have come out of difficult years.

Chapter 12

High Finance and High Farming

Until now the personal affairs of the Cartwright family have not taken up very much of this History. This has been deliberate: it is a history of the village, not of the Cartwrights, and family matters have seldom affected the village very closely. Nor has much been said lately of the farmers: as villagers ceased to farm, and as the squire's farms came to be larger and their tenants more professional, so the farmers came to be men of the world rather than men of Aynho, happier mixing with their peers in the markets of Banbury, Brackley and Chipping Norton than with other villagers in the taproom of the Cartwright Arms.

But neither the farmers nor the family can be passed over altogether, and this chapter concerns both. In the middle of the nineteenth century two squires died within four years, with profound consequences for the family and for the estate. At the same time, at least three members of the family were becoming increasingly enthusiastic about 'high farming', about the latest advances in steam threshing, improved implements and stock, field drainage and artificial fertilisers that were becoming something of a mania among more forward-looking Victorian landowners.

Much of this can be followed in a series of letters between the family and their agent, written over these few years. They concern family business, the conflict between the old farming and the new, the disturbances to the household inevitable on the death of the squire, village gossip and rural politics, and the coming of the railway. There has been a good deal of quotation from documents in the book already, and this chapter consists of much more. But these letters can mostly be allowed to tell their own story; their immediacy conveys the pressure of successive crises, both of the grand ones and of the small day-to-day problems that seemed large at the time, and the overall atmosphere of the times comes over better in these letters than it could in a summary told at second hand.

The principal *dramatis personae*, so to speak, are:-

William Ralph Cartwright, the old squire. Gouty since 1820, and an object of awe to his children who referred to him in their letters as 'the governor' but not, one suspects, to his face;

Julia Cartwright (née Aubrey) his second wife. Called Mother by the children of William Ralph's first marriage;

Sir Thomas Cartwright, William Ralph's eldest son and heir. A career diplomatist, currently H.M.'s ambassador in Stockholm. In 1826 he married Marie Sandizell, daughter of a German Count. She was always known as Lili in the family;

William Cornwallis Cartwright, Sir Thomas's eldest son, born in 1826 and already embarking on a career of European travel that would absorb him for many years;

Colonel William Cartwright, William Ralph's second son, enthusiastic, a trifle interfering, but always anxious to help in a crisis. As a young man he had fought at Waterloo;

The Revd. Stephen Cartwright, William Ralph's youngest son by his first marriage. Probably a spoilt child; the rector of Aynho, a bachelor, and disliked by his brothers;

Samuel Field, a partner in Churchill and Field, Solicitors and Land Agents in Deddington;

The Willifers. Valentine Willifer, in his late 60's, was the bailiff on the Home Farm. His eldest son, called after him, was always referred to as Val.

Others who make their appearance will, so far as is possible or necessary, be identified as they occur.

In the later years of William Ralph's reign the Aynho estates were not well run, though only after his death would it be revealed quite how badly. Willifer had a good deal of authority, Samuel Field collected the farm rents, and many of the books were kept, after a fashion, by the old squire himself. But the general state of things may be gathered from a rent agreement of 1835, probably for Aynho Grounds farm:-

> William Ralph Cartwright agrees to let the farm at Aynho and Souldern now in the occupation of William John Scott to William Scott from the 6th of April, 1836, at the present rate, on condition that William Scott abstains from using abusive language towards Mr. Willifer & behaves properly to him, also that he do not take down any pollard trees without his landlord's consent, also that he do his utmost to get rid of the thistles now growing so shamefully & in such numbers on his farm.

Hardly the sort of conditions to encourage progessive husbandry.

Sir Thomas was well aware of the state of affairs. In 1844, probably feeling that his son William Cornwallis was old enough to know how things stood, he wrote to him:-

Sir Thomas Cartwright to William Cornwallis Cartwright

Stockholm, 4th April, 1844

My dear Willy . . .

If I should survive my father I should have about £9000 a year to spend, for I should not give up diplomacy. I have made up my mind on that head. The Aynho property wants a little nursing. Between ourselves my Father has spent a great deal of money. He succeeded to the property after a long minority so that when he attained his majority he must have been in very flourishing circumstances. The expenses of rebuilding the house, making the place what it is, his [election] contests, must have taken much money, and in point of fact if Mrs. Elizabeth Cartwright had not stood his friend and left him all she had to leave, I really do not know what turn things would have taken . . .

My father had debts of about £50,000 on the estate, or personal to him, £35,000 he paid off, & £16,000 still remains upon the property . . . If I come into the property I may reckon, as I calculate, upon some £5500 clear from the estate, & my salary being £3400 a year I may take my income at about £9000. I have told you that I should not give up Diplomacy. I have been accustomed to it, and it is entirely with this determination of making an effort to retrieve the property that I mean to cling to it as long as it will cling to me, *under all circumstances.* My expenses in this arrangement would not be much greater than they are now, but by putting all my wants and expenses at about £6000 a year I should be able still to put by £3000 annually towards liberating the estate . . .

Mrs. Elizabeth Cartwright may have been the widow of squire William who had died in 1768. A good deal of village property had been entailed to her, and she had lived until 1803.

In any case, Sir Thomas did not have long to wait.

Colonel William Cartwright to Sir Thomas Cartwright

Aynhoe, 4th January 1847

My dearest Thomas

My poor Father breathed his last this morning at 5 o'clock without a struggle. A most happy and peaceful end. I can write no more now, but trust Lili to give you every particular. My poor Mother is as calm and resigned as possible. We have much to go through yet but trust to Providence to bear her up in her affliction & all of us in our everlasting loss.

Lady Cartwright's (Lili's) presence at Aynho was, perhaps, because the old squire's death had not been wholly unexpected. He had been ill for many months, though he had rallied towards the end and given some hopes for a recovery. For the moment, however, the Colonel took charge, with Lili's help in discharging those expenses that must necessarily now fall to Sir Thomas as the new squire and to her as his wife. Much of the Colonel's correspondence is about day-to-day financial arrangements, of little interest now, but first there was the funeral to be taken care of and then, among much else, the future of the Aynho staff and of his step-mother, the old squire's widow.

Colonel William Cartwright to Sir Thomas Cartwright

Aynhoe, 7th January 1847

My dearest Thomas

It is now my duty to tell you how our mournful arrangements are proceeding. The whole of the family are now assembled that we can expect and on Wednesday next the last duty is to be performed . . . We have agreed that the funeral shall be strictly confined to the family, but if the tenants offer to attend they may do so. It is to be entirely spontaneous on their part. My Mother bears up most wonderfully & seems to reflect upon the happy end of my Poor Father & upon the suffering he has been spared . . .

You will see that my Poor Father has left his servants very well off. I presume that my Mother will keep Gillam [butler] and Powell [housekeeper] and Skelton [cook]. My poor Father told me as a deathbed request to ask you to keep Millard as Park Keeper, but all these sort of things we can talk over when you think it right to come . . .

We have the happiness of knowing that we are all united and all feel that you will be to us a kind and affectionate brother . . .

From *Jackson's Oxford Journal*, 16 January, 1847

The remains of the Fine Old English Squire, who died at the age of 75, were interred in the family vault at Aynho on Wednesday last and we never remember to have witnessed a man descend to the grave with such a manifestation of respect and regret. The funeral took place at 12 o'clock. The duty was performed by Archdeacon Clarke, nephew of the deceased, and the procession composed of the principle of the deceased's family and relations, 38 of the tenants, and the servants of the household, about 40 in number. Most of the labourers of the village joined in the procession on the way to church. The interior of the sacred edifice was hung with black cloth, and crowded with a congregation who appeared to share in the universal grief at the loss of a man who had faithfully served his country for a long period — been an upright landlord — a kind friend — a liberal benefactor to the poor — and a kind and indulgent master to his household.

Colonel William Cartwright to Sir Thomas Cartwright

Aynhoe, 18th January 1847

My dear Thomas

I am now going to write a letter of business to you . . . [there follows a summary of the liabilities of the estate — mortgages, legacies, annuities and settlements, amounting to just over £40,000].

The only thing we wish to know if you do not come is what to do about the establishment. Gillam is waiting for your orders. He is an excellent servant & will do nothing until he hears what you wish to do. Powell will not go to my Mother, who had taken Miss Carter's maid . . . The under-butler goes to my Mother, as also the housemaid and groom. This is all that is at present arranged. My Mother's movements are marked out. She goes first to Edgecote where Aubrey will remain with her until she takes a house in London . . .

There was much to be decided about the future organisation of the Aynho household, for if Sir Thomas was to spend much time abroad a full staff at Aynho would not be required. A note, probably by him, puts the full household expenses of the great house at £4000, made up as follows:-

Household, living, etc.	£1560
Wine	£242 . 10s
Beer	£120
Stables	£300
Servants' wages	£420
Liveries	£120
Firing	£250
Keepers	£324
Gardens	£350
Household wear & tear	£220
Various	£93 . 10s
	£4000 . 00

and the figures are so very precise that they must derive from the actual expenditure in William Ralph's last years.

Edgecote was the home of Julia Cartwright's own eldest son,

Aubrey Cartwright. It was fortunate for the children of William Ralph Cartwright's second marriage that his wife's relations were dying out, and their wealth descending to her children. She was the sister of the last Aubrey baronet, and the family also inherited the property of the Carter family of Chilton in Buckinghamshire. It is hard to see now how William Ralph's younger children would otherwise have been provided for.

Colonel William Cartwright to Sir Thomas Cartwright

Aynhoe, 1st February 1847

Mr dear Thomas . . .

My Mother is most extraordinarily well and her mind as firm and collected as possible . . .

The squire's widow left for Edgecote in early February, leaving Aynho to Lady Cartwright and to the Colonel.

Julia Cartwright: On leaving Aynhoe in Heavy Affliction,

February 1847

Farewell — loved scenes of such domestic bliss
As few experience in a world like this —
Giver of good, for those unclouded days
Accept the tribute of my grateful praise!
Oh! My beloved, hard to be repressed
Are tears & vain regrets, tho' thou art blessed.
Thy voice no longer with affection's power
Soothes my sad heart, & cheers each passing hour;
Lost is my tender Counsellor & Guide,
In whose indulgent love I could confide . . .

With magic art fond memory oft portrays
In vivid tints, the charms of other days;
The joyous groups that o'er the level green
Desported gaily, on a summer even
Till on the terrace wide, the rising moon
Shed her soft rays; then to the gay saloon
They all resort, where song and mirth resound
And all is harmony and peace around.
Yet 'tis not these bright scenes I would recall,
'Tis not for these my rising tears still fall . . .

To him, tranquility and peace were given
And e'en a foretaste of the joys of Heaven!
Oh! When my race is run, my conflict o'er
May we Beloved meet to part no more.

The next passages concern the son of the bailiff at the Home Farm, of whom we shall hear more in due course:-

Banbury Guardian, 4th February, 1847
ACCIDENT AT AYNHO. Mr. Valentine Willifer, a few days ago,
was riding round his farm, when in consequence of the snow on
the ground his horse slipped and fell on his side, fracturing Mr.
Willifer's thigh in two places . . .

Colonel William Cartwright to Sir Thomas Cartwright

Aynhoe, 4th February, 1847

My Dear Thomas
      Poor Val Willifer broke his leg the other day in two places.
He is going on very well. It will confine him some weeks. Willifer
has some barley and Wheat in the yard. What do you want done
about brewing? Would you have the usual quantity brewed?

      Naturally the servants in the great house were supplied with
beer, and probably a superior brew was made for the family, but
of course a reduced establishment would not require so much.
      The next letter shows how difficult things might get when
squire and parson were not on the best of terms.

Colonel William Cartwright to Sir Thomas Cartwright

Aynhoe, 26th February 1847

Dear Thomas . . .
      There is one point I wish to lay before you and which came
to my knowledge . . . only yesterday, and therefore I beg you will
not mention as coming from me [My informant] told me he had
read an advertisement for a curate for Aynhoe, to undertake the
School, & applicant to apply to S.B.C. Now upon this subject I
talked with my poor father and he was quite aware of the immense
importance of knowing who was to be selected for the school now
vacant, as you may get into the parish someone who may hereafter
plague you most exceedingly . . . Stephen has never mentioned the
subject to any of us as I know of, but put this advertisement into
the Ecclesiastical papers, and I think that rather *infra dig* . . .

      That the reverend Stephen Cartwright was something of a
family butt is confirmed by the next letter, which also touches on
one of the sources of the latest ideas in up-to-date farming, and on
the complications of protocol among the servants:-

Colonel William Cartwright to Sir Thomas Cartwright

Aynhoe, 5th March 1847

My dear Thomas . . .
      Why keep the coachman, he is totally useless . . .

Your idea of the post boys being in the Hall [i.e. servants' hall] at Aynhoe is the same as mine & which I took from Whittlebury where no post boy is allowed to enter the house, but they receive 1s from the house steward to go to the public. [i.e. public house] I shall talk this over with Gillam . . .

Should you wish to be a member of the Royal Agricultural Society I will ask Lord Spencer to propose you . . . As they meet at Northampton this July I thought you would wish to be a member at once . . .

I hear the Rector is going to enlarge his house, so I suppose he thinks of enlarging his establishment by a wife although from whence she is to come I cannot imagine.

In view of the uncertainty of Sir Thomas's plans — of when he would be able to spare time to visit Aynho — a similar uncertainty continued with regard to the Aynho household. But with the most pressing matters, such as his step-mother's future, now settled, the Colonel was increasingly able to turn his attention to the farms.

Colonel William Cartwright to Sir Thomas Cartwright
Aynhoe, 11th March 1847

My dear Thomas . . .

I had a good deal of conversation with Gillam as to the establishment and I do not see that you could do with less servants than you have . . . Gillam at present does the housekeeper's work and can do it until you arrive, & the kitchen maid sends up very nice tidy dinners. The brewing will commence this week and the quantity to be brewed will be 12 hogsheads at 9 bushels of malt pr. h. and one hogshead for your own drinking at 6 which will be ready for you on your arrival . . .

I think your plan of taking the Warren Farm in hand very good. It is just the sort of land to be cultivated by artificial manure & the *Yard* will be very handy to *your own farm*. You will find the whole of the Aynhoe farms require remodelling, and that part of your own near the Camp should go to Gardners, which would enable you to take the Warren, & the horses when put to double horse plough instead of done at length would be almost enough for the extra ploughing, besides the advantage of having so much grass land as you have in hand to get stock ready for feeding at stall there in the winter. I cannot imagine a nicer farm than yours if you take the Warren & place such a man as Val Willifer there.

These are only *my ideas* of the thing, but they seem to correspond with your own. I think highly of Val Willifer. He is an extraordinary youth as to stock, & if he had a chance of seeing good arable farming I think he would be a superior servant. What ought to be done with him is to let him go for a season either to the Lothians or to Norfolk . . .

I cannot imagine Gardner doing any good, as he has sold all his stock & is buying very inferior stock now in its place. It never answers to let a man farm land who has not £10 *per acre of good land* to lay out upon it.

The wheat which is in the field towards Old Down & Padbury bottom looks very badly, and I have desired Willifer to put some nitrate of soda & sow over about 2 acres, just to show what it will do. I have also sent for seed for 2 acres of Mangold Wurtzel, which he is to sow near the Pest House. I am obliged to you for thinking of the Swede Turnip seed — it will be a very good thing to get it as a change is very useful. Hillyard intends to sow it if it comes to make a show for the great Agricultural at the show at Northampton. I hope they will get the best sort, with *little* top and *large* bottom.

I think I have answered all your questions to me. As I am very fond of farming you only add to my amusement by any orders you may send me . . . I told Willifer to buy about 12 *Scots* oxen for your own feeding thinking you may wish to have them & if not no great harm will be done, but I could not advise more as they are not the most profitable sort of stock, being bought in dear and not standing stall feeding . . .

Gillam's wife is in service & if she were not I think you would not act prudently in taking her as man & wife pull too much together some times, whereas strangers keep each other in order . . . Gillam tells me that you wish to know how to send things down here. If wine is in a *double* case it should come by water by Pickfords, if in hampers from King's Arms Snow Hill.

I can find no man to live at the lodge belonging to Aynhoe — which does not say much for a population of 600. I think I can find you plenty elsewhere, but Stephen & Willifer both say they cannot recommend anyone here so what shall I do about it . . .

Colonel William Cartwright to Sir Thomas Cartwright

Aynhoe, 28th March 1847

My dear Thomas . . .

I find the farm as usual. Old Willifer not having got the nitrate of soda, being rather a bigotted old fellow I shall have perhaps to get it myself & sow it also, but I am determined to have it done. The wheat requires stimulating, owing to its having been sown so late in the season. The rest of the farm goes on well. The land works most beautifully & spring cropping is carrying on in force. He has sown the field by Millard's with Spring wheat & the field running from the 3 cornered covert to the Buckingham road with peas and beans. The barley is not yet in, but there is no hurry for that at present. The weather has changed and a most lovely rain is now descending.

I think you will find the cropping pursued by the tenants requires attention & also that they have purchased too many Welsh sheep, replacing their old Leicester flocks by sheep of this description — a decided mistake as I know well they are the curse of the Country in Wales & will certainly here be very injurious to the growing crops.

Mrs Skelton [? the former Aynho cook] who went to Pennant has been discharged having only stayed 14 days. She must be a bad one — & it is not much to the credit of the Aynhoe establishment to have concealed her faults from my Father, as they now appear to have been so flagrant. Gillam says you write to him to say that you are surprised the coachman is not gone . . . He has now however had his warning . . .

I have desired Willifer to buy some sheep for immediate consumption, as he had only 11 left of the South Downs & they are not half fat & will come in nicely for you when you come . . . Val Willifer showed me the meat account for last year & I find it amounted to £437 for meat delivered to the house . . .

I have given Willifer seed for two acres of Mangold Wurtzel, & if he gets the Swedish turnips seed from you he will be supplied with green crops. You will find that all the present improved system of farming is not carried out here. Liquid manure pumps and carts not being in existence & Artificial manure being unknown, Scotch ploughs unheard of and no horse hoe in the parish. All this it will take time to bring forward, & you will no doubt yourself wish to introduce them when you come over . . .

They tell me old Willifer was overheard to say to Millard 'they say we want new implements. Bless my soul we have got plenty of wagons & carts & what do they want more?' he is an awkward old fellow to manage I think, but I have said nothing to him but with caution and your authority . . . I am now going to get my stick and walk round the farm . . .

Willifer will want about £250 by the end of April for *Store*

Oxen. Where is he to get it? It is about the value of the Wheat kept back. He has at last sent for the nitrate of soda.

Colonel William Cartwright to Sir Thomas Cartwright

Aynhoe 31st March 1847

My dear Thomas . . .

Willifer went to Chipping Norton today where he sold 6 Devon oxen for £18 each, this will give him plenty of money to go on with at present & there are 5 or 6 more fat beasts to sell.

I do not think Lili could have lived any cheaper anywhere than here & she does much good by her attention to the Villagers — and her presence is of great importance from every point of view . . .

When you get possession of the Warren Farm I think you will find bone dust the best manure you can use, & you should work it with South Down sheep which would give you good mutton for your table . . .

You have not said anything about Val Willifer, which I am sorry for as I could have got him to the same place Doigue was at for £100 for one year, which would have made him a tip top bailiff, and he might be made to serve for 2 years at a reduced salary to cover the amount paid for his apprenticeship to the Lothians. He can never learn anything as to arable farming at Aynhoe where they go on in the system of their forefathers . . .

Pray do not put Jack in the Old Down Pond. They will ruin your trout fishing. Put in *trout*. If you put Jack in the young Jack will get down the brook & destroy every trout & I believe trout will do well in the pond & feed the brook with young trout.

Colonel William Cartwright to Sir Thomas Cartwright

Aynhoe 22nd April 1847

My dear Thomas

By your letter of the 9th inst I find you in a state of excitement against Willifer. I do not mean to say that he has not been somewhat indolent as regards your affairs, but I think you are rather inclined to overate his sins of omission & commission . . .

As to the barley he certainly told me that you had advised him not to sell it & I will look to his letter when I go over on Monday next. I do not think Barley will fall just yet although it has fallen since the malting season, but wheat looks up so much that it must affect Barley also . . .

If I were you I should most decidedly not let Willifer mow

the part of the park railed in for the deer, as it has already been mown too much & the grass in consequence is coarse. The middle ground between the Hill & the Mill should be substituted for it. You may manure a field very highly every year but you cannot encourage the better grasses as you can by feeding it off.

I told Willifer to put Watts (Millard's man) in the cottage as a stop gap and you may arrange when you come what to do with it afterwards. Young Knight would take the situation at £30 and a suit of Clothes but I did not like to say anything definitive as it had better wait till you come . . .

As to the sheep being in the plantations as long as you or your tenants have Welsh sheep they will destroy every fence in the property & so I told you before. When you come you may readily make an arrangement with the Deddington farmers about shooting. I will tell Millard about the hole in the Wall altho' I think it rather premature as the railroad navvies will have the best of it until the game is looked after . . .

There will be much more, later, about the railway from Oxford to Banbury, now building.

Sir Thomas Cartwright to Colonel William Cartwright

Stockholm, 30th April 1847

My dear William . . .

I think that for the present Val Willifer had better remain where he is & think more of his leg than of active farming. He must get well. I wished to place him under Doigue for some time, which I should think would be better than sending him far off, but I am for doing nothing in a hurry, & shall see what is best when I get to England. I am only afraid that he has too much of his father's blood in him to get him easily to adopt enlightened notions. At present he is a second Willifer himself & is just as prejudiced and narrow-minded as Papa and is as much against change & improvement as any Old-Gone-By farmer . . .

There is a break now in the correspondence, presumably because of Sir Thomas's arrival home. No doubt he found much to do: there are indications that he found the Willifer family as difficult face-to-face as when their actions (or inaction) had been reported at second hand. The Colonel we hear less of; he had taken a lease on the house at Floore, towards Daventry, and during his time at home Sir Thomas established good relations with Samuel Field. And he clearly, too, felt obliged to do something for the villagers. There is no reason to suppose that under the old squire the family had neglected their moral obligations, but it may be that the prospect of his own long absences prompted Sir Thomas to place certain things on a more regular footing.

Allotments, which had existed in some form at least since 1830 (then called Potato Ground) were newly laid out where they have lain ever since — in the north-east angle of the Croughton cross-roads. A notebook entitled 'Aynho blankets 1848' survives, with the names of 40 poor villagers given blankets that Christmas. A list of repairs to cottages to be undertaken by estate workmen in the summer of 1848 runs to 27 names — a quarter of the houses in the village — and inevitably prompts comparison with the list of presentations for dilapidations before John Cartwright's manor court over two hundred years before. The circumstances were very different. The 27 include

Mary Watts	Back room window to be re-leaded
	Back kitchen do.
	Slates out of place
Wm. Howes	Casement to be leaded & repaired
	Lean-to to be roofed
George Turner	Thatch round chimney to be repaired
	Plastering inside to be done
Thos. Turner	New window frame for bedroom — old
	Board along bottom of door
Ann French	Privy door & lintel to be mended
	Old paling to garden

The other repairs are similar, and it was clearly Sir Thomas's wish to have everything placed in good order against his departure.

The colonel's letters have already indicated Sir Thomas's interest in taking the Warren Farm in hand. There were no difficulties about this: the tenants of the estate held on annual tenancies, and Mrs. Perkins at the Warren made no more difficulties with Samuel Field than might be expected when — in lieu of formal notice to quit at a Michaelmas or a Lady Day rent day — she agreed to leave the farm whenever she was required to do so, in return for the usual compensation at valuation. Some time in 1847 or 1848 the Warren was taken in for complete modernisation. Modernisation meant a complete new set of farm buildings to accommodate the best stock in ideal conditions; the building of cottages for farm workers; rebuilding the farm house to a standard at which an 'enlightened', up-to-date and progressive farmer might occupy it; and a stationary steam engine to drive threshing machines, chaff mills or whatever other power-driven machinery modern agriculturalists

20. General William Cartwright, c.1860

Second son of William Ralph Cartwright, and a keen agriculturalist (see chapter 12). He married an heiress, and his sons both died childless. He was thus able to leave a substantial amount back to the Aynho branch of the family, enabling William Cornwallis Cartwright and his descendants to live at Aynho despite the impoverishment of the estate by William Ralph Cartwright and William Ralph's eldest son, Sir Thomas.

21. The Great House, 1949, from the North East

22. The Drawing Room at the Rectory, 1846
Drawn by Lady Cartwright (Lili). The home of the Revd. Stephen Cartwright.

23. Cottages on the Charlton Road, 1949: 'Paradise Row', built by William Ralph Cartwright in about 1800 (see pages 187, 256). Each front door leads into a cross passage common to a pair of two-bedroomed cottages.

24. The almshouses, 1949: built in 1821–23, under the terms of the Will of John Baker who died in 1816 (see pages 214–5).

25. The Square, c.1910

26. The church, 1949
Edward Wing's church, with the tower of the medieval church at its west end.

might contrive. The architect was a man called Milne, but Franklin, the builder from Deddington who did much of the work, seems to have provided some of the designs for the farm buildings as well. Local craftsmen and tradesmen also did a good deal, contracted directly to the estate and paid by Samuel Field.

Old Willifer died in late 1848 or early in 1849, when Sir Thomas was in England, but Sir Thomas was in London in March when Field wrote to him about Willifer's affairs. Sir Thomas replied:-

Sir Thomas Cartwright to Samuel Field

30, Albemarle Street, 30th March 1849

Dear Mr. Field,

I shall not think of admitting these new claims upon me from Willifer's Executors till I have been to Aynho and examined my Weekly Farm book, for from the slovenly habits of Willifer in keeping his accounts it is very probable that some of these have already been settled . . . If Willifer chose to keep his accounts in disorder it is not my fault & I wish to have my affairs with his estate closed once and for all. There is no knowing how many of these little slips of paper they may find around the house . . . I think we have had now sufficient proof in many ways how totally unfit Willifer was to manage the Farm, let alone the Estate . . .

Sir Thomas's normally regular handwriting became positively frenzied as he wrote, some evidence of his state of mind.

Sir Thomas's concern for up-to-date farming extended to the tenanted farms, and while he was unwilling to disturb existing tenants he was extremely keen to get better ones when old farmers were giving up. His letters to Field are full of remarks on the existing farmers on the estate and on applicants to succeed them, and together with his remarks on the Willifers are a commentary on rural politics and on the contrast between the old farming and the new. He was back in post in Stockholm in the early summer of 1849, and the length of time taken for letters to pass between there and Deddington — even by the Diplomatic Bag — means that his and Field's letters do not always seem to answer one another.

Samuel Field to Sir Thomas Cartwright

Deddington, 18th May 1849

Sir Thomas . . .

Young John Bygrave of Aynho spoke to me for [the Warren Farm]. He dislikes keeping an Inn & wishes to leave the White

Hart. I think this is a farm that would suit him, & if you would like to let it to him as an Aynho man I think the other applicants would not feel as much disappointment . . .

It may be that John Bygrave was far-sighted enough to forsee the effects that the railway, now building, would have on the business of his Inn.

Samuel Field to Sir Thomas Cartwright

Deddington, 24th May 1849

Sir Thomas . . .

Shall I offer [a certain farm] to Mr. Billing? From what I know of him I think him an eligible tenant & one that will not lower the farm in cultivation. I remembered what Mr. Beasley had said to you & I therefore asked him to tell me plainly what was alleged against them & all I could get was that 'there was something not quite satisfactory on the father leaving Holkham.' It so happens that at Leicester lately I met with a gentleman who knew the Billings & without his knowing the object of my enquiries I learnt from him that the reason for the elder Mr. Billing leaving Holkham was that on his first coming there Lady Leicester had taken a great dislike to him . . .

I fear that your tenant John Harris of Clifton is like to die of a bad fever & if he does, I apprehend that his nephew who is so fond of racing & coursing is not an eligible tenant to succeed him . . .

I have fixed the Rent Day for 19th June. The state of the markets and the general scarcity of money make me very apprehensive that we may have some defaulters on the day. As there are none I believe among them who are not responsible men, a little indulgence as to time may be reasonably allowed them if required especially for a Lady Day rent in these times.

The cottage on the Warren is getting on & I have allowed Secull two additional men, for Underwood is rather in haste to have the new hovelling in the yard finished.

The next two of Sir Thomas's letters concern, among others, Robert Gardner, the tenant of Nell Bridge Farm, whose selling off his good stock and buying bad has been mentioned in a previous letter, two years before. A constant theme of Sir Thomas's letters is the necessity for progressive farmers to have sufficient capital, which Gardner clearly did not have:-

Sir Thomas Cartwright to Samuel Field

Stockholm, 8th June 1849

Dear Mr. Field . . .

I am not much in favour of Mr. Billing jnr. I do not think that the late Lord Spencer [sic] would have removed the father merely to favour the whim of Lady Leicester. He who was a thorough agriculturalist would not have removed a thoroughly good bailiff, the superintendant of as great a concern as Holkham, at the caprice of a Lady. But that matter only in point of fact affects the Father. I wish to have a thorough Agriculturalist, a man whose whole attention is in his farm. Now I suspect that Mr. Billing jnr is a Sporting Farmer . . . Moreover I do not much like the tone of his speech in the Banbury Guardian of the 24th ult. responding to the toast of 'The Agricultural Interest' . . .

Gardner's farm is in excellent condition and as to farming, he is the best tenant I have, and will on that account be a great loss, but I do not see how he can remain . . .

If the Scotts are to remain another year so let it be, but I have been much surprised to see in the Banbury Guardian & Oxford Journal the Advertisement that I enclose . . . As you have not mentioned that you have allowed them to sell by auction any part of the Pasture on their farm, I fancy that it must have been done without your knowledge. It is perhaps too late to object but in this way we may have the Cattle disease all over the place by having the farm stocked with strange cattle. This matter settles the question about the farm, for never was it allowed nor can it be allowable for a tenant to underlet his land. This is a highly objectionable proceeding and ought to be stopped if possible. I know that they have had losses, but in part by their own fault for the loss of the sheep was owing to their choosing to take to Welsh sheep and keep them too long on ground that was too good for them . . .

The Scotts were the tenants of Aynho Grounds, the beneficiaries of the remarkable tenancy agreement of 1835 quoted at the beginning of this chapter. The Cattle Disease is probably foot-and-mouth, known from 1839 onwards and already widespread.

Sir Thomas felt obliged to explain matters to Gardner himself:-

Sir Thomas Cartwright to Robert Gardner

Stockholm, 19th June 1849

Mr. Gardner . . .

You have unfortunately got into pecuniary embarassments which are such, that you have found it necessary to come to an arrangement with your creditors, & they have consented to take, either ten or twelve shillings in the pound (for I do not exactly remember which) in lieu of their just due.

Now it is self evident, that if you had become so deeply involved, that you are compelled to make a Composition of this nature with your Creditors, you cannot be in possession of the Capital necessary to enable you to manage & stock a farm of the extent & description of that which you have held for many years under my Father & now hold under me . . . You must recollect that this is the second time that you have, within a few years, become involved in considerable pecuniary difficulties . . .

Sir Thomas was decided in his prejudices, which were probably not unjust:-

Sir Thomas Cartwright to Samuel Field

Stockholm, 9th June 1849

Dear Mr. Field . . .

I really forget whether I answered that part of your letter respecting Harris when I wrote a week ago. I therefore — at the risk of repetition — state that should I lose the present tenant I am not disposed to take the sporting nephew. I want tenants with Capital, forward agricultural minds, & who are wrapped up in their trade . . .

Samuel Field's misgivings (above May 24th) about the Rent Day were not realised:-

Samuel Field to Sir Thomas Cartwright

Deddington, 20th June 1849

Sir Thomas . . .

The Rent Day . . . went off very well, scarcely any arrears and none of the tenants asking for any abatement of rent though they certainly complain of the times . . .

while in his next letter he refers again to matters that have arisen already. Also to a little business of the Rector's, which he is clearly uncertain whether to take seriously nor not:-

Samuel Field to Sir Thomas Cartwright

Deddington, 30th June 1849

Sir Thomas,

Gardner came & paid his rent and then said that he hoped he should be allowed to continue on the farm, for he had got a friend who would come forward and guarantee to find him sufficient money to carry it on properly & who would be bound for the payment of the Rent. He says he would bring him to me . . . I told him that if he would bring his friend to me I would hear what he had to offer and would then judge of the propriety of submitting his application to you . . .

I wrote to Billing, declining any negotiation with him for the farm. I afterwards saw him when he wanted to know the reason which of course I declined giving. I have heard that the late Lord Leicester left by his Will to each of his servants a year's wages & that old Mr. Billing claimed under that bequest, a year's salary, £350 or some such sum, that the Executors refused to pay & that he then commenced an action against them, when they paid the demand & that he was then dismissed . . . I cannot vouch for the truth of this story . . .

Mr. Stephen spoke to me the other day about the Park Wall which you know is fallen down between you and him . . . I must moreover tell you what Mr. Stephen said in the matter. He said 'he did not know that he would much object to take it on himself for if he did he should take it quite down & substitute an iron fence so as to let in a view of the Park to the Garden & Close' & he added 'besides there will be lots of hares which will then come into my Close & then I may as well shoot them'. I can't imagine that either the iron fence close to your garden walk or the shooting of the hares would be agreeable to you. It might have been without a real intention of doing one or the other, & with a view of its being reported to you & thus getting you to repair the wall . . .

Your tenant John Harris at Clifton is dead . . . His nephew has applied for it for his mother & himself. I gave him no hopes. Women are not desirable tenants & he himself is not yet of age . . .

Milne has been at the Warren & Underwood expects the plans of the new buildings next week. The cottage is getting on. I hope you will not think it too well done. It is a great set off to the Road and the Plantations there . . .

The Grass crops are very heavy about here and the weather has been very fine for them.

It is uncertain which farm the following refers to:-

Samuel Field to Sir Thomas Cartwright

Deddington, 11th July 1849

Sir Thomas . . .

I could not get over to see Timms until this week . . . He says he would live better out of business than by holding the farm at the present rent with these prices, & he asked me to 'present his duty' to you & say that he will do anything for your accommodation & that if he leaves the farm there shall be nothing disagreeable on his part — that he shall leave it a poorer man than he came 21 years ago and the farm in better condition (the latter is always said by an outgoing tenant) . . .

Timms too complains of the game & foxes. He has had a fat sheep stolen & is going to Northampton to assizes tomorrow to prosecute a railway labourer whom Morgan has apprehended for taking it . . .

Timms's pasture was very badly out of condition, covered in tussocks, and Sir Thomas was anxious to get rid of him if he could.

Sir Thomas Cartwright to Samuel Field

Stockholm, July 15th

Dear Mr. Field,

I received your two letters of the 30th June and 2nd July by the last post from England. I am happy to learn that the Rent Day went off well. If farms are let fairly — which they ought to be — and if Farmers have the Capital which their farms demand (& without which they ought never to hold them) a year of *low prices* ought not to make any difference in the payment of rent. The loss on one year of low prices ought to be amply covered by the gain on other years of good prices. But years of short harvests, when the crops are half ruined through the elements and give bad returns both in quantity and quality, demand some consideration, for then when combined with low prices in consequence of the bad quality of the produce, the farmer does not suffer through the caprice of the Market but from causes beyond his control. In such a case, there ought to be some consideration for him if the following harvest does not right him . . .

I am quite ready to accept or rather continue Gardner as tenant for the farm he now holds upon the terms you have mentioned, if he can procure bona fide capital sufficient to stock his farm as it ought to be stocked, & continue the management as it ought to be managed. He is an excellent agriculturalist and as to the management of his land he is the best tenant I have. The farm will demand a Capital of near £3000 to be managed properly . . .

You were quite right not to give any reason to Mr. Billing for declining to take him as a tenant. I do not see that I am called upon to state why I will not let a farm to the first person who may choose to apply for it . . .

Stephen's threats are perfectly ridiculous but they are like him. He has always been accustomed to have everything done for him, and thinks now the system should be continued. I do not mean to do any one thing but what I am strictly compelled to do, as far as the Rectory and its appurtenances are concerned. If the repair of this wall positively falls on me of course I shall undertake it. But it must be made quite clear to me that it is my wall . . . As to Stephen's threats about the hares it is too childish to deserve any notice being taken of it . . .

It was never my intention to have Milne to Aynhoe for the Hovels & other additions which I wish to make at the Warren. I should have been quite satisfied with leaving the matter in Franklin's hands & I thought I had made both him and Underwood understand that such was my intention. But no inconvenience will accrue from Mr. Milne being called in except a little additional expense. In future however I think that Franklin for all our farm buildings will be the best person to employ. Underwood probably thought Milne indispensible from his having given the plan of the original buildings.

The whole expense of the Cottage and the new additional buildings at the Warren — the steam engine, threshing machine & so on will be defrayed out of the receipts of the farm. I hope Franklin is keeping to the plan I saw of the cottage & has made the alterations I pointed out. The cottage was very neat, but I thought there were too many doors, and made a change in this respect which I hope he has adhered to.

I have every reason to be satisfied with Underwood, and next year (and my farm year dates from the 1st of Oct to the 1st of Oct) will bring me a good return out of which the steam engine and the additional expenses at the Warren will be covered. Underwood has carried all my hay at a period when old Willifer had hardly even commenced mowing, and I have 50 acres to Swedes up & growing well, when Willifer last year had not commenced sowing my Swedes . . . I think I shall want to buy a few more oxen and some more sheep and I shall then be set up in stock. He tells me that my what is looking very well indeed as also the barley. I think prices are likely to get up & I have desired him to sell the remaining quantity of wheat, on hand from the last harvest . . .

Underwood was Willifer's successor at the Home Farm, apparently managing the Warren Farm as well while the alterations and improvements were in progress. Gardner at Nell Bridge farmed 294 acres, so the capital of £3,000 that Sir Thomas thought it necessary for him to have was almost exactly the £10 an acre that the Colonel had also thought was needed.

Samuel Field to Sir Thomas Cartwright

Deddington, 21st July 1849

Dear Sir Thomas . . .

Millard has just been here with his monthly account . . . He says his pheasants get on well & that he thinks it will be a fair season for game. He wishes me to mention that he had not yet had an account of the venison to be given away, he wants the names of the persons to whom he is to send . . .

A haunch of venison from the squire was a gracious rural compliment to farmers, leading tradesmen and any poorer gentry whom he wished to assist, and had probably come to be expected by many of them as a regular, annual present.

Work at the Warren was progressing, but it was slow. In several of the letters between Field and Sir Thomas during the autumn of 1849 complaint is made about the lack of progress, and it may be that Sir Thomas was becoming apprehensive about the expense. There were some small things that were irritating. Field had persuaded Sir Thomas to take on James Secull the mason for a year at £45 ('I consider him worth all the money' he had written) but Sir Thomas doubted that this was a bargain. There was, too, the question of whether work should be contracted by the piece or by measured day work; in any case the cost was mounting up. By the spring of 1849 the cost had already approached £3,000, and there was still enough to do to keep men employed into the following year.

Sir Thomas Cartwright to Samuel Field

Christiania, 19th September 1849

Dear Mr. Field . . .

I do not wonder at the building getting on slowly. If the arrangement with Secull proves practically disadvantageous put an end to it, but I thought that we should always have work for him independent of great undertakings which he might assist, if not otherwise employed . . .

Samuel Field to Sir Thomas Cartwright

Deddington, 22nd October 1849

Sir Thomas . . .

The new buildings at the Warren are complete & if the weather continues a few days longer it will be all covered in & will be quite ready for the Engine before it arrives. Mr. Milne has been over & is quite satisfied with it. The Chimney is up, & that part of the building is finished & the open hovels across the yard are covered in . . .

I rode over to the Warren Farm with Underwood last week. He has got some splendid Mangold Wortzel. The weather here is very fine & I should think a finer Harvest cannot be remembered.

Many thanks for a fine haunch of venison you desired to be sent to me . . .

This letter will have crossed with another from Sir Thomas about another matter altogether — the railway. Building the line between Oxford and Banbury had begun two years before; the exploits of navvies have been touched on already, and a fuller account of the building of the line follows in the next chapter. In Aynho and Souldern the Company had to acquire their land from the Cartwright estate, and by the time Sir Thomas wrote the letter which follows next he was clearly persuaded that the Great Western was playing fast and loose. The letter concerns the origin of the present pub by the station, the Great Western Arms;-

Sir Thomas Cartwright to Samuel Field

Christiania, 28th October, 1849

Dear Mr. Field . . .

It appears that the Railway Company have purchased Rutter's House [i.e. the Alfred's Head public house] the garden & some of the stabling for £1000 of the Canal Company and that after taking as much of the ground as they may require for their own purposes, damaging the convenience of the house to a great extent, and blocking up the front, they have offered to sell me the house so damaged & that portion of the premises which they do *not require*, for the same sum which they have given for the whole. This mode of treating me, & treating with me, has thoroughly disgusted me. A more exorbitant demand, could not have been made. I do not think that in our transactions with the Company we have ever been otherwise than straightforward, fair, & reasonable, and I considered therefore that we had every reason to expect to be treated in a similar manner . . .

With regard to the question of the necessity of an Inn to be built or arranged at the station, it appears to me that public convenience requires that a small Inn or Public House should be established there with sufficient stabling to enable travellers to put up their horses & vehicles, and the innkeeper to keep a fly or two or a gig and a fly.

I once thought that the best thing would be for the person occupying the Cartwright Arms to rent also this small inn, & then less stabling might be required at the station. But this requires consideration and one indispensible arrangement to it would be that I should have another tenant at Aynho instead of Mrs. Holloway who is a screw & has been a very bad occupant of the Cartwright Arms & would not be able to carry out my intentions or understand her own advantages. We must have a man there & not a woman . . .

Admitting then that a Public House such as I have described be required for Public convenience it cannot be for my interests that that public house should belong to anyone but myself.

The question then is, whether the present premises, circumscribed as they are all to be by the Company's works, & hemmed in on all sides, & blocked up in front by the wall which is necessary to hold the sloping, can be made available as they stand for such a purpose, & are worth purchasing with that view . . .

It strikes me . . . that it will be most advisable to pull the present premises down & build what is required quite afresh. We do not want a large inn — a small house with merely a couple of good rooms, a good tap, kitchen & such outbuildings as may be necessary with stabling to suit the traffic. I should think that with £500, the materials of the present premises & my own timber & stone we should be able to make a very good job . . .

The Company should be made to comprehend that they had so impaired the present premises that they would no longer be available for the object I wanted. The Company ought to understand that it is in their interest that there should be a good public house there with good accommodation, & if they had put it out of my power to arrange this — for I am not disposed to throw away money for them — they will be the sufferers . . .

Leave nothing to verbal understanding for we may find ourselves duped. The ground should be measured, & the ground *to a yard* specified in the agreement. Take good care that we are not done in this business.

Sir Thomas's next letter reverts to farming matters:-

Sir Thomas Cartwright to Samuel Field

Stockholm, 4th November, 1849

Dear Mr. Field . . .

I have heard . . . that my turnips were very good indeed. The Swedes have been grown in a field where I was told by Willifer it would be *useless to attempt* to grow them, for that the land was not suitable for them.

Underwood thinks that he has great reason to complain of the decision of the judges for the turnip prize at the Banbury Agricultural meeting. They awarded the prize to Mr. Neville of Tew and Underwood tells me that his turnips were neither so *large* nor as *clean* as my turnips. I can very well imagine that there was partiality in the decisions. The Gentlemen have never been well looked on in that Society. I am contemplating withdrawing from the Society altogether — not on account of any of their decisions respecting the prizes, partial or unfair as many think they have been, nor on account of Politics at the dinner, though against the rules, but on account of the tone taken against the landlords. I think that if Gentlemen support a society in which the tone of the farmers at the annual meeting is directly abusive of them, and is directed against their interests, they are very great simpletons. It will be a great misfortune if the Society should be broken up, through the proceedings of these persons, but I for one will not submit to be tutored, or lectured, or browbeaten by them. The labourers will be great losers by Mr. Bozes & co. will be the cause . . .

The right mode where a farm is out of condition is precisely as you propose, to let it for the first year or two at a lower rent than the land ought to bear, which will give the tenant the means of getting it about. I think that with the exception of Gardner's & perhaps Holloway's farm there is no one of my farms in the state in which it ought to be . . .

The point made by Sir Thomas about the labourers suffering by the winding-up of the local agricultural society is probably that the Banbury society, like most others, gave awards and prizes to farm workers who were recommended for them, and these windfalls of a guinea or two were very welcome indeed.

Sir Thomas Cartwright to Samuel Field

Stockholm, 4th December 1849

Dear Mr. Field,

In your letter of the 30th June you said that at the Rent Day on the 19th of June some of the tenants said that they hoped on a future occasion that low prices would meet with consideration, and as the next rent day is approaching & some of the tenants may ask for reductions of rent in accordance with what may seem to be the clamour of the day, I think I may as well send you my sentiments on the subject.

I see no reason whatever to grant anything of the kind . . .

I know that on my own farm I have in my rickyard *full* one third more corn than I had last year, partly from the effects of a good Harvest and partly the effects of *a better system of cultivation.* I presume that my case is not exceptional, but that others in our district might with the same attention & care have had the same results. If they however farm slovenly or haven't the Capital enough to cultivate their farms well, I do not see that I ought to be the sufferer . . .

Sir Thomas's absence did not make him forget what was due at Christmas to the villagers, as his next letter to Field shows. Following that are a couple of invoices from Mrs. Holloway at the Cartwright Arms for rent-day entertainments, suitably graded, for cottagers and for farm tenants on successive weeks:-

Sir Thomas Cartwright to Samuel Field

Stockholm, 13th December 1849

Dear Mr. Field . . .

My sister Mrs. Gunning has written me word that the Poor feel our absence very much. No one has been thrown out of work through my absence, and I think some of the Ayno cottagers a grumbling and complaining set, but there may be families that be in real want and deserve and require succour. I think that the best charity is to give in kind — coals, blankets, soup or bread, for money often goes to the ale house. I request you to do in this matter as may be necessary and as you may think fit, without further reference to me . . .

Sir Thomas Cartwright dr. to S. Holloway		
Cottage tenants		
Dec. 21	77 dinners @ 1s 6d each	£5 16 0
	Ale to do. @ 6d each	£1 18 0
	Fire to do.	2 6
		£7 16 6
Rent Day		
Dec. 18	41 dinners @ 2s 6d each	£5 2 6
	Wine to do. @ 5s each	£10 5 0
	Fire to do.	2 6
		£15 10 0

It is evident from the next letters that work was still dragging on at the Warren, and that George Walton, one of the Aynho crafts-men, was to blame:-

Sir Thomas Cartwright to Samuel Field

Stockholm, 1st February 1850

Dear Mr. Field . . .

I hear from Gillam that one of the almshouses has become vacant and that Stephen has taken on himself without one single line to me to put someone into it. I suppose that I shall next hear of his establishing himself in Aynhoe House . . .

I am afraid Walton is not equal to the charge he has under-taken. Franklin last year always complained that the carpenters were behind hand, & when I spoke to him, his answer was always that 'it would be ready before it was wanted' . . . Underwood says that he had spoken to Walton about these things often, but that he had never taken the least notice of what he had said, but had al-ways replied that all would be ready by the time they would be wanted. This is always his answer, and then when the time comes the things are never ready . . .

Sir Thomas Cartwright to Samuel Field

Stockholm, 14th February 1850

Dear Mr. Field . . .

With regard to the Clifton farm, I leave you to select the tenant, only I will on no account take Joseph Willifer, even if he should have the necessary capital, which I doubt. I have had enough of the Willifers. John Willifer is the best of them and a good far-mer, but I do not want anything more to do with them and have no opinion of Joseph Willifer's knowledge of farming.

There are two things indispensible whenever there may be question of new tenants. The one is undoubted possession of *ample* capital, for in these times all farming will go to the wall without a reserve to draw upon during low prices, & without the means to enable the tenant to farm in good style. And secondly, which is full as necessary as the first point, the certainty that the applicant is a thorough good farmer, alive to improvements, and has a thorough knowledge of the best system of cultivation. I have few tenants of this description . . . I hope that what I am doing myself will lead to a better system on the part of the tenants, but many of them are far behind hand . . .

Now with regard to the future. I hope that I now have got to the end of borrowing. I should like however to have a summary of the Receipts and payments you have made since the accounts were last made up, when you have leisure to forward it to me. It is possible that I may require, to put things quite straight, £500 more, but this must be decided hereafter when I know how the balance may be . . .

With regard to my own farm I have done with building for the present. The Warren buildings are not yet as complete as I mean them to be, but next summer I mean to do nothing more than complete the buildings which are already erected, and arrange the yards & interior of the buildings, hovels etc, where the carpenter and others may still have work to do. But I shall leave the stables as they are for another winter or two for if the horses have passed two winters in them they may well pass two more. Therefore as to brick and mortar next summer I shall require little use of them for my own farm . . .

Sir Thomas Cartwright to Samuel Field

Stockholm, 9th April 1850

Dear Mr. Field,

I merely write a few lines to tell you that since I last wrote to you, I have been a *great* invalid . . .

I think when a farm is henceforward to be let the new tenant should be made perfectly to understand that he takes it at the rent fixed at his own risk . . . I want that the rents shall be *stable* and a moderate rent, which the tenant may be certain will not be altered . . .

I think you should take steps to apply for a sum out of the money which the Government is to lend out on loan for draining. Apply for £1500. We shall want it on the various farms . . .

Eight days later Sir Thomas was dead.

The heir, William Cornwallis Cartwright, could not at once be found. (His father had earlier upbraided him for his peripatetic habits and his tendency not to leave addresses behind him.) To him, a young man of 24, who must have been looking forward to many carefree years before he in turn would in the natural course of things succeed his father, Sir Thomas's death must have come as a great shock. When at length he was traced, he hastened with all speed to Stockholm to comfort his mother and to look at his father's affairs. Here there were immediate problems, the most pressing of which were the meeting of his Father's liabilities in Sweden and the provision of his mother and himself with the wherewithal to live. He wrote soon after his arrival, as soon as he had taken stock of the situation, to Field:-

William Cornwallis Cartwright to Samuel Field

Stockholm, 28th May 1850

My dear Field,

On arriving here I found your letter. Since then I have examined all my late Father's papers here amongst which no Will or testamentary paper of any description was found. This was all done by me in the presence of the Consul who had put his seal on the room, and I have his certificate of the same. I myself proceed with my mother to Germany the day after tomorrow and after drinking the Homburg waters I shall come to England in the end of June or the beginning of July.

Now for business. The personal property is to be sold to cover Stockholm debts. You must let me know what moneys may exist in any banks, in short what property there is to cover his debts. I have taken myself the moneys furnished by the bankers here since his death for the establishment and have given a bill on Hoare at three months' date, for £356. 18s. 1d. I am afraid there is a great deficit in my Father's finances. Tell me when by Mother's dowry begins? . . .What moneys remain to me? . . . I feel that the income of Aynhoe is fearfully curtailed and I must consequently live with great economy . . . I have only enough ready money to last a fortnight — tell me I have a right to draw on Hoare . . .

It is not my intention to continue the Warren Farm. I mean to dispose of the Stock and let it. Such a thing cannot be done directly but I suppose there need be no great delay in arranging a sale and I suppose that its produce will be my own. You have done quite right to stop all buildings etc at Aynhoe but I wish to know about the state of things there for in fact I know nothing whatever. Let Underwood & Millard etc. write to me if they have anything to say. You will understand from this letter how I am in want of information on every point . . .

Between travelling day and night, the anxiety about my Mother and the whole wear and tear of the present circumstances I am not quite well and therefore I have determined before proceeding to England to drink the waters as there is no such pressing business that a month could not be spared. That death truly came like a thunderbolt upon me . . .

P.S. If my brother comes out you had better give him £100 because I want some and my mother also — ready money is drained. She especially wants some.

There was only one more matter to attend to while waiting for fuller information from Field:-

William Cornwallis Cartwright to Samuel Field

Stockholm, 30th May 1850

My dear Field,

These few lines written on the point of starting will inform you that I have made the agreement with Capt Allen of the *Sykes* to carry my poor Father's remains to Hull for £15 and incidental expenses of landing etc. to be consigned to George Malcolm at Hull. Put yourself in communication with him, announce yourself as my agent and should you hear of the arrival of the Corpse before you get any further instructions from me, as the ship sails in a day or two, consult Mr. Stephen.

Colonel William, who had acted for his brother on the death of the old squire three years before, was keen once more to do what he could:-

Colonel William Cartwright to Samuel Field

Flore, June 13th 1850

My dear Sir,

I presume you have been made acquainted with the last intellegence that I have received — which is that the remains are on the road home and that Mr. William is to remain in Homburg till the end of July. I shall go out to him the beginning of the month and shall also see his mother. As she will be in want of money most probably, would it not be advisable for you to pay £250 to her account with Messrs Hoare when you get the rents . . . I know nothing about Mr. W.C's arrangements, but as he appears to be thinking of taking a separate house for Lady Cartwright I cannot imagine that he is aware of the small sum which without her assistance will be left to him to keep up Aynhoe . . .

This time, however, the Colonel's interference was not welcome. Samuel Field wrote to the young heir at Homburg with fuller information which William Cornwallis did not find encouraging.

William Cornwallis Cartwright to Samuel Field

Homburg, June 17th 1852

My dear Field,

Col. Cartwright has no authorisation from me to inquire into or manage my affairs. I have received letters from him in which he never mentioned having examined them. I am therefore more than astonished at your supposing that the information which I had asked for in my letter to you would have been sent to me by him or by any third person . . .

As far as I can at present understand the Rent Roll at Aynhoe after the 25th June is subject to the following deductions. The interest on the £40,000 mortgage, the doweries & my brother's portion . . . I must say that the other charges had staggered me for I always understood that the only encumberance was the mortgage which I had made on the understanding that it was to pay off all debts, & as the law does not force me to raise money to pay them off I will only deal with them as I am forced. I cannot keep up Aynhoe on a pittance of £2000 a year which alone would remain. The debts are not of my making . . .

As you say you want directions about many things, name them. I shall be in England in the middle of next month. I am better than I was but I want rest. Plain business letters no trouble but the communications of crude advice on all hands is of no earthly help & only gives trouble . . .

The unavoidable commitments of the estate came to over £7,000 annually. The principal ones were doweries of £1,000 to his grandmother, William Ralph's widow, and of £1,500 to his mother Lady Cartwright, £1,100 to his brother Thomas and to the Revd. Stephen, £1,500 interest on the mortgage, numerous annuities and pensions to old servants and the like, and the irreducible costs of managing the Aynho estate which, even if William Cornwallis did not occupy the great house, would come to close on £1,000. Sir Thomas would have found things extremely tight without his salary, and his own expenditure had considerably increased the estate's liabilities. As the heir of an entailed estate, William Cornwallis must have assented to the consolidation of many liabilities into a huge mortgage (with the Norwich Union company at 3¾ per cent) only a few years before, but had probably failed to realise the additional commitments resulting from his grandfather's death. His inheritance must have seemed deeply flawed, as indeed it was, and his enjoyment of it highly problematical. It will have been difficult for him to think without a trace of bitterness about the old squire or about his Father whose extravagances had to be paid for by a new generation. In the long term, of course, the situation would improve as those in receipt of pensions and doweries died and the sums reverted to the estate, but there was no cause for immediate comfort.

This series of extracts from letters is approaching an end. The letters themselves continue, now from William Cornwallis's brother, Thomas Cartwright, who with his allowance of £600 a year settled in the neighbourhood to farm on his own account and to be his brother's agent, taking over much of the day-to-day work that had formerly been done by the bailiff of the Home Farm (Willifer and latterly Underwood) and by Samuel Field. Having frequent contact with Field, Thomas seems to have been less impressed by him than Sir Thomas had been at a distance, and when Field's partner, William Churchill, absconded in 1870 with some hundreds of Cartwright money unaccounted for (besides a good deal of other people's) it must have seemed some consolation that Thomas had taken an increasing amount of estate business on himself.

There could be no question of the squire's continuing to live at the great house. Even if the £4,000 a year that Sir Thomas had considered necessary had been an over-estimate (and in view of Sir Thomas's expansive notions it probably was) £2,000 could not be nearly enough. Consequently there was no point keeping the Warren or the Home Farms in hand: the Home Farm's prime function had been the supply of the household in the great house, and profitable farming for market a secondary consideration only; the Warren was an expensive whim of Sir Thomas's but had now to be let on a sound business footing. Even if William Cornwallis has been interested in farming, and there is no great evidence to suppose that he was, high farming was not always highly profitable. William Cornwallis spent many of the succeeding years abroad, in Rome and elsewhere, and only towards the end of his life came to Aynho for any length of time.

To tie up a few loose ends. The squire cancelled his subscription to the Banbury Agricultural Society, with consequent embarrassment to all concerned when in the autumn of 1850 Underwood's turnips (exhibited, of course, in the squire's name) did win the prize they deserved. The Revd. Stephen did marry, in the summer of 1848, Lady Fanny Hay, daughter of the Earl of Erroll, but this seems to have done nothing to reconcile him to his family nor to save him from the continuance of their snide remarks. The Willifers vanish from the scene, though at the Census of 1851 Joseph with his young family was living with one of the Aynho farmers and was described as 'out of employment'. The railway will be discussed more fully in the next chapter; the Great Western Arms, the pub that Sir Thomas built, still stands.

Extracts from four letters of Thomas's and one from the new squire may close the chapter, since they bring us down from the lofty schemes of Sir Thomas and his easy ways with money, from high finance and high farming, to the day-to-day life of the village. To rural crime, in fact: to poaching. In the autumn of 1850 the squire had written to Samuel Field 'I must have the Home Farm measured, and that immediately, as a person has applied, a Mr. Cox, who I think is likely to get it'. Clearly Mr. Cox impressed him favourably. The impression was not to last.

Thomas Cartwright to William Cornwallis Cartwright

Merton College, Oxford, 4th December 1851

My Dear Willy . . .

I saw Cox on Monday. On the Saturday I told him quite quietly that I thought he ought to have spoken to me before he went shooting in the way he did, because he promised you so long as the game was in your hands he would leave it to Millard, which he denied as I told you in my former letter. He also said he had placed the guns outside & the beaters went to drive the rabbits and hares out . . .

I saw Millard afterwards who took his oath that he saw three hares shot in the cover. I therefore saw Cox again on Monday to tell him this and I had hardly said it when he got into a towering passion & quite trembled with rage, said he was not going to be dependant on me or to be made my slave nor be bullied by the keeper and me. I told him he had no right whatever to shoot hares and rabbits in the covers, he could only ferret them which means, turning ferrets into the holes & catching them in nets as they come out, & not go with beaters and dogs and disturb all the covers. He said ferreting meant to search for rabbits in any way, that he had his bargain and would stick to it . . . I told him that if he came into the covers again in the same way I would have him up for trespass . . . Would you mind writing to Cox about it? He says if you had been here nothing of the sort would have happened . . .

What will you give away to the poor people at Xmas this time? Some ought to have coals & some blankets . . .

William Cornwallis Cartwright to Edwin Cox (draft)

n.d.

Mr. Cox.

It is with astonishment which transcends expression that I

this day have received information of actions and words of yours towards me and my brother which are of such wanton and unprovoked violence that I fear I have all along been duped by you. I do not know what scruple you may have about denying in acknowledging conversations you had with me about the destruction of the game but I know for my own personal satisfaction that as the shooting was in my hands you would not interfere with it, all which you undoubtedly remember as much as I do. If you . . . having received from me every consideration that a tenant can desire make use of these priveleges with the most wanton disregard of any consideration for the wishes I expressed to you, you must not be surpised that after having been startled out of the unbounded confidence which I delighted in reposing in a tenant of your standing and education henceforth from an unfortunate necessity that suspicion which is hateful to me should rule my conduct . . . When after every indulgence my right is attacked I am as obstinate in defending it as I had before been willing to grant concessions.

An expression of righteous indignation of which the old squires in the seventeenth century might have been proud.

During the following year the brothers were already considering how Cox was to be got rid of. The difficulty was that while William Ralph Cartwright and Sir Thomas had both let farms by the year, William Cornwallis had granted Cox a seven year lease, to break which the landlord would have to pay compensation unless it could be proved that the tenant had in some way or other unfitted himself to continue farming. A year later they were still in a quandary about it. But as to poaching by lesser folk, that could be dealt with in a very much more summary fashion.

Thomas Cartwright to William Cornwallis Cartwright

Tew Park, Enstone. 22nd January, 1853

My dear Willy,

I have delayed writing till now in hopes that I might give you more decided news about Cox, but I am sorry to say it is not yet settled . . .

Millard has been very active catching poachers. I told him I knew poaching was going on and I insisted on his trying to catch them. The consequence was that one morning he caught Lambert of Nell Bridge & a Clifton man shooting without a license. They will most probably be fined £10 each or 3 months at the jail. Three nights ago Adkins, the man who lives at the lodge, caught a Souldern man in the act of shooting a hare. He took hold of him and in the act of doing so the gun went off & the charge carried away the pocket of Adkins's coat. He had a very narrow escape indeed. I have laid the information against the man for night poaching which is 3 months imprisonment & to find two sureties in £10 to keep the peace for 12 months, in default of which he is to be imprisoned another 6 months. As he is a very bad character most likely no one will stand surety for him. If that is the case we get rid of him for 9 months. There is a regular gang of poachers beginning to form around Aynhoe — the policeman knows them.

Cox's downfall would be sealed sooner than either brother, at the present moment, could know. It is uncertain whether Cox was farming the Warren as well as the Home Farm or whether the Warren was still in hand, still being farmed by Underwood with Thomas Cartwright's active supervision. In any case a further extract from this same letter is worth quoting: it may refer to the Warren or it may concern some farm that Thomas had taken at Newbottle, but in either case his enthusiasm for farming is as infectious as was that of his uncle, the Colonel, while his obvious success is ironic: it shows what could have been done at the Warren to reward the enthusiasm of Sir Thomas had he lived:

The farm is going on as well as well as it can be considering the weather we have had, in fact a great deal better than many farmers in the country, as I had all the wheat and beans sown a fortnight before the rain began in October & since then I have done all the winter ploughing except about 20 acres, which wants draining. This I have done & now it is being ploughed & as soon as the land is dry enough to get onto it I mean to begin sowing barley when half the farmers in England will be only sowing their wheat. I sold 85 bacon pigs the other day at 8/6 the score which will be about £5 apiece. In a fortnight I begin to send them to the butcher who bought them. I send 15 a week. Besides these I have about 40 porkers & all which will be worth about £50 the lot. The wheat I am keeping, the oats I am going to sell . . . The wheat is looking very well considering the season we have had. I am not quite certain whether it was before you went abroad or not that I sold a bull calf 7 months old for £17. 10s. The steam engine is at work almost every day, if not on the farm, threshing for other people . . .

Cox's time, however, was up.

Thomas Cartwright to William Cornwallis Cartwright

Aynhoe, 24th February 1853

My dear Willy . . .

Millard told me that Cox had again been into the Pesthouse
covers beating for hares, in the same way he did a year ago, that he
said he had a right to do so & began to abuse Millard, called him a
all manner of names & said he would worm him out of the place
before long & that he had written to you to tell him what sort of
man Millard was . . .

I had a good case against Cox for beating the covers & I have
taken out a summons against him to appear before the magistrates
next Monday for trespass in search of game. Before I took his step
I went over to Litchfield's, who is the senior magistrate of the
bench. He told me that if he was in my position he should certainly
take out a summons & advised me to retain Francillon of Banbury
to conduct the case as it would hang a good deal on points of law
& Francillon is a very crafty lawyer & sure to be retained against
me if I did not retain him . . .

If he gets convicted, of which I am almost certain, I think he
would give up the farm for a very small claim . . .

Lambert & Stillgoe, who I said in my last letter had gone to
Australia, did not go & last Monday were convicted at Brackley &
fined £2. 18s. 9d & in addition were surcharged for not having a
license, which made it about £8 more. The Souldern man Bond,
by whom Adkins was nearly shot, has run away. The warrant is
out against him, as soon as he appears again . . . The Bonds are
the worst family in Souldern. One of them is in jail for an assault,
a warrant out against a second, the third is coming up on Monday . . .

It may seem unethical, to put it mildly, going and seeing the magistrate who is likely to try your case, but presumably neither Thomas
Cartwright nor Francis Litchfield (whom we have encountered
before) saw anything amiss. Thomas's next letter reported the
result of Cox's appearance — and continued with some family
gossip:-

Thomas Cartwright to William Cornwallis Cartwright

3rd March, 1853

My dear Willy . . .

You will no doubt be glad to hear that I gained the case
against Cox yesterday & he was convicted & had to pay the fine.
Litchfield was the senior magistrate on the bench & gave Cox an

immense long lecture about his conduct & touched on the case being made much worse by a person of his position & of his intelligence misconstruing the terms of his lease wilfully . . . Litchfield spoke to Cox afterwards and hoped there would be no ill feeling between us all, but all Cox's answer was that you liked one sort of tenant & I liked another . . .

Dreadful weather last week. Tremendous storms, snow with it, especially last Saturday. The wind has blown down a great many more trees at Old Down . . .

I have a great piece of family news to tell you which I forgot to mention last time. Lady Fanny is going to have a baby in July — the Rector don't fancy it at all I believe. I suppose he had congratulated himself in thinking the ill chance over by this time.

I have lost two or three litters of pigs at the farm from the great cold. They were born just in the middle of it & were brought in to the fire, but it would not do . . .

Cox did indeed consent to leave the Home Farm: with such relations as now subsisted between him and the Cartwright brothers it is difficult to see how he could well have continued. He took £1,200 as compensation for the severed lease and for the loss of his crops on the ground. Poaching went on, and the state of the game laws continued to harass the farmers since, with the example of Cox to show them what might happen to farmers who attempted to control the vermin on their farms, they were reluctant to take even such limited action as the law allowed them. Twenty years later Mr. Bennett, the tenant of Aynho Grounds, was in much distress over this: the tenant of the great house, Mr. Fullerton, rented the shooting over the entire estate, and a friend wrote to the squire:-

Bennett is in a sad way about the rabbits. I don't think Fullerton is behaving well — he ought to compensate him. Bennett cannot make up his mind to stay the Holy Communion with a man whom he thinks is robbing his children. It is most sad & grievous . . .

The great house was let for the simple reason that the squire could not afford to live there. The Fullertons who occupied it in the 1870's were perhaps not ideal tenants. The same correspondent wrote disparagingly

The Fullertons have had the house full lately for the Bicester & Westbury ball . . . they had had numerous carpet hops which I have escaped I am thankful to say . . . He drinks more claret than

Aynho

Map 8. Land use, c.1860.

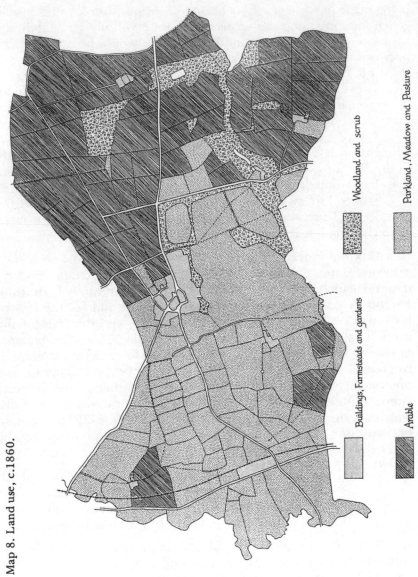

Woodland and scrub

Parkland, Meadow and Pasture

Buildings, Farmsteads and gardens

Arable

ever & she is more artificial & superficial

There was a great to-do when the Fullertons left the house, since they had stocked the garden with a great many rose trees, which they claimed the right to remove: Thomas Cartwright denied this, and there was a great row at the end of which he and the Fullertons were not on speaking terms.

Thomas Cartwright took the manor at Newbottle and farmed there, visiting Aynho frequently to look after his brother's interests during the squire's many absences. In 1858 he married Elizabeth, daughter of the Earl of Leven and Melville, and it was probably because of this Scottish connection that he found at last a good Scots tenant for the Warren Farm, William Patullo. Perhaps it was slightly ironic, in view of the Colonel's having tried to get young Willifer sent to Scotland to learn farming. The Patullos were succeeded by the Maclarens, who are still there.

Lady Fanny's pregnancy, so lightly announced, sadly seems to have killed her, for she died that year, though the baby, Augusta, survived. The Revd. Stephen, perhaps understandably, spent an increasing amount of time away from the village, and died in 1862. His successor at the Rectory was his half brother, youngest son of his father's second marriage, Frederick William Cartwright.

The squire himself lived largely abroad over the next twenty years. He had begun to be a traveller when young; in the 1840's, when still in his teens, he had made a tour of the Balkans with introductions to all the local potentates provided for him by Lord Palmerston through his father Sir Thomas. On succeeding to his empty inheritance he lived for much of the time in Rome, where he made the acquaintance of many of the leaders of the *Risorgimento* and became an intimate of Browning, Frederick Leighton and the rest of the English colony. Like his father, he married a German wife. His financial circumstances improved as time went on, and in 1868 he was able to stand, successfully, as Liberal M.P. for Oxford (to become which he had to live down his family's reputation for high and unflinching Toryism). In Parliament he never achieved office, but his knowledge of the world gave him a standing in the Party's inner councils that was greatly valued. 'He has the longest head in Europe' said Gladstone of him.

But in the long term, the financial embarassments in which William Ralph Cartwright and Sir Thomas had involved the estate were never resolved. By 1896 the mortgage on the estate stood at £88,000 at 4 per cent, and the income from Aynho properties had fallen, owing to the agricultural slump of the late 1870's, from

£6,160 to £3,890. It was only the family's possession of a substantial income from property in London that kept the estate afloat; that, and the fact that by the end of the century no-one wanted to buy land and mortgagees preferred a safe though low interest to foreclosing on unsaleable assets. That was ironic, since one of the threads running through this history has been the slow but constant acquisition of land by the Cartwright family. As Lady Bracknell is made to say in *The Importance of Being Ernest*, written in 1895, 'Land gives one a position without the means of keeping it up. That is all there is to say about land.'

There is one thing, however, for which (though without being able to prove it) we may have to thank Sir Thomas, and that is the famous apricot trees growing against the fronts of many of the cottages in the village. The tradition that they have been there since the middle ages is, of course, not credible: many of the houses where they grow were only built in the eighteenth century or bought by the squire in the nineteenth, and the villagers would never have got together to plant apricots outside their houses on their own account: they were far too individualistic, and would have thought such a notion was a lot of nonsense. William Ralph Cartwright is a possible candidate: he was keen on trees (he put up notices all over the place threatening dire penalties against anyone who damaged trees or cut wood without permission) and the improvement of the village's appearance in this way might have appealed to him. But it seems to accord more with Sir Thomas's mixture of benevolence and gratuitous extravagance, the trees look as though they could be that old (those that remain) and one feels, too, that it is slightly un-English, more the sort of thing that Sir Thomas might have seen during his travels abroad. In the absence of any documents that mention these famous trees (which one cannot pass over in a history of Aynho) it is he who may, tentatively, be given the credit for them.

There is a story that has gained currency, that cottagers paid their rent in apricots. Given the unpredictableness of the English climate, this would hardly have been possible; Aynho tenants paid their rents in money like tenants did anywhere else, and they were entitled to keep the produce of their apricot trees, to eat or to sell as they chose. But a few cottagers would neglect their trees, and then a gardener from the Park would come at the right time of year to do what pruning and training was needed, and would return later, when the fruit was ripe, to take two or three of the choicest for the table of the squire.

Chapter 13

A Close Village

Writers in the nineteenth century often distinguished between two different kinds of village, the open and the close. The open village was one where there were numerous landlords, no squire, and where rural slums and overcrowding proliferated. The close village was 'a show village, where . . . none but persons who are needed as shepherds, gardeners, or gamekeepers are allowed to live, regular servants who receive the treatment usual to their class.' Add to these the labourers on the farms that belonged to the Cartwright estate and the village tradesmen and craftsmen, and Aynho meets the description fairly well.

On the other hand Aynho never became, so to speak, an ideal closed village. The population was too great even after the emigrations of the 1830's and 1840's, the squire's ownership still too partial, and a legacy of earlier generations had been numbers of small cottages run up by other owners before their purchase by the squire. The incentives to create closed villages were several, not all of them discreditable to their landlords. There was the wish to get rid of slums and bad characters, both of which would have been seen as corrupting the mass of the village population as well as creating trouble for the authorities. There was the wish to reduce the unemployed population for the greater good of those in work, even though the bad characters and the unemployed would then be compelled to find lodgings in the nearest 'open' village. There was, too, often an element of ostentatious philanthropy in being seen as the landlord of a clean, well-housed village, even though the model cottages that some owners built for their tenants were as pokey for their occupants as they appeared picturesque to the visitor. The cottages that William Ralph Cartwright erected were functional rather than decorative, and there remained in Aynho plenty of farm labourers who were at least spared the longer walk to their employment that they would have had to endure had they lived in another village.

Much of what William Ralph Cartwright and his successors did was cosmetic, probably affecting the village structure very much less than did the actions of some other landowners elsewhere. He pulled down several groups of poor, slum cottages, notably on

255

Blacksmith's Hill and on the east and south-west sides of the Square, but left others standing in which the accommodation was probably little better. He named the streets for the first time, in the 1820's, with names that sound an odd mixture of industrial town and leafy suburb: Wapping (off Blacksmith's Hill), Prospect Terrace (looking towards Deddington), Paradise Row (William Ralph Cartwright's new cottages on the Charlton road), Spring Gardens (the group above and to the south of the Causeway), Hart Lane (the lane leading up to the present school from the Square) and others; a rather silly exercise of authority (though no sillier than the Rural District Council's imposition of equally arbitrary street names a few years ago) but one that did nobody any harm. And some time in the 1820's the name of the Red Lion was changed to the Cartwright Arms.

Even after the great emigrations the fall in population was not great — from 664 in 1831 to 611 in 1851, and overpopulation makes itself felt in various ways, not all concerned with jobs. There remained throughout the nineteenth century a great deal of over-crowding in many of the village cottages. Few of the labourers' cottages had more than two bedrooms, very few had been built since 1800, and many of the larger ones had been subdivided. It is difficult to identify with certainty all the houses listed in the nine-teenth century censuses with those that stand today, but one group that one can recognise is numbers 62 to 75 on the Charlton Road: Paradise Row. In 1841 these fourteen cottages were occupied by 92 people — an average of over six in each, parents, boys and girls and even in a couple of cases, lodgers. Even in 1871 the number was still 86 — scarcely a fall of any significance, and there were eight or nine in several of these households. It is almost impossible to imagine how such families crowded into houses with two small bedrooms and a kitchen and living room equally small.

No wonder that children had to leave the village when they grew up: apart from the lack of work, there was simply not room for them. There must have been many who would have liked to stay in Aynho and could not, and many who would have liked to marry and for whom there was no cottage. But if one is inclined to blame the squire for failing to provide sufficient cottages, he would have seen no point in housing villagers for whom no work was available, and if he failed to build cottages as large as were needed, he would have pointed out that his tenants could not, many of them, afford an economic rent even for those small cottages that they did occupy.

In the 1860's the squire's cottages let at between 1s and 3s a week; the Paradise Row ones let at 1s 6d. It was not much, but on a wage of 9s – 12s a week it was as much as a labourer could afford (in Paradise Row all tenants were labouring families). It left little enough for other necessities. We have no details of their meals and diet, but these were probably little different from those of two labouring families in Bodicote, four miles away, that were recorded in the 1860's:-

	I	II
Number in family (over 10/under 10)	6/5	4/3
Household income, per week	19s	18s
Bread	84 lbs	43 lbs
Flour	7 lbs	7 lbs
Peas (dried)	3½ lbs	–
Potatoes	30 lbs	28 lbs
Green vegetables	18 lbs	28 lbs
Sugar	1 lb	1 lb
Butter	1 lb	1 lb
Suet	½ lb	1½ lbs
Bacon	6 lbs	3 lbs
'Meat & bone'	2 lbs	2 lbs
Skim milk	3 pts	6 pts
Tea	2 oz	4 oz
Beer	1 pt	2 pts
Eggs	–	4

The second family ate a reasonable quantity of green vegetables, but otherwise their diets were uniformly appalling, both nutritionally and in terms of sheer monotony. The huge quantity of carbohydrates may have been of some value to farm workers doing heavy labour in cold weather, but the lack of protein must have been dire for growing children. Surprisingly, neither family seems to have eaten cheese. The diet of two other Oxfordshire families reported on sounds very slightly better, but set out below, meal by meal, it sounds hardly any less boring:-

III

Breakfast:	Tea, bread and butter or bread and dripping
Dinner:	Vegetables and bread; bacon three days a week
Tea & supper:	Bread and tea

IV

Breakfast:	Tea, bread and butter or bread and treacle
Dinner:	Bread and cheese or potatoes and herring
Tea & supper:	Bacon and vegetables.

The essence of the close village was that it was a well organised place, with the rich man in his castle, so to speak, and the poor man at his gate: a place where due regard was had to what was felt to be the proper social order. Such villages might well give the impression of changelessness: the outsider (or someone looking back on the Victorian village from a century later) might easily think that nothing had altered there since time immemorial. But one of the themes of this history has been that change is continuous and always has been, and that only the speed of change has sometimes varied. Change did not stop in Victorian Aynho, and a cause of much change was the improvements in transport and in communications with the outside world that had begun in the eighteenth century.

Little has been said until now about transport: roads have been taken for granted. The fact of Aynho's lying on two main roads, Buckingham–Chipping Norton and London–Bicester–Banbury, was the reason for the continued presence in the village of two Inns, the Red Lion that was re-named the Cartwright Arms and that had existed at least since the beginning of the seventeenth century, if not before, the Bell until the early eighteenth century and the White Hart from a little later. The documents are full of casual references to comings and goings, to goods and messages being sent to and fro. Richard Grafton, Richard Cartwright's man, writing in 1616 a letter about estate business to his master in London, sent with it by the Warwick carrier 'two great Cakes and 6 Banburie cheeses, the Carriage paid for'. A hundred years later, Joseph Wasse the rector asked John Bridges in London 'If you meet with any old edition of Lactantius, which may be ventured into the Country, Mr. Cartwright's servant, or the Banbury carrier Barrett at the Ram in Smithfield will safely convey him to Aynho, and I will return him in a Month's time.' Public transport existed and could be relied on.

But the roads of the time were extremely bad, and progress was slow. Travel was uncomfortable, too; if one could afford it a coach was probably more genteel than riding, but had little else to commend it. The queasy, lurching motion imparted by the leather thongs of the suspension and the pot-holes of the roads took some getting used to, and is supposed to be the origin of the expression 'being coached' — meaning, to be schooled to something difficult. Most sensible people, genteel or not, travelled on horseback. Roads were maintained by the parishioners of each parish they passed through, and in theory all inhabitants had to put in five days' work a year on them. Men were presented at the Manor Court for having the footpaths outside their own houses out of repair, while the Overseers of villagers where the roads were neglected were presented before the magistrates. The system was unfair on those villages (like Aynho) that lay on much-used roads, and was inefficient.

The solution was the establishment of turnpikes. The first turnpikes were introduced in the seventeenth century, but it was only in the mid-eighteenth that the Aynho roads began to be improved. By then they badly needed to be. The road from Deddington for example, through Clifton, over the Cherwell meadows and up the hill, was a constant source of trouble. There was a wooden bridge and a causeway of some sort across the fields, for which Richard Cartwright had left £40 in his will, but this was constantly out of repair and then carts and waggons would abandon it altogether and make their way over the meadows as best they could until they reached higher ground and the road once more. Some of the measures taken in the eighteenth century to prevent this sound so drastic as to have seriously hindered the passage of traffic:

> If the causeway be not repaired by All Saints next the fieldsmen do nevertheless cause the ditch before the Cherwell to be opened well and sufficiently to hinder carriages coming through

and four years later

> Fieldsmen to cause a Wall to be built at Clifton Mill so as to stop Carts Wagons and other Carriages from coming up the Meadow as soon as possibly can be

The London road was no better, carrying as it did a good deal of the traffic between the metropolis and the burgeoning towns of the Midlands — Birmingham, Coventry, and the growing industrial regions beyond. As early as 1728 the House of Commons was told of its terrible state beyond Banbury, half destroyed by waggons of coals and iron, and by returning loads of barley and wheat from Buckinghamshire and Oxfordshire. These conditions were probably taken for granted by the people of Aynho, and possibly even welcomed after a fashion: breakdowns meant work for wheelwrights and carpenters and business for the Inns. But improved roads elsewhere made people more aware of local deficiencies. In 1790 Sir Stephen Cotterel wrote to the young squire from London

> I begin to think travelling in the dark not so very tremendous as I had imagined, but observe I speak of the road this side of Oxford,

for between Oxford and Aynho I should have expected my neck
to be broken infallibly

On a stormy night a fortnight earlier, William Ralph Cartwright
had ridden back to Oxford from Aynho with a party of Christ
Church friends, and his step father had written to him anxiously
the next day,

The first news I heard this morning was that the Birmingham coach
had overturned in Aynho fields, and some of the passengers much
hurt

The improvement of the roads was slow and piecemeal. The
Deddington road was the first, as a spur of the Burford to Banbury
Turnpike under an Act of 1770; the road from Croughton to Nell
Bridge formed a part of the Buckingham and Hanwell Trust established in 1777, while the Bicester and Aynho Turnpike Trust was
not set up until 1791, and the Act of Parliament establishing it
caused, it will be remembered, some difficulty at the time of the
Enclosure. Under the Turnpike Acts, Trustees were empowered to
maintain the roads and to recoup themselves out of the receipts at
toll gates. It is not certain where the gates were on the Aynho
roads; the toll collectors' cottages that often survive elsewhere (at
the bottom of the hill west of Hempton, for instance) at Aynho
have been pulled down. But one was known as Clifton Gate and
the other as Croughton Gate, and it seems likely that one was either
at the bottom of the hill on the Deddington road or somewhere
near Clifton Bridge, and the other close to where the Buckingham
road leaves the road to Bicester.

The improved roads made travel very little cheaper for those
who had to use public transport — stage coaches or post horses —
but made it vastly quicker and more comfortable. In 1750, mail
coaches (the fastest) had taken thirty hours between Banbury and
London. By the 1820's a coach leaving Banbury at 7.30 at night
would reach London at 3 o'clock the next morning: time to snatch
a little sleep and still get to business without having wasted any of
the working day in travelling. And the roads were busier than ever:
there were by then twenty coaches a week in each direction between Banbury and London, most of them passing through Aynho,
besides others on cross-country routes, the waggons of numerous
carriers, and an ever-increasing number of private travellers taking
advantage of the better roads.

But roads remained a relatively expensive way of carrying
heavy and bulky goods about the country, and there was by then

CANAL FROM NELL BRIDGE AYNHO 33

27. The Canal, c.1910, from Nell Bridge, looking South East towards Nell Bridge Farm. Taken in winter or in early spring, with flooded water-meadows between the canal and the railway.

28. The railway station, c.1920
The low level station, on the Oxford to Banbury line, taken from the up side platform. Trucks in the goods station indicate a fair amount of local business. Station staff and others stand on the opposite platform; the station master on the left with white gloves and gold braid to his cap, the station lad next to him.

29. The Cartwright Arms, c.1900
Fan-trained apricot trees are on the walls of the inn and on the houses beyond.

30. The Post Office, c.1895
William Buckingham standing outside the former post office, where he lived.
The board over the window reads 'Post Office Aynhoe'.

31. Prospect Terrace, c.1905

Houses built by William Ralph Cartwright, c.1800, looking towards Deddington. The name is that bestowed by him (see page 256) and had probably already lapsed when this picture was taken. The cart bears the name 'Hopcraft', possibly the Deddington carrier.

32. The stocks, the hill trees and a waggon, c.1910

33. Coronation Sports, 1910. Ladies' race.

34. Flower Show, 1908. Pillow fight.

an ideal alternative — the canal. The Oxford and Coventry Canal was first proposed in the late 1760's, and the promoters of the Burford and Banbury Turnpike adopted the old road that led from the Swerford turn, through Hempton and Deddington to Aynho, in the expressed hope that it would give access to the wharf that they foresaw being built at Aynho. But it was not until 1778 that the canal was opened between Coventry and Banbury, and only after several more years' delay that the Company began to build the last stage of the route. Aynho may have been reached in the spring of 1787, but the first receipts at Aynho wharf were collected in early 1791 by which time the canal was open all the way through to Oxford. Aynho was the centre for the immediate neighbourhood, including the decayed market town of Deddington, and justified at last the turnpiking of the road over the water-meadows. There was a pub on the canal, the Alfred's Head, and an account book of 1824 kept by the landlady records credit run up by regular visitors from Deddington, Charlton and Croughton as well as from places nearer at hand. The amount of business done by the wharf in its early days can be imagined from the sums collected there as the Company's dues. They increased rapidly to a peak of over £2,000 in 1798 and 1799. It may be that in these years the canal was carrying a good deal of the traffic between Birmingham and London, and that Aynho, on the new turnpike, was a good place to land it to carry it further by road. The Grand Junction Canal, linking London and Birmingham by water direct, was not opened throughout until 1803.

For long the Oxford Canal remained highly profitable, paying in some years over 30 per cent to the investors (Robert Weston and William Ralph Cartwright among them) who had put their money into it. It was of enormous benefit to the country round: besides cheap coal, slates, bricks, lime and other bulk merchandise from the industrial Midlands which were now available in greater quantity and cheaper than ever before, there were useful, regular passenger services: fly-boats and market boats on scheduled runs between Oxford and Banbury, travelling at faster than walking pace and having priority at the locks. One of the more unlikely kinds of traffic has been mentioned already: the wine that Sir Thomas Cartwright wanted sent down to Aynho in 1847 — unlikely, that is, until one realises how much safer it must have been at the bottom of a smoothly, slowly moving boat than bumped about on a carrier's waggon. (It should perhaps be added, however, that the benefits were not clear to everyone, and perhaps indeed were not universal. In the early 1790's, when prices were soaring and farmers were suspected of profiteering, a mob from Deddington had seized a flour barge and only given it up on the miller's promising to sell the flour at a reduced price. It was widely believed that the canals were making it possible for farmers to export their corn for a higher price than they could get for it at home.)

But the days of the canal's affluence were numbered by the advent of the railway. The first moves to build a line from Oxford to Banbury and beyond were made in 1844, and a Bill for an Oxford and Rugby railway, to be leased to the Great Western, got through Parliament in 1845. There was initially hot debate both locally and in the House of Commons about whether the new line should be built to the standard gauge or to the broad: the Great Western was the broad gauge line (7′) but the London and North Western, its great rival, hoped for a standard gauge (4′ 8½″) down which it could run its own trains from Birmingham to Oxford. It mattered a great deal to some people: a correspondent to the leading Oxford newspaper wrote —

> The London markets are the ones we send to, if we do not sell at home; we none of us send to the north . . . we gain more by sending our fat stock to town without a change of carriage than by having our coal brought from the north without such a change . . . we receive our guano and other imported manures from the port of London more frequently than from any other . . . I believe that butter is sent from these parts to the Metropolis and that a quick transit and delivery . . . is far from unimportant

Others were ready to argue the reverse, while others again, not without justice, regarded the matter of gauges as a great battle for territory between the two mighty Companies, a war in which local interests were mere pawns. Some in their exasperation missed the point of it entirely, like Francis Litchfield who addressed a meeting in Banbury

> as for the question between broad gauge and narrow, in his opinion [the promoters] must take the meeting to be so many *green gages* to lay so much stress on the matter

while in despair William Tancred, the M.P. for Banbury, wrote to his agent while the debate was in progress

> [I am told] that you are head and ears engaged in railroads and that I am threatened if I do not support the wishes of my constituents. I only wish to know what those wishes are, for I am absolutely indifferent upon the subject of broad gauge and narrow and am only sorry I cannot vote for both

The Great Western won in the end, and work started in 1845 with the making of the necessary detailed survey of the line of the route. Local people complained of delay, that nothing was to be seen except a 'gigantic game of cribbage made by those who have made holes and stuck pegs in the middle of cornfields and meadows', that the prospect of earning high wages on the railway was keeping men from regular employment, that landlords and tenants were having their relations soured by the uncertainty of the railway's plans, and that the engineers were being prodigal of time, wasting the dry summer months when the Cherwell valley was free from flooding.

Construction began in earnest in the summer of 1846. Old hands, the regular navvies who for upwards of fifteen years had been following the railway building boom as the mania spread through the country, could make 4s a day; even tyros could earn 2s 6d which was 4s a week more than they could earn as farm labourers. But the work was extremely hard, cuttings and embankments had to be dug and built entirely with picks and shovels, wheel-barrows and muscle-power, and many who tried their hands at navvying were back on the farm by harvest. The great invasion of workmen was anticipated in the neighbourhood with dread: as early as 1846 Sir Thomas had written nervously to Samuel Field about reports that had reached him of their activities. There were near-riots in Banbury when the original contractor for the line was known to be pressed for money and there was fear that wages would not be paid, and landowners clearly regarded their game as virtually beyond preservation while the navvies were in the district. But otherwise they tended to keep themselves to themselves, living at a pace and working with an energy that set them apart from the common people. A sympathetic contemporary wrote of them

> The ploughman, or thresher, who plods through his day's work would be amazed to see the rapid movements and prodigious energy of these men. A careless and thoughtless race they are, resembling much the sailor in character: highly paid for their herculean labourers, they spend their few hours of leisure recruiting their strength for the next effort by feasts of the most substantial kind, in which even expensive luxuries are not forgotten — young ducks, and green peas, for instance, at a time of year when such delicacies command high prices.

When pay-day came, an orgy of eating and drinking would be indulged in until their money was gone, after which they would run up credit for necessities at the contractor's tommy-shop until pay day came round again. But to the Cartwrights the behaviour of the Great Western company proved as exasperating as the navvies': the episode of the Alfred's Head that occupied a long letter of Sir Thomas's that has been quoted in the last chapter was merely the climax of a long history of shifty dealings by the railway over the acquisition of the land they required for the line.

The line was opened between Oxford and Banbury in 1850; in 1852 it was extended to Leamington to provide a through route to Birmingham. The official opening, however, was marred by what might have been a serious accident. To celebrate the achievement a special train was laid on to run from Paddington to Birmingham and back, the expedition to be crowned by a 'sumptuous dejeuner' at Leamington for the Company's directors and their friends. The Great Western's crack engine, the Lord of the Isles, recently shown at the Great Exhibition in Hyde Park, hauled the train, a band of the Guards was provided to make music at stops, and the importance of the occasion and the eminence of the passengers made the authorities forgetful of such banal details as timetables. The personages inspected the new station at Oxford while the band played, and the special train was already half an hour late by the time it reached Aynho.

Unfortunately, the train before it, a local from Didcot to Banbury comprising both goods vans and passenger carriages, was even later. Approaching Aynho at forty miles an hour, those on the footplate of the special (who included the great engineer Brunel) were appalled to see the local train standing in the station. The driver sounded his whistle, screwed on his brakes and threw the engines into reverse. The driver of the local managed to get his own train under way — but with the violence of the acceleration he broke the couplings of the last two waggons of his train. The Lord of the Isles was still travelling at fifteen miles an hour when she struck them, and the accounts of the accident make the most of the crash. In point of fact little damage was done and no one was hurt, but it was half past five before the Directors got to Leamington for their lunch.

(Not that the older, more leisurely canal was necessarily safer. There had been a bizarre and rather beastly accident three or four years earlier at Nell Bridge, when a bargee had the tow-rope of his barge stretched across the main road in contravention of safety regulations. At that moment a runaway horse charged down the hill and into the taut rope, snapping it. Lashing back, one end struck the old mother of the canal foreman, killing her on the spot.)

Aware of the good business done by the canal, in 1852 the

Company added a goods station to the one already built for passengers; indeed, even before the death of the old squire his more far-sighted heir Sir Thomas had written to Samuel Field asking him to take up the desirability of such a development with the Company. Further local complaint was that the station was initially called Aynho only, with no mention of Deddington where strenuous local efforts were being made to revive the former market. 'Aynho for Deddington' appeared in the course of time on the station name-boards, but the station remained plain Aynho in most people's minds.

The high line was built much later, early in the present century, as a move in the Great Western's continuing rivalry with the London and North Western. The L.N.W.R. had always, until then, provided the fast route between London and Birmingham. With its new line from Paddington through Bicester and Banbury the Great Western was now able to complete for the Birmingham traffic on more than equal terms, while local trains contributed yet further to the railway's monopoly of communications. (There were by then a good many intermediate stations on the Banbury to Oxford line; originally there had been only Aynho, Heyford and Kirtlington, then called Woodstock Road.) The station for the high line at Aynho was no more than a halt; one bought one's tickets in a separate building by the roadside and then walked up a long, cindered slope to the platform on the embankment. The halt was called Aynho Park to distinguish it from the station on the lower line, and the Cartwrights are said to have had the right to have expresses stopped there whenever they required it as part of the price paid by the Company for the land.

In one way, paradoxically, the railways increased the village's air of changelessness mentioned at the beginning of the chapter, for it meant the end of the old turnpike roads and a great falling-off of road traffic. The turnpikes had depended for their income on receipts from travellers at the toll bars and gates, and as the stage and mail coaches were driven off by the railways, as private carriages were increasingly used for short journeys only and to meet the nearest train, and as even flocks and herds were as often carried by train as driven along the highways, so income from the tolls fell rapidly off. The trusts responsible for the Aynho turnpikes were wound up in the 1870's, and the roads themselves were probably by then emptier than they had been for a hundred years. The White Hart closed down at some time during these years; it was always second to the Cartwright Arms in trade and, probably, in esteem, and the traffic on the deserted roads could no longer support two inns. Aynho in the latter part of the nineteenth century must have seemed sleepier and quieter than it had done for many years.

But profound changes had nevertheless occurred, not all of which can be described from documents. Changes in people's outlook and way of life do not often leave records behind them. Late in the eighteenth century a traveller riding through Oxfordshire was prompted by what he observed of the country people to complain

> I wish with all my heart that half the turnpike roads of the kingdom were ploughed up, which have imported London manners and depopulated the country. I meet milkmaids on the road, with the dress and looks of Strand misses . . .

and though he (John Byng) lived in London and had then, as townsman have now, a somewhat romantic and exaggerated idea of rustic simplicity and virtue, there must have been substance in what he wrote. (The country people themselves, of course, must have seen it very differently: they must have welcomed these developments that put them in touch with news and fashion.) It is difficult to think of an old rustic, born in Aynho when Victoria was on the throne, and then to realise how very much more sophisticated he must have been than his great-grandfather born a century before, but so he must have been.

Another effect of improved communications, however, easier to document and which must have affected every other village in the country, is their impact on employment and rural occupations. Better roads, the canal and the railway provided a number of jobs that had not existed before, but at the same time led to the loss of some other jobs that the village had provided for centuries. The new jobs were those created by improved transport itself and by the services that better communications made possible, such as postman, railwayman, coal merchant and brickmaker. Jobs lost were in those callings where villagers could no longer compete with the cheap, easily transported products of the new factory towns, and occupations recorded in the eighteenth century that had vanished by the second half of the nineteenth included tailor, breeches-maker, cutler, apothecary, hempdresser, weaver and cooper.

Down by the wharf and the railway a little industrial centre sprang up. In the 1870's the landlord of the Great Western Arms (the pub that had been built to replace the Alfred's Head) was a coalmerchant as well, and there was another coalmerchant too:

between them they probably supplied Deddington as well as Aynho. Sometime probably in the 1860's a small brickworks arose, and bricks with AYNHO impressed in the frog can still be found. In 1867 the squire had leased a field close to the station to a firm of auctioneers, Paxton and Clerk, for use as a cattle market, the squire providing the buildings. For many years the market flourished: an announcement of 1894 of the firm's 450th sale included details of the slip carriage to be attached to the morning fast train from Oxford to Banbury, and this may have been a standard facility since the market's patrons were said to come from all the counties round. It still flourished in the 1920's, with sales on the first Monday and third Tuesday of every month, and the remains of the market buildings still stood until recently, some brick walls in a field just on the Aynho side of the Park station.

The railwaymen themselves were of course a new class that the railway had created. Only porters, the more lowly of railway staff, are recorded in the censuses as living at the station; the station master, a man of importance, probably had a house in Clifton or Deddington. The mobility that the railway encouraged was reflected in the origins of its staff. In 1861 one of the porters was a Gloucestershire man, while the railway policeman, Moses McIlwain, was Irish. These new jobs helped Aynho men as well: in 1866 Edward Letch Walton, son of an Aynho carpenter and probably grandson of the last of the Letch family, wrote to Samuel Field about the sale of his cottage in the village from the goods station at Swansea, and the fact that he wrote on the Company's headed paper suggests that he was something above a humble clerk.

Improvements in postal services antedated the railway. There had been a letter carrier in the village since at least the 1790's, and before the railway was built John Tebby the postman would walk to Brackley and back daily with his satchel for letters, a little keg for his beer and a small brass post-horn which he would blow at the front gate of anyone for whom he had letters. In 1852 the old postman retired, and the principal inhabitants petitioned the postmaster-general:-

> We, the undersigned inhabitants of Aynho in the County of Northamptonshire, humbly petition that James Tebby may be appointed Letter Carrier from Brackley to Aynhoe in the place of his father John Tebby who is now incapacitated from ill-health after having faithfully performed the office for nearly thirty years. The above named James Tebby is in every respect trustworthy and has borne a good character and is quite competent to fulfil the office.

Successfully, apparently, since James Tebby appears as postman in
the next census, and his father, Old John, promoted to the dignity
of parish Beadle. One cannot be surprised at his ill-health, if he
had walked that journey daily in all weathers for thirty years. The
farm labourers at least had work under cover, such as threshing, in
really bad weather.

It is unlikely that young James will have had to walk to
Brackley for long after the coming of the railway. With the railway,
too, there came another, still more rapid means of communication,
the telegraph. The railways pioneered the telegraph, because of the
need for stations and signal-boxes to inform each other of the arrival
and departure of trains, and for many years telegrams could be
sent to the station whence they would be delivered to the village
by hand. (A letter of 1878 from the squire to the Great Western's
head office at Paddington conveys his wrath at a telegram's having
taken more than an hour to reach him from the station: it appeared
that the station lad had stopped on his way up the hill to watch
Farmer Buckingham's sheep shearers at work.)

There were a few other novel employments beside these.
There were Thomas Robbins and Thomas Watts who both kept
threshing machines, and who must have rented them out to local
farmers who lacked them: a fair number to judge by Sir Thomas
Cartwright's strictures on the backwardness of Aynho's farming.
There was, too, a sprinkling of retired people, the most surprising
of whom in the 1851 census being John Walton, described as a retired cheese-monger. He had spent his working life in London,
though born in Aynho, and one would like to know both the circumstances that took him away from the village (apprenticeship,
presumably) and the considerations that brought him home again
in old age. In the 1841 census appears Mary Letch, farmer's widow,
aged 85 and living in a two-roomed cottage behind John Walton's
(number 19), and Susannah Boxall, widow of the local excise
man. In 1871 one finds Charles Millard set down as retired game-
keeper — we have met him in the last chapter.

The farmers of Aynho for the most part left the village when
they left off farming. They often came from far away, and in the
course of their careers might have farmed three or four farms in as
many counties. The only men who stayed were those with ties in
the place. In 1871 appears Richard Mayo, retired farmer: the
Mayos had been butchers and farmers in Aynho for three hundred
years, though never owning more than a few freehold acres themselves. Another retired farmer in that year was Joseph Buckingham,

but the Buckinghams too were by now an old Aynho family. Thomas Buckingham, schoolmaster, had bought number 25 in 1798, and had filled various village offices as his superior literacy qualified him to do: he was Overseer in 1831 when with the squire he gave evidence to the Poor Law Commissioners on the state of things in Aynho. Joseph's son William was also a small farmer with 28 acres, and it was his sheep that the unfortunate station lad had been distracted by when he delayed the squire's telegram. William Buckingham was the local tax collector as well (for the land tax and the duties on such things as man-servants, carriages and dogs) and kept the village post-office; the photograph at plate 30 shows him outside his house with AYNHOE POST OFFICE written up over the window. And in each generation it seems to have been the Buckinghams who, as Overseers, were the enumerating officers for the census each ten years. Men such as the Buckinghams and Richard Mayo would have no call to leave the village when they retired, but they were not in the same farming league as the tenants of the principal farms. And it was still very many years before anyone unconnected with the place would come to live in Aynho in their old age.

A great many trades continued as they had long existed, such as wheelwrights, blacksmiths, carpenters, shopkeepers, innkeepers, farmers and labourers. Many of these occupations have only disappeared in the present century, when the return of traffic to the roads has completed the revolution that the turnpikes and the railway began, and some trades that were present in Victorian Aynho would seem to have been over-supplied. Three carpenters are recorded from the 1841 census, four from 1871. Four masons in 1841, three still in 1871. Family traditions still counted for much, and perhaps held men at home when without ties they might have ventured away from the village. Of the four masons in 1841, three were members of the Secull family, and three of the four carpenters in 1871 were Waltons. A further reason for the numbers in these two trades, at least, was that there were always odd jobs to be done on the park walls and about the buildings of the estate. Sometimes (as with James Secull, mentioned in the last chapter) the estate might contract with a good man for a whole year; on other occasions jobs would be done by piecework, as when in 1868 John Secull was paid £20 for laying the stone setts to the road that leads up to the church (they are still there); on other occasions again men would be employed by day work: a day book of the Secull family survives from the 1880's, when two men of the family were earning 3s 6d a day working for the estate, and a lad 1s 9d.

Butchers and shopkeepers might also seem over-supplied, considering the comparative poverty of most of the population. Here again family traditions were still important. Richard Mayo, set down in the 1871 census as a retired farmer, had been a butcher in 1841; an ancestor had been a farmer in the 1790's and had had the contract to cull the deer in the Park; another Mayo was a butcher in the 1750's and there had been a Richard Meow living in the village in the early sixteenth century. Mayo's trade was more than local: in the 1820's he regularly attended Banbury market. Thomas Bygrave was another butcher in the 1840's, supplying the great house with whatever meat they did not obtain from Willifer at the Home Farm. Thirty years later Thomas Bygrave was still a butcher in Aynho, and had been joined by his relative John who, it may be remembered, had kept the White Hart in the 1840's and had written to Samuel Field to express a preference for farming to innkeeping. Butchery and innkeeping often went together, it seems, and the reasons may have been both the desire to furnish good cuts of meat to one's guests and the need to have a few acres of pasture for one's own and for travellers' horses, acres that might also be used for finishing a few beasts.

The Bygrave family continued to dominate the village's inns for most of the century, despite John's aversion. In the 1840's a Mrs Holloway kept the Cartwright Arms, but we have heard Sir Thomas's opinion of her and when she left the inn William Bygrave succeeded her there. In the 1870's it was described as a Commercial Inn, offering good stabling and well-aired beds, and with horses, phaetons and dog-carts for hire. (Mrs Holloway was not a favourite with Samuel Field, either; when a cottage fell vacant in 1866 he wrote to the squire advising him not to let her have it: 'it would be letting a hornet take a lodging in one's side' he wrote.) And in the 1860's an elderly woman, Sophia Bygrave, kept an alehouse at number 17 at the turn in the Banbury road.

At the shop in the square, Quakers continued as they had done for at least a hundred years before. The Wycherley family ran it until the 1850's, and to judge from his bill heads James Wycherley kept at least as general a shop as Erasmus Banbury had done in the eighteenth century. He described himself in addition as a collector of honey and dealer in metheglyn, which presumably he brewed himself. James Lardner, who appears as a shopman in the 1851 census, had taken the shop over by the next decade, and he too was probably a Quaker — he dates bills '8th mo.' and so forth rather than using the months' usual names. There were other shops in the village, though these were less permanent. In the 1840's one of the terrace on the Banbury road, numbers 20 to 24, was kept as a grocer's by George Spiers who had probably been a carpenter; in 1841 the house next to the Cartwright Arms on the east side (the grammar school side) was another small shop, kept by Mrs Watts the widowed mother of the blacksmith. Ten years later it was occupied by a labourer, William Wrighton, but by 1871 he had re-opened the shop and called himself a grocer. It was seldom that a labourer would have been able to amass even the small amount of capital that a little shop would require, but he and his wife seem to have had no children and they may have been able to save for their old age. Wrighton was in his 60's before he turned shopkeeper.

The labourers formed some two thirds of the population. A few were employed on the roads, but for the most part they worked on the farms, an eleven hour working day, six days a week, and those (almost all of them) who lived in the village rather than in outlying cottages had to walk perhaps a mile or more at the beginning and end of the day. The term labourer clearly included the more skilled, the carters, cowmen, ploughmen and so on (though a good man could turn his hand to several specialisations) and only the shepherds, who spent all their working day with their flocks, are separately described in the censuses. The farmers employed plenty of people. In 1871 William Patullo at the Warren farmed 694 acres with 14 men, 6 boys and 3 women; Edwin Wilson at Nell Bridge, 216 acres, 9 men and 3 boys; Samuel Hawkes at College Farm, 285 acres, 8 men and 5 boys; William Austin, Aynho Grounds, 420 acres, 13 men, 2 boys; William Bygrave, who besides keeping the Cartwright Arms farmed 540 acres as well, probably the Home Farm, 18 men and 3 boys.

The Victorian censuses record for the first time the occupations of many of the village women. Some of these must have been followed for generations, though others sound comparatively novel. To earn their own living was essential for single women and for widows, while for childless wives it was a valuable way of raising a couple's standard of living. For those with the skill there was lace making, probably long practised in the village and still made in the present century until machine-made lace and changing fashions drove it out. Laundry work must also have called for skill, to judge by the high wages paid to laundrymaids in the great house (more than housemaids and much more than kitchen maids) and in 1851 the blacksmith's wife and 16-year-old daughter were both set down as laundresses. There were other jobs that were probably less traditional: the 1841 census records a glove maker and a mantua-maker, both perhaps outworkers for some milliner in Banbury, and later on one of the Wrighton family appears as a confectioner. Perhaps she supplied her relation's shop between the pub and the grammar school: there were pennies for children to earn by open-ing gates and running errands for their betters, and at harvest there was work for absolutely everyone still. For women without such skills as these there was charing, while several households (not necessarily the largest houses) took in lodgers. And for all Samuel Field's prejudices against women farmers, there were some who farmed, like Sarah Holloway of the Cartwright Arms and Mrs. Perkins who farmed at the Warren before Sir Thomas took it in hand.

Children left school early. There was no compulsory educa-tion until the 1880's, and though labourers' children increasingly were sent to the village school, there were always some families for whom the powers of example and pressures from their betters (from the schoolteacher and the rector, for instance) were insuf-ficiently strong. Nevertheless, if the railway and the roads had done much to increase villagers' knowledge of the world and to reduce the distance of the village from the town, education was probably doing more. The schools have been spoken of already: the grammar school, founded under Mary Cartwright's Will, and the beginnings of what would now be called primary education — the teaching of the 3 R's (or at least one or two of them) to the village children.

The small payments that the squires had made to one of the better educated villagers for giving children a smattering of ele-mentary knowledge continued throughout the eighteenth century. In 1806 William Ralph Cartwright was paying Thomas Buckingham £5 to teach village children, perhaps in his own house. Those children who could afford it probably brought him a penny or two: others were taught for nothing. But any organisation is likely to have been very informal — many parents probably only sent their children to school when there was no chance of their earning a few pence by crow-scaring — and in 1812 a more systematic method of teaching the village children was introduced.

This was the 'Madras' system, employed by the National Society for the Education of the Poor in the Principles of the Church of England — the cumbersome title of an organisation founded the year before as a rival to the non-denominational

British and Foreign School Society. The National Society must have had the support of the squire; reform of the village school could not have been undertaken without it. William Ralph. Cartwright was an unflinching Tory and dissenters tended to be Liberal, and though there was no dissent in the village the squire was probably determined that there should be none. The Madras system was so called from its having been originally introduced into a school for military orphans in India, and it involved the teacher's teaching the leading pupils who in turn then taught what they had learnt to the other children in the school. In this way, and after a fashion, one master could teach more children than could be organised into a single form, and by 1813 the Aynho school had 50 children. Such a school was too large for anyone's house, and since as yet no building existed it was conducted in a farm barn. At first only boys attended. The rules for the National Schools laid down that children were to be at school at nine in the morning, again at two, 'clean, washed and combed', and that the day should always begin with prayers. They were to learn to read and write and — if they stayed long enough — the four rules of arithmetic. They were to spend half an hour each day learning by heart the Lord's Prayer, collects and the Catechism, 'entire', and as to discipline, it was said that 'a few rewards skilfully administered and a few marks of disgrace judiciously applied' were all that was wanted. It was a system that imparted facts rather than the power to think, but it was probably well enough contrived for the basic grounding that was thought sufficient for the children of the poor.

In the 1840's the National School at Aynho won glowing reports. It was said to be 'a perfect model of what a village school should be' and in 1849 the schoolmistress, Catherine Ekins, was awarded one of the Society's national prizes. In reply she wrote 'to return most grateful thanks for the valuable prize which they had awarded her' and to assure them that 'no exertion shall be wanted on her part to merit the continuance of their approbation'. But there was as yet no compulsion on parents to have their children educated, and education was not free: although the Society paid much of the school teacher's salary, children were required to contribute something too. The children of the better-off villagers probably did not attend Miss Ekins's school at all, however good the education. In 1851 the census records a widow, Mrs. Prophett, as a 'preparatory school mistress' and she probably kept some kind of a dame school for those children whose parents preferred them to be taught in a smaller class, or who did not want them to rub shoulders with rough labourers' children.

Involvement by the State was slow in coming, but a great step forward was with the introduction of the Education Department's 'Revised Code' in 1861. The State was now prepared to pay local schools 12s a head, of which 4s was based on attendance and 8s on annual examination results. The teaching required for the examinations remained mechanical: the standards laid down to be attained each year were both unimaginative and low, and since grants depended so much on the exam results the system placed a premium on pushing the dull pupils and neglecting the bright ones. Teaching was exclusively in the 3 R's, and it was only in the examinations for the final standard (at 12 years old) that children were expected to be able to read aloud a piece they had not previously prepared in class with the teacher's help. Writing was mostly learnt in slow dictation; only in arithmetic was progress slightly better with practice in adding up money bills in the final year.

In 1871, probably for the first time, a government inspector visited the school. There were 112 places, and it is likely that almost every child of school age (who was not at the dame school) attended sometimes. But attendance was far from regular, which may explain the monotony of the syllabus: perhaps it was the most that could be expected. Over the previous six months, average attendance had been only 49. There was a separate infant school by then, which the inspector commented favourably on. The schoolmaster, Richard Poole, had come to Aynho at the age of 26 in 1859. His salary in 1871 was £74. 18s, made up of £60 from the National Society plus the contributions of the pupils which varied with their parents' means from 4d a week downwards. Most paid 1d.

However, gradual improvements in the manner in which government help was given did, slowly, begin to improve the curriculum. The grants for the mechanical subjects were reduced, and new ones introduced such as history, geography, grammar and plain needlework. Education was made compulsory in 1870 and free to the poor. By 1890, when Richard Poole was still in charge, there was an average attendance of 98, and he must have had at least one assistant. By then, children in the top form were expected to be able to read a passage from Milton or Shakespeare at sight and to work out sums in percentages, stocks and discounts, but few children stayed at school that long. They could still leave after the third standard, when even their basic reading and writing was not far advanced. (The minimum standard for leaving varied from one place to another; at Aynho it probably meant an age of ten.)

But though to most people in the village the National School was probably 'the school' and the only one they bothered about, it was the old grammar school that presented greater problems for the authorities. By the late nineteenth century it was a white elephant. Some ancient grammar schools had adapted themselves to the times and blossomed into fully fledged public schools, but Aynho was not one of them. Since its foundation it had continued a humdrum existence, little known and leaving small record behind. The better educated villagers in the eighteenth century may have attended it, though to judge even by their educational achievements (they kept the Constables' and Fieldsmen's books, for instance) they had not learnt very much.

In the middle of the nineteenth century the headmaster was a certain Revd. Enoch Reddall, who was chaplain to the Brackley Workhouse as well. He may have had several day pupils, but only two boarders are mentioned in the 1851 census. In the 1870's it was recalled that there had formerly been as many as forty boys in the school, but that had been many years before. Reddall was succeeded by J.T. Cooke, who came to Aynho as a working retirement from a school he had formerly kept in Banbury. Cooke was unexpectedly cosmopolitan: he described himself as 'Professor of the University of St. Petersburg' and had a Swiss wife with whom in the late '60's he retired to the Lake of Geneva. It was said that he had made his fortune, but he is not likely to have done so out of the school at Aynho. A few years before his departure one visitor had found only five boys in attendance, four of them foundationers (i.e. free pupils) and one a fee-paying boy from the next parish. All were 'above the rank of the poor' and all could read well, two could write well at dictation, and the fee-paying child knew a little French and Latin grammar. Their arithmetic was poor. Apart from the Latin and French, these attainments hardly raised the children above the academic level of those in the National School. One boy suffered from St. Vitus' Dance, while another was almost dumb.

Cooke's successor was Charles Davies, a Welshman from Abergavenny. It was later said of him that 'he seems by report to have belonged to a class more often to be found in the small country grammar schools a generation or two ago than now. He had a smattering of many kinds of knowledge, taught drawing and surveying besides Latin and French, took his scholars into the fields for practical instruction and acted as well maker, consulting landagent and right-hand-man to the whole parish.' Things at the school improved at first under this attractive-sounding man: in 1871

Davies had 21 pupils of whom nine were boarders, varying between the ages of 8 and 14. But the times were against him: the new school at Bloxham and the fast-reviving, old school at Brackley were creaming off the farmers' sons who were the natural recruits to the grammar school at Aynho. Davies died in 1888, and by then the numbers had again declined to a mere three or four.

On Davies's death the sole trustee, the squire, realised that there was no point in trying to maintain it in view of its manifest failure. Winding it up was not easy: both the Charity Commissioners and the Board of Education required to be consulted, and there was also the matter of disposing of the old school buildings. Negotiations took some time. Representatives of both bodies came successively to Aynho to see for themselves how things stood and to consult with those who might be interested.

The Department of Education's representative was a Mr. Edis, and in the evening of the day of his visit the squire called a meeting of leading villagers in his house. Besides the squire and his brother Thomas, there was the Rector, the Revd. Frederick Cartwright (the squire's uncle), the curate, and some fifteen tradesmen and farmers, 'a number which may be said practically to exhaust the whole population above the rank of labourer' said Edis. The farmers adopted Thomas Bygrave, landlord of the Cartwright Arms, as their spokesman, and Bygrave made no secret of views that would now be thought snobbish. The principal reason why the farmers wished to retain the school was so that they might send their own sons to it, 'farmers and tradespeople objecting to their children being educated with the children of the poor' reported Edis. Some thought that a successful school would bring business to the village.

It was a poor argument, and though Edis listened with sympathy and politeness, the opposition made all the running. Mr. Gibbs the shoemaker, 'a man of considerable ability' wrote Edis, blamed the decline of the Aynho school on the successes of Bloxham and Brackley: he had a child of his own at the National School and clearly resented the aspersions that the farmers cast upon it. The farmers apparently believed the school to have been founded for their own class, and were surprised to be told that it had not. The old school had not failed for want of opportunity, and there was no reason to suppose that it could succeed in the future. Edis certainly was left in no doubt about what should be done: it was simply a matter of arranging the legal formalities. He had some suggestions to make himself, however: that the endowment fund might be used to give scholarships to other secondary schools or to support Aynho boys who were already there. Even the school's supporters had to admit that this was reasonable, and so the meeting adjourned, everyone having spoken (said Edis) with 'outspoken frankness', despite the inhibiting presence of the squire and the parson.

Such indeed were to be the general lines of the scheme that the Charity Commissioners finally approved (and published in the local newspaper and printed for sale in the village shop at 3d a copy): the school funds were to endow scholarships of £10 to £30 a year at an approved boarding schoool or at a day school in Banbury. The principal asset of the school, the school house, was little changed since the time it had been built. The master's house had two rooms on the ground and first floors and three good attics. On the school side was a kitchen that had been taken out of the school room, the schoolroom itself, 'dismal and badly lighted', and a dormitory on the floor above. There was almost an acre of land attached to it, and the squire was at first sanguine about its prospects of sale, particularly since his son, Thomas, was interested in buying it. It was in fact not until 1894 that it was finally disposed of, by auction, following numerous flattering advertisements in the local papers, and then his son did buy it, for £600.

The slow improvement in the village school was one institutional change that the nineteenth century brought about. Another was a change in the treatment of the poor. It will be remembered how a Government enquiry of 1833 had collected evidence from Aynho, among other places, into the workings of the existing Poor Laws, and the general tenor of its conclusions — in common with those of everyone else who responded to the enquiry — was that the existing system was bad in principle and disastrous in practice. The Poor Law Amendment Act of 1834 was the result: the law that established the workhouses whose harsh management was made so notorious by Dickens and others. Under the new law, the able-bodied unemployed were only to receive relief if they entered the workhouse, where families were divided by age and sex, where paupers were set tasks that were generally tedious and frequently pointless, and where their diet, while sufficient to keep body and soul together, was devised with the idea that if sufficiently unattractive it would be a further disincentive to those who might otherwise seek help from the authorities. In the Poor Law Commissioners' words, the situation of the pauper 'must not be really or apparently so eligible as the situation of the independent labourer of the lowest class.'

The new Poor Law provided for the grouping of neighbouring parishes into Unions, and each Union was to be governed by a Board of Guardians and to provide a workhouse for its poor. Aynho was a Parish of the Brackley Union, and added to the misery of its poor was the distance of the workhouse from the village. Not, perhaps, that that mattered, since the poor were only eligible for support if they remained within the workhouse's walls and forfeited any claim for assistance if they ventured outside it. But though the regulations were laid down centrally, by the Commissioners in London, they were not always quite so harshly administered. They provided for out-door relief — i.e. for local relief for the elderly and the infirm, and it is clear that even the able-bodied were not always forced into the workhouse if their unemployment seemed only temporary. Probably a mixture of humanity and economics sometimes persuaded the authorities that there was no point in sending a man to the workhouse if he had a greater chance of finding work outside it, though the fact that the authorities were not always so moved is shown by the case of the man Watts, quoted already on page |211. But it is clear from the difference in sums paid for indoor and for outdoor relief that the number of Aynho people supported in the workhouse was always very much smaller than the number assisted in the village, and a few instances will serve to show how things might work in practice.

Outdoor relief was generally given as a combination of bread and a small allowance of money. In 1854 Mary Chilton, widow of a shoemaker, was aged about 60 and living alone. That summer she was to be given 2s a week and two 8d loaves until further notice. Four years later when she was ill, she was allowed 1s 2d worth of mutton in addition, and later 1s worth of gin. Two years later she was ill again and given wine, then gin again (she was probably more used to it) and allowed a nurse.

Richard Howes, a farm labourer with a wife and four children, was ill at the end of 1848 and was allowed six 4¾d loaves. In January next year he died, and the allowance paid to his widow was increased to 4s a week and six loaves; perhaps she had been working during her husband's last illness, and now had to stay at home and look after the children herself. In the summer she was ordered to the workhouse, but then the authorities changed their minds and gave her 1s a week and five loaves: one at least of her children was working, and was probably bringing in sufficient for the family to subsist on with the authorities' additional help.

The elderly might be sent to the workhouse if there was no-one to look after them, but much seems to have depended on whether they were able to look after themselves. John Jones, for instance, was an old shepherd whose wife died in 1848 when he was 78. For a year he was allowed two loaves and 2s 6d, but the following December the authorities paid 5s for his removal to the workhouse. But perhaps he had been allowed home to relatives for Christmas, for on Boxing Day the Guardians made a fresh order for his removal. By the end of January he was in Aynho again, and two years later he was receiving his old allowance and living with his grandson, Henry Williams, a young farm labourer and his wife. They must have come to his assistance feeling that they could not allow him to die in the workhouse alone. The guardians allowed the old man another 1s a week for nursing some time afterwards, and £1 for his funeral in 1853. The Williamses themselves were not well off: Henry Williams was in need of help a few years later and was allowed money, bread, 1s 2d worth of mutton and 1s 9d of porter.

There were other kinds of help that were also available. By the 1850's there was a doctor to see the poor, a Mr. Gee, who would see patients in the schoolroom each Monday morning at ten. What he prescribed was given free to paupers, while a loan for the cost of the prescription might be given by the Oversears to those who seemed to have a chance of repaying it. (There were many calls for trusses and elastic kneecaps: farm work was often heavy, and there were no mechanical aids for lifting great sacks of corn or coal.) The Overseers, the parish officers with charge of the money made available for outdoor relief in the village by the Guardians, could help in other cases with grants and loans. John Holland was given 15s for his charges in taking his wife to North-ampton Infirmary in 1848, and £1 for bringing her home again a few weeks later; six months later he was given a further sum for her funeral. Holland was a farm worker with a family of seven, living in a cottage on the Charlton Road, and it is most unlikely that he would have been able to repay sums such as these.

The Poor Law Unions were among the first fruits of a new approach to local government that by the end of the nineteenth century was to have created most of the existing machinery of local administration. The Victorians were obsessed with good government in a way that would have seemed quite alien to earlier ages. Partly it was a matter of the State's assuming responsibility for powers that earlier generations had not considered appropriate for government action: sanitation and education, for instance.

Partly, the scale of the tasks that the state had to fulfil had changed as population grew, as with the new Poor Law. Partly it was a matter of replacing earlier authorities that had withered away, so to speak. There had been no body representing the village as a whole since the decay of the Manor Court in the eighteenth century. Concern with local government had started with reforms in the way that towns were administered, but spread to the country: County Councils were set up in 1888, Parish Councils in 1894.

The Act that established them laid down that there was to be an annual parish meeting, and that Parish Councillors were to be elected by the voters of the village (who by then comprised almost all the men, though as yet none of the women.) They were to take over all the powers of local government that the churchwardens had exercised, such as keeping footpaths and bridleways in good order, powers to appoint various village officials such as the Overseers, and to supervise any charities that were not specifically concerned with the church. And in one notable way it differed from the meetings of village officials a century before: it was forbidden to meet in a pub.

The Parish Council tended to be run by the great men of the village, though by no means exclusively so. At the first meeting William Bygrave, landlord of the Cartwright Arms, farmer and Overseer, proposed and William Howes the baker seconded that the squire should take the chair. The first Councillors (elected after Mr. Bennett, the elderly tenant of Upper Aynho Grounds, had demanded a vote rather than a show of hands) were E. Baughan, carpenter and farmer; William Bygrave; Bennett; Mr. Gibbs the shoemaker, the man 'of considerable ability' whom Edis had remarked upon; T.H. Hawkes, farmer of the College Farm; J. Watts, blacksmith; Mr. Woolnough, agent to the Cartwright estate; William Howes, and a single labourer, J. Lambert. From the first there was some dissension over the elections to vice-chairman, clerk and treasurer, opposite factions being led by Woolnough and Bennett, Woolnough narrowly losing: interestingly, since he might as the squire's representative be thought to be expressing the squire's point of view. Nor next year were all the squire's candidates elected, his son and heir, Thomas, getting in but his brother, old Thomas who had so often managed the estate in his past absences, losing.

The Council had few direct responsibilities, but among these were the paving and lighting of village paths. There were ditches to be cleaned out alongside bridleways, and paths themselves to be put in order. Even where responsibility lay with the District Council (another recently created body) the Parish Council could make recommendations, as when they urged that the footpaths in the village itself should be repaired with flagstones in character with the old paving — an early example of rural conservation? But the most important of their actions in their early years was the lighting of the village with oil lamps.

It was not to be supposed, in Aynho, that even so uncontroversial and beneficent a measure as street lighting could be introduced without debate. In 1896 a sub-committee was appointed to consider the matter, and in due course they reported back, recommending that six street lamps of 50 candle-power each should be erected, on posts or brackets and with a ladder rest to each. The cost, they said, would be about £2 each for the lamps, with oil at 1½d a night. There was immediate argument. Two farmers, including Bennett, moved that 'the village be not lighted'; the two labourers on the Council, Lambert and Frederick Wrighton who had just been elected, moved that there should be seven lamps instead of six, and there for a year matters stood.

But it seems likely that street lighting was becoming a matter of public concern in the village, for at the next elections Bennett and Hawkes, the farmers, were voted off and two villagers, Robert Oakey (butcher and baker) and Frederick Dunn (labourer and groom) were voted on. A second lighting sub-committee was appointed, on Mr. Woolnough's motion, which recommended six lamps as their predecessors had done. This time there was no dissent. One was to be in the Hollow Way, one on the corner of William Secull's cottage in the square (number 44), and one on the Banbury Road at the corner of the engine pond opposite the College Farm. The others were probably placed at intervals along the main road. By mid October the lamps were ready, and Samuel Gibbs the shoemaker gave up his post as Parish Councillor to be lamplighter. Two candidates were proposed for the vacant place, Bennett and the curate, but Bennett only received one vote to the curate's four.

The business the next year (when Bennett scraped in at the bottom of the poll) included such items as petitioning the Post Office for a Sunday delivery, the levying of a lighting rate and the re-election of the lighting sub-Committee, and the choice of a successor to William Buckingham as the local Assessor of Taxes. The parish council was well launched, doing business that was not spectacular but which was useful. It provided a mouthpiece whereby village grievances could reach the ears of higher authority. And

in April 1901 when the Lord Lieutenant wrote to ask for a subscription towards the Queen Victoria Memorial Fund, even Mr.
Woolnough and Mr. Bennett came together in volunteering to collect the donations.

Epilogue

Looking back, life in Aynho before 1914 takes on an elegiac quality. There are still distant memories to be had of people who are long gone, and still people living whose childhood impressions of life before the first World War, added to knowledge of the changes since then, gives a peculiar poignancy to their reminiscences.

The village even looked more settled than it does now. There were few houses less than a century old, and most were already far older than that. The roads were white, dusty and empty, and the only sounds beyond those of the farms the occasional echo of a distant train when the wind was in the right direction. There were far more trees, many more even than there were before Dutch Elm disease took so heavy a toll of some of the finest trees in the parish. There were the Hill Trees, a clump of great elms where Blacksmith's Hill and the Hollow Way meet and where there are still fragments of the walls built to hold their roots. Opposite the Grammar House was the Town Elm, and it may have been there that the village elders had formerly met for their periodic inspection of the open fields more than a hundred years before. The enclosure hedges were now a century old, and contained many trees by now well grown. There were limes between the great house and the main road, and the house could hardly be seen through them.

The old houses of the village have for the most part been altered since then, to make them more comfortable than their old occupants could ever have imagined their being, and sometimes too to make them 'cottagey' in ways that correspond more to modern myth than to rural reality. Ceilings were lime washed, walls colour washed or perhaps covered in a cheap (and probably rather garish) paper. A cottager with a pig often cured his own hams and smoked his own bacon, but the open fireplaces of former times had mostly, by 1914, been filled with cast-iron grates with side ovens. Tenants would request one from Mr. Woolnough the agent, who would (if necessary) visit the cottage to see what was wanted: a left-handed or right-handed grate, depending on which way the light came from. The appropriate grate would then be ordered from Banbury and delivered by the twice-weekly carrier and installed by one of the Seculls. But Woolnough need seldom have inspected beforehand; he must have known the insides of all the squire's cottages well, and though his request to inspect a tenant's cottage would have been politely made, it is not one that a cottager would have dreamed of refusing.

Furniture was simple: a table, a few wooden chairs, one or two with arms, perhaps, in front of the fire, a home-made rag rug on the stone flagged floor, a simple dresser, and a bit of pottery, a pretty tin, a pair of brass candlesticks and an almanack on the mantlepiece. There might be a geranium in the window, and light after dark from an oil lamp hanging from the ceiling. Many cottages had outside shutters which would help to keep the warmth in on cold nights. In one corner of the living room there might be a sack of grain if the owner kept a pig or chickens, with a stick in it to keep it stirred up and to prevent it from over-heating if the grain was damp. Running water, of course, was quite unknown in cottages. People fetched water from one of the wells and heated it in a boiler. A shallow sink in an outhouse served for all kitchen purposes, and a daily wash and a weekly bath would be taken in tin tubs by the living room fire.

Rents varied, 1s 9d to 2s 6d a week according to the size of the cottage and the income and status of the tenant. Many people paid in addition a small annual rent for an allotment on which to grow greens or potatoes or a little barley for the pig in his stye behind the cottage. (Gardens were attached to most cottages, but several tenants had gardens elsewhere in the village and these detached plots sometimes continued to be let with distant cottages for generations.) After paying his rent, a labourer might be left with ten or eleven shillings for everything else: bread at 6d a large loaf, a pound of cheese at 6d, eggs at ½d each, tea at 6d a quarter. There was not much left for luxuries.

The old squire, William Cornwallis Cartwright, lived until 1915. The great house was not often let in his later years, but he was none the less often away. He had a game leg, and the first that villagers might know of his visits to the village was seeing the flagstones leading to the church sprinkled with sand to stop him slipping. He was a fine-looking old man, walking slowly with his rubber-tipped stick, and in the village he had a reputation for a peppery temper. Most of the day-to-day running of things fell to the rector and to the agent, Mr. Woolnough.

The upper servants at the great house were almost as much figures of awe as was the squire himself. There was Mr. Bennett the butler, a stately individual who might be asked to serve on such occasions as the flower show committee. He had a French wife and later they tried (not very successfully) to run the Cartwright Arms. Mr. Brown, the head gardener and invariably addressed as 'Sir' by his staff, had a white beard and always wore a dark suit, a bowler hat and a stiff white collar even on the hottest days. His wife had been in service as a ladies' maid. These and others of the village aristocracy would be addressed as 'Sir' or as 'Mr.' so-and-so by everyone, and titles mattered: the village policeman was Mr. Carter (a big, jovial fellow who looked after Croughton as well), the blacksmith, Mr. Watts (whose shoeing of their horses was vital to the village farmers). The farmers themselves, of course, were 'Mr.' as well.

The estate owned everything except the College Farm; the last outstanding freehold in the village had been No. 25 where for over a century the Buckingham family had lived, and this was bought by the squire in 1902. Similarly, the estate provided a good deal of employment. At the timber yard, Joe and Tom Humphris were constantly on call for repairs to houses, fences and waggons. Edwin Baughan was the wheelwright, on the corner where wheelwrights had worked for well over a century past; Fred Baughan was a carpenter, who made 'Aynho' tables, long and narrow, six sided, with the date carved on one side and sometimes the name Aynho carved on the other. There were two thatchers to attend to the cottage roofs, and the Seculls were still – two hundred years after Arthur's arrival – the village masons. The keeper Westbury (perhaps not a 'Mr.') lived by the brook off the Bicester road, and reared his pheasants in coops on the grass beside the water. There too, next to his house, he kept chained up three dogs which were the terror of the village children. (The house had been a part of the mill, and Westley still worked the sluice that controlled the flow of water to Souldern Mill lower down the stream.) But for most of the villagers work was still work on the land, ten or eleven hours a day, six days a week, with perhaps one week's holiday in the year and that not paid; some men could probably afford no holiday even if their master allowed it.

Women worked as well as the men. With their powdery, lime washed walls, their greasy oil lamps, their rugs and uneven floors, cottages were harder to keep clean than they are now, and of course there were none of the facilities that now one takes for granted. Carpets had to be beaten or brushed, floors scrubbed on hands and knees, hot water heated in a copper, ranges raked out and stove-blacked, clothes to be made by hand, boiled to wash them, mangled to dry them, and carefully mended to preserve them. In moments of relaxation, while women stood at their doors to talk to neighbours, socks would be growing on their knitting needles. At harvest the women would still work with the men, returning home to see to their children's dinner and then back to the field with something for their husbands. And harvest work was hard, binding and stocking the corn or pulling and stacking the beans.

There were always chores to be done in spare moments: wood to find for firing, for instance, and the women would wear a man's old cloth cap to carry bundles home on their heads. There were blackberries in September, for jam or home-made wine. Some people made mead and metheglin from honey; it is said that though this left the head quite clear it had a disastrous effect on the legs, and that once things had got so bad that the brewing of it was stopped. There were others, though, who claimed it was stopped because the landlord of the Cartwright Arms feared the competition.

There was pin money to be earned as well: a few of the older women still made lace, sitting outside their cottage doors on sunny days to get the best light, working with their lace pillows on their laps and the bobbins clicking. There were those who were good at dressmaking and could work for the less handy. Mrs. Lambert, who always wore a black hat, kept the Parish Room and the school clean, and was reputed to be able to move enormous weights. Mrs Savings, in blue cotton frock and apron, did laundry work in the washhouse near the Parish Room on Little Lane. One wife, whose husband was in the village fire brigade (men from the estate whose fire engine was a hand pump on a cart) was rumoured to have started a few fires herself, as the men were paid 5s a fire for turning out and 5s an hour for putting it out. One day she did the job rather too well, and raised a blaze that threw her into a terrible consternation: there were said to have been rather fewer fires in the village after that. But despite these small extras, efforts orthodox or less so to add to family earnings, budgets were still tight. Women would walk into Banbury and back to save a few pence on a purchase, and jumble sales were of the greatest importance for shoes, shirts or an old piece of lino for a bedroom floor. There was keen competition for bargains, and a firm line taken by stall holders backed up|by the presence of the policeman.

Children, too, could earn a little by running errands and doing other odd jobs. The old rector until 1906, Frederick Cartwright (William Ralph's youngest son by his second marriage) was a keen fisherman, and the child who carried his basket and rod home for him would be given 3d and a piece of cake by the Rectory butler. Occasionally the rector himself might give them half a crown, which seemed to the children untold wealth. It was said too that sometimes, driving back from Banbury in his brougham, he would have his pockets full of sweets which he would throw out to them; if someone opened a gate for him and he knew the family was in difficulties, he would unobtrusively let fall a coin as he passed; the recipient could sometimes be seen dodging along the other side of the hedge to reach the next gate before the rector arrived.

The school was much larger than it is now, since it took children right up to the age at which they left; it was only in 1930 that the older children went to a secondary school at King's Sutton, walking down the hill (in all weathers) to catch the 8.43 train. There were medals for good attendance, and a watch for any child with an unbroken record until his schooling was finished, but few children can have stayed long enough at school to have earned one even if they were never away ill. Many still left at 11 or 12 to learn a trade, to work as a farm lad or (for the girls) to go into service.

People worked for as long as they were able: the idea of retirement had not yet reached the farm labourer. Those without relations to care for them might still have to end their days in the workhouse — 'the Union' — at Brackley, but those who stayed in the village were paid 2s 6d, or 3s 6d for a couple. Those who went to the almshouses were fortunate, with two rooms of their own and six or seven shillings a week. One old man, still remembered until recently, was George Tuckey. Born in 1804, he lived until 1898. He had been a labourer all his working life, and verger in the church until he was over eighty. In his last years he was no longer able to go to church on a Sunday, but when he heard the church bell he would sit outside his house and follow the service, including the Lessons and the Collect for the day.

There were other charities, too. The bread charity that Richard Cartwright had endowed provided 2 lb and 4 lb loaves to a few old people. The rent from the allotments was spent on coals for the poor. The rector provided white dresses for the girls' Confirmation. Lady Elizabeth Cartwright of Newbottle gave the children a treat at Christmas, when every boy would return home with a length of cloth for a suit and every girl with material for a dress. The rector would give fruit for a pudding and some tea.

Sunday was the one day off from work, and many children went to bed early on a Saturday night so that their clothes might

be washed and ironed for Sunday morning. Children went to
Sunday School at 10 o'clock, for some time held in Church Cottage
(where the curate lived) off the Square. Everyone went to the 11
o'clock service, announced first by a peal of bells and then by a
five-minute bell, the smallest and oldest of the bells, called the
'hurry-up bell' by the villagers. As time for service approached the
Rector would lead the children across from Church Cottage, and
in church they would sit on their own, on forms down the side,
under the watchful eye of the Verger. When there had still been
boys at the Grammar School, they had sat in the gallery at the
back, dressed in Eton suits and mortar boards. There would generally be a sermon (the church bell rang at half past nine if there
was going to be) and the children must have thought it unfair that
the old squire always left before it. None of them would have dared
try.

After church came Sunday dinner, for many families the high
spot of the week and the one day when they ate fresh meat. A
cheap cut, costing 6d or so, was put on a stand in a baking tray
above plenty of Yorkshire pudding to eke it out; before service it
was taken to Oakey's or to Howes's bakehouse to be cooked for
1d or 2d, or it was done at home in a Dutch oven in front of a bar
of coals. After the morning service the men would fetch the dinner
carefully home, each eyeing his neighbour's tray to see how it
compared with his own. After lunch the post office was open for
an hour in case anyone had letters to fetch or send, the men might
play skittles, while the children might go up the road to skirmish
with the children from Charlton — which was their idea of spending
an agreeable afternoon.

Sundays apart, there were few breaks in the annual round.
Even Good Friday was not considered a holiday: on that day, the
men either went to church or worked, and the agent saw to it that
they did one or the other. But there were high spots scattered
through the year: the crowning of the May Queen, the flower
show, cricket matches, the rent dinner, the pig club dinner and
Christmas.

Whether the crowning of the May Queen was an ancient tradition is doubtful. In 1913, when one of the Garrett children was
chosen as Queen, the ceremony was organised by Mrs. Pollard, the
infants' school mistress. The chosen girl and her attendants would
process round the village, calling at each house with a verse or a
song, collecting pennies as they went, and finally returning to the
school for buns and lemonade. The Queen wore a veil thrown back

from her face, she and her girl attendants carried bouquets and wore sprays of flowers, and were accompanied by four boys each carrying a bell-shaped garland of blossom on a pole decorated with ribbons and streamers. It was not always easy to find the true may on the first of the month; if none could be found the children made do with blackthorn instead.

The annual flower show was the high spot of the year, held in the grounds of the great house. Everyone dressed in their best, the men (in old photographs, anyway) looking uncomfortable and ill-at-ease in starched collars and their best jackets and in boots that had probably taken half an hour to polish, the children wearing clean pinafores or knickerbocker suits and threatened with dire punishment for soiling them, the women in their prettiest dresses. There was a marquee with grand shows of flowers and vegetables, spreads of bread and home made cakes and needlework, prizes for such practical things as 'the best dinner for four people costing no more than 6d' (one could count the produce of one's allotment as free) and frivolities such as a hat dressing competition for the men. There were sports: men tried to knock each other off a horizontal bar with pillows and bowled for a pig, and ladies' races, despite the hobbling of a long skirt. There were merry-go-rounds and swing boats, and a band from King's Sutton. Then there was the prize giving on the lawn of the great house, presided over by the Rector, and in the evening dancing by the light of home-made fairy lights: night lights in jam jars tied to poles.

There were cricket matches with neighbouring villages in the summer, 'games away' gone to in waggonettes whose horses' coats glistened and whose harness had been polished until it shone. Later in the year came the Michaelmas rent dinner for the farmers. There was usually venison, there were always speeches, and then the squire (if he had been present) would tactfully withdraw and leave the tenants to a convivial evening (any new tenant had to be 'shod' by tapping him on the heel with a bottle of whisky). Before the end of the century a rent supper had been held in the big barn behind the Cartwright Arms, decorated for the occasion, and afterwards there had been dancing to the music of an accordion, a whistle and perhaps a mouth organ. This may have been a supper for the cottagers as well.

Through the winter there was the occasional excitement of a Meet of the Bicester and Walden Hunt, the road thronged with horses, traps and carriages, bicycles and even an odd motor car. And at Christmas there was mumming.

On Christmas Eve the boys and lads went mumming, dressed up in borrowed clothes and armed with flue brushes. They would knock on each cottage door in turn, scrub away at the doorsteps with their brushes, and cry 'make way, make way for my great gentleman' and Old Mother Christmas, also with a broom, would call up a motley collection of characters: 'Come in King George and Duke of Cumberland, Dr. Gullet and Dr. Phinny, also Beelzebub and short shirt Jinny, old big yead Jack with his bag on his back'. There followed a good deal of pantomine mumbo-jumbo in which Mother Christmas poked fun at Dr. Phinn and his miraculous pills, and the performance ended with a song and a step dance. They had a collecting box, said to have been made out of a beam from the old church, and people put in a penny or two before the mummers moved on to the next cottage.

There were other festivities of various kinds. There was, for instance, the annual dinner of the pig club. The pig club was an insurance club against the death of a member's pig. If the pig fell ill, its owner would summon the officials of the Club who might advise killing it there and then: if the pig should die, the carcass was worthless and the club would have to pay up. The killing itself was a bloody and a noisy affair, usually carried out on a bench on the street; it was not a scene for the squeamish, but was of the greatest interest and excitement to the village children. The Pig Dinner was an important occasion, usually attended by the agent and the Rector, and it was a good solid meal with roast beef and a boiled pudding to follow. On one occasion, probably when it was held at the Cartwright Arms, some practical jokers managed to get a donkey up the stairs and into the Club Room. There was a smaller annual party for the Fire Brigade. And there were spontaneous entertainments, like a mock trial in a barn of an evening, with a fine of a pint of beer from each prisoner. Sometimes there were gatherings to sing in the square. And there were quieter entertainments: a reading room and library run by the Rector, Digby Cartwright and his wife, and a night school for older villagers whose mastery of the 3 R's had been neglected before the days of compulsory education. There were special occasions for celebration such as Coronations, and events in the squire's family: marriages and comings-of age, and family funerals too, when the blinds were drawn in village shops and houses, a muffled peal was rung, and the grave lined with moss and fresh flowers by the gardeners from the great house.

Since two world wars the life of the village has changed utterly.

The old employments that tied men to the land have gone, and old village families have gone with them. The squire has gone, and the place now belongs to a hundred and fifty different people. Many of the old cottages have been so altered as to make them almost unrecognisable, and since 1950 the number of houses in the place has doubled, a rate of growth unequalled in the past. There are few people now who expect to spend their lives in Aynho, and it is unlikely that many people now even spend all their working lives in the village. The life of the village is still as strong as ever but it is bound by new forces and new customs, as vital as the old but suited to people with money, transport, refrigerators, telephones and jobs in towns, and without the need to grow their own food, to pinch and save for a day's holiday, and with more than the schooling that, for most people, had been barely enough to enable them to pick their way through the church services.

Many of those who came back from the 1914–1918 War came back with broader horizons, with other ideas about the established order. Children would spend longer at school, but not in Aynho itself but in King's Sutton or Brackley. There would be council houses built, houses which the villagers would welcome as warmer and dryer than anything they had ever known, with hot and cold water and bathrooms, and the old houses would slowly be bought by a class of people who would once never have dreamed of living in an old cottage. There would be tractors on the farms, and ever fewer hands needed as mechanisation increased. There would be buses to make even the walk to the station an unnecessary hardship, and soon almost everyone in the place would have a car. The Park would be ploughed and the deer sold. Houses would be re-numbered and streets re-named, and the great house divided up into flats.

The Aynho farmers made their last service of gift-cart in 1920, to bring ice from the canal to the ice-house in the Park. There was a last coming-of-age for the young heir, Richard Cartwright, in 1924. The last Cartwright rector died in 1926, and the last traditional village celebrations were for the Jubilee in 1935, the Coronation in 1937 and for Victory in 1946. The mortgage on the estate remained as a drain on the family's resources, and much of the village was sold in 1940, the remainder in 1946. Only a few houses were kept back for the occupancy of old family servants and the great house for themselves. The family had already severed all but emotional connections with the village when, on a night at the end of March, 1954, the squire and his only son were driving home from London and ran into the back of a stationary timber lorry. Both were killed instantly.

The history of the recent years must still be written. The evidence is all round, in the lives and memories of people living, and despite the revolutions of the last few years there is no break: the story is continuous, even though the speed of change has been more rapid than ever before. To understand how and why these changes have taken place is a debt that we owe to the old villagers of the past, and one that we should honour if their lives and the life of the old village community are not to be left in limbo, of no value save to serve our curiosity. The remote and the recent past deserve understanding if we are to know how people do, can and should live now and in the future.

Time is a dragon that devours all its riders. Yet we must all ride, though few can see the destination to which we are born as it recedes always before our now slow, now hectic flight.

Appendix 1

Poll Tax, Tenures and Rents, 1544/5

Tax	Name	Tenure	Holding	Rent	Note
–	Rowland Shakerley (Rector)	Lord Glebe	2 virgates		
–	George Keble	Freehold	2 vv.	£ 0 0 1	
–	Richard Leche	Freehold	1 v.	£ 0 7 0	
–	Richard Burberye	Freehold	1 v.	£ 0 16 0	
£20	Joan Boughton	Lease	Demesne: 10 vv.	£20 13 4	
	"	Freehold	1 v.	£ 0 16 0	
	"	Freehold	½ v.	£ 0 6 0	
	"	Freehold	Small		
	"	Copyhold	1 v.	£ 0 18 0	
	"	Copyhold	1 v.	£ 0 16 0	
	"	Copyhold	½ v. + small	£ 0 6 0	
£20	Thomas Hanslape	(Taxed on goods)			
£20	Edward Love	College Lease	6 vv.		College Farm
£15	Richard Cowley	Copyhold	2½ vv.	£ 2 3 4	
£9	Thomas Burton	Copyhold	2 vv.	£ 1 12 0	
£8	Thomas Sparry	Copyhold	2 vv.	£ 1 14 0	
£7	Henry Leche	Copyhold	1½ vv.	£ 1 6 0	
£7	Thos. Bartford als. Baker	Copyhold	1½ vv.	£ 1 4 0	
£7	William Longstaffe	Copyhold	1½ vv.	£ 1 4 0	
£5	Thomas Bele	Copyhold	1½ vv.	£ 1 4 0	
			Sheepcote	£ 0 1 0	
£4	Robert Grene	Copyhold	2 vv.	£ 1 12 0	
£3	John Brignell	Copyhold	1½ vv.	£ 1 4 0	
£3	John Brignell	Copyhold	1 v.	£ 0 16 0	
£3	James Bewley	Copyhold	1 v.	£ 0 16 0	
£3	John Burton	Copyhold	1½ vv.	£ 1 4 0	
£3	Thomas Gevis	Copyhold	1½ vv.	Note 1	
£3	William Bricknell	Note 2			
£3	William Canch				
£3	William Cowley	Note 2			
£3	Thomas Grene	Note 2			
£3	John Leche	Note 3			
£3	George Powle				
£3	John Warlow				
£2	Christiana Baker	Copyhold	1½ vv.	£ 1 4 0	
£2	Peter Parker	Copyhold	2 vv.; Note 4	£ 1 12 0	
£2	William Harberd	Cottager	Cottage	£ 0 3 0	Mason?
£2	Ric. Milward als. Spencer	Cottager	Cottage + 1 acre	£ 0 4 0	
£2	Agnes Bricknell	Note 2			
£2	John Brignell	Note 2			
£2	Thomas Kyrby				
£2	Richard Side				

Tax	Name	Tenure	Holding	Rent	Note
£1	John Clerke	Cottager	Cottage	£ 0 3 0	
£1	Richard Elyott	Cottager	Cottage	£ 0 3 4	
£1	Christopher Pemberton	Cottager	Cottage + 4 acres	£ 0 4 0	
–	Agnes Warde	Cottager	Cottage	£ 0 1 4	
£1	Richard Watkyns	Cottager	Cottage + 1 acre	£ 0 4 0	
£1	Thomas Westly	Cottager	Cottage + 4 acres	£ 0 4 4	
£1	Robert Wilkyns	Cottager	Cottage + 1 acre	£ 0 3 4	
£1	George Wyssewaye	Cottager	Cottage + 1 acre	£ 0 3 4	
£1	Thomas Allowe				
£1	Richard Bricknell	Note 2			
£1	Thomas Brickmore				
£1	Thomas Elys				
£1	Gyles Franklin				
£1	Thomas Fynson				
£1	Elizabeth Grene	Note 2			
£1	William Gubbins				
£1	James Mills				
£1	James Warclow				
£1	(indecipherable)				
£1	”				

Notes

1. Thomas Gevis seems to have been a tenant of Joan Boughton's probably renting her freehold rather than the copyhold which she would not normally have been allowed to sub-let.
2. Not recorded as renting land or cottages, but possibly a member of a landholder's family.
3. Landholder's son (Henry Leche's).
4. Not recorded as holding land in 1544; renting 2 virgates in 1545. It is not clear whose land this was, i.e. whether it has been entered twice in the table.

It seems likely, from the identities of names, that many of those taxed were living in the houses of people to whom they were closely related, and that the number of households in the village is substantially less than the names recorded in the poll tax. Towards the bottom of the list, particularly among those assessed at £1, there is less duplication of names. It cannot be assumed that all are servants, since one or two farmers are known to have paid rent for more than one messuage and therefore probably had subtenants, but the majority are probably the servants of the better-off.

Freeholders appear to have been omitted from the Poll Tax for Aynho: it is uncertain why. Agnes Warde, however, paying the smallest rent for her cottage (1s 4d) is also left off, and it may be that even householders (and certainly servants) escaped taxation if they were too poor.

The list prompts comparison with the details given in an Inquisition of 1369. The valuation included chief rents from an unspecified number of freeholders (*redditu liberorum tenentium*), £20 from 25 messuages and virgates held *in bondagio*, 26s from two further virgates similarly held, 47s from 18 cottages held at will (*ad voluntatem Dni.*) and nothing from 9 further cottages *ruinosa et vastata*.

Appendix 2

Households, Tenures and Rents, 1618

Name	Tenure	Holding	Acres	Rent
Richard Cartwright	Lord	Demesnes, etc.	807	
Edward Love	College lease	6 yardlands	162	
Thomas Hanslape	Freehold	4 yy.	110	£ 2 7 6
Thomas Drope	Freehold	3 yy.	99	Note 1
” ”	Glebe	2 yy.	45	
Giles Southam	Freehold	2½ yy.	62	Note 1
Peter Parker	Freehold	2 yy.	58	Note 1
Richard Stanton	Freehold	2 yy.	58	Note 1
William Wyatt	Freehold	2 yy.	54	£ 0 0 1
Robert Hobcroft	Freehold	1 yy.	40	Notes 1, 2
William Howes	Freehold	1½ yy.	41	Notes 1, 3
Jane Bricknell	Freehold	1 yy.	32	£0 0 1
George Collins	Freehold	3/4 yy.	22	Note 1
Lawrence Watts	Freehold	3/4 yy.	20	Note 1
Edward Jarvis	?	?		Notes 1, 4
Mark Gardner	Copyhold	2 yy.	68	£ 1 14 0
John Grene	Copyhold	2 yy.	61	£ 1 12 0
William Bower	Tenant	1½ yy.	45	£17 0 0
				Note 5
Richard Bewdley	Tenant	1½ yy.	46	£10 0 0
William Burton	Tenant	1½ yy.	44	£15 0 0
Ralph Jarvis	Copyhold	1½ yy.	51	£ 1 4 0
John Loe	Tenant	1½ yy.	45	Note 6
John Young	Copyhold	1½ yy.	45	£ 1 6 0
Thomas Swetnam	Copyhold	1 y. + shop	29	£ 0 18 0
Richard Collins	Lease	House + land	6	£ 0 8 0
Bridget Bell	Lease	House + land	8	£ 2 6 0
Thomas Deverill	Tenant	House + land	1	£ 0 4 0
William Herne	Tenant	House + land	10	£ 2 1 0
Elizabeth Hobcroft	Tenant	House + land	5	£ 1 6 0
Robert Loveday	Tenant	House + land	2	£ 0 10 0
Edward Meowe	Tenant	House + land	1	£ 0 4 0
George Pemtone	Tenant	House + land	4	£ 0 13 4
Nicholas Stilgoe	Tenant	House + land	4	£ 0 10 0
William Barton	Cottager	House		£ 0 0 1
Walter Bayliss	Cottager	House + garden		£ 1 0 0
Richard Bett	Hanslope's cottager	House		
Henry Brackley als. Bulckely	Cottager	House		£ 0 5 0
Widow Collyer	Drope's cottager	House		
Robert Crackley	Cottager	House + shop		£ 0 8 0
Robert Gardner	Love's cottager	House		
John Garye	Drope's cottager	House		
Widow Green	Cottager	House		£ 0 3 0

Name	Tenure	Holding	Acres	Rent
Widow Hobcraft	Love's cottager	House		
John Howse	Hanslope's tenant	House		Note 7
John Jarvis	Drope's cottager	House		
Widow Meade	Cottager	House		£ 0 5 0
Thomas Mott	Cottager	House		£ 0 4 0
Widow Osborne	Hanslope's cottager	House		
Roger Perian	Hanslope's cottager	House		
Fulke Rowsam (?)	Hanslope's cottager	House		
William Shomaker	Drope's cottager	House		
Edward Swetnam	Love's cottager	House		
William Toogood	Love's cottager	House		
Widow Watkins	Love's cottager	House		
Crescent White	Cottager	House		£ 0 4 0
John Whighte	Cottager	House		£ 0 1 6
William Yonger	Hanslope's cottager	House		

Notes

1. Freeholds purchased from Shakerley Marmion.
2. Hobcroft bought 1½ yardlands from Marmion originally, and later sold ½ yardland to Southam.
3. Let to William Howes.
4. Recorded by Richard Cartwright as having bought 1 yardland from Marmion, but holding no identifiable land in the 1618 survey.
5. Lands bought from Marmion by Thomas Skillman, and subsequently sold by Skillman to Richard Cartwright.
6. Lands bought from Marmion by Loe, subsequently sold by him to Richard Cartwright but possibly leased back to him.
7. Probably farming Hanslope's lands.

Direct comparison with Appendix 1 (land holdings in 1544/5) is difficult since the absence of many Court Rolls for the intervening years makes it impossible to trace holdings from the first recorded tenant to the next. The amount of land in each list is not precisely the same, since in 1544 most if not all of the demesne, probably as yet unenclosed, was leased out, while in 1618 Richard Cartwright seems to have been farming it himself. Furthermore, in addition to enfranchising copyholders, Shakerley Marmion apparently sold off a small amount of the demesne. Nevertheless the number of farmers appears almost precisely the same, and the average size of farms little changed if at all.

The impression of mobility that may derive from changes in names between the two tables may be slightly misleading, since it is clear that names could be temporarily 'lost', only to recur later. Thus for instance, while there is no-one with the surname Letch/Leche appearing in 1618, against three in 1544/5, in fact John Young was married to a Letch widow, probably farmed her land, and his stepson Henry Letch was farming on his own account only a few years later. It is likely that different names disguise other close relationships between villagers at the two dates.

No allowance is made in the table — because no calculations were made by the surveyors of 1618 — for the interest that the larger farmers had in meadow and in grazing the commons.

'Cottagers' (so described) appear already to have been tenants at will rather than copyholders.

Appendix 3

Farmers: Households and Tenures, 1740–45

Name	Age, 1740	Household, 1740 (family/servants)	Tenure	Holding, 1744
John Pruce	57	8/4	tenant	Inn (?), 5½ yardlands, closes, 27 cows' commons
Edward Homan	56	8/5	tenant	Inn (?), 5 yardlands, closes, 25 cows' commons
Chas. Marshall	35	6/3	?	3 yardlands, closes, 18 cows' commons
Edward Letch	about 25	5	freehold	3 yardlands (?), closes, 15 cows' commons
John Reynolds	about 30	5/2	?	3 yardlands, closes, 12 cows' commons
Thomas Smith	36	8/1	?	2½ yardlands, closes, 12 cows' commons
Thomas Bower	24	6	mixed	2½ yardlands, close, 12 cows' commons
Wm. Tomkins	about 68	4/3	?	2¼ yardlands, meadow, 10 cows' commons
John Bricknell	about 56	5/2	freehold	2 yardlands, closes, 15 cows' commons
John Borton	about 40	9	tenant	2 yardlands, closes, 10 cows' commons
John Burberow		8/1	tenant	1½ yardlands, meadow, closes, 12 cows' commons
Samuel Mayo	about 30	3	tenant	Deer park (?), 9 ridges, close
Thomas Bricknell	about 40	3	freehold	closes, 18 cows' commons
Samuel White		2/1	?	14 ridges, closes, 2 cows' commons
John Baker	(? absentee)		freehold	meadow, 4½ cows' commons
Jos. Wagstaff		5/2	?	4 ridges, close, 1 cow's common
Wm. Borton	about 25	3	?	ridges (few), meadow, 1 cow's common
Robt. Addington	63	2	tenant	4 ridges, meadow, 1 cow's common
Ben Coates		6	freehold	close, 2 cows' commons
John Smith	(old)	1	?	1 cow's common
Widow Aris		1	tenant	1 cow's common
Wm. Phillips			tenant	3 ridges

Appendix 4

Farmers: Post-enclosure Holdings and Rents, 1794

Name	Acreage	Rent (1)
Robert Wagstaff (Nell Bridge Farm)	283 (2)	£306
John Aris (Lower Aynho Grounds)	282½	£420
William Howes (Upper Aynho Grounds)	271½	£208
Samuel Mayo (Aynho Park)	225 (3)	£280
Edward Dunn (Warren Farm)	210	£130
William Tibbetts (College Farm)	208	
Matthew Borton (Borton's Farm)	196	£130
Mary Letch	103½	£ 93
Thomas Smith	92	£ 93
Timothy Burberow	59 (4)	£ 70
Mary Bygrave (Red Lion Inn)	37	£ 64
George Hunt (Alfred's Head Inn)	20	£ 21
William Bull (? butcher)	17 (5)	
Edward Bygrave	16 (6)	
Thomas Walker (wheelwright)	9 (7)	
Henry Bolt	1½	£ 2 10s.

Notes

1. Rent paid to William Ralph Cartwright. Rents to other proprietors are not known.
2. Including 92 acres rented from John Baker senr. and John Baker jnr.
3. Including 21 acres rented from Sarah Burton.
4. Including 16 acres of his own.
5. 13 acres of his own, 4 rented from Mary Banbury.
6. Rented from Mary Merry.
7. Rented from John Gardner.

Mary Letch surrendered her new farm almost immediately, and the land seems to have been distributed among other, existing tenants rather than re-let as a separate unit. It seems probable that some of the small farms, including hers, represent the recognition of pre-existing tenancies, and that when these lapsed the opportunity was taken for consolidating farms further.

Appendix 5

Occupiers of Houses, 1790

Occupants of Aynho property, circa 1790 (the numbers correspond to those of the map on the rear end-paper). A number of buildings are barns and other farm buildings, though not indicated as such; presumably those at a distance from an occupant's main premises.

*Tenants of the Cartwright estate
†Tenants of other landlords

1	John March†	31	John Bridge†
2	Thomas Smith*	32	Thomas Wagstaff*
3	William Wrighton*	33	Valentine Austin*
4	William Peckover*	34	Samuel West*
5	Matthew Borton*	35	Joseph Ayris*
6	William Watts	36	James Betts*
7	John Leach	37	John French*
8	William Alcock	38	William Seccull*
9	Samuel Goode†	39	Moses Collins*
10	Thomas Kimber†	40	Benjamin Clemens*
11	John Turvey*	41	Betty Baldwin*
12	Richard Kitteridge†	42	The school: Revd.
13	Richard Terry†		Mr. Oliver
14	John Watts	43	Mrs. Ely*
15	– Gibberd	44	Martin Harris*
16	Thomas Bygrave (malting)	45	Widow Ayris*
17	John Steanes†	46	Timothy Hall*
18	William Buckler†	47	John Gurney*
19	John Turbit	48	Widow Knott*
20	Ralph Palmer*	49	Robert Malins*
21	Edward Fathers†	50	Valentine Austin*
22	Thomas Wagstaff*	51	Martin Watson†
23	Joseph Wagstaff*	52	William Burton†
24	John Boxall	53	William Franklin
25	Thomas Knott*	54	John Collins*
26	Thomas Bygrave	55	Widow Cross*
27	Susannah Prowett	56	William Turner*
28	William Knott†	57	Mrs. Winkle
29	John Bolton†	58	Francis Collins†
30	William Baldwin†	59	Mrs. Acome†

60	Mrs Banbury	98	George Whetton†
61	William Bull (malt house)†	99	Thomas Walker
62	Richard Bolt	100	Thomas Marsh
63	William Dry*	101	Thomas Gregory†
64	Edward Spiers*	102	John Turner†
65	Mrs. Bird†	103	John Bowers
66	Martha Priest†	104	Rev. Mr. Mabletoft
67	Widow Hawtin†	105	William Ralph Cartwright
68	Richard Dimock*	106	Robert Weston*
69	Richard Anstee†	107	William Ayris†
70	Robert Upton*	108	John Buckingham†
71	– Whitby*	109	– Shelton
72	Widow Horwood*	110	Benjamin Tyrrell†
73	Thomas Baldwin*	111	William Smith†
74	William Stanley		Robert Walton†
75	John Polton	112	Thomas Wrighton†
76	Widow Whitby		Thomas Marsh†
77	William Wrighton	113	John Goode†
78	Widow Leach†	114	Timothy Burberow*
79	John Baker	115	– Tyrrell†
80	Ann Jackson†		– Smith
81	Timothy Hulbird	116	John Turbitt†
82	Daniel Taylor*	117	William Bull†
83-4	Samuel Mayo*	118	John Nicolls†
85	Mrs. Merry†	119	William Galloway†
86	John Baker	120	Thomas Silver†
87	Emery Walker*	121	Thomas Collins†
88	Samuel Mayo*	122	Matthew Borton*
89	Mr. Markham	123	John Collins*
90	Mr. Burbidge	124	Ezekiel Dolton*
91	Henry Farring†	125	Widow Coates*
92	William Bull†	126	Mary Jones*
93	William Watson†	127	– Pollard†
94	William Borton†	128	Mary Ford†
95	Thomas Steel†	129	– Tibbets†
96	Thomas Goodger	130	Mrs. Wodhull†
97	John Turbit		

Appendix 6

Field and Furlong Names in the Early Eighteenth Century

1	Hemp piece	37	Church Mead
2	Wards Ash	38	Nomans Hill
3	Wensdon	39	Berry Slade
4	Butts piece	40	Catsbrain
5	Six acres	41	Norris grass
6	Arslong	42	Cotman meadow
7	Irish Butts	43	Cotman Hook
8	Walton Hedge furlong	44	Depden Head
9	Short lands	45	Short Clays
10	Butts	46	Great Depden
11	Demcsne	47	Norcot Hill
12	Fifty acres	48	Whethill
13	Rainsbury furlong	49	Sparrowhill
14	Long furlong	49a	Sparrowhill Butts
15	Stanhills	50	Woollands
16	Six Butts	51	Towards Sheep Bridge
17	Deadlands	52	Shooting into Mill Brook
18	Picked furlong	53	College Grass
19	Middle Sands	54	College Mill and Mead
20	Long Sands	56	Merry's Corner
21	West Buglow	57	Willmore Mead
22	Lower Buglow	58	Hockley Piece
23	Middle Buglow	59	Between the Mills
24	East Buglow	60	West of Greenway
25	Spitchill furlong	61	Crabtree west of
26	Spitchill leys		Greenway
27	North Fulwell	62	Crabtree furlong
28	Fulwell Slade	63	Elderbush furlong
29	Coniger	64	Blackbush furlong
30	Coniger middle furlong	65	Blackwell furlong
31	Warren	66	Blackwell head
32	Furze close	67	Smannell furlong
33	Ryelands furlong	68	Smannells common
34	Ryelands Hill three furlongs	69	Langford furlong
		70	Long sands
35	Ryelands Hill middle furlong	71	Long reel
		72	Five lands
36	Ryelands Clay	73	Long irondown

74	Little irondown
75	Pye furze furlong
76	Pye furze common
77	Twenty lands
78	Armley acres
79	Handley acres
80	Kings Moore head
81	Binley acres
82	Truckingham mead
83	Clifton mead
84	Smatts
85	West mead
86	Croton meadow
87	Warren hook
88	Radford hook
89	Crooked doles
90	Ripham smatts
91	College mead
92	Dunny doles
93	Cullimore leys
94	Flaggy doles
95	Pill doles
96	Well doles
97	Broad doles
98	Mead broad doles
99	Oxhey cowpasture
100	Summer cowpasture
101	John Spruce's cowpasture
102	John Spruce's spinney
103	Robert White's spinney
104	Sentum mead
105	Peartree hill
106	Little Cotlow
107	Great Cotlow
108	Warren ground
109	Little Barnhill
110	Warren ground
111	Lawley's leys
112	Spencer's close
113	Paddock
114	Messers mead
114a	Messers mead copse

115	Little Noore
115a	Little Moor copse
115b	Little Moor pool
116	Bingham's Moor
116a	Bingham's Moor copse
117	Hopyard
118	Horse close
119	Mill cot
120	Silwells
121	Nether church pasture
122	Over church pasture
123	Drope's close
124	Fisher's leys
125-6	Closes
127	Parsonage close
128-9	Closes
130	William Boarton's close
131	William Howes' close
133	Edward Letch's close
134	Haslop's close
135-7	Parsonage close
138	Mary Stanton's close
139	Mrs Drope's close
140	Hanslop's close
141	College close
142	Spittle Hatch
143	John Spruce's close
144	John Bricknell's close
145	Tim Burberow jnr's close
146	Tim Burberow snr's close
147	Samuel Barding's close
148	Spencer's close
149	Henry Letch's close
150	Spencer's close
151	Thomas Tomkins's close
152	Edward Letch's close
153	Edward Jarvis's close
154	Mrs Drope's close
155	Hanslop's close
156	Edward Letch's close
157	John Southam's close
158	John Spencer's close

159   Thomas Tomkins' close   164   Edward Homan's close
160   William Boarton's close   165   John Spruce's close
161   Thomas Tomkins' close   166   William Boarton's close
162   William Boarton's close   167   John Spencer's close
163   William Addington's close

The names are taken from two maps, dated 1696 and 1720. The closes are almost without exception in the former Lower Fields — the open fields west of the village enclosed in 1620, and the names by which they were known before their enclosure had been lost (or at least passed out of use) by the time the maps were made.

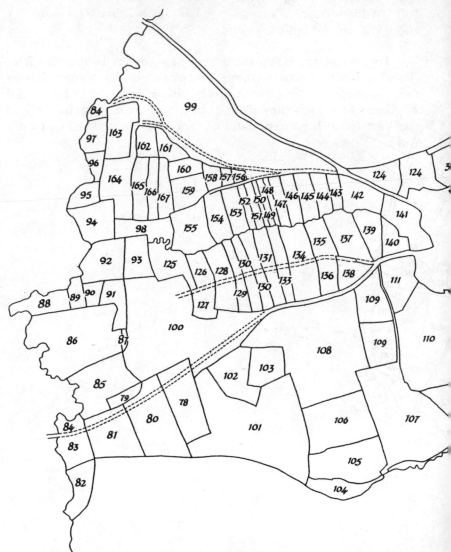

Map 9. Field and furlong names in the early 18th century.

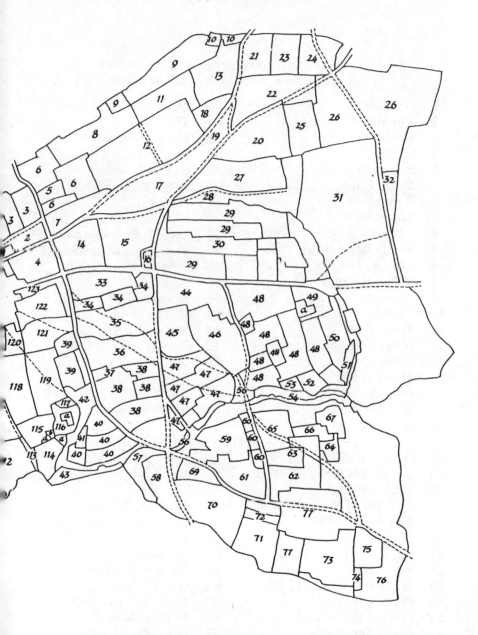

Appendix 7

Field Names, circa 1960
from information given to Miss M. Kennedy

1	Wensden	36	Northcotehill Covert
2	The Butts	37	The Clays
3	Little Butts	38	Long Clays
4	Glebe	39	Double Gate Ground
5	Stone Pit	40	Old Mill Ground
5a	Spion Copse	40a	Three Corner Spinney
6	Barn Ground	41	Wheat Hill
7	Limekiln	42	Old Down Covert
8	Camp Ground	43	Lime Kiln Ground
9	Bridle Road Field	44	First Lime Kiln Ground
10	Letches Ground	45	Further Lime Kiln
11	Magro Ground		Ground
12	Burglar	46	Keeper's Hill
13	Rectors Field	47	Mill Ground
14	Poors Piece	48	Middle Covert
15	Walton Ground	49	New Wood
16	Close	50	Sheep Walk
17	Standell Pits	51	Smanhill Covert
18	Spittals	52	Swan Hill
19	Barn Ground	53	Sandy Ground
20	Middle Cross Road	54	Lime Kiln Ground
	Ground	55	Barn Ground
21	Corner Wall Ground	56	Long Reel
22	Bricklands Cub	57	Irondown
23	Slade Ground	58	The Firs
24	Croughton Road Ground	59	Holloway's Flat
25	Ten Acre Field	60	Cotmoor Hooks
26	Long Sands	61	Park Flat
27	Big Warren Top Field	62	Cotlands
28	Big Warren	63	Sansom Meadow
29	Little Warren and Ley Plat	64	Great Peartree Hill
30	Pesthouse Wood	65	Little Peartree Hill
31	Pesthouse Ground	66	Collins Ground
32	Great Spetchells	67	Great Cow Pasture
33	Barn Ground	68	Little Cow Pasture
34	Smith's Close	69	Great Barn Hill
35	Northcote Hill	70	Little Barn Hill

71	Whites Close	90	Middle Merchants Meadow
72	Little Close Paddock	91	Top Merchants Meadow
73	Great Spinney	92	Brickyard Close
74	Little Spinney	93	Drawbridge Ground
75	Three Corner Close	94	Railway Field
76	Old Common	95	Bank Meadow
77	Cow House Ground	96	Midsummer Ground
78	Tuppings Close	97	Goosham Meadow
79	Clap Gate	98	Ryans Meadow
80	Merry's Close	99	Home Field
81	Foot Road Paddock	100	Great Close Meadow
82	Cattle Sale Grounds	101	Little Oxey Meadow
82a	Sale Yard	102	Oxey Meadow
83	Aynho Meadow	103	Arnold
84	The Meadow	104	Inkerman
85	Croughton Meadow	105	Gee's Close
86	Boat Meadow	106	Burberow's Close
87	Middle Meadow	107	Wycherley's Close
88	Weir Lock Meadow	108	Ben Watts's Close
89	Merchants Meadow	109	Picket Field

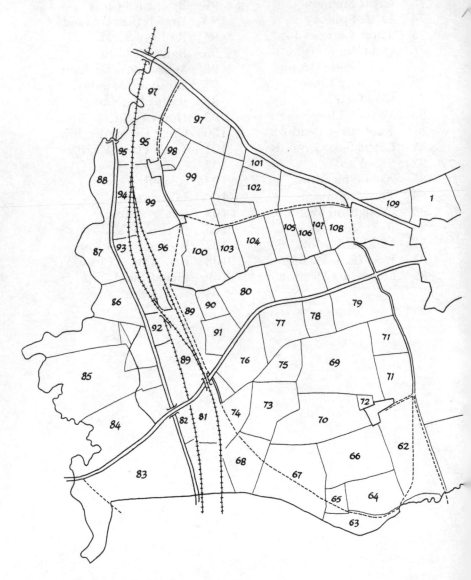

Map 10. Field names c.1950.

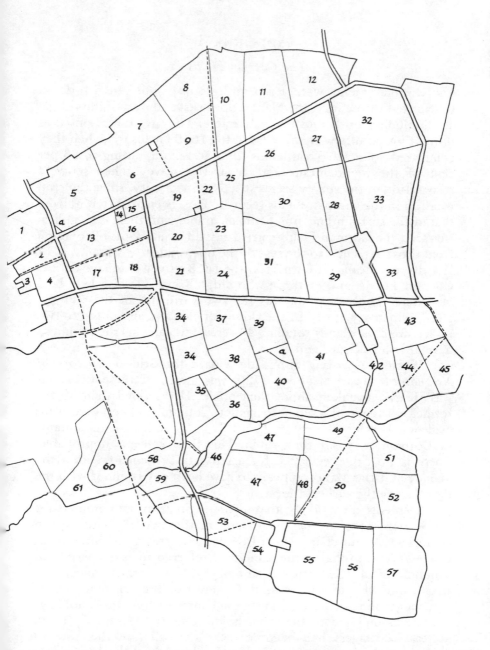

Appendix 8

The Cotman Fields

The Cotman Fields were a separate group of open-field furlongs distributed throughout the Manor, both east and west of the village, and including both meadow and arable. They were recognised as distinct in the survey that preceded the 1619 enclosure, when they comprised some 10½ yardlands, 292 acres, amounting to 23 per cent of the non-demesne acreage in the survey. Their separate recognition in the survey seems strictly unnecessary, since the crop rotation in the Cotman Fields seems to have been no different from that in the surrounding, non-Cotman, arable, and there is no indication that the Cotman Fields carried any different rights of common from those attached to the rest of the open fields.

By no means all farmers in the 1618 survey held lands in the Cotman Fields, and of those who did, all save one also held land elsewhere. The exception was the two yardlands of the rectorial glebe, which lay solely in the Cotman fields and amounted to two rather small yardlands totalling 46 acres, but carrying the commons normal to a full yardland.

Wasse, in writing about the village for Bridges' *History of Northamptonshire* in about 1720, was aware of these fields but was clearly mistaken about their origin. He ascribed them to the former existence of a separate hamlet, Cotnam (sic) and gave as his evidence a sixteenth century Court Order directing the inhabitants of Cotnam to scour their ditch. This theory seems improbable. There is no other evidence for a separate settlement within the Manor, and the Manor appears to have been coterminous with the Parish since the earliest times.

It seems most likely that their origin is in land granted for the settlement of *bordarii* and *servi* in the twelfth or thirteenth centuries. A quitclaim of 1314 relates to two half virgates *in Cotemanfeld*, probably the same land referred to as one virgate in a quitclaim of 1391 and a grant of 1478. It is thus conceivable that a half virgate represents the amount of the original grant, if this suggestion is correct, and that in course of time these holdings became assimilated to the other holdings of the Manor. By 1369, at least, cottagers had become tenants-at-will (see the note to Appendix 1) without substantial land holdings, yet the 1314 document seems to prove that the creation of the Cotman Fields was not, as otherwise it might have been, a response to the crisis of the late fourteenth century.

The occasion for the glebe lying solely in the Cotman Fields may, however, be some rearrangement of holdings after the Black Death. The 1369 Inquisition is evidence for the existence of vacant land that might make possible such redistribution, though it is not easy to suggest reasons why the glebe should have been consolidated in these particular furlongs.

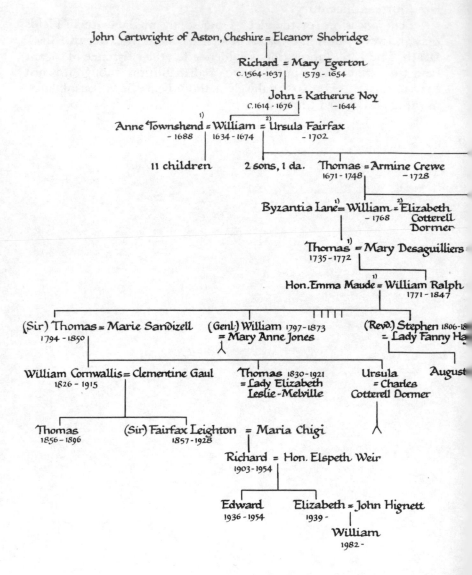

John Cartwright of Aston, Cheshire = Eleanor Shobridge

Richard = Mary Egerton
c.1564-1637   1579-1654

John = Katherine Noy
c.1614-1676   -1644

Anne Townshend =¹⁾ William =²⁾ Ursula Fairfax
-1688   1634-1674   -1702

11 children   2 sons, 1 da.   Thomas = Armine Crewe
1671-1748   -1728

Byzantia Lane =¹⁾ William =²⁾ Elizabeth
-1768   Cotterell
Dormer

Thomas ¹⁾ = Mary Desaguilliers
1735-1772

Hon. Emma Maude ¹⁾ = William Ralph
1771-1847

(Sir) Thomas = Marie Sandizell   (Genl.) William 1797-1873   (Revd.) Stephen 1806-18
1794-1850   = Mary Anne Jones   = Lady Fanny Ha

William Cornwallis = Clementine Gaul   Thomas 1830-1921   Ursula   August
1826-1915   = Lady Elizabeth   = Charles
Leslie-Melville   Cotterell Dormer

Thomas   (Sir) Fairfax Leighton = Maria Chigi
1856-1896   1857-1928

Richard = Hon. Elspeth Weir
1903-1954

Edward   Elizabeth = John Hignett
1936-1954   1939-

William
1982-

314

THE CARTWRIGHT FAMILY TREE

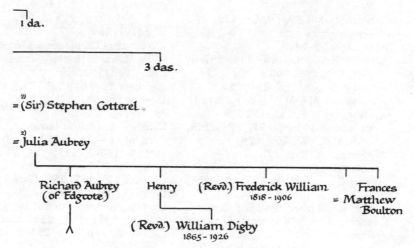

1 da.

3 das.

= 2) (Sir) Stephen Cotterel

= 2) Julia Aubrey

| Richard Aubrey (of Edgcote) | Henry | (Revd.) Frederick William 1818 - 1906 | Frances = Matthew Boulton |

(Revd.) William Digby 1865 - 1926

Index of Subjects

(including Places within Aynho)

Accidents 122, 152, 222
Canal and Railway 264
Advowson 26, 71–2
Agricultural Societies 214, 223, 239, 246
Aleshouses 36, 38, 54, 88, 168, 270
see also Inns
Ale tasters 53, 149
Alfred's Head inn 199, 204, 237–8, 261, 263, 266, 300
Allotments 205, 228, 284, 287
Almshouses 214–5, 241, 287, *Plate 24*
Apothecary 115, 133, 152
Apprentices 114–5, 121, 124, 149, 159, 166, 202, 206, 226
Apricots 254, *Plate 29*
Archery 25, 38
Aynho Grounds farm 217, 231, 251, 271
see also Lower (Aynho) Grounds farm, Upper (Aynho) Grounds farm
Aynho Park railway station 265, 267
Aynho railway station 265, *Plate 28*

Bakehouse (manorial) 23, 38
Bakers 22, 113, 116, 126, 128, 288
Balks 48, 51
Banbury Agricultural Society 239, 246
Bankruptcies 101, 116, 158
see also Mortgages
Barns 140, 144
Beer — see Almshouses; Brewing; Food and drink; Inns
Bell inn 43, 46, 111–3, 147–8, 258
Black Death 20–3, 27
Blacksmith 46, 110, 116–7, 152, 164
Books 28, 159
see also Education
Bordars 13, 22
Borton's Farm 300
Boundaries 1–2, 26, 47
Brackley Volunteers 197–201

Breeches maker 121
Brewing 56, 148–9, 222–3
Bricklayer 166–7
Brickyard 267
Building 1–2, 112, 144–5, 156, 164–8, 193, 214, 228–9, 233, 235–6, 241–2, 261
see also Carpenters; Church; Dilapidations; Houses; Masons
Bull — see Livestock
Butchers 22, 38, 104, 109, 117, 270
Butterman 158

Canal — see Oxford Canal
Carpenters 121, 133, 144–5, 153, 164, 166–7, 198, 214, 241, 269, 285
Carriers 117, 158, 258, *Plate 31*
Carts 111, 225, *Plates 31, 32*
Cartwright Arms inn 43, 46, 64, 214, 216, 238, 240, 256, 258, 265, 270–2, 276, 280, 285–6, 289–90, *Plate 29*
see also Red Lion
Charities 175–6, 213, 228, 240, 247, 287
see also Allotments; Friendly Societies; Hospital; Schools
Cherwell river and valley 1–2, 7–8, 23, 38, 82, 175, 259
Children 86, 128, 204–6, 256, 288
see also Apprentices; Household size; Orphans; Schools
Church (old) 26–9, 31, 50, 65, 70, 91, 132, 150, 162–4, 172, *Plate 4* (new) 107, 114, 153, 163–6, 168–9, 183, 208, 219–20, 283, *Plate 26*
Church Cottage 288
Churchwardens 70, 149, 164, 170–1
Cider 149
Clifton bridge and gate 260
Clothing 28, 34, 38, 117, 128, 156–7, 198, 227, 287, 289
Coachmaker 115

Coal — see Heating
College farm 29, 31, 33, 43, 47, 58, 60, 69, 110, 136, 179–80, 185, 189, 195, 214, 271, 280–1, 285, 293, 300
College mill 149
Commons 46, 49–50, 58–9, 65, 104, 108–9, 125, 168
  Cottagers' cows commons 59, 109, 190
Commutation 21, 23
  see also Services
Confectioner 272
Constable 53–4, 89, 129, 149, 172–3
Cooking — see Heating
Cooper 124
Copyhold — see Tenure
Cows — see Livestock
Cricket 197, 289
Crime 22–5, 30, 37, 53–4, 88–9, 172–3, 212–3
  see also Constable; Poaching
Crops 49–50, 52, 56, 103, 106, 108, 224–6, 235, 237, 239, 249
  see also Farming; Open fields
Crop rotation 8, 14, 16, 49, 60, 103, 106–7, 312
Crop yields 14–5, 20
Croughton gate 260
Customs 16, 21, 35, 52, 87
  see also Commutation; Services; Manor court
Cutler 199
Cuttle brook 1, 6, *Plate 1*

Danes 9, 13–4
Deer 227, 236, 270
Demesne 9, 13, 15, 20, 22, 39–40, 57, 107–8, 297
Dilapidations 52, 62–4, 228
Disease 85, 116, 151–2, 155, 161
  see also Accidents; Black Death; Smallpox
Dissenters 123, 151, 171–2, 273
  see also Quakers
Dog Kennel — see Pest house
Domesday 13–4, 20, 26
Dovecote 23, 140
Ducking stool 22, 88

Earth building 144
Education 158–9, 176
  see also Grammar school; Schools
Emigration 129, 209–10, 256
  see also Mobility
Enclosure (Walton) 39
  (1561) 39–40, 47, 57
  (1619) 57–60, 103, 178, 312
  (1792) 134, 177–92, 202
Engineer 134
Entertainments 196, 207–8, 214, 288, 290–1, *Plates 33, 34*
  see also Cricket; Fairs; Festivals; Flower Show; Friendly Societies; Harvest supper; Morris dancing; Mummers; Music; Pig Club; Rent dinner; Volunteers
Excise officer 110

Fairs 15–6, 22, 24, 30, 56, 206
Fairslade House 154–5
  see also Pest house
Farmers 33–4, 41–8, 101–4, 121, 133–4, 189–92, 216, 222, 229–32
Farming 8–9, 14–5, 21, 23, 37, 39, 45–7, 49–51, 58–9, 103–6, 109–11, 158, 184, 193, 216–7
  see also Crops; Grazier; Livestock
Farms 31, 33–4, 41, 43, 47, 101, 103–4, 134, 185–90
  see also individual farms: Aynho Grounds; College; Home; Lower Grounds; Nell Bridge; Upper Grounds; Walton Grounds; Warren
Fertiliser 222–3, 225–6
  see also Manure
Festivals 15, 76, 149–50
Fields and other land names 303–11
  Arslong 48
  Buglow (field) 48, 106
  Conigree field 106
  Cotman fields 22, 312–3
  Crabtree 48
  Croughton meadow 30
  Deadlands 23, 48
  Elderbush 48
  Flaggy Doles 50
  Glebe 178
  Lower fields 49
  Middle field 106

Fields, etc., *continued*
Middle Sands 48
Mill mead 37
Nomans Hill 23
Norcott Hill 48
Old Down 158, 184, 194, 224, 251, *Plate 1*
Padbury Bottom 224
Pill Doles 50
Potato Ground 228
Radford Hook 50
Raynebury Furlong 48
Ripham Smatts 50
Six Acres 48
South field 106
Sparrow Hill 48
Spetchill Leys 48
Spichwell 36
Stanford 37
Truckingham mead 50
Turner's Plank mead 145
Upper fields 49
Wainmore Hook 36
Warren, the 47, 57-8, 154, 175, 184, 187; see also Warren farm
Wensden 48
see also Commons; Open fields
Fieldsmen 48, 51, 62, 109-11, 114, 149, 158
Fines 15, 24, 50
Fire brigade 286, 290
Fishing 23, 30, 38, 175, 226, 287
Flower Show 289, *Plate 34*
Food and drink 46, 112, 116-7, 149, 155-7, 194-5, 200, 202, 205, 208, 257, 278, 284, 286, 288
see also Alehouses; Brewing; Cider; Heating; Inns; Malnutrition; Metheglyn; Water supply
Foot-and-mouth disease 231
Freehold — see Tenures
Friendly Societies 207-8, 214, 235
Fuel — see Heating
Fuller 157
Furlongs — see Open fields
Furniture 33-4, 43-6, 145-6, 160, 195-6, 283-5
see also Houses

Game 268, 285
see also Poaching

Gardener 128, 285
Gift cart 107, 165, 291
Glazier 141, 214
Glebe 66, 170, 178, 312-3
Glove maker 272
Grammar school 115, 136, 140, 145-6, 159-63, 275-7, 283, 288, *Plate 5*
see also Education; Schools
Grazier 112
Great House 82, 84, 193-4, *Plates 1, 2, 3, 10, 21*
Great Western Arms inn 208, 237-8, 246-7, 266
Guns 38, 114

Harvest supper 196
Hayward 51-2
Headsilver 50
Hearth Tax 136
Heating 107, 148, 283
Hemp dresser 170
Heriots 15-6, 60-1
Hill Trees 283, *Plate 32*
Hiring fair 206
Ho brook 1, 60
Hogherd 51
Home farm 43, 136, 196, 217, 221-54, 270-1
Horses — see Livestock
Hospital 17, 21, 24-5, 29-32, 48
Household size and composition 104, 121-6, 142, 256
Houses 1, 15, 22, 34-5, 43, 52, 88, 102, 114, 132-48, 228, 255-6
by number, individual houses
10: 128   74: 123, 127
13: 115, 123   79: 114
17: 128   86: 134, 136-7, 146-8, *Plates 6, 18*
20-24: 187
25: 269   87-91: 140
64-71: 187   92: 123
62-75: 256
Burberow's (house north of Post Office): 113-4
Drope's: 136
Hanslope's: 135-6
Jarvis's — see No. 86
Houses with less than four acres of land attached 88
Occupants in 1790 301-2

Houses, *continued*
see also Building; Dilapidations; Furniture; Heating; Lodgers
Hue and cry 175
Hundred and Hundred court (King's Sutton) 9, 14, 174
Hunting 107, 175-6, 289, *Plates 1, 10*

Inheritance 16, 99, 101, 113-5
see also Heriots
Inmates — see Subletting
Innkeepers 112-3, 270
see also Index to Personal Names: Bell, Bennett, Bygrave, Collins, Herbert, Holloway, Homan, Hunt, Norris, Pruce, Rutter
Inns 36, 43, 54-5, 110, 112, 121, 149, 172, 198, 204, 258, 265
see also under names of individual inns: Alfred's Head, Bell, Cartwright Arms, Great Western Arms, Red Lion, White Hart
see also Alehouses; Entertainments; Food and drink
Inquests 68-9, 149

Joiner 202
Jury 52, 109

King's Sutton hundred 9, 14, 174

Labourers 46, 108, 120-1, 169-70, 188, 190, 203-6, 263, 271
see also Poor; Wages
Lace making 272, *Plate 19*
Land Tax 105
Lanford bridge 109
Laundress 272
see also Servants (Great House)
Livestock 2, 14-6, 34, 39, 47, 49-51, 57-8, 106-8, 111, 177, 224-6, 235, 249, 283-4
see also Farming; Manure; Tithes
Lodgers 125, 256, 272
see also Subletting
Lower (Aynho) Grounds farm 187, 190, 300

Magdalen College, Oxford (as landowner) 31, 47-8, 59, 65, 178-9, 181

Malnutrition 21, 257
Malthouse 137
Maltster 113, 129
Manor 9, 12, 15-8, 20-2, 31-3
Manor court 9, 37-9, 50, 52, 61, 67-8, 84, 87-8, 109, 150, 153, 172, 191-2, 259, 280
Manor house (medieval) 31
Mantua maker 272
Manure 14, 21, 106, 108, 112, 225, 262, 269
see also Fertiliser
Market and market house 15, 22, 56, 159
Cattle market 267
Marriage 53, 124
Masons 34, 110, 114-5, 124, 133, 137, 144-6, 152, 165, 202, 214, 236, 285
May queen 288
Meadow 14, 23, 30, 36, 49, 108, 312
see also Field names; Pasture
Medicine 110, 115, 152
see also Disease
Mercer 114, 123
Metheglyn 270
Militia 57, 121, 128, 152, 169, 201
see also Soldiers; Volunteers
Mills, millers 13, 21-2, 30, 38, 110, 117, 149, 154
Mobility 122-4, 129, 206-7
see also Emigration
Mole catcher 51, 110
Morris dancing 150
Mortality 151-2
see also Disease; Smallpox
Mortgages 115, 120, 142, 144, 156
Mummers 290
Music 95, 150

National School 272-5, 287
Nell Bridge 82, 248, 260, 264, *Plate 27*
Nell Bridge farm 187, 230-3, 236, 271, 300, *Plate 27*
Normans 12
Northamptonshire Agricultural Society 214

Open fields 8, 16, 39, 46–9, 103, 177, 184, *Plates 1, 2*
see also Enclosure; Farming; Field names
Orphans 155–6
Overcrowding — see Household size
Overseers of the Poor 115, 120, 125, 149, 154–7, 202–6, 211, 269, 280
Oxen — see Livestock
Oxford Canal 204, 224, 261–2, 264, *Plate 27*

Paradise Row 256–7, *Plate 23*
Parish 26
Parish clerk 168
Parish Council 280
Parish Room 286
Park 24, 57, 136, 185, 227, 233, 300, *Plates 2, 3, 10*
Parliament 175, 179, 181–2, 253
Pasture 14, 21, 23, 47, 49, 51, 57, 66, 108
see also Meadow
Pest house (Dog Kennel or Fairslade House) 154–5, 224, 250
Pigs — see livestock
Pig Club 290
Pillory 22
Plane maker 202
Plasterers 116, 133, 145–6, 214
Ploughs 13–4, 21, 61
Plumber 214
Poaching 38, 175, 227, 234, 247–51
Poor 119–21, 125, 136–7, 140, 157, 202–6, 211, 277–9
see also Labourers; Poor relief; Unemployment; Wages
Poor relief — see Overseers; Removals; Roundsmen; Settlement; Workhouse
Population 3–4, 13, 20, 33, 104, 119, 125, 134, 140, 158, 190–1, 201, 209, 256
Postman 267–8
Post Office 269, 288, *Plate 30*
Pound 52, 69–70
Prehistoric remains 2–4
Prices 20–3, 104, 110–1, 120, 193, 202, 204
Prospect Terrace 256, *Plate 31*
Puritanism 77, 93–4

Quakers 114, 123, 129, 169–71, 270
Quarter Sessions 174

Rabbits 38, 57, 59
see also Field names: Warren; and Poaching
Railways 227, 230, 234, 237–8, 262–7, *Plate 28*
Railwaymen 267, *Plate 28*
Rainsborough Camp 2–4, 48, 97, 223
Rates (fieldsmen) 106
(poor) 106, 155, 157–8, 204–5
Rectors 24, 27, 90–8
see also Advowson; individual rectors (in Index to Personal Names): Robert Bright (1532), Reginald Burdyn (1635–43), Frederick William Cartwright (1862–1906), Stephen Ralph Cartwright (1830–62), William Digby Cartwright (1906–26) Ralph de Diceto (d. 1210), Thomas Drope (1588–1633), Matthew Hutton (1677–1711), William Lambton (C15), James Longman (1643–46, 1662–77), Francis Mabletoft (1770–1807), Richard Pearson (1508–32), Joseph Wasse (1711–38), Robert Wilde (1646–62)
Rectory 136, *Plate 22*
Red Lion inn 36, 43, 63–4, 112–3, 119, 121, 133, 149, 155, 157–8, 181, 183–4, 195–6, 203–4, 207–8, 214, 256, 258, 300
see also Cartwright Arms
Reformation 28–9
Removals 155–7
Rents 22, 33–6, 40–1, 46, 60–1, 120, 122, 191, 230, 232, 234, 257, 284, 293–7, 300
Rent dinner 240, 289
Retirement 268, 287
Roads 1–2, 37, 43, 47, 132, 177, 258–60, 269
Banbury road 163, 270–1, 281
Bicester road 47, 185, 260, 285, *Plate 1*
Blacksmith's Hill 43, 47, 117, 132–3, 256, 283, *Plates 14, 16, 18*
Buckingham road 225, 260
Butts, the 25

Roads, *continued*
Causeway, the 150, 187, 256, 259
Charlton road 47, 127, 132, 147, 256, 279, *Plate 23*
Cross, the 52
Croughton crossroads 228
Deddington road 47, 132, 174, 187, 260
Hart Lane 256
Hollow Way 281, 283, *Plate 13*
Little Lane 137, 286
Lower Green *Plates 15, 17*
Mansion Street 187
Oxford road 47
Paradise Row 256-7, *Plate 23*
Port Way 2, 6, 39, 47, 185
Prospect Terrace 256, *Plate 31*
Skittle Alley 117, 133
Spring Gardens 256
Square, the 43, 137, 256, 288, *Plates 12, 25*
Wapping 256
Watson's yard *Plate 19*
Romans 4-7
Roundsmen 202
Royal Agricultural Society 223
Royal Society 96-7, 152

Sawyer 46
Schools 27, 56, 163, 222, 272-5
see also Grammar school; National School; Sunday school
Schoolmasters 115, 152, 159, 163
see also Schools
Schoolmistress 273
Serfs 13, 22
Servants 34, 120-1, 206
(in the Great House) 117-9, 133, 152, 220, 222-3, 225, 285
Services 9, 20, 22-4, 30, 35, 37, 61, 107
Settlement 155, 173, 203
Sheep — see Livestock
Shepherds 44, 121, 126, 166, 170, 271
Ship Money 68, 73, 76
Shoemakers 152, 157, 163, 276
Shops, Shopkeepers 114, 116, 155-6, 204, 270-1, *Plate 12*

Slaters 116, 133, 214
Smallpox 123, 152-4, 168, 207-8
Soldiers 25, 79-82, 97, 128, 173, 201
see also Militia; Volunteers
Speculative building 137-8
Springs — see Water supply
Stocks 88, 174, *Plate 32*
Street lighting 280-1
Street names 256
Subdivision of properties 101-2, 104, 109, 128, 133, 136-7
Subletting 35, 53, 88-9, 125, 140
see also Household size; Lodgers
Sunday school 288
Surgeon 152

Tailors 117, 124, 137
Taxation 9, 22, 33, 125, 269, 281, 293-4
see also Hearth Tax; Land Tax; Rates; Ship Money
Telegraph 268
Tenures 9, 17, 35-6, 41, 47, 58, 60-1, 99, 102-4, 293-4, 296-7, 299
Thatchers 285
Threshing machines 268
Timber building 140
Tithes 60, 66-7, 90, 106-8, 110, 112, 169, 171, 178, 180, 183
Tokens 112
Tollgates 110
Tombstones 145
Tournaments 18, 25
Town elm 283
Tradesmen 133, 158, 207, 266
see also under individual trades
Transport — see Oxford Canal; Railways; Roads; Travellers; Turnpikes
Travellers 16, 24, 29-30, 53, 68, 129, 172, 258, 266
Turkeys 65
Turnpikes 180, 204, 260-1, 265

Unemployment 104, 140, 158, 191, 201-5, 209, 211, 255
see also Poor relief; Population
Upper (Aynho) Grounds farm 187, 300, *Plate 1*

Vagrants 53, 173–4
Victualler 113
   see also Innkeepers
View of Frankpledge 50, 123
Village Hall 155
Villeins 13–4
Volunteers 197–201

Wages 23, 117, 120–1, 163, 202,
   204–5, 236, 263, 269
Walton Grounds farm 39
Wardship 18
Warren farm 187, 190, 223, 226,
   228–54, 271–2, 300
   see also Field names, etc.: the
   Warren

Water supply, wells 1, 134, 150–1
Wharf, the 156, 214, 261
Wheelwrights 117, 128
White Hart inn 113, 133, 197, 204,
   208, 258, 265, 270, *Plate 12*.
Wills 28–9, 33–4, 114, 119, 126, 128,
   140
Windmill (Old Down) 117, *Plate 1*
   see also Mills
Woods 47
Workhouse 157, 277–9, 287

Yeomen — see Farmers

Index of Places

For places in Aynho, see the Index of Subjects

Places near Aynho

Adderbury, Oxon 24, 35, 84, 96, 146, 197, 214, *Plate 1*
see also Twyford
Alauna or Alchester, Oxon 4
Aston, North, Oxon 4
Astrop (King's Sutton), N'hants 81, 85, 167, 200, 213

Banbury, Oxon 2, 54, 77, 79–80, 82, 84–5, 89, 97, 110, 146, 158, 202, 227, 258, 260–2, 264, 267, 272, 275, 283, 286–7
Castle 81, 83–5, 89–90
Baynard's Green, Oxon 82
Begbroke, Oxon 24
Bicester, Oxon 2, 4, 24, 152, 180, 258, 260
Bladon, Oxon 24, 156
Bloxham, Oxon 78, 96, 168
School 276
Bodicote, Oxon 257
Brackley, N'hants 25, 34, 55–6, 79, 83, 110, 150, 153, 164, 166, 179, 198–9, 213, 250, 167–8, 276, 291
Union and Workhouse 211, 278, 287
Broughton, Oxon 78
Buckingham 2, 43, 124, 206, 258, 260
Burford, Oxon 146, 160–1
Byfield, N'hants 199

Charlton, N'hants 13, 23, 212–3, 261, 288
Chipping Norton, Oxon 2, 226, 258
Clifton (Deddington) 85, 230, 233, 241, 248, 259, 267
Mill 259
Compton Winyates, Warw 78–9
Cropredy Bridge (battle), Oxon 82
Crouch Hill, nr. Banbury, Oxon 79
Croughton, N'hants 4, 8, 13, 24, 28, 80, 101, 124, 175, 212–3, 260–1, 285

Daventry, N'hants 79, 201, 227
Deddington, Oxon 2–4, 25, 43, 56, 82, 202, 207, 217, 227, 229–54, 259, 261–2, 265, 267
see also Clifton, Hempton, Idbury

Easton Neston, N'hants 39
Edgecote, N'hants 25, 220–1
Edgehill (battle), Warw 80
Eydon, N'hants 206
Eynsham, Oxon 24

Farthinghoe, N'hants 82, 211
Fenny Stratford, Bucks 167
Floore, nr. Daventry, N'hants 227
Fritwell, Oxon 107

Galley Hill (King's Sutton, N'hants ?) 213

Hanwell, Oxon 77–8, 260
Hempton (Deddington), Oxon 260–1
Heyford, Oxon 265
Hinton-in-the-Hedges, N'hants 178, 213
Hook Norton, Oxon 82
Hornton quarries, Oxon 146

Idbury (nr. Deddington, Oxon) 3

King's Sutton, N'hants 4, 7, 9, 23, 39, 47, 73, 82, 116, 124, 145–6, 156, 175, 199, 207, 212–3, 287, 289, 291, *Plate 1*
Hundred 9, 14, 174
see also Astrop, Walton

Kirtlington, Oxon 265

Middleton Cheney, N'hants 82
Middleton Stoney, Oxon 194
'Middleton' (?county) 27
Milton (nr. Adderbury), Oxon 146

Newbottle, N'hants 167, 249, 253, 287
Newington, South, Oxon 157
Northampton 56-7, 68, 70, 74-5, 77, 82, 89, 183, 197, 202, 223, 234
  gaol 169-70, 212
  infirmary 279

Oxford 80, 90-2, 95-6, 124, 153, 168, 181, 183, 214, 227, 253, 259-62, 264, 267
  Balliol College 20
  Bodleian Library 96
  Magdalen College 31, 47-8, 59, 65, 178-9, 181
  Merton College 247

Rollright, Oxon 2
Rousham, Oxon 80

Shipton (which ?) 152
Somerton, Oxon 24

Souldern, Oxon 4, 7-8, 13, 24, 82, 128, 137, 182, 217, 237, 248-50
  Mill 285
Steeple Aston, Oxon 115
Stoke Lyne, Oxon 7
Stowe, Bucks 194
Studley, Oxon 24
Stukely or Stewkley, Bucks 207
Syresham, N'hants 35, 150

Tackley, Oxon 24
Tadmarton, Oxon 3
Tew and Tew Park, Oxon 239, 248
Thame, Oxon 45
Towcester, N'hants 4, 168, 202
Twyford (Adderbury), Oxon 82

Walton (King's Sutton), N'hants 7, 39, 47, 73, 133
Whittlebury, N'hants 223
Woodstock, Oxon 25, 34, 128

Other Places

Abergavenny, Wales 275
America 209-10
  New Jersey 129
Amsterdam, Holland 96
Ardington, Berks 145
Ashendon, Bucks 155, 157

Bath, Som 180
Birmingham (Warw), King's Arms, Snow Hill 224
Brill, Bucks 157
Burton-on-Trent, Staffs 179-80

Cambridge 92, 96
  Catherine Hall 152-3
Canada 209-11
Chilton, Bucks 221
Christiana, Sweden 236
Coventry, Warw 261

Deene Park, N'hants 22
Deneshanger, N'hants 30
Dunwich, Suffolk 20

East Indies 129
Eton, Bucks 176

Germany (Homburg) 243-4
Gloucester 82

'Hamstead' 151
Hanslope, Bucks 201
Holkham, Norfolk 230
Hull, Yorks 244

Langley Abbey, Norfolk 20
Leamington, Warw 264
Lewknor, Oxon 24
Liverpool, Lancs 210
London (general references not indexed)
  Barn Elms 77, 81, 86
  Smithfield, The Ram 258
Long Compton, Warw 17

Mercia, Kingdom of 9

Newport Pagnall, Bucks 83-4

Oundle, N'hants 94

Paris, France 27
Pennant (Wales ?) 225

Reading, Berks 114
Roade, N'hants 202
Rome, Italy 253

St. Ives, Hunts 92
Sandwich, Kent 25
Sawbridgeworth, Herts 24
Scotland 96

Southwark, Surrey 115
Stamford, Lincs 25
Stratford, Warw 168, 202
Stockholm, Sweden 217-44.
Swansea, Wales 267

Tamworth, Warw 179, 181

Walden Priory, Essex 26-7, 29, 71
Wales 25
Warwick 25, 107, 153, 165, 201, 258
  Castle 79
Wellingborough, N'hants 55
Woburn, Beds 25

Index of Personal Names

Acome, Mrs (1790) 301
Adderbury, John (?C14) 24
Addington, Robert (1740) 299
William (1723) 153, 305
Adkins, -, lodge-keeper (1853) 248–50
Aegon 7–8
Alcock, William (1790) 301
Alexander, warrener (?C13) 24
Allen, Captain, of the 'Sykes' (Stockholm-Hull) (1850) 244
Allowe, Thomas (1544) 294
Amner, Lord (1618) 68–9
Anstee — see Anstey
Anstell, - (emig. 1842) 210–1
Anstey, Ansty, Anstee, James, 'architect' (1701) 110, 159
Richard (1790) 302
Archer, Thomas, architect (C17/18) 166, 193, *Plate 10*
Aries, Thomas (d. 1722) and family 154, 157–8
Aris, John, farmer from Weedon Lois (1793) 190, 300
Widow (1740) 299
see also Ayris, Harris
Arrowsmith, Mrs (1753) 155
de Arundel family, Lords of Aynho (C14–16) 20, 30–2, 35, 37
Asgar the Staller (C11) 12–3
Asplin, William, Vicar of Banbury (d. 1758) 97
Aubrey, John (C17) 77
Julia (C19) — see Cartwright
Austin, Valentine (1790) 301
William, farmer (1871) 271
Ayris, Joseph (1790) 301
William (1790) 302
Widow (1790) 301
see also Aries, Aris, Harris

Baber, Sir John (C17) 94

Baker, Christiana (1544) 293
John, snr. (C18) 155, 158, 214, 299–300, 302
John, jnr. (d. 1816), glazier of Oxford, endowed almshouses 181, 185, 214, 300, 302, *Plate 24*
Thomas and son Thomas (C16) 36, 293
Goody (1670) 144–5
Baldwin, Betty (1790) 301
Samuel (?C18) 128
Sarah (early C18) 151
Thomas, shoemaker (C18) 157, 302
Walter (1740) 121
William (mid-C17) 88, 123
William, shoemaker (C18) 176, 301
Ball, Thomas (C16) 34
Banastre, Sir Robert, Sheriff of Northants (1635) 73–6, 101
Banbury, Erasmus, mercer (mid-C18) 114, 116, 155(?), 270
Mary (wife of Erasmus), formerly of Reading (later C18) 114, 300, 302
William, shopkeeper (C17/18) 114, 155–6
William (C18) 113, 155(?)
Barding, Samuel (C17/18) 304
Barrett, -, Banbury to London carrier (early C18) 258
Bartford, Thomas (1544) — see Baker
Barton, William (1618) 296
Barwell, Mr, Parliamentary draughtsman (1792) 182
Baudwen, William (C16) 37
Baughan family, wheelwrights (C19–20) 117, 285
Edwin, wheelwright, carpenter and farmer (1894) 280
Baxter, Richard (C17) 92

Bayley, Corporal (C17) 83
Baylis(s) family (C16-18) 121
    John (1723) 165
    Walter (1633) 62, 296
Beasley, Mr (1849) 230
Bele, Thomas (d. 1554) 29, 121, 293
Bell, Bridget, innkeeper (1616) 47,
    53, 63-4, 296
Bennet(t), William, carpenter (1723)
    165
    Mr, farmer (1870) 251, 280-2
    Mr, butler to Cartwrights, later
    innkeeper (C19/20) 285
Bentley, Dr Richard, Master of
    Trinity College Cambridge (C18)
    96
Berdnell — see Brudnell
Bett(s), James (1790) 301
    John and Elizabeth (1671) 44
    Richard (1618) 296
    Thomas (1755) 155
Bewdley, Bewley, James (1544) 293
    Richard (C16) 34-5, 68
    Richard (1616) 68, 296
Billing, -, farmer, and nephew (1849)
    230-1, 233-4
Billington, James, of Charlton (1815)
    213
Bird, Mrs (1790) 302
Birds, Elizabeth, maidservant (1679)
    118
Blencowe, Francis, mason (1723)
    165-8
    Major (late C18) 200
Boarton — see Borton
Bolt, Henry (1794) 300
    Richard (1790) 302
Bolton, John (1790) 301
Bond, - poacher, of Souldern (1853)
    248-50
Borton/Burton family (C16-18) 121,
    189
    Henry (d. 1683) 111, 128
    Henry, shepherd (early C18) 152
    John, Quaker (emig. 1674) 129,
    169-70
    John, shepherd (1740) 126, 299
    John, carpenter (C18) 133, 165,
    (C19) 212, 214

Borton/Burton continued
    Matthew (1670) 144
    Matthew, farmer (1792) 189-90,
    300-2
    William (1633) 62
    William, carpenter (1663) 160
    William (C17/18) 304-5
    William (1740) 299
    William, shopkeeper (C18) 116,
    155, 302
    William, carpenter (C18) 156, 174,
    302
    see also Boughton, Burton
Botcher, John, of Brackley (C16) 34
Boughton, Henry (d. 1538) and Joan
    33-5, 293-4
    see also Borton, Burton
Bower(s), George (1723) 165
    John, butcher (C18) 117, 302
    Thomas, butcher (1740) 104, 299
    William (1618) 296
    - (late C17) 141
Boxall/Boxold, George, plane-maker
    (1790) 202
    John (1790) 301
    Mr, exciseman (C18) 110; and
    widow Susannah (1841) 268
Bozes, Mr, farmer (1849) 239
Brackley, Henry (1618) 296
Bratford, Thomas (C16) 37
Brett, John, Quaker (1659) 169-70
Brickmore, Thomas (1544) 294
Bricknell, Brignell, Agnes (1544) 293
    Jane (1618) 296
    John (1544) 35, 293(2)
    John and family (mid-C17) 74,134
    John (C17/18) 304
    John, infant (early C18) 151
    John (mid-C18) 104, 127, 129,
    299
    Richard (1544) 294
    Thomas (d. 1614) 126
    Thomas (1740) 299
    William (1544) 293
Bridge, John (1790) 301
Bridges, John, historian (C18) 97,
    258, 312
Bright, Robert, Rector of Aynho
    (1532) 28

Brignell — see Bricknell
Brooke, Lord (C17) 79
Brown, Mr, head gardener (C19/20) 285
Browning, Robert, poet (C19) 253
Brudnell, Berdnell, Brudenell, Richard (C14) 22
    William (C15) 31
Brunel, Isambard Kingdom, engineer (1806-59) 264
Buckingham family (C19) 268-9, 285
    John, of Croughton (1732) 175
    John (C18/19) 214, 302
    Thomas, schoolmaster (C18/19) 269, 272
    William, farmer and tax collector (C19/20) 268-9, 281, *Plate 30*
    2nd Marquess and 1st Duke (C18/19) 194
Buckler, William (1790) 301
Bulckley, Henry (1618) 296
Bull, William, maltster (1790) 302
    William, butcher (1790s) 300, 302
Burberow, Burbery, Burborough, family (C16-18) 113-4, 170, 189
    John (1740) 299
    Richard (C16) 36, 113, 293
    Timothy (d. 1729), Quaker, baker, and family 113-4, 137, 147, 170-1, 189, 304
    Timothy (1790) 300, 302, 304
    'Old' (1642) 80, 113
Burbidge family (C18-19) 115-6, 123
    Edward, apothecary (later C18) 115, 133, 152, 155, 199, 302
    John, Master of the Grammar School (C18) 115-6, 124
Burborough — see Burberow
Burdyn, Revd. Reginald (d. 1643), Rector of Aynho 1634-43 72, 85, 90, 164
Burnell, Robert, bishop (C13/14) 19
Burton, Francis, Cartwright agent (mid-C18) 115, 120, 155, 177-8
    John (C16) 34, 293
    Sarah (1794) 300
    Thomas (1544) 293
    William (1618) 296
    William, timber-yard (C18) 117, 301
    see also Borton, Boughton

Butler, Richard (C16) 37
    William, farmer (C18) 110
Bygrave family (C18-19) 112, 189, 270
    Edward (son of Thomas), maltster and innkeeper (C18) 113, 300
    John, innkeeper (1849) 229-30, 270
    Mary, innkeeper (1794) 300
    Thomas (son of Thomas), butcher, (C18) 113, 117-8, 155, 301
    Thomas (son of Thomas, butcher, farmer, victualler, and innkeeper, (C18/19) 113, 189, 270, 276, 301
    William, innkeeper and farmer (1871) 271, 280
    Mrs, innkeeper (1813) 204
Byles, William (1815) 213
Byron, Sir John (1642) 79-80
Byng, John, Viscount Torrington (d. 1813) 266

de Camera, Geoffrey (C14) 22
Canch, William (1544) 293
Carter family, of Chilton, Bucks (C19) 221
    Mr, policeman (C20) 285
    Miss (1847) 220
Cartwright family, 42 -315 — *passim*; pedigree 314-5
    Aubrey — see Richard Aubrey
    Augusta Emma (b. 1853), dau. of Stephen and Lady Fanny 253
    Digby — see William Digby
    Edward Fairfax (1936-54), son of Richard 291-2
    Mrs Elizabeth (née Cotterell-Dormer), 2nd wife of William (d. 1768) 181-2, 218
    Lady Elizabeth (d. 1892; dau. of Earl of Leven and Melville), mar. Thomas 253, 287
    Lady Fanny (d. 1853; née Hay, dau. of Earl of Errol), mar. Revd. Stephen 246, 251, 253
    Revd. Frederick William (1818-1906), Rector of Aynho 1862-1906 253, 276, 286-7
    John (c1614-1676), son of Richard 60, 74-7, 80-1, 85-6, 88-91, 99, 103, 145, 159-60, 162, 228, *Plate 8*

Cartwright, *continued*
Mrs Julia Frances (d. 1856)(née Aubrey), 2nd wife of William Ralph 217–8, 220–1, 245
Mrs Katherine (d. 1644; dau. of Sir William Noy), mar. John 76–7, 80–1
Lady Marie ('Lili') (d. 1902; née Sandizell), mar. Sir Thomas 217–9, 221, 226, 242–5, *Plate 22*
Mrs Mary (née Egerton), mar. Richard (d. 1637) 61, 66–7, 71, 76, 81, 86, 91, 159, 272
Mrs Mary Catherine (née Desaguilliers), mar. 1765, Thomas; mother of William Ralph; mar. 2ndly, Stephen Cotterel (later Sir) 179–80, 206
Richard (d. 1637) 42–4, 46–7, 52, 54–73, 99, 101–3, 106–8, 121, 125, 129, 177, 180, 190, 213, 258–9, 287, 296–7, *Plate 7*
Richard Aubrey (1811–91) of Edgcote, eldest son of William Ralph and his second wife Julia Frances Aubrey 220–1
Richard Fairfax William (1903–54) 291–2
Revd. Stephen Ralph (1806–62), Rector of Aynho 1830–62 217, 222–4, 233, 235, 241, 244–6, *Plate 22*
Thomas (c1671–1748), son of William 97, 99, 101–3, 107, 113, 117–8, 150, 168, 175–6, 258, *Plates 9, 10*
Thomas (1735–72), son of William 176, 178
Sir Thomas (1794–1850), eldest son of William Ralph, Minister Plenipotentiary to the Diet of Frankfort, and Ambassador at Stockholm 217–42, 245–8, 253–4, 261, 263–5, 268, 270, 272, *Plate 20*
Thomas Robert Brook (adopted additional surnames of Leslie-Melville) (1830–1921) 2nd son of Sir Thomas 243, 245–51, 253, 276, 280

Cartwright, *continued*
Thomas (1856–96), son of William Cornwallis 277, 280
Mrs Ursula (née Fairfax), wife of William (d. 1674) 94–5, 99, 112, 118, 120
William (1634–74), son of John 86, 89, 99
William (d. 1768), son of Thomas 176, 178, 218
William (b. 1797), of Flore House; colonel, later lieut.-general 201, 217–28, 244–5, 249, *Plate 20*
William Cornwallis (1826–1915) 217–8, 242–53, 276–7, 284, 289, *Plate 20*
Revd. William Digby (1865–1926), Curate of Aynho 1893; Rector, 1906–26 290–1
William Ralph (1771–1847) 176–8, 180, 185, 193–8, 200, 203–6, 213, 216–8, 220–1, 253–6, 260–1, 272–3, 277, 286, 300, 302, *Plates 11, 13, 20, 23, 31*
Carvell, Simper, butler to Cartwrights (1740) 117
Castle family (1723) 154
John, tailor, mercer and cooper in Oxford and Buckingham 124
Cauldrey, John, plumber and glazier (1821) 214
Chilton, Mary, widow of shoemaker (1850s) 278
Churchill, John (C17) 76
William, Deddington solicitor (1870) 246
Clavering family, Lords of Aynho (C12–14) 17–20, 22, 29–31, 36
Clarke, Archdeacon, nephew of William Ralph Cartwright (1847) 219
Clemens, Benjamin (1790) 301
Clerk(e), John (1544) 294
Mr (1815) 213
–, auctioneer (1867) 267
Coates, Benjamin, Quaker, baker (C18) 114–6, 299
Timothy, Quaker, baker (C18) 113, 155
Widow (1790) 302

Collins, Colyns, Francis (1790) 301
  George (1618) 296
  John, hayward (C17) 51
  John (1790) 301-2
  Jo. (1680s) 118
  Moses (1790) 301
  Richard, innkeeper (1616) 47, 53,
    61, 296
  Thomas, innkeeper (d. 1607) 46
  Thomas (1790) 302
  William, of Croughton (1544) 24
Collyer, Widow (1618) 296
de Columbariis, Matthew (C14) 19
Colyns — see Collins
Compton, Spencer, 2nd Earl of
    Northampton (1601-42) and
    family 78-9, 83
  Sir Charles (d. 1661) 83
  Sir William (d. 1663) 80, 83, 91
  Major (1664) 82
Cooke, J.T., headmaster of Grammar
    School (later C19) 275
Cope, Sir John, of Deneshanger
    (1390) 30
Cosby, - (C17) 86
Cotterel, Sir Stephen, step-father of
    William Ralph Cartwright (C18)
    178, 185, 194, 259-60; see also
    Cartwright, Mary Catherine
Councer, Mrs, housekeeper to Cart-
    wrights (1740) 117
Cowley, Margaret (d. 1558) 29
  Richard (1544) 34-5, 293
  William (1544) 293
Cox, Edmund, farmer (1851) 247-51
  Stephen, Woodstock baker (1778)
    128
Crackley, Crackloe, John (1650) 88
  Richard (C17) 55
  Robert (C16/17) 37, 296
Cross, Widow (1790) 301

Danvers, Sir John (C17) 57
Dark, Hannah (early C19) 212
Davies, Bridget — see Bell
  Charles, last headmaster of Gram-
    mar School (d. 1888) 275-6
Davis, Thomas (1636) 75
Davy, Thomas, of Souldern (1544) 24
Deferill — see Deverill

Derby, Earls of (C16) 17
Deverill, Deferill, Thomas (early C17)
    62, 296
de Diceto, Ralph, Rector of Aynho
    (d. 1210) 27
Dimock, Richard (1790) 302
Doigue, - (1847) 226-7
Dolton, Ezekiel (1790) 302
Dormer, John (C17) 80-1
Drope family (C18) 178
  Thomas (d. 1633), Rector of
    Aynho 1588-1633 47-8, 58-
    60, 64-7, 69-73, 90, 136, 163,
    180-1, 214, 296-7
  Thomas (son of Rector Drope) 54,
    78, 85, 136
  William (d. 1693) 101, 114
  Mrs (wife of Rector Drope) 70,
    304
Dry, William (1790) 302
Dryden, John, poet (C17) 93
Dunn, Edward, farmer (1792) 189-
    90, 300
  Frederick, parish councillor
    (1890s) 281

East, Philip (C17/18) 174
Eastmont, Daniel, bricklayer at Fenny
    Stratford (C18) 167
Edis, Mr, representative of Depart-
    ment of Education (C19) 276-7,
    280
Edmonds, Thomas, and wife, of
    Ashendon, Bucks (1720s) 155-7
Edward, Prince (later King Edward I)
    25
Eely, Jethro, cutler (1794) 199, *Plate
    18*
Ekins, Catherine, schoolmistress
    (1849) 273
Ely, Mrs (1790) 301
Elly, Henry, and family, emig, to
    Canada (1830s) 210
Elyot(t), Richard (1544) 294
  Robert (1653) 88
Elys, Thomas (1544) 294
Ennis, Major, of Newport Pagnell
    (C17) 84
Erroll, Earl of — see Cartwright,
    Lady Fanny

Essex, Earl of (1643) 82
Evans, William (C16) 36

Fairfax — see Cartwright, Ursula
Farring, Henry (1790) 302
Fathers, family, masons (C18) 133
    Bet (C18) 156
    Edward (1790) 301
    Thomas, mason (late C18) 202
Fermor, Richard (1537) 39
    William and Henry (1764) *Plate 1*
Field, Samuel, Deddington solicitor
    and land agent to Cartwrights
    (C19) 217, 227, 229–47, 263, 265,
    267, 270, 272
Fiennes, William, 1st Viscount Saye
    and Sele (d. 1662) and family 78–9
Fletcher, Peter (late C17) 145
Ford(e), Mary (1790) 302
    Richard, shepherd (1740) 126
Foxley, Thomas (early C19) 212
Fowler, –, Quaker (1684) 171
Francillon, Francis (b. 1794), Ban-
    bury solicitor 250
Franklin, Giles (1544) 294
    William (1790) 301
    –, Deddington builder (mid-C19)
    229, 235, 241
Freeman, Thomas, carpenter (late
    C17) 145
    – (C17) 86
French, Ann (1848) 228
    John (1790) 301
    Robert, baker (1750) 116, 126
Fullerton family, lessees of Great
    House (1870s) 251, 253
Fynson, Thomas (1544) 294

Galloway, William (C18/19) 214, 302
Gardner, Faulke (1652) 88
    John (1794) 300
    Mark (early C17) 62, 103, 296
    Robert (1615) 296
    Robert, farmer (1840s) 223–4,
    230–4, 236, 239
    Thomas, aletaster (C17) 53
    Widow (1633) 62
Garrett family (1913) 288
Garye, John (1618) 296
Gaveston, Piers (d. 1312) 25

Gee, Mr, doctor (1850s) 279
Geoffrey of Croughton (?C12–13) 24
George, John and Ann (emig. to
    Canada, 1833–4) 209–10
Gevis, Thomas (1544) 293–4
Gibberd, – (1790) 301
Gibbs, Samuel, shoemaker (1888)
    276, 280–1
Gillam, –, butler to Cartwrights
    (1840s) 219–20, 223–4, 241
Gladstone, W.E., prime minister
    (d. 1898) 253
Golder, Henry (1740) 125–6, 154
Goode, John (1790) 302
    Samuel (1790) 301
Goodger, Thomas (1790) 302
Goodier, Goodyer, Alice (1663) 128
    Ed., groom (1680s) 118
    Elizabeth, teacher (C17) 163
    John (early C18) 151
    William, Quaker (1683) 170
Goodman, Elizabeth, laundrymaid
    (1740) 117
Goodyer — see Goodier
Gough, Drope, of Fritwell (C18) 178
Goylyn, John (C15/16) 39–40
Grafton, Richard, agent to Richard
    Cartwright (1616) 61, 258
Grant, John and family (1753) 155
    William and family (1740) 122–3
Green(e) — see Grene
Gregory, John, labourer (1749) 121
    Thomas (1790) 302
Grene, Elizabeth (1544) 294
    John (C16) 36
    John (1618) 296
    Margaret (C16) 37
    Robert (1544) 293
    Thomas (1544) 293
    Widow (1618) 296
Griffin, Mr, Bicester physician (C18)
    152
Gubbins, William (1544) 294
Gunning, Mrs Mary Catherine (d.
    1877; née Cartwright, mar. Revd.
    Henry John, later Sir; sister of Sir
    Thomas Cartwright) 240
Gurney, John (1790) 301
Gytha (C11) 12

Haddon, Mr, farmer (1815) 213
Haines — see Haynes
Hall, Thomas, Mary and family
    (1734) 122-3, 156
    Timothy (1790) 301
Hanley, Ed. (1670s) 144
Hanslape, Hanslope family (C17)
    101, 103, 134, 136, 187
    Nicholas (C16) 34-5, 38-40
    Roger (1485) 31, 34
    Thomas (1535) 28, 293
    Thomas (C17) 47-8, 52, 54-5,
    59-60, 62, 64-5, 78, 85, 192,
    296-7
Harberd, William (1544) 293
Harold, Thomas, gardener (1680s)
    118
Harris, John (early C18) 151
    John (d. 1849), Clifton farmer
    230, 233
    Martin (1790) 301
    Nicholas, Ardington window-
    maker (late C17) 145
    Mr, schoolmaster (C17) 163
    see also Aris, Ayris
Hartha-Canute, King (C11) 12
Hatley, William, of Warwick (1723)
    153
Hatton, Sir Christopher (C17) 90
Hawkes, Samuel, farmer (1871) 271
    T.H., farmer and parish councillor
    (1894) 280-1
Hawley, Edward, Quaker, shepherd
    (1660s) 170
Hawtin, Widow (1790) 302
Hay, Lady Fanny — see Cartwright
Haynes, Richard (emig. 1682) 129
    Widow (C18) 156
Hearne, Thomas (C18) 96
Hedges, -, of Stukeley (C18/19)
    206-7
Henry III, King 25
Herbert, George, innkeeper, formerly
    of Bladon (late C18) 156
    William, stonemason, and dau.
    Joan (1544) 34
Herne, William (1618) 296
Higman, Edward, joiner of 'Hamsted'
    (early C18) 151

de Hikkeholte, William (d. 1293),
    Master of the Hospital 30
Hill, Christopher, guild priest of
    Croughton (C15/16) 28
Hobcraft, Hobcroft family (C17)
    101, 152, 157
    Elizabeth (1618) 296
    Henry, mason (C18) 133, 137,
    152
    John, Quaker, and family (mid-
    C17) 128, 170
    Joyce (mar. Arthur Secull, 1697)
    114
    Joyce (C18) 122, 156
    Mary (1719) 154, 170
    Robert (1618) 296-7
    Thomas (1658) 147
    Thomas (1725) 168
    William (1723) 154
    Widow (1618) 297
Holland, John and wife (1848) 279
Holloway, Edward, innkeeper (C19)
    197, 204, 210
    Mrs Sarah (widow of Edward),
    innkeeper 238-40, 270, 272
Holyfield, Richard, of Kings Sutton
    (1726) 175
Homan, Edward, innkeeper (C18)
    109, 113, 149, 154, 157, 165,
    299, 305
Hopcroft, Mr T. (1816) 212
Horseman, John, Rector of Souldern,
    enclosure commissioner (1792)
    182-3
Horwood, Widow (1790) 302
Howes, Howse, Abraham and family,
    emig. to Canada (1845) 211
    Frances (1723) 153
    John (1636) 75, 297
    Richard (C16) 34
    Richard (d. 1849) and family 278
    William (1611) 41, 59, 296-7
    William, curate (1620) 71
    William (C17/18) 304
    William (1794) 300
    William, baker (C19) 228, 280, 288
    - (C17) 87
Hudson, Dr, of Oxford University
    (C18) 96

Hughes, Samuel, baker (1813) 204
Hulbird, Timothy (1738) 116
  Timothy (1790) 302
Humphris, Joe and Tom, estate carpenters (C20) 285
Hunt, George, innkeeper (1794) 300
Hutchins, Mary, hayward (C17) 52
Hutton, John, of Adderbury (C16) 35
  Dr Matthew (d. 1711), Rector of Aynho 1677-1711 90, 94-5, 110, 150, 170-1
  Roger (C16) 35
  Mr, of Somerset House (C18) 97
Huwes, William (?C13) 24

Jackson, Ann (1790) 302
Jameson, John, painter (late C17) 113
Jarvis, Edward, engineer and constable (C17) 54-5, 101, 134, 136, 174, 296, 304
  Edward, grandson of Edward (1713) 101
  John (1618) 297
  Ralph (1618) 296
  Widow (1618) 68-9, 149
Jeffs, Jeffes family (C18) 116-7
  John and Elizabeth (1653) 88-9
  John, tailor (1720s) 150
  Peter (1723) 165
  William (d. 1730), tailor 128
  William (d. 1768) 128
Jenkyns, John (1653) 88
Jennens, Thomas (1723) 165
Jersey, Lord (C18/19) 194
Jones, John, shepherd (C19) 279
  Mary (1790) 302
Jordan of Eynho, of Sawbridgeworth (C13) 24

Keble, George (1544) 293
Kempster, Christopher, master mason of Burford (late C17) 146
Kenning, John, Banbury mason (late C17) 146
Kimber, Thomas (1790) 301
Kitteridge, Richard (1790) 301
Knight, -, farmer (1847) 227
Knot(t) family, blacksmiths (C17-18) 116, 118

Knott, *continued*
  Edward, blacksmith (C18) 110, 152
  Henry, gardener (1680s) 118
  John (1616) 61
  Margaret (C17) 54-5
  Thomas (1790) 301
  William, blacksmith (late C17) 164, 174
  William (1790) 301
  Widow (1790) 301
  - (C17) 87
Kyrby, Thomas (1544) 293

Lambert, J., parish councillor (1894) 280-1
  -, of Nell Bridge (1853) 248, 250
  Mrs (C20) 286
Lambton, William, Rector of Aynho (C15) 24
Lamprey, Sarah (d. 1723) 153
Langton, William, bishop (C13/14) 19
Lardner, James, shopkeeper (1851) 270
Lawley, John, grazier, and wife (1704) 103, 112
Leache, Leche — see Letch
Leicester, Lady, of Holkham (C19) 230-1
Leighton, Frederick (C19) 253
Leland, John (d. 1552) 39
Lestrange, Earl Hamo (C13) 25
Leonard, -, schoolmaster (1794) 198
Letch, Leche, Leach family (C17-19) 123, 140, 147, 178, 267
  Edward (C17) 45
  Edward (C18) 106, 121, 126, 170, 299, 304
  Elizabeth, widow of Edward (C17) — see Young
  Elizabeth, wife of Henry (1652) 89
  Henry and family (C16) 35-6, 45, 293-4
  Henry (son of Edward, C17) and family 45, 74, 85, 88-9, 111, 123, 134, 140, 170, 297, 304
  John (1544) 35, 293
  John (d. 1787) 104, 111, 178
  John (1790) 301

Letch, *continued*
Mary (widow of John, C18/19) 189, 268, 300, 302
Richard (1544) 293
Litchfield, Revd. Francis (d. 1876), Rector of Farthinghoe and J.P. 211–2, 250–1, 262
Loe, John (early C17) 41, 61–2, 64, 69–70, 73, 110, 296–7
Longman, Revd. Dr James (d. 1677), Rector of Aynho 1643–46, 1662–1677 90–2, 94, 110
Longstaffe, William (1544) 293
Lothian family (1840s) 224, 226
Love, Edward, farmer (1552) 29, 33, 293
Edward (d. 1618), farmer 58, 296–7
Richard, farmer (1618) 69
Loveday, Robert (1618) 296
Lovell, George (c1816) 212–3
Luckars, Lukas, Surgeon (C18) 152
Luke, Sir Samuel (C17) 83
Lukenore, R. (?C14/15) 24
Lukin, Mary, wife of Shakerley Marmion — see Marmion
Lyne, Richard, Quaker (1683) 170

Mabletoft, Revd. Francis (d. 1807), Rector of Aynho 1770–1807 181–2, 195–6, 199, 302
Maclaren family, farmers (C20) 253
Magdalen College, Oxford (landowner in Aynho) 31, 47–8, 59, 65, 178–9, 181
Makepeace, John (early C18) 152
Malcolm, George, of Hull (1850) 244
Malins, Robert (1790) 301
Manchester, Earl of — see Montagu
de Mandeville family, Lords of Aynho (C11–12) 12–3, 16–7, 26, 30
Manvers, Lord (C19) 194
March — see Marsh
Markham, Mr (1790) 302
Mrs (C18) 133
Marmion, Mary (née Lukin, mar. Shakerley Marmion, 1600) 40
Mary (d. 1605; dau. of Rowland Shakerley, mar. Thomas Marmion) 40

Marmion, *continued*
Shakerley (b. 1568, son of Thomas), Lord of Aynho 40–2, 44, 58, 60, 66, 134, 297
Shakerley (1603–39, son of Shakerley), playwright 42
Thomas (d. 1583), Lord of Aynho 40–1
Marsh, March, John, fuller (C18) 157
John (1790) 128, 301
Thomas, shoemaker and schoolmaster (C18) 152, 163, 176, 302
Marshall, Charles (1740) 299
James (C18) 97, 165
William, of London, mason to the King (later C17) 146, 193, *Plate 3*
Mayo, Meow(e) family (C17–18) 189, 270
Edward (1618) 296
Mary (1740) 125, 128
Richard (C16) 270
Richard, farmer and butcher (C19) 268–70
Samuel, butcher (C18) 111, 117, 299
Samuel, farmer (1792) 189, 300–2
Timothy (?C18) 128
McIlwain, Moses, railway policeman (1861) 267
Meade, Widow (1618) 297
Mellycome, – (1633) 62–3
Meow(e) — see Mayo
Mercer, Thomas, Quaker, hempdresser (1660s) 170–1
Merevale, Agnes and John (C16) 37
Merriman, Susannah (1780) 128
Merry family, millers (C18) 117; 149
John, miller (C18) 110
Mary (1794) 300
Nathan (1740) 299
Samuel, miller (1794) 198
William, miller (1723) 154
Mrs (1790) 302
Millard, Charles, park keeper (C19) 219, 225, 227, 236, 243, 247–8, 250, 268
Miller, Sarah (1723) 153
Mills, James (1544) 294
Milne, Mr, architect (1848) 229, 233, 235, 237

Milward, Richard (1544) 293
Monck, General George (later Duke of Albemarle) (C17) 93
Montagu, Sir Edward, of Boughton, and family (C17) 78
Moore, Richard, steward to Richard Cartwright (1616) 67
Mordaunt, John, Earl of Peterborough, and family (C17) 78
Morgan, - (1849) 234
Mott, Thomas, sawyer (d. 1632) 46, 297
Mumford, Richard, of Astrop (1815) 213

Neal, John, mason (late C17) 145-6
Nelson, James (C18) 110
de Neville, Ralph (C14) 20, 22
Mr, farmer of Tew (1849) 239
Newers, John, of Tackley (C15) 24
Nichols, Nicolls, George, at Eydon (C18/19) 206
John (1790) 302
Norman, Joseph and family (early C19) 201
Norris, Thomas, and Mary (d. 1700), innkeepers 112-3, 171
Northampton, Earl of — see Compton
Norwood, Ann (early C18) 151
Noy, Katherine) see Cartwright
Sir William (d. 1634), Attorney-General, and father-in-law of John Cartwright 76-7

Oakey, Robert, butcher and baker (1890s) 281, 288
Oliver, Revd. Mr, schoolmaster (1790) 301
Osborne, Widow (1618) 297
Osmund, brother at Hospital (?C12/13), 24
Oxford, Earl of (C17) 95

Palmer, Ralph (1790) 301
Palmerston, Lord, prime minister (d. 1865) 253
Parker, Margaret, Quaker (1660s) 170
Peter (1544) 293
Peter and family (C17) 41, 70, 134, 296
Thomas (1652) 88
Parry, John, curate (C17) 70-1

Patullo, William and family, farmers (later C19) 253, 271
Paxton, -, auctioneer (1867) 267
Pearson, Richard, Rector of Aynho 1508-32 28
Peckover, Jane and family (C18) 122-3, 156-7, 176
Samuel (early C18) 152
William (1790) 301
Pemberton, Pemtone, Christopher (1544) 294
George, aletaster (C17) 53, 61, 296
Perian, Roger (1618) 297
Perry, Goodwife (C16) 37
Pepys, Samuel, diarist (1633-1703) 93
Peterborough, Earl of — see Mordaunt
Perkins, Mrs, farmer (1847) 228, 272
Philips, William (1740) 299
Pirkins, Mr, of Charlton (1815) 213
Pollard, Sergeant, in Volunteers (C18/19) 201, 302
Mrs, infants' schoolmistress (1913) 288
Polton, John (1790) 302
William (1743) 156
Poole, Richard, schoolmaster (1859-90) 274
Pope, Sir Thomas (1635) 73-4
Porter, Mr (1792) 184
Pottinger, James (C18/19) 201
Powell, -, housekeeper (1847) 219-20
Powle, George (1544) 293
Priest family (1720s) 154
James, carpenter, and son James (1723) 129, 153, 155
Martha (1790) 302
Roger, Quaker (C17/18) 154, 170
William, carpenter (C18) 158
Priour, William (d. 1723) of Catherine Hall, Cambridge 152-3
Prophett, Mrs, preparatory schoolmistress (1851) 273
Prowett family (C18) 189
Mr, and Susannah, farmers (C18) 155, 189, 301
Pruce, John (son of Peter), innkeeper (C17/18) 56, 112, 149, 299
Peter (d. 1682), innkeeper 87, 111-2, 147
Mrs (1740) 109

Pryse, Robert, servant to Richard Howse (C16) 34–5
Purcell, Henry, 'spinet-master' (d. 1695) 150, 176

Queeny, Richard (C16) 35, 37

Reddall, Revd. Enoch, headmaster of Grammar School (1851) 275
Reeve, Reve, Thomas (C16) 37
  William (C14) 22
Reynolds, Edward (C17) 92–3
  John (1740) 299
Righton — see Wrighton
Robbins, Thomas, theshing machine owner (C19) 268
  – (emig. 1842) 210–1
Round, –, partner of Edward Wing (C18) 167
Rowsam(?), Fulke (1618) 297
Russell, Mr, Brackley surveyor (1790) 179, 183–4
Rutter, –, innkeeper (C19) 237
Rymill, John (1790s) 158

St Valery, Thomas de (C13) 18
Salter, Mr, coroner from Northampton (1618) 68–9
Sandizell, Marie ('Lili') — see Cartwright
Savings, Mrs, laundress (C20) 286
Saye and Sele, Viscount — see Fiennes
Scambler, Edmund (d. 1594), Bishop of Peterborough 1560–84 77
Scott, William, farmer and churchwarden (mid–C19) 210, 217, 231
  William John (1836) 217
  Mr, of Hinton (1815) 213
Secull, Seacole, Seccull family, masons (C17–20) 114–6, 124, 128, 133, 269, 285
  Arthur (d. 1758), mason 114–6, 124, 128, 144, 147, 154, 158, 285
  Elizabeth (1753) 155
  James (1849) 230, 236, 269
  Joyce (née Hobcraft, mar. Arthur, 1697) 114
  Thomas (C18/19) 110, 114–5, 214, 230

Secull, *continued*
  William (1790) 301
  William (1890s) 281
Shakerley family (C16) 40
  Rowland (d. 1564/5) 29, 32–3, 36, 38–40, 45, 47, 57, 177, 293
  see also Marmion
Shelton, – (1790) 302
Shomaker, William (1618) 297
Sibthorpe, Dr Robert (d. 1662), Vicar of St Sepulchre, Northampton 1618–22 70–1
Side, Richard (1544) 293
Silver, Thomas (1790) 302
Simpson, Elias (late C18) 116
Skelton, Mrs, cook (1847) 219, 225
Skillman, Thomas (1618) 297
Smith family (C18) 189
  Catherine (C18/19) 206–7
  George (1540) 38
  James (1740) 121–2
  John (C17/18) 125
  John (b. 1704), farmer, and family 124, 299
  Mary — see Banbury
  Thomas, schoolmaster (C18) 176
  Thomas, farmer (1740) 299
  Thomas, farmer (1790) 189, 300–1
  William (early C18) 152, 154
  William (1790) 302
  Mr, of Charlton (1815) 212
  – (1790) 302
Soane, Sir John, architect (C18/19) 193
Southam family (late C17) 101
  Giles (d. 1645) 67–8, 149, 159, 296–7
  John (C17/18) 304
  Thomas (C17) 85
Sparry, Thomas (1544) 293
Spencer, John (1704) 107, 165, 304–5
  Lord (1847) 223, 231
Spiers, Spires, Edward (1790) 302
  George, carpenter (1794) 198, 202
  George (son of George), grocer (C18/19) 202, 271
  John, carpenter (1821) 214
  Nathan and Abigail (1742) 157
  – (emig. 1842) 210–1

Spruce, John (C17/18) 304–5
Stanley, William (1790) 302
Stanton, Mary (C17/18) 304
Richard (d. 1619) 41, 53, 58, 62, 296
William (d. 1672) and family 54–5, 59, 75, 101
Staunton, William (1816) 212–3
Steanes, John (1790) 301
Steel, Stele, Thomas (1790) 302
Goodman, of Woodstock (C16) 34
Stilgoe, Stillgoe, Nicholas (1618) 296
- (C17) 64
- (1853) 250
Stutchbury, Francis (1740) 126
Summerton, Thomas (?C13/14) 24
Swetnam, Swetman, Edward (1618) 297
Giles (son of Thomas), smith (C17) 46, 54, 62
Thomas, blacksmith (C17) 46, 296
Thomas (son of Thomas; 1630s) 46, 52, 75, 88
Will. (C17) 112, 174
Widow (1633) 62
- (C17) 87
Swift, Thomas (C18) 123, 154

Tailor, Taylor, Daniel (1790) 302
Thomas (early C18) 151
Dr (C17) 91
Mr, of Charlton (1815) 213
Tancred, William (d. 1860), M.P. for Banbury 262
Tebby family (emig. 1842) 211
John, postman (retired 1852), and son James, postman (from 1852) 267–8
Terry, Richard (1790) 301
Thomas, George, Banbury cutler (early C19) 210
Tibbetts, James, farmer (1791) 180, 189, 195
William (1794) 300
- (1790) 302
see also Tippets
Tims, Timms, Peter, churchwarden (1660s) 170
, farmer (1849) 233–4

Tippets, –, ensign in Volunteers (18/19) 200
Tofig the Proud, and Gytha (C11) 12
Tomkins, Thomas (early C18) 152, 304–5
William (1740) 126, 299
Toogood, William (1618) 297
Tuckey, Edward (early C19) 212
George, verger (1804–98) 287
Turbert, Vicar of Aynho (C13) 27
Turbet, Turbit family, slaters and plasterers (C17–19) 116, 133
Francis, slater and plasterer (1821) 214
John (1784) 144, 301–2
Thomas, plasterer, of Kings Sutton (late C17) 145–6
Turner, George (1814) 228
John (C18/19) 212, 302
Thomas (1848) 228
William (1790) 301
Turpin, Mary and Susanna (early C18) 151
Turvey family (C18/19) 206
John (1790) 301
Tyrrell, Benjamin (1790) 302
- (1790) 302

Underwood, Hesther (early C18) 151
- (C17) 87
–, Cartwright agent and tenant at Home Farm (C19) 230, 233, 235–7, 239, 241, 243, 246, 249
Upton, Robert (1790) 302

de Valence, William (C13) 18

Wagstaff(e) family (C18) 189
Joseph (d. 1723) 153
Jos. (1740) 299
Joseph (1790) 301
Robert (1794) 300
Thomas. and son Thomas (1790s) 189, 207, 301
Walker, Emery (1790) 302
Thomas, wheelwright, and Sarah (mar. 1778) 117, 128, 300, 302
Mr, Parliamentary draughtsman (1792) 182

atte Walle, Simon, of Middleton (?C14/15) 27

Waller, Sir William (1644) 82

Walton, Edward Letch, railway executive (1866) 267
George, carpenter (1849) 241
John, retired cheesemonger (1851) 268
Robert (1790) 302

Warclow, James (1544) 294

Warde, Agnes (1544) 294

Warlow, John (1544) 293

Wasse, Revd. Joseph (d. 1738), Rector of Aynho 1711–38 90, 95–8, 110, 151–4, 164, 166–7, 258, 312

Watkins, Watkyns, Richard (1544) 294
Mr, tenant of College Farm (C18) 176, 179–81, 185, 195
Widow (1618) 297

Watson, John, carpenter of Kings Sutton (1811) 207
John Martin, surgeon and apothecary of Steeple Aston (C18/19) 115, 199?, 301
William (1790) 302

Watts family, blacksmiths (C18–19) 116, 123
Benjamin (d. 1663), son of Lawrence, and family 74, 101, 136–7
James (1652) 88–9
John (1790) 301
J., blacksmith (1894) 280, 285
Lawrence (d. 1634), shepherd, and Elizabeth 44–5, 74, 101, 133, 296
Mary (1848) 228
Richard, blacksmith (1676) 99
Thomas, theshing machine owner (C19) 268
Timothy (early C19) 212
William, blacksmith (C18/19) 214, 301
– (emig. 1842) 211
– (in workhouse 1846) 210–1, 278
–, Millard's man (1847) 227
Mrs, widow, shopkeeper (1841) 271

Wayneflete, Bishop of Winchester (1485) 31

Welch, Mr, Kings Sutton farmer (1815) 212–3

Wellington, Duke of (d. 1852) 201

Wells, Mr (1616) 66

West, Samuel (1790) 301

Westbury, William (1807) 212
–, keeper (C20) 285

Westly, Thomas (1544) 294

Weston, Robert, Cartwright agent (late C18) 136, 177–83, 185, 187, 195, 199, 206, 261, 302

Whetton, George (late C18) 116, 302

Whitby, Widow (1790) 302
– (1790) 302

White, Whighte, Whyte, Crescent (1618) 297
John (C16) 37
John (1618) 297
Richard (C17) 87
Robert (C17/18) 304
Samuel (1740) 299

Wigson, Joshua, mason (1723) 165

Wilde, Revd. Dr. Robert (d. 1679), Rector of Aynho 1646–62 90, 92–5, 160, 169

Wilkins, Wilkyns, George, of Kings Sutton (1815) 213
Robert (1544) 294

Willes, Mr (1815) 213

Williams, Henry (1850s) 279
Thomas and Ann (1652) 88–9

Willifer, John, Joseph and family (1850) 241, 246
Valentine snr. (d. 1848/9), bailiff of Home Farm 212, 217, 224–7, 229, 235, 246, 270
Valentine jnr. ('Val.', son of Valentine snr.) 212, 217, 221–4, 226–7

Willis, Browne, antiquary (C18) 167
Rev. Thomas (d. 1732), Vicar of Newbottle 167

Willoughby, –, servant to the earl of Northampton (C17) 91

Wilmot, Henry (1643) 82

Wilson, Edwin, farmer (1871) 271

Wing, Edward (1683–1755), carpenter and designer of Aynho church 164–9, 176, *Plate 26*

Wing, *continued*
John, carpenter, and son John (C17/18) 144-5, 166
Prudence (early C18) 151
Winkle(s), William (d. 1780), gardener to Cartwrights 128
Mrs (1790) 301
Wisdom, Mr, Shipton physician (C18) 152
Wodhull, Mrs (1790) 302
Wolfe, Sir Edward (d. 1535), Curate of Aynho and guild priest of Croughton 28
Woolnough, Mr, Cartwright agent (C19/20) 280-4
Wren, Sir Christopher, architect (d. 1723) 146
Wrighton, Righton, family (C18-19) 116, 128, 272
Abraham (early C18) 128, 151
Alice (early C18) 152
Frederick, parish councillor (1896) 281
Thomas (1708) 128
Thomas (1790) 302
William (early C18) 151

Wrighton, *continued*
William (d. 1780) 196
William (1790) 301-2
William, grocer (1871) 271
Wyatt, Wyet, Alice (d. 1663) and dau. Hannah 128
Thomas, Adderbury window-maker (late C17) 146
William (C16) 34
William (d. 1663) and family 61, 65, 101, 104, 121, 123, 296
Mr., enclosure commissioner, of Burton-on-Trent (1791) 179-80, 182-3
Wycherley family, Quakers (C19) 172, 270
James, maltster (C18/19) 128
James, shopkeeper (C19) 204, 270
Mary, Quaker (1813) 171-2
Wyssewaye, George (1544) 294

Yonger, William (1618) 297
Young, Elizabeth (d. 1639), widow of Edward Letch and John Young of Thame 45-6, 48-9, 62
John (1618) 296-7

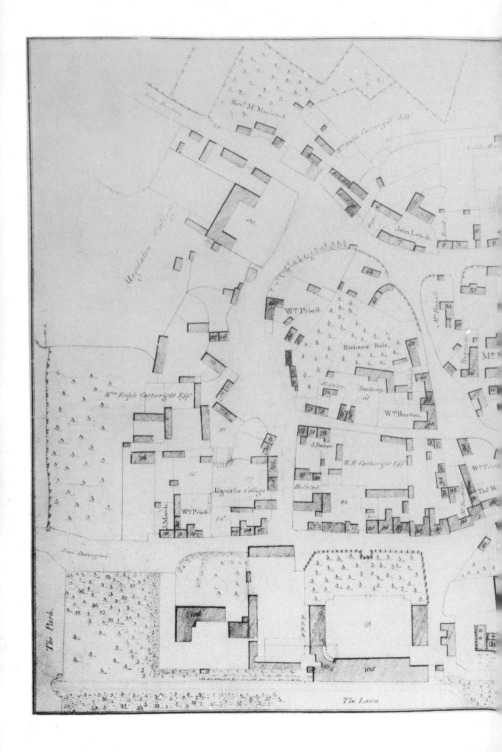